TEXTBOOK

Employment Law

THIRD EDITION

ALISON HOUGH
LLB, Barrister

OLD BAILEY PRESS

OLD BAILEY PRESS
at Holborn College, Woolwich Road,
Charlton, London, SE7 8LN

First published 2001
Third edition 2006

© The HLT Group Ltd 2006

All Old Bailey Press publications enjoy copyright protection and the copyright belongs to the HLT Group Ltd.

All rights reserved. No part of this publication may be reproduced or transmitted in any form or by any means, electronic, mechanical, photocopying, recording or otherwise, or stored in any retrieval system of any nature without either the written permission of the copyright holder, application for which should be made to the Old Bailey Press, or a licence permitting restricted copying in the United Kingdom issued by the Copyright Licensing Agency.

Any person who infringes the above in relation to this publication may be liable to criminal prosecution and civil claims for damages.

ISBN 1 85836 596 1

British Library Cataloguing-in-Publication.
A CIP Catalogue record for this book is available from the British Library.

Acknowledgement

The publishers and author would like to thank the Incorporated Council of Law Reporting for England and Wales for kind permission to reproduce extracts from the Weekly Law Reports, and Butterworths for their kind permission to reproduce extracts from the All England Law Reports.

Printed and bound in Great Britain

Contents

Preface *v*

Table of Cases *vii*

Table of Statutes and Other Materials *xix*

1 Introduction to Employment Law *1*

Introduction – Historical background – The European Union

2 The Concept of Employment *9*

Introduction – Employee or independent contractor? – Continuity and delegation – Special categories of workers – Fixed-term contracts – Vicarious liability

3 The Contract of Employment *30*

Introduction – Written particulars of terms – Express terms – Implied terms – Collective agreements – Company handbook/rule book – Variation of contractual terms – Post-termination obligations – Whistle-blowing

4 Dismissal *63*

Introduction – Termination by agreement or operation of law – Dismissal: definition and language of termination – Wrongful dismissal – Constructive dismissal – Automatically fair reasons for dismissal – Automatically unfair reasons for dismissal – Potentially fair/unfair reasons for dismissal – Excluded categories – Reasonableness and the importance of procedure – Notice – Time limits – Remedies

5 Redundancy *114*

Introduction – Dismissal – Rationalisation or restructuring – Alternative employment – Misconduct – Lay-off and short-time working – Redundancy payments – Consultation – Selection criteria – Role of the employment tribunal – Transfer of undertakings

6 Discrimination in Employment *148*

Sex discrimination – Race discrimination – Disability discrimination

7 Equal Pay *206*

Introduction – Equal Pay Act 1970

8 Employment Law and the Family *224*

Introduction – Ante-natal care – Maternity rights – Parental leave – Time off for dependants

9 Remuneration *236*

Introduction – Statement of pay – Payment of wages/deductions from wages – National minimum wage – Guarantee payments

10 Health and Safety   *246*
Introduction – Common law duty – Statutory regulation – Working Time Regulations

11 Trade Unions   *267*
Definition and legal status – Trade unions and their members – Trade union membership and employers – Employment Relations Act 2004 – Trade union duties – The government of trade unions – Collective bargaining – Union recognition

12 Industrial Action   *293*
Introduction – Inducing a breach of contract – Statutory immunity – Trade dispute – Secondary action – Picketing

13 Employment Tribunal Procedure   *310*
Introduction – Procedure – The hearing – ACAS unfair dismissal arbitration

Index   *323*

Preface

This book aims to provide the basic principles of employment law for those who, by reason of work or study, come into contact with the legal aspects of employment.

The study of employment law is challenging and stimulating; it is subject to constant change and refinement as recently enacted law evolves through case law. Whilst such change serves to keep us on our toes it can be difficult to keep abreast of all developments. In this book I have tried to state as simply as possible the general principles which define current employment law, looking at the nature of the contractual relationship between an employer and an employee and the rights and obligations that arise out of that contract.

Consideration is given to contracts of employment, sex, race and disability discrimination, maternity rights, equal pay, unfair dismissal, redundancy and transfer of undertakings.

The book also attempts to provide a coherent understanding of the legal parameters in relation to the role of trade unions and industrial relations. It takes into account the reforms to trade union recognition provided by the Employment Relations Act 1999 and the Employment Relations Act 2004.

In addition to covering recent changes in employment law, the text also includes detailed consideration of new rights contained within the Employment Act 2002, including paternity leave, adoption leave and changes to maternity leave and the Fixed-term Employees (Prevention of Less Favourable Treatment) Regulations 2002, which give new rights to more than one million workers in the UK. The Employment Act 2002 (Dispute Resolution) Regulations 2004 are also considered in detail.

I would like to thank my family, friends and Old Bailey Press for their support and patience throughout the writing of this textbook. Any errors contained within the text are, however, entirely my own.

I have endeavoured to state the law as at December 2005.

Alison Hough

I dedicate this book to Peter and Michael.

Table of Cases

A v Chief Constable of West Yorkshire Police *see* Chief Constable of West Yorkshire Police v A
Abadeh v British Telecom plc [2001] ICR 156   *195*
Adams v Charles Zub Associates Ltd [1978] IRLR 551   *79*
Addis v Gramophone Company Ltd [1909] AC 488   *74*
Addison v London Philharmonic Orchestra [1981] ICR 261   *11*
Ahmed v United Kingdom [1999] IRLR 188   *7*
Ainsworth v Glass Tubes & Components Ltd (1976) The Times 19 November   *213*
Air Canada v Lee [1978] IRLR 392   *122*
Airfix Footwear v Cape [1978] IRLR 396   *13*
Alabaster v Barclays Bank and the Secretary of State for Social Security [2005] EWCA Civ 508   *216*
Alamo Group v Tucker [2003] IRLR 266   *147*
Alcan Extrusions v Yates [1996] IRLR 327   *70*
Ali & Others v Christian Salvesen Food Services Ltd [1995] IRLR 624   *37*
Alidair v Taylor [1978] ICR 445   *88*
ALM Medical Services Ltd v Bladon [2002] IRLR 807   *62*
Archibald v Fife Council [2004] IRLR 651   *199*
Archibald v Rossleigh Commercials Ltd [1975] IRLR 231   *119*
Armstrong Whitworth Rolls v Mustard [1971] 1 All ER 598   *50*
Arnold v Beecham Group Ltd [1982] ICR 744   *210*
Asda Stores Ltd v Thompson [2002] IRLR 245   *110*
Ashford v Association of Scientific, Technical and Management Staffs [1973] ICR 296   *277*
ASLEF v Lee [2004] EAT/0625/03   *276*
Associated Newspapers Ltd v Wilson [1995] 2 AC 454   *279*
Avonmouth Construction Ltd v Shipway [1979] IRLR 14   *121*

Badger v Transport and General Workers Union [1974] ITR 80   *277*

Bahl v Law Society [2004] IRLR 799   *154*
Bailey v BP Oil (Kent Refinery) Ltd [1979] IRLR 287   *101*
Bainbridge v Circuit Foil UK Ltd [1997] IRLR 305   *50*
Baker & Others v Rochdale Helath Authority (1994) (unreported)   *219*
Balgobin v Tower Hamlets London Borough Council [1987] IRLR 401   *165*
Bamsey v Albon Engineering Ltd [2004] IRLR 457   *262*
Banerjee v City and East London AHA [1979] IRLR 147   *94*
Barber v Guardian Royal Exchange Assurance Group [1990] IRLR 240   *207*
Barber & Others v NCR (Manufacturing) Ltd [1993] IRLR 95   *218*
Barber & Others v RJB Mining (UK) Ltd [1999] IRLR 308   *259*
Barclays Bank plc v James [1990] IRLR 90   *151*
Barclays Bank v Kapur [1995] IRLR 87   *182*
Barratt Developments Ltd v UCATT [1978] IRLR 403   *127*
Barretts & Baird (Wholesale) Ltd v Institution of Professional Civil Servants & Duckworth [1987] IRLR 3   *297*
Barry v Midland Bank [1998] IRLR 138   *160*
Barton v Investec Henderson Crosthwaite Securities Ltd [2003] IRLR 332   *169, 170*
Bass Leisure v Thomas [1994] IRLR 104   *117*
Batisha v Say [1977] IRLR 13   *150*
Baxter v Glostal Architectural Anodising Ltd (1976) (unreported)   *164*
Benton v Sanderson Kayser [1989] ICR 136; [1989] IRLR 19   *121*
Beneviste v University of Southampton [1989] ICR 617   *218*
Berriman v Delabole Slate Ltd [1984] ICR 636; [1984] IRLR 394   *83, 142*
Betts & Others v Brintel Helicopters Ltd (Defendants) and KLM ERA Helicopters (UK) Ltd (Defendants/Appellants) [1997] IRLR 361   *135–136, 136*
BG plc v O'Brien [2001] IRLR 496   *38*
Bilka-Kaufhaus GmbH v Weber von Hartz [1986] ICR 110   *160*

Table of Cases

Billington v Michael Hunter & Sons Ltd [2003] EAT/05780/03   42
Birch v University of Liverpool [1985] ICR 470   115
Birch and Humber v University of Liverpool [1985] IRLR 165   65
Birmingham District Council v Beyer [1977] IRLR 211   278
Blackburn v Gridquest Ltd (t/a Select Employment) [2002] IRLR 604   264
Blackman v Post Office [1974] ICR 151   89
Blackpool and The Fylde College v National Association of Teachers in Further and Higher Education [1994] ICR 648   300
Blackstone Franks Investments Management Ltd v Robertson (1998) The Times 4 May   237
Bliss v South East Thames Regional Health Authority [1985] IRLR 308   42
Blue Circle Staff Association v Certification Officer [1977] ICR 224   268
Bonner v Gilbert Ltd [1989] IRLR 475   122
Bonsor v Musician's Union [1956] AC 104   276
Boston Deep Sea Fishing & Ice Co v Ansell (1888) Ch D 339   42
Bournemouth Borough Council v Meredith [2003] ELR 1   101
Boychuk v H J Symons Holdings Ltd [1977] IRLR 395   90
Bracebridge Engineering v Darby [1990] IRLR 3   164
Brennan v J H Dewhurst Ltd [1983] IRLR 357   163
Brennan & Ging v Ellward (Lancs) Ltd [1976] IRLR 378   280
Briggs v North Eastern Education and Library Board [1990] IRLR 181   157
Brindley v Tayside Health Board [1976] IRLR 364   164
British Aerospace plc v Green and Others [1995] ICR 1006; [1995] IRLR 433   130, 132
British Aircraft Corporation Ltd v Austin [1978] IRLR 332   247
British Airways Engine Overhaul Ltd v Francis [1981] ICR 278   281
British Coal Corporation v Smith [1996] 3 All ER 97   214, 215
British Gas Services Ltd v McCaull [2001] IRLR 60   201
British Home Stores v Burchell [1978] IRLR 379   91, 92
British Labour Pump v Byrne [1979] IRLR 94   102, 129
British Leyland v Ashraf [1978] ICR 979   65
British Leyland v McQuilken [1978] IRLR 245   47
British Leyland v Swift [1981] IRLR 91   100
British Sugar plc v Kirker [1998] IRLR 624   202
British Telecommunications plc v Reid [2004] IRLR 327   190
Bromley & Others v H & J Quick Ltd [1988] IRLR 456   209
Brookes v Borough Care Services Ltd [1998] IRLR 636   134
Brooks v BT [1992] IRLR 66   96
Broome v DPP [1974] AC 587   307
Brown v Southall & Knight [1980] IRLR 130   69
Brown v Stockton-on-Tees Borough Council [1988] IRLR 263   83
Buchan and Ivey v Secretary of State for Employment [1997] IRLR 80   17
Bullivant Ltd v Ellis [1986] IRLR 491   58
Bullock v Alice Ottley School [1992] IRLR 564   151, 155
Burdett-Coutts v Hertfordshire County Council [1984] IRLR 91   50
Burton Allton & Johnson Ltd v Peck [1975] IRLR 87   115
Burton and Rhule v De Vere Hotels [1996] IRLR 596   183
Byrne & Others v Financial Times Ltd [1991] IRLR 417   217, 315

Cambridge and District Co-operative Society v Ruse [1993] IRLR 156   121
Cantor Fitzgerald International v Bird and Others [2002] IRLR 867   78
Capper Pass Ltd v Lawton [1976] IRLR 366   208
Carlson v Post Office [1981] ICR 343   279
Carmichael v National Power plc [1998] IRLR 4   23, 24
Cassidy v Ministry of Health [1951] 1 All ER 574   10
Cast v Croydon College [1998] IRLR 318   177
Catherall v Michelin Tyres plc [2003] IRLR 61   203
Celtec Ltd v Ashley Case C–478/03 [2005] IRLR 647   140
Chamberlin Solicitors v Emokpae [2004] IRLR 592   170
Chapman v Goonvean and Rostowrack China Clay Co Ltd [1973] 2 All ER 1063   118
Chappell v Times Newspapers Ltd [1975] IRLR 90   75

Chessington World of Adventures Ltd v Reed [1997] IRLR 556   *165*
Chessington World of Adventures Ltd v Reed (Restricted Reporting Order) [1998] ICR 55; [1998] IRLR 56   *316*
Chief Constable of Bedfordshire v Liversidge [2002] IRLR 651   *162*
Chief Constable of West Yorkshire Police v A [2004] ICR 806; [2004] IRLR 573   *166, 173*
Church v West Lancashire NHS Trust [1998] ICR 423   *120*
Clapson v British Airways [2001] IRLR 184   *310*
Clark v Novacold Ltd [1998] IRLR 420   *196, 201*
Clarke v Eley (IMI) Kynoch Ltd [1982] IRLR 482   *157*
Clay Cross (Quarry Services) v Fletcher [1979] ICR 1   *217*
Clements v London & North Western Railway Co [1894] 2 QB 482   *20*
Coates v Modern Methods and Materials [1982] ICR 763   *82*
Cocking v Sandhurst (Stationers) Ltd [1974] ICR 650   *314*
Cole v Fred Stacey Ltd [1974] IRLR 73   *31*
Cole v Midland Display Ltd [1973] IRLR 62   *38*
Colen & Another v Cebrian (UK) Ltd [2003] EWCA Civ 1676   *32*
College of North East London v Leather (2001) Judgment of 30 November (unreported)   *263, 264*
Collier v Sunday Referee Publishing Co Ltd [1940] 4 All ER 234   *45*
Colwyn Borough Council v Dutton [1980] IRLR 420   *95*
Commissioner of Police of the Metropolis v Ekpe [2001] IRLR 605   *195*
Commissioner of Police of the Metropolis v Harley [2001] IRLR 263   *203*
Connick Tree Care v Chapman (1997) (unreported)   *135*
Connolly v Sellers Arenascene Ltd [2001] IRLR 222   *18*
Coomes (Holdings) Ltd v Shields [1978] IRLR 263   *208*
Coote v Granada Hospitality Ltd [1998] IRLR 656   *168*
Coral Leisure Group Ltd v Barnett [1981] IRLR 204   *32, 98*
Council of Civil Service Unions v Minister for the Civil Service [1985] IRLR 28   *81*
Courtaulds Northern Spinning v Sibson [1988] IRLR 305   *36, 39*

Coxall v Goodyear Great Britain Ltd (2002) The Times 5 August   *250*
Creswell v Board of Inland Revenue [1984] IRLR 190   *43*
Crofter Hand-Woven Harris Tweed Co v Veitch [1942] AC 435   *296*
Crossley v Faithful & Gould Holdings Ltd [2004] IRLR 377   *41*
Crown Suppliers v Dawkins [1993] ICR 517   *181*
Cruickshank v Vaw Motorcast Ltd [2002] IRLR 24   *195*
Curr v Marks & Spencer plc [2003] IRLR 75   *16, 124*

Dacas v Brook Street Bureau (UK) Ltd [2004] IRLR 358   *22*
Daley v Allied Suppliers [1983] ICR 90   *19*
Davies v Presbyterian Church of Wales [1986] 1 WLR 323   *19*
Davison v Kent Meters [1975] IRLR 145   *89*
Day v T Pickles Farms Ltd [1999] IRLR 217   *227, 257*
De Francesco v Barnum (1890) 45 Ch D 430   *20*
De Souza v Automobile Association [1986] IRLR 103   *182*
Dedman v British Building & Engineering Appliances Ltd [1974] ICR 53   *108*
Defer-Wyatt v Williams [2003] EAT/0270/03   *108*
Defrenne v Sabena (No 2) Case 43/75 [1976] ECR 455   *6, 214*
Dekker v Stichting Vormingscentrum voor Jong Volwassenen [1991] IRLR 27   *149*
Delaney v Staples [1992] 1 All ER 944   *240, 241*
Dentmaster (UK) Ltd v Kent [1997] IRLR 636   *53*
Derby Specialist Fabrication Ltd v Burton [2001] IRLR 69   *182*
Devis v Atkins [1977] IRLR 314   *102*
Dibro Ltd v Hore [1990] IRLR 129   *212*
Dietman v London Borough of Brent [1987] IRLR 259   *73*
Din v Carrington Viyella Ltd (Jersey Kapwood Ltd) [1982] IRLR 281   *180*
Discount Tobacco and Confectionary Ltd v Williamson [1993] IRLR 327   *238*
Dixon v The Automobile Association Ltd [2004] All ER (D) 127   *199*
Dixon & Constanti v BBC [1978] ICR 281   *27*
DJM International v Nicholas [1995] IRLR 76   *145*

Dobie v Burns International Security Services [1984] IRLR 329 *95*
Doble v Firestone Tyre and Rubber Co [1981] IRLR 300 *69*
DPP v Fidler [1992] 1 WLR 91 *308*
DPP v Marshall [1998] ICR 518 *313*
Dryden v Greater Glasgow Health Board [1992] IRLR 469 *45, 247*
D'Souza v London Borough of Lambeth [1997] IRLR 677 *189*
Dugdale & Others v Kraft Foods Ltd [1976] IRLR 368 *208, 209*
Duncan Web Offset (Maidstone) Ltd v Cooper [1995] IRLR 633 *138*
Dunnachie v Kingston-upon-Hull City Council [2004] IRLR 727 *74, 113*
Duport Steels Ltd v Sirs [1980] 1 WLR 142 *305*

Eagland v British Telecommunications [1992] IRLR 323 *35*
Eastwood and Anothr v Magnox Electric plc [2004] IRLR 733 *41*
Eaton v Nuttall [1977] IRLR 71 *208*
Eaton v (1) Robert Eaton Ltd (2) Secretary of State for Employment [1988] ICR 302 *17*
EC Commission v United Kingdom Case 61/81 [1982] ICR 578 *211*
EC Commission v United Kingdom Case C-373/92 [1994] IRLR 142 *126*
ECM (Vehicle Delivery Service) v Cox and Others [1999] IRLR 559 *136*
EEPTU v Times Newspapers [1980] QB 585 *270*
Egg Stores v Leibovici [1977] ICR 260 *67*
Electrolux Ltd v Hutchinson & Others [1976] IRLR 410 *209*
El-Hoshi v Pizza Express Restaurants Ltd [2004] IDS 768 *80*
Elkouil v Coney Island Ltd [2002] IRLR 174 *131*
Elliott v Richard Stump Ltd [1987] IRLR 215 *121*
Ely v YKK Fasteners (UK) [1994] ICR 164 *94*
Enderby v Frenchay Health Authority [1993] IRLR 591 *218*
Equal Opportunities Commission v Robertson [1980] IRLR 44 *164*
Esso Petroleum Co Ltd v Harper's Garage (Stourport) Ltd [1968] AC 269 *52*
Express and Echo Publications Ltd v Taunton [1999] IRLR 367 *12*
Express Newspapers v McShane [1980] AC 672 *305*

Faccenda Chicken Ltd v Fowler & Others [1985] IRLR 69 *56, 57, 58*
Fairchild v Glenhaven Funeral Services Ltd [2002] 3 WLR 89 *249*
Falconer v ASLEF and NUR [1986] IRLR 331 *301*
Falkirk Council v White & Others [1997] IRLR 560 *157*
Faramus v Film Artistes' Association [1964] 1 All ER 25 *272*
Ferguson v John Dawson & Partners (Contractors) Ltd [1976] IRLR 346 *13*
Fitch v Dewes [1921] 2 AC 158 *53*
Fitzpatrick v British Railways Board [1991] IRLR 376 *278*
Fleming v Secretary of State for Trade and Industry [1997] IRLR 682 *18*
Ford Motor Co v AUEWF [1969] IRLR 67 *46*
Foster v Hampshire Fire and Rescue Service (1998) 43 BMLR 186 *194*
Frames Snooker Centre v Boyce [1992] IRLR 472 *92*
Francisco Hernandez Vidal SA v Gomez Perez & Others [1999] IRLR 132 *136*
Francovich v Italian Republic [1992] IRLR 84 *6*
Franks v Reuters Ltd & Another [2003] IRLR 423 *22*
Freud v Bentalls Ltd [1982] IRLR 443 *129*
Fu v London Borough of Camden [2001] IRLR 186 *200*
Fytche v Wincanton Logistics plc [2004] IRLR 817 *257*

Galt v Philip [1984] IRLR 156 *308*
Gardner (FC) Ltd v Beresford [1978] IRLR 63 *44*
Garry v London Borough of Ealing [2001] IRLR 681 *182*
Gascol Conversions Ltd v Mercer [1974] IRLR 155 *35*
Gee v Shell UK Ltd [2003] IRLR 82 *318*
Gemmell v Darngavil Brickworks Ltd [1967] 2 ITR 20 *117*
General Cleaning Contractors Ltd v Christmas [1952] 2 All ER 1110 *247*
Gibson v East Riding of Yorkshire Council [1999] IRLR 358 *262*
Glasgow City Council v Marshall [2000] ICR 196 *207*
Glendale Managed Services v Graham & Others [2003] IRLR 465 *43*
Gogay v Hertfordshire County Council [2000] IRLR 703 *42*

Goodwin v Patent Office (1998) The Times 11
  November *194*
Grant v South West Trains Ltd [1998] IRLR 206
  166
Greater Manchester Police Authority v Lea
  [1990] IRLR 372 *158*
Greenwood v British Airways plc [1999] ICR 696
  195
Greig v Community Industry [1979] IRLR 158
  151

Haden v Cowan [1982] IRLR 314 *119*
Haddon v Van Den Burgh Foods Ltd [1999]
  IRLR 672 *101*
Hadjioannous v Coral Casinos [1981] IRLR 352
  105
Hagen v ICI Chemicals and Polymers Ltd [2002]
  IRLR 31 *145*
Halford v Sharples [1992] 1 WLR 736 *316*
Halford v United Kingdom [1997] IRLR 471 *7*
Hall v Woolston Hall Leisure Ltd [2001] 1 WLR
  225; [2001] ICR 99 *31, 32, 98*
Hamilton v Futura Floors Ltd [1990] IRLR 478
  47
Hampson v Department of Education & Science
  [1989] IRLR 302 *160*
Hannen v Ryman [1979] EAT/478/79 *97*
Hare v Murphy Brothers Ltd [1974] ICR 603
  68
Harrods Ltd v Remick [1997] IRLR 583 *185*
Hart v A R Marshall & Sons [1977] IRLR 51 *67*
Hayward v Cammell Laird Shipbuilders Ltd (No
  2) [1988] AC 894 *213*
Health and Safety Executive v Cadman [2004]
  IRLR 29 *160*
Heath v Longman (Meat Salesmen) [1973] IRLR
  214 *82*
Heatons Transport (St Helens) Ltd v Transport
  & Genral Workers' Union [1972] 3 WLR 431
  271
Hendricks v Commissioner of Police for the
  Metropolis [2003] IRLR 96 *182*
Herbert Morris Ltd v Saxelby [1916] 1 AC 688
  52
Hewcastle Catering Ltd v Ahmed and Elkamah
  [1991] IRLR 473 *31, 98*
Hewlett Packard Ltd v O'Murphy [2002] IRLR 4
  16
Higgins v Cables Montague Contracts Ltd [1993]
  EAT/564/93 *238*
High Table Ltd v Horst [1997] IRLR 513 *117*
Hill v C A Parsons & Co Ltd [1972] 1 Ch 305
  46, 75

Hilton Hotels v Protopapa [1990] IRLR 316 *80*
Hitchcock v Post Office [1980] ICR 100 *17*
Hivac Ltd v Park Royal Scientific Instruments
  [1946] Ch 169 *39, 40*
HM Prison Service v Beart [2005] IRLR 171
  204
Hogan v Cambridgeshire County Council [2001]
  IDS B699/10 *67*
Holman v Johnson (1775) 1 Cowp 341 *31, 97*
Home Office v Holmes [1984] IRLR 299 *157*
Hopkins v National Union of Seamen [1985] ICR
  268 *273*
Horsey v Dyfed County Council [1982] IRLR
  395 *154*
Hough v Leyland DAF Ltd [1991] IRLR 194
  127
Hugh-Jones v St John's College, Cambridge
  [1979] ICR 848 *174*
Hurley v Mustoe [1981] ICR 490 *158*
Hutchings v Coinseed Ltd [1998] IRLR 190
  59

Iceland Frozen Foods v Jones [1983] ICR 17;
  [1982] IRLR 439 *100, 197*
Igbo v Johnson Matthey Chemicals Ltd [1986]
  IRLR 215 *65*
Igen v Wong [2005] IRLR 258 *169*
Inland Revenue Commissioners v St Hermans
  Estate Co Ltd [2002] IRLR 788 *244*
Inland Revenue Wales and Midlands v Bebb
  Travel plc [2002] IRLR 783 *243*
Insitu Cleaning Co Ltd v Heads [1995] IRLR 4
  152
Irani v Southampton and South-West Hampshire
  Health Authority [1985] IRLR 203 *75*

Jackson v Ghost Ltd [2003] IRLR 824 *99*
James v Eastleigh Borough Council [1990] IRLR
  288 *150, 153*
John Brown Engineering Ltd v Brown & Others
  [1997] IRLR 90 *130*
Johnson v Nottinghamshire Combined Police
  Authority [1974] IRLR 20 *119*
Johnson v Unisys [2001] IRLR 279 *38, 113*
Johnston v Bloomsbury Health Authority [1991]
  2 WLR 1362 *258*
Jones v Associated Tunnelling Co Ltd [1981]
  IRLR 477 *49*
Jones v The Post Office [2001] ICR 805 *197*
Jones v Tower Boot Co Ltd [1997] 2 All ER 406;
  [1997] IRLR 168 *29, 162, 183, 184, 187*
Jones v University of Manchester [1993] IRLR
  218 *160*

Table of Cases

Kalanke v Freie Hansestadt Bremen [1996] ICR 314   *174, 175*
Katsikas v Konstantinidis [1993] IRLR 179   *142*
Kavanagh v Hiscock [1974] QB 600   *307*
Kenneth McRae & Co Ltd v Dawson [1984] IRLR 5   *124*
Kenny v Hampshire Constabulary (1998) The Times 22 October   *201*
Kent County Council v Mingo [2000] IRLR 90   *200*
Kerr v Lister Co Ltd [1977] IRLR 259   *209*
Kerr v The Sweater Shop (Scotland) Ltd [1996] IRLR 424   *238*
Kerry Foods v Creber [2000] IRLR 10   *147*
Kidd v DRG (UK) Ltd [1984] IRLR 190   *158*
Kirkton v Tetrosyl [2002] IRLR 840   *194*
Kwik-Fit v Lineham [1992] ICR 183   *72*

Ladbroke Racing Ltd v Arnott [1983] IRLR 154   *90*
Laing Limited v Yessin Essa [2004] IRLR 313   *189, 190*
Lancashire Fires Ltd v S A Lyons & Co Ltd and Others [1997] IRLR 113   *57*
Langsten v AEUW [1974] 1 All ER 980   *45*
Langston v Cranfield University [1998] IRLR 172   *133*
Lasertop Ltd v Webster [1997] IRLR 498   *172*
Law Stores Ltd v Oliphant [1978] IRLR 251   *107*
Lawlor v Union of Post Office Workers [1965] Ch 712   *274*
Lawrence v Regent Office Care Ltd [2002] IRLR 822   *214*
Lawson v Serco [2004] IRLR 206   *99*
Lee v Showmen's Guild of Great Britain [1952] 2 QB 829   *273*
Lesney Products Ltd v Nolan [1977] IRLR 77   *119*
Leverton v Clwyd County Council [1989] 2 WLR 47   *215*
Levez v T H Jennings (Harlow Pools) Ltd [2000] ICR 58   *222*
Lewis v Kingston Royal London Borough Council (2001) Judgment of 3 May (unreported)   *318*
Lewis v Motorworld Garages Ltd [1985] IRLR 465   *40, 77*
Lewis Shops Group v Wiggins [1973] IRLR] 205   *89*
Lister v Romford Ice and Cold Storage Co [1957] AC 555; [1957] 1 All ER 125   *39, 250*

Litster v Forth Dry Dock & Engineering Co Ltd [1989] ICR 341; [1989] IRLR 161   *133, 139, 140*
Littlewoods Organisation Ltd v Harris [1978] 1 WLR 1472   *53*
Livingstone v Hepworth Refractories [1992] IRLR 63   *100*
London Ambulance Service v Charlton & Others [1992] ICR 773   *284*
London Borough of Southwark v Afolabi [2003] IRLR 220   *188*
London Borough of Waltham Forest v Omilaju [2004] EWCA Civ 1493   *77*
London Transport Executive v Clarke [1981] ICR 355   *80*
London Underground v Edwards [1997] IRLR 157   *158*
London Underground v Edwards (No 2) [1998] IRLR 364   *159*
London Underground Ltd v National Union of Rail, Maritime and Transport Staff [1995] IRLR 636   *301*
Lonrho v Shell Petroleum Ltd [1982] AC 173   *297*
Lord Chancellor v Coker [2001] IRLR 116   *155*
Lucas (T) & Co Ltd v Mitchell [1972] 3 All ER 689   *55*
Luce v London Borough of Bexley [1990] ICR 591   *284*
Lumley v Gye (1853) 2 E & B 216   *294*

Macarthys v Smith [1980] ICR 672   *215*
MacDonald v Advocate General for Scotland [2003] IRLR 512   *166*
MacLelland v National Union of Journalists [1975] ICR 116   *273*
Malik v Bank of Credit and Commerce International SA (In Liquidation) [1997] IRLR 462   *40, 74*
Managers (Holborn) Ltd v Hohne [1978] IRLR 230   *117*
Mandla v Dowell Lee [1983] ICR 385   *181*
Market Investigations Ltd v Minister of Social Security [1969] 2 QB 173   *13*
Marley Tile Company Ltd v Shaw [1980] ICR 72   *280*
Marriott v Oxford & District Co-operative Society [1970] 1 QB 186   *49, 115, 116*
Marschall v Land Nordrhein-Westfalen [1998] IRLR 39   *174, 175*
Marshall v Harland & Wolff Ltd [1972] IRLR 90   *115*
Marshall v N M Financial Management Ltd [1997] IRLR 449   *55*

Marshall v Southampton and South-West Hampshire Area Health Authority [1986] ECR 723; [1986] ICR 335 *97, 149*
Marshalls Clay Products Limited v Caulfield [2004] IRLR 564 *264, 265*
Martin v MBS Fastenings (Glynwed) Distribution Ltd [1983] IRLR 49 *68*
Martin v Yeoman Aggregates Ltd [1983] IRLR 49 *71*
Mason v Provident Clothing and Supply Co Ltd [1913] AC 724 *52*
Massey v Crown Life Insurance [1978] ICR 590 *14, 15*
McAlwane v Boughton Estates Ltd [1973] 2 All ER 299 *64*
McCabe v Cornwall County Council; [2004] IRLR 733 (HL) [2003] IRLR 87 (CA) *41*
McCaffrey v Jeavons & Co Ltd [1967] 2 ITR 636 *115*
McFarlane v Glasgow City Council [2001] IRLR 7 *12*
McMeechan v Secretary of State for Employment [1997] IRLR 353 *21*
Meade v Haringey London Borough Council [1979] 1 WLR 637 *297*
Mears v Safecar Security [1982] IRLR 183 *35*
Mediguard Services Ltd v Thame [1994] IRLR 504 *207*
Menzies v Smith & McLaurin Ltd [1980] IRLR 180 *284*
Mercury Communications Ltd v Scott-Garner [1984] Ch 37 *298*
Meridian Ltd v Gomersall [1977] IRLR 425 *107*
Michael Peters Ltd v Farnfield [1995] IRLR 190 *139*
Midland Bank v Madden [2000] IRLR 827 *101*
Midland Cold Storage v Turner [1972] ICR 230 *267*
Millbrook Furnishing Industries Ltd v McIntosh [1981] IRLR 309 *77*
Mingeley v Pennock and Another (t/a Amber Cars) [2004] ICR 727 *186*
Ministry of Defence v Jeremiah [1980] IRLR 436 *151, 182*
Mohmed v Virgin Trains (2004) (not reported) *192*
Monie v Coral Racing Ltd [1980] IRLR 464 *92*
Moonsar v Fiveway Express Transport Ltd [2004] EAT/0476/04 *154*
Moore v C & A Modes [1981] IRLR 71 *93*
Morgan v Middlesborough Council [2004] EAT/0375/04 *208*

Morgan v Staffordshire University [2002] IRLR 190 *193*
Morrish v Henleys Ltd [1973] IRLR 61 *38*
Morrow v Safeway Stores plc [2002] IRLR 9 *79*
Morse v Wiltshire County Council [1998] IRLR 352 *197*
Morton v South Ayrshire Council (2002) The Times 1 March *214*
Morton Sundour Fabrics v Shaw [1967] 2 ITR 84 *69, 70, 115*
Motorola v Davidson [2001] IRLR 4 *21, 22*
MPB Structure Ltd v Munro [2003] IRLR 350 *264, 265*
Mugford v Midland Bank [1997] IRLR 208 *129, 130*
Murphy v Epsom College [1985] IRLR 271 *118*
Murray v Foyle Meats Ltd [1999] ICR 827 *120*
Murray v Newham Citizens Advice Bureau [2003] IRLR 340 *193*

NALGO v Killorn and Simm [1990] IRLR 464 *274, 275*
Nagarajan v London Regional Transport [1999] 3 WLR 425 *184*
Napier v National Business Agency [1951] 2 All ER 264 *97*
Narich Proprietary Ltd v Commissioner of Pay-Roll Tax [1984] ICR 286 *14*
Nash v Mash Roe Group plc [1998] IRLR 168 *96*
National Coal Board v Sherwin [1978] IRLR 122 *209*
National Heart and Chest Hospital v Nambiar [1981] IRLR 196 *104*
National Power plc v Young [2001] ICR 328 *221*
National Vulcan Engineering Insurance Group v Wade [1978] ICR 800 *219*
NCB v Galley [1958] 1 All ER 91 *46*
Nelson v BBC [1977] IRLR 148 *117, 119*
Nelson v Carillion Services Ltd [2003] IRLR 428 *171*
Nethermere Ltd v Gardiner [1984] IRLR 240 *15*
Newham London Borough Council v NALGO [1993] ICR 189 *303, 305*
Newland v Simmons & Willer (Hairdressers) Ltd [1981] IRLR 359 *97*
News Group Newspapers Ltd v SOGAT 82 [1986] IRLR 337 *297*

Nokes v Doncaster Amalgamated Collieries Ltd [1940] AC 1014   *141*
Nordenfelt v Maxim Nordenfelt Guns & Ammunition Co [1894] AC 535   *52*
North Essex Health Authority v David-John [2004] ICR 112   *18*
North Yorkshire County Council v Fay [1986] IRLR 247   *120*
Northern Joint Police Board v Power [1997] IRLR 610   *182*
Norton Tool Co Ltd v Tewson [1972] IRLR 86   *113*
Nottinghamshire County Council v Meikle [2004] IRLR 703   *199, 203*
Nova Plastics Ltd v Froggatt [1982] IRLR 146   *40*

O'Brien v Associated Fire Alarms Ltd [1988] 1 All ER 93   *38*
O'Brien & Others v Sim-Chem Ltd [1980] ICR 573   *210*
Octavius Atkinson & Sons Ltd v Morris [1989] IRLR 158   *109*
Office Angels Ltd v Rainer-Thomas and O'Connor [1991] IRLR 214   *54*
O'Kelly v Trusthouse Forte [1983] ICR 728   *15*
Oliver v J P Malnick & Co Ltd [1984] 3 All ER 795   *20*
Ottoman Bank v Chakarian [1930] AC 277   *38*
Owen v Professional Golfers' Association (2000) (unreported)   *153*
Owen and Briggs v James [1982] ICR 618   *179*
Owusu v London Fire & Civil Defence Authority [1995] IRLR 574   *152, 182*

P v National Association of School Masters [2003] ICR 386   *282*
P v S and Cornwall County Council [1996] IRLR 347   *165, 313*
Paggetti v Cobb (2002) The Times 12 April   *112*
Palmer v Southend-on-Sea Borough Council [1984] IRLR 119   *108*
Paris v Stepney Borough Council [1951] 1 All ER 42   *247*
Parkinson v March Consulting Ltd [1997] IRLR 308   *105*
Pay v Lancashire Probation Service (2003) The Times 27 November   *105*
Payne v Spook Erection Ltd [1984] IRLR 219   *38*
Peake v Automotive Products Ltd [1978] ICR 968   *150, 151*

Pearce v Mayfield School [2003] IRLR 512   *166*
Pepper v Webb [1969] 2 All ER 216   *72*
Petrie v MacFisheries [1940] 1 KB 258   *48*
Photostatic Copiers (Southern) Ltd v Okuda and Japan Office Equipment Ltd [1995] IRLR 11   *140, 141*
Pickford v Imperial Chemical Industries plc [1998] IRLR 435   *248*
Pickstone & Others v Freemans plc [1988] 3 WLR 265   *213*
Piddington v Bates [1960] 3 All ER 660   *307*
Polkey v A E Dayton Services [1988] AC 344; [1988] IRLR 503   *102, 129, 130*
Porcelli v Strathclyde Regional Council [1986] ICR 564   *152, 164*
Port of London Authority v Payne [1994] ICR 555   *316*
Porter v Oakbank School (2004) 19 March Case No XA52/03   *91, 92*
Post Office v Fennell [1981] IRLR 221   *105*
Post Office v Foley [2000] IRLR 827   *197*
Potter v Hunt Contracts Ltd [1992] IRLR 108   *238*
Poussard v Spiers (1876) 1 QBD 410   *66*
PowerHouse Retail Ltd & Others v Burroughs, Bartlett & Others [2004] EWCA Civ 1281   *221*
President of the Methodist Conference v Parfitt [1984] QB 368   *19*
Preston v Wolverhampton Healthcare NHS Trust (No 2) [2001] ICR 217   *220, 221*
Preston & Others v Wolverhampton Healthcare NHS Trust & Others; Fletcher & Others v Midland Bank plc Case C–78/98 [2000] IRLR 506   *220, 221*
Price v Civil Service Commission [1977] IRLR 3   *157*

Quinn v Leathem [1901] AC 495   *294*
Quinn & Others v Calder Industrial Materials Ltd [1996] IRLR 126   *44*

R v Associated Octel Co Ltd [1997] IRLR 123   *252, 254*
R v Attorney-General for Notrthern Ireland, ex parte Burns [1999] IRLR 315   *260*
R v Gateway Foodmarkets Ltd [1997] IRLR 189   *252*
R v London (North) Industrial Tribunal, ex parte Associated Newspapers Ltd [1998] ICR 1212   *317*
R v Secretary of State for Employment, ex parte Equal Opportunities Commission [1994] IRLR 176   *161*

R v Secretary of State for Employment, ex parte Seymour-Smith [2000] IRLR 263 *97*
R v Swan Hunter Shipbuilders Ltd [1981] IRLR 403 *254*
Rainey v Greater Glasgow Health Board Eastern District [1987] AC 224; [1987] IRLR 26 *160, 217*
Rask & Christensen v ISS Kantineservice [1993] IRLR 133 *134*
Rayware Ltd v TGWU [1989] 1 WLR 675 *309*
RCO Support Services Ltd v Unison & Others [2002] ICR 751 *137*
Ready Mixed Concrete v Minister of Pensions and National Insurance [1968] 1 All ER 433 *12, 17*
Relaxion Group v Rhys-Harper; D'Souza v London Borough of Lambeth; Jones v 3M Healthcare [2003] IRLR 484 *168, 203–204*
Rendell v University of London Institute of Education (1977) (unreported) *175*
Retarded Children's Aid Society v Day [1978] 1 WLR 763; [1978] ICR 437 *90, 107*
Ridout v TC Group [1998] IRLR 628 *198*
Rigby v Ferodo Ltd [1987] IRLR 516 *49*
Robb v Leon Motor Services Ltd [1978] IRLR 26 *279*
Robb v London Borough of Hammersmith and Fulham [1991] IRLR 72 *75*
Roberts v West Coast Trains Ltd [2004] IRLR 788 *70*
Robertson v British Gas Corporation [1983] ICR 351 *35, 47*
Roe v Minister of Health [1954] 2 All ER 131 *247*
Roebuck v National Union of Mineworkers (Yorkshire Area) (1976) The Times 28 July *274*
Rookes v Barnard [1964] AC 1129 *296*
Rotsart de Hertaing v J Benoidt SA and IGC Housing Services SA [1997] IRLR 127 *141*
Rowe v Radio Rentals [1982] IRLR 177 *103*
Royal National Orthopaedic Hospital Trust v Howard [2002] IRLR 849 *162–163*
RS Components v Irwin [1973] 1 All ER 41 *94*
Rummler v Dato-Druck GmbH [1987] ICR 774 *210*
Rutherford and Another v Secretary of State for Trade and Industry [2004] IRLR 892 *96*

Sagar v Ridehalgh [1931] 1 Ch 310 *44*
Sainsbury v Savage [1981] IRLR 109 *104*
Saunders v Richmond-upon-Thames London Borough Council [1977] IRLR 362 *163*

Savoia v Chilktern Herb Farms Ltd [1982] IRLR 166 *78*
Scally & Others v Southern Health & Social Services Board [1991] IRLR 478 *37, 41*
Schmidt v Austicks Bookshops [1977] IRLR 360 *152, 153*
Schmidt v Spar [1995] ICR 237 *135*
Secretary of State for Employment v ASLEF & Others [1972] 2 All ER 949 *43, 48*
Secretary of State for Employment v Spence [1987] QB 179 *139*
Secretary of State for Trade and Industry v Bottrill [1999] ICR 592 *18*
Secretary of State for Trade and Industry v Cook [1997] IRLR 150 *141*
Securicor Omega Express Ltd v GMB [2004] IRLR 9 *128*
Seide v Gillette Industries Ltd [1980] IRLR 427 *179*
Shamoon v Chief Constable of the Royal Ulster Constabulary [2003] IRLR 285 *155*
Sheffield v Oxford Controls Company Ltd [1979] ICR 208 *65*
Shell UK Ltd v Lostock Garages Ltd [1977] 1 All ER 481 *38*
Shepherd v Jerrom [1986] IRLR 358 *68*
Shillito v Van Leer (UK) Ltd [1997] IRLR 495 *255*
Shirlaw v Southern Foundries Ltd [1939] 2 KB 206 *38*
Showboat Entertainment Centre Ltd v Owens [1984] IRLR 7 *180*
Sim v Rotherham Borough Council [1986] IRLR 391 *43*
Simmons v Hoover Ltd [1977] IRLR 266 *122*
Sinclair v Neighbour [1967] 2 QB 279 *72*
Skyrail Oceanic Ltd v Coleman [1981] IRLR 226 *154*
Sloan v Strathclyde Regional Council (1978) (unreported) *164*
Smith v Safeway [1995] IRLR 132 *152, 153*
Smith v Secretary of State for Trade and Industry [2000] IRLR 6 *7*
Snoxell and Davies v Vauxhall Motors Ltd [1977] ICR 700 *222*
Sogbetun v Hackney London Borough Council [1998] ICR 1264 *312*
Spafax v Harrison [1980] IRLR 443 *79*
Spijkers v Gebroeders Benedik Abbatoir CV Case 24/85 [1986] 3 ECR 1119 *134*
Spring v Guardian Assurance plc [1995] 2 AC 296 *41*
Squibb UK Staff Association v Certification Officer [1979] ICR 235 *268*

Table of Cases

Stanley Cole (Wainfleet) Ltd v Sheridan [2003] IRLR 52   *80*
Steel v Union of Post Office Workers [1977] IRLR 288   *159*
Stevenson v Teeside Bridge and Engineering Ltd [1971] 1 All ER 296   *44*
Stevenson & Others v MacDonald and Evans [1952] 1 TLR 101   *10, 11*
Stewart v Cleveland Guest (Engineering) Ltd [1994] IRLR 440   *153*
Stichting (Dr Sophie Redmond) v Bartol [1992] IRLR 366   *137*
Stratford v Lindley [1965] AC 307   *296*
Stubbs v Trower, Still & Keeling [1987] IRLR 321   *31*
Susie Radin Ltd v GMB and Others [2004] IRLR 400   *131*
Sutherland v Hatton [2002] IRLR 263   *249*
Suzen v Zehnacker Gebaudereinigung GmbH Krankenhaus Service and Lefarth GmbH [1997] IRLR 255   *135, 136*
Swaine v Health & Safety Executive [1986] IRLR 205   *96*
Sybron Corporation v Rochem Ltd & Others [1983] IRLR 253   *42*
Symbian Ltd v Christensen [2001] IRLR 77   *60*
System Floors (UK) Ltd v Daniel [1982] ICR 54   *35*

Taff Vale Railway Company v Amalgamated Society of Railway Servants [1901] AC 426   *269, 294*
Tanner v Kean [1978] IRLR 110   *71*
Taylor v Alidair [1978] IRLR 82   *39*
Taylor v Kent County Council [1969] 2 All ER 1080   *120*
Tennants Textile Colours Ltd v Todd [1989] IRLR 3   *213*
TGWU v McKinnon [2001] IRLR 597   *147*
TGWU v Webber [1990] ICR 711   *275*
Thomas v Hillingdon London Borough Council (2002) The Times 4 October   *100*
Thomas v Jones [1978] ICR 274   *117*
Thomas and Others v National Union of Mineworkers [1986] Ch 20   *307*
Thompson v Department for Work and Pensions [2004] IRLR 348   *153*
Thomson v Deakin [1952] Ch 646   *295*
Timex Corporation v Hodgson [1981] IRLR 522   *173*
Todd v British Midland Airways [1978] ICR 959   *99*
Torquay Hotel Co Ltd v Cousins [1969] 2 Ch 106   *295*

Treganowan v Knee [1974] ICR 405   *95*
Turvey v C W Cheney & Sons Ltd [1979] IRLR 105   *122*

United Bank Ltd v Akhtar [1989] IRLR 507   *36, 39*
University of East London v Hinton [2005] ICR 1260   *66*

Vakante v Governing Body of Addey and Stanhope School (No 2) [2004] ICR 279   *186*
Vaux Breweries v Ward [1968] 3 ITR 385   *118*
Vento v Chief Constable of West Yorkshire Police (No 2) [2003] IRLR 102   *176, 189, 190*
Virgin Net v Harper [2004] IRLR 390   *73*
Vokes Ltd v Bear [1974] ICR 1   *121*

Waite v Government Communication Headquarters [1983] IRLR 341   *96*
Walden Engineering Co Ltd v Warrener [1993] IRLR 420   *145*
Walker v Northumberland County Council [1995] IRLR 35   *45, 253*
Wallace Bogan & Co v Cove & Others [1997] IRLR 453   *58*
Waltons & Morse v Dorrington [1997] IRLR 488   *247*
Wandsworth London Borough Council v National Association of Schoolmasters and Union of Women Teachers [1993] IRLR 344   *299*
Warner v Adnet Ltd [1998] ICR 1056   *143*
Waters v Commissioner of Police of the Metropolis [1997] IRLR 589   *29, 161*
Way v Latilla [1937] 3 All ER 759   *46*
Webb v EMO Air Cargo (UK) Ltd [1994] QB 718; [1993] IRLR 27   *149, 160, 216*
West Midland Co-operative Society v Tipton [1986] IRLR 112   *103, 104*
Western Excavating v Sharp [1978] IRLR 27   *76, 77, 80*
Wheeler v Quality Deep Ltd t/a Thai Royale Restaurant [2004] EWCA Civ 1085   *32, 98*
White & Others v Chief Constable of South Yorkshire [1998] 3 WLR 1509   *248*
White & Others v Kuzych [1951] AC 585   *273*
Whitehouse v Chas A Blatchford & Sons [1999] IRLR 492   *143*
Wignall v British Gas Corporation [1984] ICR 716   *284*
Wilkins v Cantrell & Cochrane (GB) Ltd [1978] IRLR 483   *81*

Wilkinson v Lugg [1990] ICR 599   98
William Hill Organisation Ltd v Tucker [1998] IRLR 313   59, 60
Williams v J Walter Thompson Group [2005] EWCA Civ 133   199
Wilson v North Cumbria Acute NHS Trust (2005)   211
Wilson & Another v United Kingdom [2002] IRLR 568   279
Wilson and Others v St Helens Borough Council [1998] IRLR 706 (HL); [1997] IRLR 505 (CA)   140, 144
Wilson and Others v United Kingdom (2002) The Times 5 July   8
Wilson & Others v West Cumbria Healthcare NHS Trust [1995] PIQR 38   145
Wilsons and Clyde Coal Co Ltd v English [1938] AC 57   44, 247
Wiltshire County Council v NATFHE [1980] ICR 455   27
Wiltshire Police Authority v Wynn [1981] 1 QB 95   19
Wishart v National Association of Citizens Advice Bureau [1990] IRLR 393   30, 75
Withers v Perry Chain Co [1961] 1 WLR 1314   250
Woodhead v Chief Constable of West Yorkshire Police (1990) (unreported)   163
Woods v W M Car Services Ltd [1982] IRLR 413   40, 78
Wylie v Dee & Co (Menswear) Ltd [1978] IRLR 103   172–173

X v Y [2004] IRLR 625   106

Yates v British Leyland [1974] IRLR 367   87
Yeboah v Crofton [2002] IRLR 634   189
Yewens v Noakes (1880) 6 QBD 530   11
Young v Canadian Northern Railway Co [1931] AC 83   47
Young & Woods Ltd v West [1980] IRLR 201   14, 15

Zucker v Astrid Jewels Ltd [1978] ICR 1088   281

Table of Statutes and Other Materials

Acquired Rights Directive *see* EC Directives 77/187/EEC and 2001/23/EC

Births and Deaths Registration Act 1953
   s10(1)   *231*
   s10A(1)   *231*

Child Support Act 1991   *238*
Children (Protection at Work) Regulations 1998   *20*
Civil Aviation (Working Time) Regulations 2004   *265, 266*
Civil Partnership Act 2004   *154*
Collective Redundancies and Transfer of Undertakings (Protection of Employment) (Amendment) Regulations 1995   *126*
Collective Redundancies and Transfer of Undertakings (Protection of Employment) (Amendment) Regulations 1999   *126*
Collective Redundancies Directive *see* EC Directive 75/129/EEC
Combination Act 1799   *1, 2*
Combination Act 1800   *1, 2*
Community Drivers' Hours Regulation (3820/85/EEC)   *266*
Conspiracy and Protection of Property Act 1875   *2, 271, 294, 307*
   s7(4)   *308*
Contracts of Employment Act 1963   *2*

Disability Discrimination Act 1995   *168, 192, 193, 194, 195, 196, 197, 200, 201, 202, 203, 204, 205, 221, 314*
   s1   *192, 193, 194*
   s1(1)   *192, 194*
   s1(2)   *192*
   s2   *193*
   s3A   *196*
   s3A(1)(a)   *196*
   s3A(1)(b)   *196, 197*
   s3A(2)   *198*
   s3A(3)   *197*
   s3A(4)   *196*
   s3A(5)   *196*
   s3B   *203*

Disability Discrimination Act 1995 (*contd.*)
   s4   *202, 203*
   s4(2)(d)   *203*
   s4(3)   *203*
   s4A(3)   *199*
   s5   *196, 197*
   s5(1)   *196, 201, 202*
   s5(1)(a)   *196*
   s5(1)(b)   *196*
   s5(2)   *200*
   s5(2)(a)   *201*
   s5(2)(b)   *201*
   s5(3)   *201*
   s6   *198*
   s6A   *203*
   s6(1)(a)   *201*
   s6(3)   *200*
   s17A   *204*
   s17A(1C)   *204*
   s55   *205*
   s58   *205*
   s59   *200*
   Pt II   *192*
   Sch 1   *193*
   Sch 3   *204*
Disability Discrimination Act 1995 (Amendment) Regulations 2003   *192, 195, 202, 203, 204*
   reg 4(2)   *196*
Disability Discrimination Act 1995 (Pensions) Regulations 2003   *192*
Disability Discrimination (Employment Field) (Leasehold Premises) Regulations 2004   *200*
Disability Discrimination (Guidance and Code of Practice) (Appointed Day) Order 1996   *194*
Disability Discrimination (Meaning of Disability) Regulations 1996   *192*

EC Directives
   75/117/EEC   *206*
   75/129/EEC   *126, 127*
      art 2   *126*
   76/207/EEC   *148, 149, 160, 165, 166, 168, 174, 175, 313*
      art 5(1)   *165*
   77/187/EEC   *6, 133, 134, 135, 139, 145*

EC Directives, 77/187/EEC (*contd.*)
    art 1(1)   *134, 137*
    art 3   *141*
    art 3(1)   *140*
    art 3(3)   *145*
  89/391/EEC   *84, 256*
  92/85/EEC   *149, 227, 228, 257*
  93/104/EC   *6, 258, 261, 262*
    art 2(4)   *261*
    art 7   *262*
  96/34/EC   *230*
  98/50/EC   *133*
  2000/34/EC   *258*
  2000/78/EC   *191, 192*
  2000/79/EC   *265*
  2001/23/EC   *133*
  2002/73/EC   *165*
  2003/88/EC   *258, 259, 260, 261, 263, 266*
EC Treaty   *3, 148, 206*
  art 138   *256*
  art 140   *3*
  art 141   *6, 149, 160, 166, 175, 206, 207, 211, 214, 216, 220*
  art 141(1)   *214, 215*
Employment Equality (Religion or Belief) Regulations 2003   *191–192*
  reg 3   *191*
  reg 4   *191*
  reg 5   *191*
  reg 7   *191*
  reg 21   *191*
Employment Equality (Sex Discrimination) Regulations 2005   *164, 165*
  reg 5   *165*
Employment Equality (Sexual Orientation) Regulations 2003   *167*
  reg 3   *167*
  reg 4   *167*
  reg 5   *167*
  reg 21   *167*
Employers' Liability Act 1880   *20*
Employers' Liability (Compulsory Insurance) Act 1969   *45*
Employment Act 1980   *288*
Employment Act 1982
  s18   *298*
Employment Act 1989   *148, 172*
Employment Act 1990   *272*
Employment Act 2002   *v, 51, 85, 105, 225, 311*
  s1   *229*
  s42   *222*
  s47   *51*

Employment Act 2002 (Dispute Resolution) Regulations 2004   *v, 70, 72, 85, 103, 105, 313*
  reg 15   *109*
Employment Protection Act 1975   *126, 268, 288*
Employment Protection (Consolidation) Act 1978   *65, 161*
  s57(3)   *129*
Employment Protection (Part-Time Employees) Regulations 1995   *161*
Employment Relations Act 1999   *v, 28, 225, 227, 230, 268, 280, 281, 282, 283, 288, 299, 300, 301–302, 302, 304*
  s1   *288*
  s7   *225*
  s8   *234*
  s10   *104*
  s29   *268*
  s32(3)   *98*
  s34   *112*
  s73   *226*
  Sch 1   *288*
Employment Relations Act 2004   *v, 3, 84, 87, 267, 279, 281–283*
  ss1–21   *281*
  s3   *281*
  ss22–28   *281*
  s24   *282*
  s26   *283*
  ss29–43   *281*
  s29   *84*
  s37   *104*
  s38   *283*
  s41   *283*
  ss44–47   *281, 283*
  ss48–51   *281*
  s51   *282*
  ss52–55   *281*
  ss56–59   *281*
  Pt 1   *281*
Employment Relations Act 2004 (Commencement No 1 and Transitional Provisions) Order 2004   *281*
Employment Rights Act 1996   *85, 86–87, 99, 103, 106, 234, 235*
  s1   *19, 33*
  s1(3)   *33*
  s1(3)(a)   *33*
  s1(3)(b)   *33*
  s1(3)(c)   *33*
  s3   *312*
  s4(2)   *312*
  s4(5)   *312*

Table of Statutes and Other Materials xxi

Employment Rights Act 1996 (*contd.*)
   s8   *236*
   s8(2)   *236*
   s8(2)(a)   *236*
   s8(2)(b)   *236*
   s8(2)(c)   *236*
   s8(2)(d)   *236*
   s9   *236*
   s11   *23, 237*
   s13   *239*
   s13(1)   *238*
   s13(1)(a)   *238*
   s13(1)(b)   *238*
   s14   *239*
   s15   *239*
   s16   *239*
   s18   *240*
   s23   *312*
   s23(2)   *241*
   s23(2)(a)   *241*
   s23(2)(b)   *241*
   s27   *239*
   s27(1)   *239*
   s27(1)(a)   *239*
   s27(1)(b)   *239*
   s27(1)(c)   *239*
   s27(1)(ca)   *239*
   s27(1)(cb)   *239*
   s27(1)(d)   *239*
   s27(1)(e)   *239*
   s27(1)(f)   *239*
   s27(1)(g)   *239*
   s27(1)(h)   *239*
   s27(1)(j)   *239*
   s27(2)   *239*
   s27(2)(a)   *239*
   s27(2)(b)   *240*
   s27(2)(c)   *240*
   s27(2)(d)   *240*
   s27(2)(e)   *240*
   s27(3)   *240*
   s28   *239, 244*
   s28(3)   *244*
   s29   *244*
   s30   *245*
   s43   *62*
   s43B   *61*
   s44   *255, 256*
   s47B   *61*
   s47C   *232*
   s48   *256*
   s55   *224*
   s55(1)   *224*

Employment Rights Act 1996 (*contd.*)
   s55(1)(a)   *224*
   s55(1)(b)   *224*
   s55(2)   *225*
   s56   *225*
   s56(2)   *225*
   s57A   *234, 235*
   s57A(1)   *234*
   s57A(1)(a)   *234*
   s57A(1)(b)   *234*
   s57A(1)(c)   *234*
   s57A(1)(d)   *234, 235*
   s57A(1)(e)   *234*
   s57A(3)   *234*
   s57A(4)   *234*
   s64   *239*
   s68   *239*
   s71   *225*
   s72   *228*
   s73   *227*
   s74   *227*
   s76   *230*
   ss79–84   *226*
   s80A   *229*
   s86   *46, 107*
   s93   *64*
   s94   *63, 73, 87, 88, 97, 98*
   s95   *28, 69, 70*
   s95(1)(c)   *75, 76*
   s98   *87, 90, 106, 129, 197*
   s98(1)   *87*
   s98(1)(a)   *87*
   s98(1)(b)   *87, 94*
   s98(2)   *87, 88*
   s98(2)(a)   *87, 88, 89*
   s98(2)(b)   *87*
   s98(2)(c)   *87*
   s98(2)(d)   *87*
   s98(3)(a)   *88*
   s98(3)(b)   *89*
   s98(4)   *88, 100, 130, 132, 133*
   s98(4)(a)   *100*
   s98(4)(b)   *100*
   s98A   *85*
   s98B   *86, 87*
   s99   *83, 150*
   s100   *84*
   s100(1)(a)   *85*
   s100(1)(b)   *85*
   s100(1)(c)   *85*
   s100(1)(d)   *85*
   s100(1)(e)   *85*
   s101   *86*

Employment Rights Act 1996 (*contd.*)
    s101A   *86*
    s103A   *61, 86*
    s104   *84, 241*
    s104C   *283*
    s108   *95*
    s109   *95, 96*
    s111(2)   *108*
    s111(3)   *109*
    s112(4)   *111*
    s113   *239*
    s114   *110*
    s115   *111*
    s117   *111*
    ss118–127A   *111*
    s120(1A)   *85*
    s122(4)   *112*
    s123   *112*
    s123(1)   *113*
    s124(1)   *275, 276*
    s128   *312*
    s130   *239*
    s131   *312*
    s132   *312*
    s135   *114*
    s136   *114, 115*
    s136(1)(b)   *119*
    s138   *120*
    s138(1)   *28*
    s138(3)   *121*
    s139   *94, 114, 116, 117*
    s139(6)   *117*
    s140   *122*
    s141   *121*
    s143   *122*
    s143(5)   *123*
    s147   *123*
    s147(2)   *123*
    s148   *124*
    s148(2)(a)   *123*
    s148(2)(b)   *123*
    s162   *125*
    s163(2)   *116*
    s165   *126*
    s182   *21, 312*
    s188   *312*
    s196   *98, 99*
    s196(2)   *237*
    s197   *25*
    s197(1)   *28*
    s203   *66, 100*
    s203(3)(B)   *66*
    s212(3)(c)   *16, 17*

Employment Rights Act 1996 (*contd.*)
    ss221–224   *263*
    s227(1)(a)   *275, 276*
    s227(1)(b)   *111*
    s230   *10, 18, 19, 22*
    s230(2)   *237*
    s234   *263*
    Pt II   *237, 239, 240*
    Pt IVA   *61*
    Pt VI   *239*
    Pt VIII   *229*
    Pt X   *61*
Employment Rights (Dispute Resolution) Act 1998   *311, 312*
    s2   *311*
    s3   *312*
    s7   *319*
    Pt I   *311*
    Pt II   *311*
    Pt III   *311*
Employment Tribunals Act 1996
    s4   *312*
    s11   *316*
    s11(1)   *317*
Employment Tribunals (Constitution and Rules of Procedure) Regulations 2001   *318*
Employment Tribunals (Constitution and Rules of Procedure) Regulations 2004   *311*
    Sch 1   *110*
Employment Tribunals (Constitution and Rules of Procedure) (Amendment) Regulations 2004   *211, 212*
Employment Tribunals Extension of Jurisdiction (England and Wales) Order 1994   *66, 241*
Employment Tribunals (Interest on Awards in Discrimination Cases) Regulations 1996   *190*
Equal Pay Act 1970   *140, 160, 161, 164, 206–223*
    s1   *216*
    s1(1)   *207*
    s1(2)   *207*
    s1(2)(a)   *207, 216*
    s1(2)(a)(i)   *207*
    s1(2)(a)(ii)   *208*
    s1(2)(b)   *210, 216*
    s1(2)(c)   *211, 212, 214*
    s1(2)(c)(i)   *213*
    s1(3)   *160, 216, 217, 218, 219, 222, 315*
    s1(3)(a)   *216*
    s1(3)(b)   *217*
    s1(4)   *208*
    s1(6)   *207, 214, 215*

Equal Pay Act 1970 (*contd.*)
    s2(4)   *220, 221*
    s2(5)   *220*
    s2ZA   *221*
Equal Pay (Amendment) Regulations 1983   *211, 213*
Equal Pay (Amendment) Regulations 2003   *222*
Equal Pay Directive *see* EC Directive 75/117/EEC
Equal Treatment Directive *see* EC Directives 76/207/EEC and 2002/73/EC
Equal Treatment Framework Directive *see* EC Directive 2000/78/EC
Equal Treatment in Occupational Pension Schemes Directive   *148*
European Communities Act 1972   *3*
European Communities (Amendment) Act 1986   *3*
European Communities (Amendment) Act 1993   *3*
European Communities (Amendment) Act 1998   *3*
European Convention on Human Rights 1950   *7, 105*
    art 6   *7*
    art 8   *7, 105, 106*
    art 9   *7, 8*
    art 10   *8*
    art 11   *8, 279*
Extension of Jurisdiction Order 1994   *74*

Fixed-term Employees (Prevention of Less Favourable Treatment) Regulations 2002   *v, 24–27, 28, 85, 220*
    reg 1   *25*
    reg 2   *25*
    reg 3   *25, 27*
    reg 4   *26*
    reg 5   *26*
    reg 6   *26, 85*
    reg 6(3)   *85*
    reg 7   *27*
    reg 8   *27*
Flexible Working (Eligibility, Complaints and Remedies) Regulations 2002   *232*
Flexible Working (Procedural Requirements) Regulations 2002   *230*

Health and Safety at Work etc Act 1974   *172, 251, 255, 256*
    s2(1)   *251, 252*
    s2(2)   *251*
    s2(3)   *253*
    s2(4)   *253*

Health and Safety at Work etc Act 1974 (*contd.*)
    s2(6)   *253*
    s3(1)   *252, 253, 254*
    s7   *255*
Health and Safety (Display Screen Equipment) Regulations 1992   *258*
Health and Safety Framework Directive *see* EC Directive 89/391
Health and Safety (Miscellaneous Amendments) Regulations 2002   *258*
Highways Act 1980
    s137   *306*
Horizontal Amending Directive *see* EC Directive 2000/34/EC
Human Rights Act 1998   *7, 105, 106, 191*
    s3   *106*

Income and Corporation Taxes Act 1988   *10*
Industrial Relations Act 1971   *35, 288, 296*
Industrial Training Act 1964   *310*

Maastricht Treaty *see* Treaty on European Union
Management of Health and Safety at Work Regulations 1992   *256*
Management of Health and Safety at Work Regulations 1999   *227, 256, 257*
Maternity and Parental Leave (Amendment) Regulations 2001   *225*
Maternity and Parental Leave (Amendment) Regulations 2002   *225, 226, 227*
    reg 8(c)   *226*
Maternity and Parental Leave etc Regulations 1999   *225, 226, 227, 230*
    reg 10   *227*
    reg 13   *230*
    reg 13(1)   *230*
    reg 13(2)   *230*
    reg 13(2)(a)   *230*
    reg 13(2)(b)   *231*
    reg 13(3)   *231*
    reg 18(1)   *231*
    reg 18(2)   *231*
    reg 19   *232*
    reg 20   *227*
    reg 20(7)   *150*
Maternity (Compulsory) Leave Regulations 1994   *228*

National Health Service (General Medical Services) Regulations 1992   *18*
National Minimum Wage Act 1998   *9, 86, 242, 243, 244, 283*
    s19(1)   *243*

Table of Statutes and Other Materials

Parental Leave Directive *see* EC Directive 96/34/EC
Part-Time Workers (Prevention of Less Favourable Treatment) Regulations 2000 *161, 219, 220, 221*
Part-time Workers (Prevention of Less Favourable Treatment) (Amendment) Regulations 2002 *219, 220*
Paternity and Adoption Leave Regulations 2002 *229*
Pensions Act 1995
    ss62–65 *161*
Personal Protective Equipment at Work Regulations 1992 *257*
Police Act 1964 *19*
    s51 *307*
Pregnant Workers Directive *see* EC Directive 92/85/EEC
Provision and Use of Work Equipment Regulations 1998 *257*
Public Interest Disclosure Act 1998 *61, 86*
    s5 *86*
Public Order Act 1986 *308*
    s1 *308*
    s2 *308*
    s3 *308*
    s5 *308*

Race Relations Act 1965 *177*
Race Relations Act 1976 *2, 18, 20, 160, 168, 178, 180, 181, 182, 183, 184, 185, 186, 190, 191, 196, 199, 314*
    s1(1) *178, 180, 182*
    s1(1)(a) *178, 185*
    s1(1)(b) *178*
    s1(1)(b)(i) *178*
    s1(1)(b)(ii) *178*
    s1(1)(b)(iii) *178*
    s1(1A) *178, 179*
    s1(1A)(a) *179*
    s1(1A)(b) *179*
    s1(1A)(c) *179*
    s1(1B) *179*
    s2 *184*
    s2(1) *184, 185*
    s2(1)(a) *184*
    s2(1)(b) *184*
    s2(1)(c) *184*
    s2(1)(d) *184*
    s3 *180, 183*
    s3(1) *180*
    s3(2) *180*
    s4 *183*

Race Relations Act 1976 (*contd.*)
    s4(1) *179*
    s4(1)(a) *179*
    s4(1)(b) *179*
    s4(1)(c) *179*
    s4(2) *186*
    s4A *188*
    s5 *187*
    s5(2) *187*
    s7 *185*
    s7(1) *185*
    s32 *183, 184, 187*
    s78(1) *186*
    Pt II *178*
Race Relations Act 1976 (Amendment) Regulations 2003 *178, 183, 187, 188*
    reg 6 *183*
Race Relations (Questions and Replies) Order 1977 *188*
Racial Treatment Directive 2000 *178*
Redundancy Payments Act 1965 *2*
Registration of Births, Deaths and Marriages (Scotland) Act 1965
    s18(1) *231*
    s18(2) *231*
Rehabilitation of Offenders Act 1974 *83*
    s4(3)(b) *83*
Road Transport (Working Time) Regulations 2005 *266*

Safety Representatives and Safety Committees Regulations 1977 *253*
Sex Discrimination Act 1975 *2, 148, 150, 151, 152, 154, 157, 158, 159, 160, 161, 162, 163–177, 178, 188, 196, 199, 207, 216, 228, 314*
    s1 *150, 156*
    s1(1) *150, 152*
    s1(1)(a) *150, 152, 158, 164*
    s1(2) *156*
    s1(2)(a) *156*
    s1(2)(b) *156*
    s1(2)(b)(i) *156*
    s1(2)(b)(ii) *156*
    s1(2)(b)(iii) *156*
    s3(1) *154*
    s3(1)(a) *154*
    s3(1)(b) *154*
    s3(1)(b)(i) *154*
    s3(1)(b)(ii) *154*
    s3(1)(b)(iii) *154*
    s3(2) *154*
    s4(1) *161, 162, 168*

Sex Discrimination Act 1975 (*contd.*)
   s4A   *165*
   s5   *155*
   s5(3)   *155*
   s6   *163*
   s6(1)(a)   *163, 164, 171, 173*
   s6(1)(c)   *171, 173*
   s6(2)(a)   *171, 173*
   s6(2)(b)   *152, 164*
   s6(4)   *149*
   s6(6)   *164*
   s7   *171*
   s7(1)   *171*
   s7(1)(a)   *171*
   s7(1)(b)   *171*
   s7(2)   *171*
   s7(2)(b)   *172*
   s7(2)(b)(ii)   *172*
   s7(4)   *172*
   s17   *174*
   s18   *174*
   s19   *174*
   s38   *164*
   s41   *161, 165, 169, 187*
   s41(1)   *162*
   s42   *169*
   s43   *174*
   s52   *174*
   s56A(10)   *170*
   s63   *175*
   s63A   *169*
   s63A(2)   *169*
   s63A(2)(a)   *169*
   s63A(2)(b)   *169*
   s74   *175*
   s74(2)   *170*
   s74(2)(b)   *170*
   s76   *175*
   s76(5)   *176*
   s76(6)(b)   *176, 177*
   Pt II   *164, 169*
   Pt III   *169*
Sex Discrimination Act 1975 (Amendment) Regulations 2003   *148*
   reg 2   *162*
   reg 3   *168*
   reg 4   *168*
Sex Discrimination Act 1986   *148*
   s2   *149*
Sex Discrimination and Equal Pay (Remedies) Regulations 1993   *176*
Sex Discrimination (Gender Reassignment) Regulations 1999   *166, 173*

Sex Discrimination (Indirect Discrimination and Burden of Proof) Regulations 2001   *156, 169*
Single European Act 1986   *5*
Social Security Act 1989   *148*
Social Security Contributions and Benefits Act 1992
   s171(1)   *226*
   Pt XI   *239*
   Pt XII   *239*
   Part 12ZA   *239*
   Part 12ZB   *239*
Statute of Artificers 1562   *1*

Trade Disputes Act 1906   *2, 295, 296*
Trade Union Act 1871   *271*
Trade Union Act 1984
   s10   *301*
Trade Union and Labour Relations Act 1974   *296*
Trade Union and Labour Relations (Consolidation) Act 1992   *8, 75, 83, 84, 126, 282, 287, 289, 296, 309*
   s1   *267, 268*
   s5   *268*
   s5(a)   *268*
   s5(b)   *268*
   s10   *269*
   s10(2)   *270*
   s11   *271*
   s12   *269*
   s28   *270*
   s29   *270*
   s30   *270*
   s30(5)   *270*
   s31   *270*
   s32   *270, 271*
   s46   *285*
   s48   *285*
   s49   *285*
   s51   *286*
   s52   *286*
   s63   *273*
   s64   *274*
   s65(2)   *274*
   s66   *275*
   s67   *275*
   s67(8)   *275*
   s67(8)(a)   *275*
   s67(8)(b)   *275*
   s69   *277*
   s137   *272, 277, 278*
   s137(5)   *277*

xxvi Table of Statutes and Other Materials

Trade Union and Labour Relations
  (Consolidation) Act 1992 (*contd.*)
    ss145A–145F   *84, 279*
    s146   *278, 279, 280*
    s146(1)   *280*
    s148   *279*
    s148(3)–(5)   *279*
    s152(1)   *84*
    s161   *312*
    s164   *239*
    s165   *312*
    s166   *312*
    s168   *283*
    s168(1)   *283*
    s168(1)(a)   *283*
    s168(1)(b)   *283*
    s168(1)(c)   *283*
    s168(2)   *284*
    s169   *239*
    s170(1)   *285*
    s174   *276*
    s174(2)   *275*
    s174(2)(a)   *275*
    s174(2)(b)   *275*
    s174(2)(c)   *275*
    s174(2)(d)   *276*
    s175   *276*
    s176   *276*
    s176(6)   *276*
    s176(6)(a)   *276*
    s176(6)(b)   *276*
    s178   *284, 287*
    s178(1)   *287*
    s178(2)   *287*
    s178(2)(a)   *287*
    s178(2)(b)   *287*
    s178(2)(c)   *287*
    s178(2)(d)   *287*
    s178(2)(e)   *287*
    s178(2)(f)   *287*
    s178(2)(g)   *287, 288*
    s178(3)   *288*
    s181   *269*
    s188   *126, 127, 128, 131, 283*
    s188(1A)   *127*
    s188(1B)   *128*
    s188(4)   *128*
    s188A   *126*
    s189   *239*
    s195   *126*
    s199   *104*
    s212A   *319*
    s219   *296, 297, 298, 301, 302, 304*

Trade Union and Labour Relations
  (Consolidation) Act 1992 (*contd.*)
    s219(1)   *296, 299*
    s219(1)(a)   *296, 297*
    s219(1)(b)   *297*
    s219(2)   *298*
    s220   *309*
    s220(1)   *309*
    s220(1)(a)   *309*
    s220(1)(b)   *309*
    s220(2)   *309*
    s224   *305, 306*
    s224(2)   *305*
    s224(2)(a)   *305*
    s224(2)(b)   *305*
    ss226–234A   *301*
    ss226–235   *299*
    s226   *301*
    s226A   *299, 300*
    s226A(2)(c)   *282, 300*
    s226A(3)(b)   *300*
    s226A(3B)   *300*
    s226B   *300*
    s226B(1)   *304*
    s226C   *300*
    s227(1)   *300*
    s227(2)   *301*
    s228(3)   *301*
    s228A   *301*
    ss229–231B   *302*
    s229(1A)   *302*
    s229(2)   *302, 303*
    s229(2A)   *302*
    s231   *303*
    s231(a)   *303*
    s231(b)   *303*
    s231(c)   *303*
    s231(d)   *303*
    s231B   *303*
    s232A   *301*
    s233   *302*
    s234A   *299, 304*
    s234A(3)(a)   *282, 300*
    s234A(5A)   *282, 300*
    s234A(7A)   *304*
    s234A(7B)   *304*
    s236   *75*
    s237(1)   *81*
    s238   *82*
    s238(3)   *82*
    s241   *308*
    s241(1)   *307*
    s241(1)(a)   *308*

Trade Union and Labour Relations
  (Consolidation) Act 1992 (*contd.*)
    s241(1)(b)   *308*
    s241(1)(c)   *308*
    s241(1)(d)   *308*
    s241(1)(e)   *308*
    s241(2)   *308*
    s241(3)   *308*
    s244   *298, 299*
    s244(1)   *298*
    s244(1)(a)   *298*
    s244(1)(b)   *298*
    s244(1)(c)   *298*
    s244(1)(d)   *298*
    s244(1)(e)   *298*
    s244(1)(f)   *298*
    s244(1)(g)   *298*
    Ch VA   *289*
    Sch A1   *289, 290*
      para 7(1)(b)   *289*
      para 10(1)   *289*
      para 10(5)   *289*
      para 11   *289, 290*
      para 12   *289, 290*
      para 14   *291*
      para 14(5)   *290*
      para 31(2)   *290*
      para 31(3)   *291*
      para 58   *291*
      para 59   *291*
      para 99   *292*
      para 156   *292*
      Pt I   *289*
      Pt IV   *292*
Trade Union Ballots and Elections (Independent Scrutineers' Qualifications) Order 1988   *286*
Trade Union Reform and Employment Rights Act 1993   *100, 126, 135, 142*
    s40   *316*
    s203   *100*
Transfer of Undertakings (Protection of Employment) Regulations 1981   *6, 43, 133, 134, 135, 136, 137, 138, 139, 140, 141, 142, 143, 144, 145, 221, 269, 284*
    reg 2(1)   *138*
Transfer of Undertakings (Protection of Employment) Regulations 1981 (*contd.*)
    reg 3   *134*
    reg 5   *139, 141, 145, 147*
    reg 5(1)   *139*
    reg 5(2)   *139*
    reg 5(2)(b)   *145*
    reg 5(3)   *139, 140*
    reg 5(4A)   *142*
    reg 5(4B)   *142*
    reg 6   *147*
    reg 7   *145, 146*
    reg 8   *142*
    reg 8(1)   *142, 143, 144*
    reg 8(2)   *142, 143, 144*
    reg 10   *146, 147*
    reg 11   *146, 147*
Treaty of Amsterdam 1997   *175, 206*
Treaty of Rome *see* EC Treaty
Treaty on European Union 1992   *3, 4*
Truck Acts 1831–1940   *237*

Wages Act 1986   *144, 237*
Working Time Directive *see* EC Directives 93/104/EC and 2003/88/EC
Working Time Regulations 1998   *9, 23, 99, 258–266*
    reg 4   *259*
    reg 4(1)   *259*
    reg 4(2)   *259*
    reg 5   *260*
    reg 5(1)   *259*
    reg 6A   *261*
    reg 10   *261*
    reg 11   *262*
    reg 12   *261*
    reg 13   *263*
    reg 16   *263*
    reg 24A   *262*
Working Time Directive (Amendment) Regulations 2003   *266*
Workplace (Health, Safety and Welfare) Regulations 1992   *257*

1
Introduction to Employment Law

1.1 Introduction
1.2 Historical background
1.3 The European Union

1.1 Introduction

Changes in the social, cultural and economic environment, coupled with the increasing impact of European Union law, have combined to make employment law one of the fastest moving areas of law, providing practitioners, academics and students with a stimulating area of study and practice.

One of the central features of employment law is the relationship between employers and employees which is based on common law principles of contract. However, more recently, statutory regulations have had a significant impact on contracts of employment and other employment issues.

1.2 Historical background

The historical background to employment law can be traced back to 1349 when, following the Black Death and the increase in demand for labour, the Ordinance of Labourers was passed to regulate wages thus preventing workers from making unrealistic wage demands from their employers.

Over the next four hundred years various legislative measures were introduced to prevent groups of workers forming associations which would put pressure on employers to improve their working conditions. The Statute of Artificers 1562 prohibited groups of workers from conspiring together to raise wages. The formations of workers' associations, later to be known as trade unions, were illegal and strict criminal sanctions, including deportation to Australia, were imposed upon those found guilty. The Combination Acts of 1799 and 1800 banned groups of workers in particular industries such as the wool, silk and leather industries from forming associations. The Friendly Societies were groups of craftsmen who joined together paying a small sum of money each week into a mutual insurance which provided benefits in the event of sickness, unemployment, retirement or death. The Family Friendly Societies groups also provided a forum for the discussion of wages and other aspects of their employment. The Combination Acts were repealed in 1824–25 and although this meant that groups of workers could create organisations rather than operate through the Friendly Societies, nevertheless pursuing their objectives through collectivism was still a criminal offence.

Despite the severe criminal penalties workers associations, which had become known as trade unions, were a significant feature of British industrial relations. Pressure from trade unions led to the passing of the Conspiracy and Protection of Property Act 1875 which removed many of the criminal sanctions regarding trade union membership and activity.

The removal of the threat of criminal sanctions led to a significant increase in the number of unskilled workers joining trade unions. By 1900 just over two million workers were members of trade unions.

Although criminal sanctions for belonging to a trade union had been removed, the courts developed tortious liability to cover liability for economic damage to an employer which resulted from industrial action. This situation was reversed by the Trade Disputes Act 1906 which provided immunity to trade unions from liability for claims based on the tort of inducing a breach of contract.

By the beginning of the twentieth century trade unions had achieved legal status and there was a period of abstentionism on the part of the state towards employment law; employers and unions were left to negotiate their own agreements. This laissez faire approach continued until the 1960s when legislation offering protection to employees hit the statute books. The Contracts of Employment Act 1963 provided for minimum periods of notice that should be given to employees in the event of termination of employment. The Redundancy Payments Act 1965 provided employees with some protection in the event of redundancy. In 1964 the employment tribunals (originally called industrial tribunals) were set up and although they initially had a predominately appellate function in respect of administrative decisions, they developed into an adjudicative tribunal providing an informal forum in which employees could bring claims against their employer.

The 1960s was also a period of weakening economic strength. British industry was plagued by wild-cat strikes and inter-union strife and demarcation issues. The Donovan Commission on Trade Unions and Employers' Associations was set up to consider the problem of industrial relations and to suggest reforms. The Labour government responded to the Commission by proposing penal sanctions for unofficial strikes, but the defeat of the Labour government in 1970 brought the Conservatives back into power which effectively shelved any proposed legislation.

In the 1970s further protective legislation was introduced which gave employees the right to bring an action for unfair dismissal, togther with the Sex Discrimination Act 1975 and the Race Relations Act 1976 which were not only designed to protect workers from discrimination but also provided a remedy in the event that a worker suffered discrimination in the workplace.

However, during the early part of the 1970s the strength of the trade unions increased – this strengthening of trade union power helped to achieve better working conditions for many union members, but negotiations for the purpose of collective bargaining between employers and unions were not always easy and the decade will be remembered as one of strikes, picket lines and industrial unrest.

In 1979 the Conservative government returned to power led by Margaret Thatcher. One of her principal goals was to reduce the number of working days lost as a result of industrial action – this she considered she could achieve by weakening the perceived power of trade unions. Legislation was introduced to remove the concept of the closed shop, and lawful strike action became much more difficult with the introduction of considerable procedural requirements before a trade union could call their members out on strike.

After 18 years in government the Conservatives were defeated by Labour in 1997. The Labour government has not fulfilled trade union hopes and expectations by reversing Thatcherite employment policies. However, the Employment Relations Act 2004 has gone some way to addressing some concerns of the trade union movement.

1.3 The European Union

Introduction

Historically, the primary source of employment law has been domestic legislation. However, more recently European Union law in the form of Treaty articles and directives have played a significant part in shaping modern employment law.

The United Kingdom became a member of the European Union in 1973. The European Communities Act 1972, as amended by the European Communities (Amendment) Acts 1986, 1993 and 1998, provides that all obligations which arise as a result of Community law shall be given effect in the United Kingdom. This means that the United Kingdom is obliged to give effect to Community legislation either by enacting further legislation or by interpreting domestic statutes in such a way as to give effect to Community law.

The Treaty of Rome 1957 established the European Economic Community with the signing of the European Economic Community (EEC) Treaty, which, following the Treaty on European Union in 1992, became known as the European Community (EC) Treaty. The Treaty on European Union also changed the name of the European Economic Community to the European Union.

The general aim of the Treaty of Rome was to create a single European market in which there would be freedom of goods, persons and services. Article 140 EC provides that the European Commission 'shall encourage cooperation between the Member States and facilitate the coordination of their action in all social policy fields under this Chapter, particularly in matters relating to employment, labour law and working conditions'.

The Treaty on European Union (more commonly referred to as the Maastricht Treaty) provided for a move towards a more integrated and federal Europe, and included provision for monetary union and a single currency.

The Treaty on European Union also provided for a Social Chapter, which included employment protection measures such as a limitation on working hours. The Social Chapter did not accord with the economic and social philosophies of the Conservative government in power at the time, and they were able to negotiate an 'opt out' from these provisions. When the Labour government came into power in 1997 they accepted the Social Chapter with the signing of the Treaty of Amsterdam, and have since legislated to give effect to its provisions.

The supremacy of European Union law over national legislation has been consistently upheld by the European Court of Justice. National legislation must be interpreted by domestic courts in such a way as to give effect to European Union law. At first the UK courts were reluctant to adopt such a purposive construction: however, more recently there has been a greater acceptance amongst the judiciary of the supremacy of EU law.

The department which deals with employment issues is the Directorate-General for Employment and Social Affairs which, according to its mission statement, 'has the task of contributing to the development of a modern, innovative and sustainable European Social Model with more and better jobs in an inclusive society based on equal opportunities'. It plays a key role in promoting positive interaction between economic, social and employment policies.

Institutions of the European Union

The Commission

The European Commission based in Brussels is responsible for ensuring that effect is given to the Treaties. It is an independent body with executive powers and wide-ranging duties. The European Commission comprises a President and 25 Commissioners, who each head up a department which has responsibility for a particular aspect of Community policy. The Commissioners are appointed by their national governments: however, once they take up their role they become totally independent and work for the good of the European Union as a whole. The Commission puts forward proposals for legislation for approval by the Council of Ministers. It also has a duty to ensure that all Member States comply with EU law, and can refer any Member State who appears to be in breach of EU law to the European Court of Justice.

The Council of Ministers

The Council of Ministers is the principal decision-making body and comprises ministers from each Member State. The composition of the Council may change dependent upon the issue for consideration at any one meeting. Meetings normally comprise prime ministers or foreign secretaries from each Member State. If an issue for consideration is more specific, for example if the matter under discussion is economic policy, then the Council will comprise finance ministers from each Member State. The difficulties caused by a changing composition are in some part overcome by the Committee of the Permanent Representatives of the Member States (COREPER), which carries out preparatory work for Council meetings and co-ordinates senior civil servants from the respective Member States.

The European Parliament

The European Parliament is the only democratically elected European Union institution, yet it has a limited role with respect to EU legislation. The Parliament sits in Strasbourg and Brussels and consists of 732 members who are elected by citizens of their respective Member States. The members are known as Members of the European Parliament (MEPs) and they generally meet once a month to consider proposals put forward by the European Commission. The Parliament generally acts in an advisory capacity, although the Commission does not have to act on any recommendations put forward by the Parliament. The Parliament can put forward its own proposals for policy reform: however, the Commission is not obliged to act upon them.

The European Court of Justice

The European Court of Justice, which sits in Luxembourg, is the supreme judicial authority in the European Union. The Court comprises 25 judges, who are appointed by the agreement of the Member States for renewable terms of six years, and nine Advocates-General. The role of the Advocates-General is to assist the judges by giving reasoned opinions on cases that come before the Court. The Single European Act 1986 created the Court of First Instance, which deals with cases that turn on fact rather than law, and which has reduced the workload of the European Court of Justice.

The European Court of Justice gives rulings on how European law should be interpreted, and may do so on the application of the Commission, Member States or individuals or corporations within Member States. After a case has been heard the Advocate-General will give his opinion on the matter, usually some weeks after the case has been heard: this ruling is given in open court. Some time later the European Court of Justice will publish its ruling and the matter is then referred back to the national courts so that the ruling of the Court can be applied to the particular case.

Sources of European law

There are four principal sources of European law: Community Treaties; directives; recommendations; and decisions of the European Court of Justice.

Treaty articles

Treaty articles provide the foundation for the passing of directives: however, Treaty articles remain important because the European Court of Justice uses a 'teleological approach' when it is considering how European Union law should be interpreted. In other words, the Court considers the purpose of the Treaty and then interprets other legislation to give effect to the spirit of the relevant Treaty article. The European Treaties should be regarded as primary legislation.

An individual may be able to rely upon a Treaty article to protect his rights under European law: this is known as direct effect. Whether or not an article can be regarded as having direct effect will depend upon whether it is unconditional, sufficiently precise in its terms so as to create individual rights and does not require any further implementation. Article 141 EC provides:

> 'Each Member State shall ensure and maintain the application of the principle that men and women should receive equal pay for equal work ...'

In *Defrenne* v *Sabena (No 2)* Case 43/75 [1976] ECR 455, the European Court of Justice ruled that art 141 EC was of direct effect, although it was said that it could only be relied upon by individuals either from the date of the judgement, or by those who had already commenced proceedings.

Directives and recommendations

Directives and recommendations are secondary legislation. When a European directive is passed each Member State is given a period of time to introduce national legislation to give effect to the directive. The UK has not always been swift to implement directives, and several directives (including the Working Time Directive) have been implemented after the date for implementation has passed. Furthermore, domestic legislation, such as the Transfer of Undertakings (Protection of Employment) Regulations 1981, which purported to implement the Acquired Rights Directive (77/187/EEC), has failed to fully implement the directive, with the result that further amending legislation has been required to give full effect to the directive.

An employee who wants to exercise a right conferred by a directive which has not been passed in UK law may only do so after the date for implementation has passed. However, a directive is only directly enforceable by an employee if he works for an emanation of the state: this includes public bodies, such as a local authority or a health authority. If a person who works for a private organisation has been deprived of a legal right as a result of the failure of the government to implement legislation in time he may, according to the decision of the European Court of Justice in *Francovich* v *Italian Republic* [1992] IRLR 84, bring his claim for compensation against the government – this is known as a 'Francovich' action. In order to bring such a claim an applicant is required to show that: the directive was intended to confer rights on individuals; the extent of those rights could be identified from the text of the directive; and that there was a causal nexus between the failure of the state to implement the directive and the harm suffered by the applicant.

Human Rights Act 1998

The Human Rights Act 1998 came into force in October 2000 and gives effect to fundamental rights and freedoms enshrined in the European Convention on Human Rights (EHCR). The Convention was signed in 1950 and many signatories incorporated the Convention into domestic law: however, the UK declined to do so until the Human Rights Act 1998 was implemented. Over the last four decades governments in the UK have, however, respected the Convention and rulings from the European Court of Human Rights in Strasbourg, but for citizens of the UK it meant that if they wished to assert a Convention right they could only do so by making an application to the Court in Strasbourg. The implementation of the Human Rights Act 1998 means that cases can now be dealt with in a UK court or tribunal. With respect to employment matters the following articles of the Convention are pertinent.

Article 6 provides that any person has the right to a fair trial. This applies to both civil and criminal proceedings. The rights under art 6 include the right to a hearing in front of an independent tribunal. In *Smith* v *Secretary of State for Trade and Industry* [2000] IRLR 6 the independence of the employment tribunals was challenged on the ground that it is the Secretary of State who appoints and pays lay members of the tribunal. However, following several changes the employment tribunals are now regarded as being sufficiently independent and impartial within the meaning of art 6.

Article 8 provides the right to respect for a person's private and family life, his home and correspondence. Clearly art 8 protects employees from any invasion of their privacy by their employer: this includes the opening up of personal mail, tapping of telephones and monitoring of e-mails. The right to privacy is not absolute, however: if an employer does infringe art 8 he will have to show that it was necessary to protect the interests of national security or public safety, to prevent crime, to protect health or to protect the rights and freedoms of others. In *Halford* v *United Kingdom* [1997] IRLR 471 Alison Halford, a senior police officer with the Merseyside Police who was pursuing a claim of sex discrimination against her employers, claimed that her telephone had been tapped. It was held by the European Court of Human Rights that this was a breach of art 8.

Article 9 provides for the right to freedom of thought, conscience and religion but is subject to the same defences as art 8. Employees are therefore free to hold a broad range of views, beliefs and thoughts as well as religious faiths. In the employment context difficulties have arisen with respect to employees who either wish to take time off work or do not want to work at times when they wish to pursue their religious beliefs. In *Ahmed* v *United Kingdom* [1999] IRLR 188 it was held that an employer infringed the rights of an employee when he refused to allow the applicant, a Muslim, to take time off work to attend Friday prayers. In this case, the employer had offered the employee the opportunity to reduce his working hours to enable him to attend prayers, and therefore had not breached art 9.

Article 10 provides for the right to freedom of expression and opinion and the right to receive and impart information. This right can also be restricted, but only in limited circumstances.

Article 11 provides for the freedom of assembly and association. Individuals have the right to assemble with other people in a peaceful manner and the right to associate with others – this right includes the right to form or belong to a trade union. The Trade Union and Labour Relations (Consolidation) Act 1992 provides strict procedures that must be followed by trade unions to make industrial action lawful and provide immunity from tortious liability. However, it is not thought that the provisions contained in the 1992 Act are in breach of art 11, although it may be argued that the ACAS Code of Practice on Picketing, which restricts the numbers of pickets outside a workplace, could be in breach of art 11. However, it must be remembered that the Codes of Practice do not have statutory force. An employer cannot limit the rights provided by art 11 by giving financial incentives. In *Wilson and Others* v *United Kingdom* (2002) The Times 5 July, in the European Court of Human Rights, Mr Wilson, a journalist, was employed by Associated Newspapers and was a member of the National Union of Journalists (NUJ). In 1989 the employers signalled their intention to de-recognise the NUJ for the purposes of collective bargaining. New contracts were issued which provided for a 4.5 per cent pay increase for journalists who agreed to accept de-recognition. Mr Wilson refused to sign his new contract, and although his salary was increased, the increase was less than for those journalists who had signed and agreed to the de-recognition. He and others presented claims arguing that the requirement to sign new contracts, and therefore lose their union rights or accept a lower pay rise, was contrary to art 11 of the European Convention on Human Rights. The European Court of Human Rights held that the employer had violated art 11 by using financial incentives to induce employees to give up their rights to trade union representation.

2
The Concept of Employment

2.1 Introduction
2.2 Employee or independent contractor?
2.3 Continuity and delegation
2.4 Special categories of workers
2.5 Fixed-term contracts
2.6 Vicarious liability

2.1 Introduction

When considering an employment matter first of all it is necessary to consider whether there is a contract of employment which gives rise to a relationship between an employer and the worker which creates certain rights and obligations for both parties. It is therefore important to distinguish between an employee and other persons who are engaged to work for an employer, such as 'temps' or independent contractors who work under a contract for services.

A contract of employment is generally referred to as a contract of service and is governed by general contractual principles as well as employment law principles. Thus, a contract of employment and the terms and conditions contained therein are legally binding.

There has been a recent trend to broaden the category of persons who benefit from certain employment protection provisions. This has been achieved by the use of the term 'workers' in certain statutes, such as the National Minimum Wage Act 1998 and the Working Time Regulations 1998, to include temporary workers and those on fixed-term contracts.

2.2 Employee or independent contractor?

It is important to distinguish between an employee and an independent contractor or agent for several reasons.

1. Employees are given some statutory protection which is not given to other workers, such as holiday entitlements, notice periods, the right not to be unfairly dismissed, maternity rights, redundancy rights and preferential rights as creditors should an employer's business collapse.
2. An employer is vicariously liable for torts committed by an employee in the course of employment (*Cassidy* v *Ministry of Health* [1951] 1 All ER 574), and therefore the victim of a tort needs to determine whether the person who caused the harm should be sued or whether a claim should be pursued against the employer.
3. Contributions paid and benefits received under the social security scheme differ according to the status of a worker.
4. An employer is required to deduct income tax from employees under Schedule E of the Income and Corporation Taxes Act 1988.

Whilst it is important to distinguish between a person who works under a contract of service (an employee) and a person who works under a contract for services (an independent contractor) it is not always easy in practice to make the distinction. Indeed, in *Stevenson & Others* v *MacDonald and Evans* [1952] 1 TLR 101 Lord Denning said:

> 'It is often easy to recognise a contract of service when you see it but difficult to see where the difference lies.'

There is no universal definition of an employee, although we may seek some assistance from s230 Employment Rights Act (ERA) 1996 which defines such a person as 'an individual who has entered into or works under (or, where the employment has ceased, worked under) a contract of employment'. This unfortunately does not take us too much further forward.

Neither is it easy to distinguish between an employee, an independent contractor and a person employed by a third party just by looking at the nature of the work that they carry out. If you are unfortunate enough to spend time in hospital you may well find yourself being treated by nurses who are NHS employees and agency nurses. The duties of the nurses are the same but they are employed by different employers.

Tests for determining whether employee or independent contractor

In order to determine whether a person is an employee or an independent contractor the courts have, over the years, formulated different tests.

Control test

This traditional test has its origins in the late nineteenth century and was originally formulated for the purpose of determining whether an employer was vicariously liable in tort for the negligence of his employees. The test provided that if an employer had control over a person as to the work he carried out and the manner in which he performed his duties that person would be deemed to be an employee.

In *Yewens* v *Noakes* (1880) 6 QBD 530 Bramwell LJ defined an employee as a person who is 'subject to the command of his master as to the manner in which he shall do his work.' Whilst this test had historical relevance, and could easily be applied to the master/servant relationship, it is not as pertinent in the modern world of employment. There are many situation where an employer does not exercise control over the manner in which an employee carries out his work. It would be most alarming if the chief executive of an NHS Trust was to direct a surgeon as to the manner in which he should carry out a surgical operation or if Rod Eddington, chief executive of British Airways, was to control the way that pilots landed their aircraft!

Although the control test is no longer used as the sole criteria for determining whether a person is an employee it is still an element of the more modern tests. In *Addison* v *London Philharmonic Orchestra* [1981] ICR 261 the issue of control was considered with respect to whether an orchestra was under the control of the conductor. However, it was held that the musicians were self-employed because they were only allowing themselves to be orchestrated by the conductor and they were able to undertake other work.

Integrational test

This test, which is also known as the organisational test, was devised to overcome the difficulties with the control test. It seeks to distinguish between an employee and an independent contractor by determining whether a worker is 'part and parcel' of the organisation and is fully integrated in the employer's business. In *Stevenson & Others* v *MacDonald and Evans* [1952] 1 TLR 101 Lord Denning said:

> 'Under a contract of service a man is employed as part of the business, and his work is done as an integral part of the business, whereas under a contract for services his work, although done for the business, is not integrated into it, but is only accessory to it.'

The problem with the integrational test is that it is increasingly common in the modern working environment for companies to contract out part of their operation. A good example of this is when companies are installing new IT systems and decide, rather than use their own employees, to use independent contractors. These independent contractors may be on site for long periods of time, carrying out functions which are integral to the operation of the company, and yet are still regarded as independent contractors.

Multiple test

It has now been recognised that the complex issue of whether a person is working under a contract of services or a contract for services cannot be determined by the application of a single test. The more modern approach taken by the courts is to take into account a number of factors: this is known as the multiple test.

Consideration will be given as to whether a worker pays his own tax and national insurance contributions, is given holiday pay, is allowed to send a substitute to work in his place and whether all other terms of the contract are consistent with it being a contract of employment or a contract for services.

In *Ready Mixed Concrete* v *Minister of Pensions and National Insurance* [1968] 1 All ER 433 the plaintiffs had dismissed contract workers and replaced them with owner/drivers of ready mixed concrete lorries. The Minister of Pensions decided that the plaintiffs were liable for national insurance contributions for these workers but the plaintiffs argued that they were independent contractors. The drivers had purchased the lorries with finance from a sister company of the plaintiffs, they wore the company uniform, they were to comply with company rules with respect to the maintenance of vehicles, their lorries were painted in the company colours and their services were reserved solely for the plaintiffs. However, there were no set hours for the drivers and they could take holidays when they wished, were allowed to employ substitute drivers and were responsible for maintenance costs for their vehicles. It was held by the High Court that the drivers were independent contractors. The court considered that the fact that drivers could employ substitute drivers was a crucial factor which pointed to the drivers being self-employed.

In determining whether the drivers were employees or not McKenna J considered that a contract of service exists if the following three conditions are satisfied.

1. The servant agrees that in consideration of a wage or other remuneration he will provide his own work and skill in the performance of some service for his master.
2. He agrees, expressly or implied, that in the performance of that service he will be subject to the other's control in a sufficient degree to make that other master.
3. The other provisions of the contract are consistent with its being a contract of service.

The requirement of personal service was endorsed by the Court of Appeal in *Express and Echo Publications Ltd* v *Taunton* [1999] IRLR 367 where the Court considered that personal service was an essential requirement for there to be a contract of service. However, in the case of *McFarlane* v *Glasgow City Council* [2001] IRLR 7 the Employment Appeal Tribunal (EAT) said that a proper interpretation of *Express and Echo Publications Ltd* v *Taunton* did not mean that in order for there to be an employment contract there could never be any delegation.

In *McFarlane* v *Glasgow City Council* the applicants were gym instructors who claimed that they had been unfairly dismissed by the defendant council. The council argued that they were working under a contract for services because the contract provided that if the instructor was unable to take a gym class a substitute taken from a list supplied by the council would be provided. The EAT relied upon the judgment of MacKenna J in *Ready Mixed Concrete* v *Minister of Pensions and National Insurance* (above) where it was said that although delegation of duties would generally be inconsistent with a contract of employment some limited delegation may exist within such a contract.

Another key factor to consider in determining whether a person is employed or self-employed is the economic reality of the situation – is the person in business on his own account?

In *Market Investigations Ltd v Minister of Social Security* [1969] 2 QB 173 Cooke J recognised that no exhaustive list of considerations had been, or indeed could be, compiled to determine the status of a worker, but he did consider that the test to be applied was 'is the person who has engaged himself to perform these services performing them as a person in business on his own account?' If the answer is 'Yes' then the contract is a contract for services. If the answer is 'No', then the contract is a contract of service. In this case the company engaged interviewers to carry out market research. The employees could choose the hours they worked and work for other companies if they so wished. It was held that because the interviewers were not in business on their own account – they bore no financial risk – they were employees and the employer was obliged to pay their national insurance contributions. If a person makes a substantial investment, for example by purchasing tools and equipment, this would be more consistent with a contract for services. However, if a worker is provided with tools and materials then the worker is more likely to be an employee: *Airfix Footwear v Cape* [1978] IRLR 396.

Other determining factors

In addition to the above tests there are other factors which the courts will take into account when considering whether a person is an employed person or an independent contractor.

Labels

In determining whether a worker is an employee the court will have regard to the way in which the worker and the employer describe the status of the worker in the contract. However, it must be noted that although the intentions of the parties will be a relevant factor it will not always necessarily be conclusive. The courts will look at all the relevant factors and consider the substance of the relationship between the parties and not just the labels given to the relationship.

In *Ferguson v John Dawson & Partners (Contractors) Ltd* [1976] IRLR 346 the appellant was engaged in a very casual fashion by the defendants as a general labourer. He was to be paid on the lump at an hourly rate with no deductions for tax or national insurance. He was, however, directed by the site manager as to what to do and when, and he was provided with tools. During the course of his work the appellant fell and injured himself and he claimed compensation from the defendant 'employers'. The defendants resisted the claim on the basis that he was not an employee but a casual worker. It was held by the Court of Appeal (Lawton LJ dissenting) that in spite of the intention of the parties that the appellant was a casual labourer, the contract was in reality a contract of service and the relationship was one of master and servant.

A similar approach was taken by the Privy Council in *Narich Proprietary Ltd* v *Commissioner of Pay-Roll Tax* [1984] ICR 286, where it was said that the most important determining criteria in establishing the employment relationship is the extent to which a worker is under the direction and control of the other party to the contract. In this case the company had argued that lecturers for Weight Watchers International Inc were independent contractors, but the Privy Council held that because they were 'tied hand and foot' by their contracts and the manuals under which they operated, they were, in reality, employees of the company.

However, the Court of Appeal has drawn a distinction between a situation whereby a person is employed under one label, although the reality proves to be different, and an employee who changes his status during the course of his employment.

In *Massey* v *Crown Life Insurance* [1978] ICR 590 the applicant was employed as a branch manager of the respondent company under a contract of service. In 1973 he entered into a new agreement with the company whereby in order to reduce his tax liability he became self-employed, calling himself John L Massey and Associates although his duties remained more or less the same. This arrangement was approved by the Inland Revenue. In 1975 the respondents terminated his employment and Mr Massey claimed unfair dismissal. A tribunal held that Mr Massey was not an employee of the respondents and was therefore not eligible to make a complaint of unfair dismissal. This decision was upheld by the Employment Appeal Tribunal (EAT) and Mr Massey appealed to the Court of Appeal. It was held by the Court of Appeal that Mr Massey was self-employed and therefore unable to pursue his claim.

According to Lord Denning, when the new agreement was drawn up although the same work was carried out by Mr Massey, the relationship was no longer that of a master and servant relationship – it was an employer and independent contractor relationship and therefore Mr Massey 'Having made his bed as being "self-employed" ... must lie on it,' said Lord Denning.

Even if it is openly agreed between the employer and employee that the employee should be treated as self-employed, and he is so treated, it does not follow that he loses an employee's statutory protection. The tribunal will consider the reality of the situation and the true legal relationship.

In *Young & Woods Ltd* v *West* [1980] IRLR 201 Mr West was employed as a sheet-metal worker. It was agreed with the employers that he should be treated as self-employed and no deductions were made from his pay for tax and national insurance, nor did he receive holiday pay or sickness benefit from the company. He was also treated by the Inland Revenue as self-employed for tax purposes. Mr West was dismissed from his employment and claimed unfair dismissal. The respondents claimed that he was self-employed under a contract for services, but this was rejected by the employment tribunal. The EAT, by a majority decision, upheld the tribunal's finding and the employers appealed to the Court of Appeal. The Court of

Appeal held that the tribunal and EAT had been correct in holding that despite the agreement that Mr West should be treated as self-employed, the reality of the situation was that he was not in business on his own account, but an employee. The Court of Appeal also took into consideration the fact that Mr West was paid an hourly rate and worked normal working hours and that the company provided him with the necessary equipment for his work.

The Court of Appeal in *Young* distinguished *Massey* on the basis that in *Massey* there had been a deliberate change in the employment contract from one of service to a contract for services, whereas in *Young* the contract had not altered. Stephenson LJ also said that to force a person who is treated as self-employed to accept that position, no matter what the reality of the situation, would amount to some kind of estoppel against invoking statutory employment protection. However, Stephenson LJ was concerned that it may appear unjust that 'Mr West should be able to get away from the bed which he has made, or to eat his cake and still keep it', and that a person should not be able to alter his status simply to evade paying taxes or to gain employment protection, and therefore he said that the Inland Revenue ought to be able to claim from Mr West the balance of taxes that Mr West would have paid as an employee working under a contract of service.

Mutuality of obligations

Another key factor considered by the courts in determining the employment relationship is that of mutuality of obligations, in other words a contractual undertaking by an employer to provide work and a contractual undertaking by a worker not to refuse any work offered. This is a particularly important factor when considering casual labour and homeworkers. In *O'Kelly* v *Trusthouse Forte* [1983] ICR 728 it was held that casual wine waiters at the Grosvenor House Hotel in London, who were dismissed for trade union activities, were self-employed because the employer had no contractual obligation to provide them with work and the casual staff were under no obligation to accept the work offered. The Court of Appeal also held that the waiters were not engaged under a separate contract of service each time they reported for work at a particular function. Sir John Donaldson MR agreed with the view of the tribunal and the EAT that there was no overall or umbrella contract between the parties, and that in that particular industry casual workers were not regarded as working under any overall contract of employment. In *Nethermere Ltd* v *Gardiner* [1984] IRLR 240 the Court of Appeal considered what was the minimum requirement of an employee for the existence of an employment contract and determined that an employee should be obliged personally to accept and perform some work for an employer in return for payment. In this case the workers operated from home, had no fixed hours and, on occasions, went weeks without work. Stephenson LJ said that there was a picture of the applicants doing the same work for the same rate as employees in the factory but in their own home and in their own time – 'for the convenience of the worker and the company'. There was therefore a sufficient, irreducible minimum of obligation for there to be a contract of service.

The factors to be taken into consideration in determining when a worker will be regarded as an employee have recently been considered by the EAT in the case of *Hewlett Packard Ltd* v *O'Murphy* [2002] IRLR 4. The applicant, Mr O'Murphy, a computer specialist, set up a company to provide IT services. The company entered into a contract with an agency to provide IT services to Hewlett Packard, a client of the agency. After a while Hewlett Packard informed the agency that they no longer wished Mr O'Murphy to continue because he was unable to carry out the work they required to be done to a sufficiently high standard. Mr O'Murphy presented a claim to the tribunal alleging that he had been unfairly dismissed by Hewlett Packard. The tribunal considered that, because of the amount of control that Hewlett Packard had over Mr O'Murphy and the sufficiency of mutuality of obligations, the reality was that he was an employee. On appeal it was held by the EAT that the tribunal had erred in their finding. There was no contract at all between Mr O'Murphy and the defendants, and the lack of any contractual nexus between the parties meant that no claim arising out of an alleged contract of employment could succeed. The EAT took into account the fact that there were two parties between the applicant and the defendant – the company set up by Mr O'Murphy and the agency.

2.3 Continuity and delegation

Continuity

The relationship between an employer and employee is generally one of a continuing nature. However, there may be circumstances in which the relationship is brought to end although both parties intend to resume the working arrangement at some point in the future. The question that has recently been raised is whether a temporary break operates to bring to an end the employment relationship.

In *Curr* v *Marks & Spencer plc* [2003] IRLR 75 the respondents operated a 'child break' scheme which provided that an employee could resign at the end of maternity leave to spend time with her children, but could return to a similar post if she returned within four years. The scheme also provided that any employees who took advantage of it would be required to work for a minimum of two weeks per year. The applicant resigned at the end of her maternity leave and took her child break. She returned, but five years later was made redundant. The respondent calculated her redundancy pay from the date upon which she returned to work following her child break. The applicant argued that this was an unlawful deduction from her wages because her earlier period of employment should have been taken into account. It was held by the EAT that the child break scheme fell within s212(3)(c) Employment Rights Act 1996 and could therefore be regarded as a continuing arrangement, even though the relationship was not governed by a contract of employment. However, the Court of Appeal considered that the scheme did not fall within s212(3)(c), as the terms and conditions clearly stated that there was a possibility that the applicant would be re-employed at the end of the child break. Therefore, according to the Court, by implication there was no continuing employment relationship during the period of time that she was on the child break scheme.

Delegation

Where a worker under a contract is able to delegate his duties to another person it is more likely that he will be considered to be self-employed. Indeed, we have already seen in *Ready Mixed Concrete* that the fact that the lorry drivers could hire others to drive their vehicles was one of the determining factors in deciding that the drivers were self-employed. In *Hitchcock* v *Post Office* [1980] ICR 100 the EAT held that a sub-postmaster was self-employed even though there was a substantial measure of control by the Post Office over his conduct of its business. The sub-postmaster provided the premises for the sub-post office, had the right to delegate duties to other staff which he employed and was, in reality, carrying on business on his own account.

2.4 Special categories of workers

There are several classes of workers who because of their profession, status or calling do not receive all the employment rights which are available to other employees.

Company directors

A director of a company is, by virtue of his appointment, an office holder; however, he may have a contract of service with the company in which case he will be deemed to be an employee of the company. In *Eaton* v *(1) Robert Eaton Ltd (2) Secretary of State for Employment* [1988] ICR 302 the EAT gave guidance on some of the relevant factors that tribunals should take into account in determining whether or not a director is an employee. The EAT said that the tribunals should look, inter alia, at whether or not the director is paid a salary or directors' fees, because the latter would tend to suggest that the director would not be an employee. Another consideration would be the duties of the director and whether or not he was subject to the control of the board of directors, in which case this would point towards his being an employee.

The question as to whether a controlling shareholder can be an employee for the purposes of s230 Employment Rights Act (ERA) 1996 has been subject to considerable doubt. In *Buchan and Ivey* v *Secretary of State for Employment* [1997] IRLR 80 the EAT held that a controlling shareholder could not be an employee for the purposes of s230 ERA 1996. However, in *Secretary of State for Trade and Industry* v *Bottrill* [1999] ICR 592 the Court of Appeal held that the applicant, who was the holder of the sole issued share in the company, was entitled to recover redundancy and other payments from the Secretary of State when the company went into voluntary liquidation. The EAT ([1998] ICR 564) had taken into consideration the view that had been expressed by the Court of Session in *Fleming* v *Secretary of State for Trade and Industry* [1997] IRLR 682 that any shareholding of a person in a company in which he is employed is only one factor that should be taken into account in determining whether that person is an employee, but is not, on its own, a decisive factor and the Court of Appeal endorsed this approach.

The Court of Appeal has endorsed its earlier view that there is no rule of law that prevents a controlling shareholder from being an employee in the case of *Connolly* v *Sellers Arenascene Ltd* [2001] IRLR 222 where a managing director who was a major shareholder was held to be an employee.

Partnerships

A partner is a person who is in business with others with a view to profit. A partner is self-employed and is remunerated by taking a share in the profits of the business which will usually be in proportion to the amount of capital that the partner has invested. There are, however, examples of partners who are employed and receive a salary. People who work for the John Lewis Partnership are called 'partners' rather than employees and they are entitled to an annual share of any profits even though they have not invested any capital in the business. Junior partners in law firms or acountants may also be salaried partners.

Many doctors who work in General Practice are also partners and share the profits. In *North Essex Health Authority* v *David-John* [2004] ICR 112 the applicant was a general practitioner who provided medical services to the health authority. The medical services were provided in accordance with the National Health Service (General Medical Services) Regulations 1992, which govern the terms of service between general practitioners and local health authorities. The applicant resigned following a dispute with the authority and submitted an application to the employment tribunal alleging unfair dismissal and race discrimination. A preliminary issue arose as to whether the applicant was an 'employee' within the meaning of s230 Employment Rights Act 1996 and the tribunal held that he was and therefore they had jurisdiction to hear the claim. The health authority appealed and it was held by the EAT that the 1992 Regulations were statutory and not contractual and therefore there was no contract governing the relationship between the parties. Furthermore, the EAT held that the applicant was not in employment or a contract worker for the purposes of the Race Relations Act 1976.

Office holders

There are certain persons who 'hold office' rather than working under a contract of service or a contract for services. An office is a permanent position which has an independent existence regardless of the persons who fill it and examples include judges, the clergy and JPs. In *President of the Methodist Conference* v *Parfitt* [1984] QB 368 it was held by the Court of Appeal that a Methodist minister could not claim that he had been unfairly dismissed because the relationship between the minister and the Church was not a contractual one and, furthermore, even if there was a contractual relationship it was not a contract of service. The House of Lords also considered the position of the clergy in *Davies* v *Presbyterian Church of Wales* [1986] 1 WLR 323. It was held that the book of rules of the Presbyterian Church did not contain terms of employment which at common law were capable of being offered and accepted. Lord Templeman considered the nature of a priest's calling and said that: 'A pastor is called and accepts the call. He does not devote his working life but his whole life to the church and his religion. His duties are defined and his activities are dictated not by contract but by conscience.'

Police officers

Police officers are employed under a contract of service but are in a different position from most workers. A police officer cannot claim unfair dismissal, nor does he have the right to an itemised pay statement, trade union rights or written reasons for dismissal. However, under s1 ERA 1996 an officer does have the right to a written statement of terms and the statutory minimum notice period and redundancy pay. In *Wiltshire Police Authority* v *Wynn* [1981] 1 QB 95, which concerned the dismissal of a police cadet, the Court of Appeal held that the Police Act 1964 provided that the police authority was to be treated as the 'employer' with respect to statutory functions and for the purposes of vicarious liability. However, the power to dismiss a cadet was conferred upon on the chief officer of police not on the police authority.

Trainees and apprentices

A person who is a trainee or an apprentice may be employed under a contract of service and, indeed, s230 ERA 1996 defines a contract of employment as a 'contract of service or apprenticeship'. However, whilst some trainees may be employed under a contract of service this is not the case with all trainees. In *Wiltshire Police Authority* v *Wynn* (above) the Court of Appeal also considered the question as to whether a trainee police cadet was under a contract of service and held that an apprentice was in a special category of an appointee for training and therefore not working under a contract of service. A similar approach was taken in *Daley* v *Allied Suppliers* [1983] ICR 90 where a person engaged on a youth opportunities programme who claimed that she had been discriminated against because she was black was held not to be an employee for the purposes of the Race Relations Act 1976. However, in *Oliver* v *J P Malnick & Co Ltd* [1984] 3 All ER 795, where a female articled clerk left her employment after discovering that a male articled clerk was earning more, it was held that she was working under a contract of service.

It is therefore difficult to determine whether a trainee is working under a contract of service or not, although key factors would appear to be how much of a contribution the 'worker' makes to the business of the employer and how much time is spent on training the person.

Minors and children

A minor is a person below the age of 18. Generally speaking a child is a person under the age of 16 and a young person is someone over 16 and under the age of 18. The Children (Protection at Work) Regulations 1998 (SI 1998/276) provide that the minimum age at which a child may be employed (other than as an employee of his parent or guardian in light agricultural or horticultural work) is now 14. A contract of employment entered into by a minor will be valid provided that the contract largely is for the benefit of the minor. In order to determine whether a contract is valid it is necessary to look at the contract as a whole and not just at individual terms. In *Clements* v *London & North Western Railway Co* [1894] 2 QB 482 a minor entered into a contract which excluded his rights to sue under the Employers' Liability Act 1880 for any injuries suffered during the course of his employment. It was, however, held after taking all the circumstances into account that the contract was beneficial to him overall and therefore valid because he was covered by the employers' own insurance scheme. A different view was taken in the case of *De Francesco* v *Barnum* (1890) 45 Ch D 430 where a young girl who wanted to be a professional dancer entered into a deed of apprenticeship. The deed was held to be unreasonable and not in the interest of the minor because it provided, inter alia, that the girl could not accept professional engagements without her master's permission, she would not receive pay unless she was employed by her master and she was not allowed to marry during the period of apprenticeship.

Agency workers

There are groups of workers who are employed by one party (an agency) but whose services are actually used by others. An example of this type of arrangement would be secretarial staff who are employed by an agency but whose services are used by businesses in need of additional support.

People who are engaged by employment agents may be employed by the agency or self-employed. Those who are employed will have normal employment rights against the agency. However, they will not have all the employment protection rights of the permanent employees of those employers who use their services. A person who is employed by an agency cannot bring a claim for unfair dismissal against the user of their services – their only claim would be against the agency.

If a person employed by an agency wishes to bring a claim against the agency he will face the usual hurdle of establishing that he is an employee and not self-employed. In *McMeechan* v *Secretary of State for Employment* [1997] IRLR 353 Mr McMeechan joined an employment agency and was employed on a series of temporary contracts. On every assignment he signed a form containing a statement of terms and conditions under which he was employed. The statement contained an express term that he was self-employed and not under a contract of service. A further term in the statement underlined that the agency was under no duty to provide him with work and that he was under no obligation to accept whatever work was offered. The agency also reserved the right to end the worker's assignment at any time without notice and without giving reasons. However, the worker whilst on assignment was 'required to fulfil the normal common law duties which an employee would owe to an employer as far as they were applicable.' The worker's payments were subject to statutory deductions and he was also entitled to invoke a grievance procedure should the need arise.

The agency became insolvent and Mr McMeechan claimed £105 that was owed to him from the Secretary of State for Employment for payment from the National Insurance Fund under s182 ERA 1996. The Secretary of State resisted the claim by stating that McMeechan was not an employee and therefore not so entitled. The EAT held that the express term in the contract between the agency and the appellant that he was self-employed should be disregarded. In arriving at their decision that he was entitled to payment they took into consideration numerous other factors, such as the grievance procedure, payments, dismissal for misconduct and common law obligations. The Secretary of State appealed.

The Court of Appeal, in upholding the decision of the EAT, stated that a worker for an employment agency could have the status of an employee even though he was only on a particular engagement. They added that the terms of the contract had to be examined and in this particular case the obligation to conform with common law duties, the method of remuneration and the imposition of disciplinary rules pointed to a contract of service despite the inclusion of the express term that the worker was self-employed.

The EAT came to a similar decision in the more recent case of *Motorola* v *Davidson* [2001] IRLR 4 which dealt with the relationship between an agency worker and client. In this case an agency advertised for employees to work for Motorola – the workers were to be employed by the agency but carry out their work fixing mobile phones for Motorola. After two years continuous work for Motorola, Mr Davidson was suspended and subsequently dismissed by Motorola who then advised the agency. Mr Davidson brought a claim for unfair dismissal against the agency and Motorola. As a preliminary matter the tribunal found that the applicant was an employee of Motorola and therefore the claim against the agency was dropped. Motorola appealed to the EAT.

In finding that Mr Davidson was an employee of Motorola the EAT took the following factors into account.

1. Motorola tools and equipment were used.
2. Absences had to be agreed with Motorola.
3. Grievances were to be addressed to Motorola.
4. The disciplinary complaint against Mr Davidson was investigated by Motorola.

The decision of the EAT may have far-reaching implications for those companies who try to circumvent the obligations owed to employees by hiring staff from agencies.

Following the case of *Motorola* v *Davidson* there was much uncertainty as to the status of persons who are employed by agencies, but who work for one company for a long period of time. Problems may arise where an employment agency and the end user expressly state that they are not to be regarded as the employer of the worker engaged by the agency. The practical effect of this would leave the worker without an employer. In *Franks* v *Reuters Ltd & Another* [2003] IRLR 423 the appellant had worked for the respondent for over six years. There was no contract between Reuters and Mr Franks but there was a contract between Reuters and the employment agency for the supply of workers, and a contract between the agency and Mr Franks which set out his hourly rate but also stated that the agency was not under any obligation to provide him with work, nor was he under any obligation to accept work that was offered by the agency. When he was dismissed he presented a claim for unfair dismissal and the tribunal and the EAT held that Mr Franks was not an employee of either the Reuters or the agency. On appeal the Court of Appeal held that in determining whether a worker is an employee within the meaning of s230 ERA 1996 it is necessary to take into account all relevant evidence to determine whether a contract of employment could be implied and the tribunal had failed to do this. The Court of Appeal said that whilst the existence of a written agreement between the agency worker and the contracting company may be useful, it is certainly not conclusive in deciding whether an employment relationship exists. The appeal was allowed and the case remitted for rehearing by a fresh tribunal.

The Court of Appeal recently expressed concern over such a situation in the case of *Dacas* v *Brook Street Bureau (UK) Ltd* [2004] IRLR 358. In this case Ms Dacas entered into a temporary worker's agreement with Brook Street Bureau, an employment agency, which clearly stated that she was not to be regarded as an employee either of the agency or of any client of the agency to whom she was assigned to work. Ms Dacas was sent to work as a cleaner at a hostel run by Wandsworth Council and she carried out these duties for six years. Following an altercation and an allegation of rudeness the employment agency advised Ms Dacas that they would no longer be able to provide her with work and she was summarily dismissed. Ms Dacas presented a claim of unfair dismissal. However, the tribunal found that although the employment agency had considerable day-to-day control over the applicant and was involved in matters of discipline, nevertheless because of the clear wording of the contract she was not employed by either Brook Street Bureau nor Wandsworth Council and therefore they did not have jurisdiction to hear the claim. Ms Dacas appealed to the EAT where it was held that there was a contract of employment between the employment agency and Ms Dacas.

On further appeal to the Court of Appeal it was held that Ms Dacas was not an employee of Brook Street Bureau because of her temporary worker status. The Court of Appeal considered that the temporary worker's agreement did not amount to a contract of service and there was insufficient mutuality of obligations between the parties. For her part, Ms Dacas was not obliged to accept work that was offered by the agency.

This situation raises several concerns, including the fact that the worker has no statutory rights and, in the event of negligence, neither party would be vicariously liable. One way around the problem would be to look at the issue of control and mutuality between the worker and the end user of their services. In *Dacas* Mummery LJ considered that a finding that the council was in fact the employer would 'accord with practical reality and common sense'. This approach, whilst clearly the most logical way forward, may impose obligations upon employers who engage temporary workers that they had not anticipated. In the event that an agency worker is with an employer for more than one year, and there is sufficient control and mutuality of obligations to imply a contract of service, that worker may then be regarded as an employee with concomitant employment rights.

Agency workers will also have rights against a company who uses their services in respect of discrimination legislation and the trend towards the use of the term 'worker' in legislation, for example in the Working Time Regulations, broadens the scope for protection of this group of workers.

Casual workers

Another group of workers whose employment status has given rise to difficulties are those who work for an employer on a casual basis for an indeterminate period of time.

In *Carmichael* v *National Power plc* [1998] IRLR 4 two casual workers were engaged by the respondents as guides showing parties around power stations in north-east England. They were supplied with uniforms by the respondents and paid tax and national insurance. They brought proceedings under s11 ERA 1996 requesting a written statement of terms. Their application was rejected by the employment tribunal and the EAT on the ground that as casual workers they were not employed by the respondents and therefore had no entitlement to employment protection or benefits or a written statement of terms. The employees appealed successfully to the Court of Appeal and the employers were granted the right to appeal to the House of Lords.

It was held by the House of Lords that there was insufficient mutuality of obligations to constitute a contract of services and therefore the workers were not employees.

When considering whether a worker is an employee or not, the courts will look for continuing mutuality of obligation. In *Carmichael* it was recognised that a worker may be an employee for a period of time when he is actually engaged in work but will not be under a continuing contract of employment during period that he is not engaged to carry out work.

2.5 Fixed-term contracts

The majority of employees within the workforce have a contract of employment of indefinite duration – indeed, historically many employees have expected a 'job for life' with their employer. However, in today's working environment the concept of a job for life is much less likely; people frequently move around in the job market or take on jobs which are for a specific period or for a specific task. It is often convenient for employers who wish to employ staff for a particular purpose to employ staff on fixed-term contracts.

A fixed-term contract must clearly define the date upon which the contract is to begin and the date the contract comes to an end. The contract can only be brought to an end before the specified date either by the agreement of both parties or by the employer in the event that the worker commits an act of gross misconduct.

Fixed-term Employees (Prevention of Less Favourable Treatment) Regulations 2002

The Fixed-term Employees (Prevention of Less Favourable Treatment) Regulations 2002, which transpose the EC Directive on Fixed-term Work into UK legislation, came into effect in 2002 and aim to protect those on fixed-term contracts from discrimination in respect of terms and conditions in comparison to permanent employees.

A 'fixed-term employee' is defined as a person with a contract of employment which is due to end when a specified date is reached, a specified event does or does not happen or a specified task has been completed.

The Regulations cover persons engaged in seasonal or casual work who have contracts for short periods of time. Employees who are engaged to cover for maternity or paternity leave, or who have been hired to cover for peaks in demand, will also be protected, as will those who are taken on to undertake a particular task and whose contract will expire upon the completion of that particular task.

The Regulations do not apply to agency workers, ie those who have an employment contract or relationship with a work agency but are placed with and do their work for a third party. However, employees directly employed by a work agency who work under the control of the agency are covered. The Regulations do not apply to apprentices or students on work experience placements of one year or less that they must complete as part of a higher education course.

Employees on fixed-term contracts now have the right not to be treated less favourably than comparable permanent employees simply because they are fixed-term, unless the different treatment can be objectively justified.

The Regulations also repeal s197 Employment Rights Act 1996 under which employees on fixed-term contracts could waive their right to a redundancy payment. Any waiver in a fixed-term contract which is renewed or extended after 1 October 2002 will be void. If a fixed-term employee signed a waiver clause before 1 October 2002, the waiver will still apply and they will not be entitled to statutory redundancy payments if their contract expired and was not renewed.

Regulation 1
This defines a permanent employee as an employee who is not employed under a fixed-term contract.

Regulation 2
A fixed-term employee can compare their treatment to the treatment of a comparable permanent employee. Regulation 2 defines a comparable employee as an employee who is employed by the same employer as the fixed-term employee who is engaged in the same or broadly similar work, having regard to levels of skill and qualification. Where a fixed-term employee does the same work as several permanent employees whose contractual terms are different, the fixed-term employee may select a comparator from one of the persons who is doing broadly similar work. However, the chances of any claim for equal treatment being successful will depend on the employee selecting a comparator who is doing work which most closely resembles their own work, and on whether there are objective reasons for different treatment.

If there is no comparable permanent employee working in the same establishment, a fixed-term employee can use a comparator in another of the employer's establishments; however, there may be objective grounds for any differing treatment because of the different locations. A fixed-term employee cannot use as a comparator a person who is employed by an associated employer.

Regulation 3
This provides that a fixed-term employee has the right not to be treated less favourably than a comparable employee with respect to the terms of his contract or by being subject to any other detriment unless such treatment can be objectively justified by the employer.

A fixed-term employee may be able to establish less favourable treatment if he can show that he does not receive a benefit, whether contractual or not, that a comparable permanent employee receives or if any benefit offered is on less favourable terms. Less favourable treatment can also occur if an employer fails to do something for a fixed-term employee that is done for a permanent employee. If, for example, an employer provides free tea and coffee facilities for permanent employees but not for fixed-term employees, that would be less favourable treatment. Similarly, if tea and coffee was subsidised for fixed-term employees but free for permanent staff this too would amount to less favourable treatment.

Less favourable treatment may also occur where fixed-term employees are offered less paid holiday than comparable permanent employees or if they are not paid for bank holidays. There may also be less favourable treatment where a fixed-term employee is subjected to disadvantages which are not imposed on permanent employees, such as redundancies or where permanent employees are given better promotion opportunities than those on fixed-term contracts.

Regulation 4
This provides that where a fixed-term employee is treated less favourably than a permanent employee with respect to any term of his contract, there may a defence of objective justification. Employers can objectively justify different terms and conditions for fixed-term employees in one of two ways.

1. By showing that there is an objective justification for not giving the fixed-term employee a particular benefit or for giving him or her the benefit on less favourable terms.
2. By showing that the value of the fixed-term employee's total package of terms and conditions is at least equal to the value of the comparable permanent employee's total package of terms and conditions.

An employer may be able to justify less favourable treatment if it can be shown that the less favourable treatment is necessary to achieve a legitimate business objective.

Regulation 5
Where an employee considers that he may have been treated less favourably he may request from his employer a written statement giving reasons for the treatment: any such statement should be provided by the employer within 21 days of the request. The statement should set out the reasons for the different treatment or, if the employee is not being treated less favourably, it should state that this is the case. If the employer justifies any perceived less favourable treatment by adopting the package approach, the statement should clearly say that this is why there is different treatment, giving as much detail as possible. If an employee wishes to pursue his claim at an employment tribunal the statement may be used by the employee at the tribunal hearing.

Regulation 6
Where an employee is dismissed by an employer, and one of the principal reasons for the dismissal relates to bringing proceedings under the Regulations or asserting a right or assisting another in asserting a right under the Regulations, then any such dismissal shall be regarded as unfair.

Regulation 7
Any employee who considers that a right conferred by reg 3 has been breached by his employer may present a complaint to the employment tribunal within three months of the alleged breach.

Regulation 8
If a fixed-term contract has been renewed or the employee is engaged on a new fixed-term contract and the employee has been continuously employed for a period of four years or more, the renewal or new contract takes effect as a permanent contract unless a fixed-term contract can be objectively justified. Any employment prior to 10 July 2002 does not count towards the four-year period.

Notice

When a fixed-term contract is coming to an end generally there is no requirement on the part of an employer to give notice. However, where a fixed-term contract is terminated before the date it was expected to expire, notice must be given: *Dixon & Constanti* v *BBC* [1978] ICR 281. Furthermore, affected employees have the right to the same minimum notice period as permanent employees.

A provision within a contract which provides that the contract can be terminated by notice by either party does not prevent it from being a fixed-term contract. In *Dixon & Constanti* v *BBC* two workers were given fixed-term contracts which provided that one week's notice of termination could be given by either side. They were dismissed by the BBC with notice and claimed unfair dismissal or redundancy. The Court of Appeal held that the contract was a fixed-term contract even though the contract was determinable by notice and therefore the respondents were dismissed and could claim for unfair dismissal or redundancy before a tribunal. The Court of Appeal said that to interpret the contract in any other way would frustrate the objectives of the employment protection legislation.

Particular task

A contract may provide that a person is employed to carry out a particular task such as putting in a new software package. However, the parties to the contract may not know exactly when the contract will end. If the contract does not specify the date upon which the contract ends it will not be a fixed-term contract. However, where a contract provides that the contract will terminate at a particular time, such as at the end of the academic year, this will be a fixed-term contract. In *Wiltshire County Council* v *NATFHE* [1980] ICR 455 a teacher claimed that she had been dismissed when her teaching contract was not renewed. The Court of Appeal held that because the contract provided that the teacher was to serve the council for the whole of the academic year the contract was sufficiently precise in terms of when it concluded for it to be a fixed-term contract and therefore she could claim unfair dismissal.

A clause within a contract which provides that the agreement will come to an end upon completion of a specific task or on a fixed date, whichever is earlier, will be a fixed-term contract even though the contract may be subject to review before the contract comes to an end.

Dismissal

At common law a fixed-term contract that is not renewed by an employer will not amount to a dismissal because the contract has come to its natural conclusion. To provide workers who are employed under fixed-term contracts additional security s95 ERA 1996 provides that an employee on a fixed-term contract will be deemed to be dismissed by his employer if the fixed term expires and the employer does not renew the contract. In order to determine whether a dismissal is fair or unfair the employer will have to show that he acted reasonably in not renewing the contract. Many fixed-term contracts, particularly those for industrial placement students, are for less than one year to preclude such workers from bringing a claim for unfair dismissal if their contract is not renewed.

An employee on a fixed-term contract used to be able to waive his right to unfair dismissal under s197(1) ERA 1996. However, this right (if it could be considered as such) has been repealed by the Employment Relations Act 1999 so that an employee can no longer waive his right to protection in the event of an unfair dismissal.

Redundancy

A person employed on a fixed-term contract may find that his contract is brought to an end and he is dismissed by reason of redundancy. An employee will not be dismissed for the purposes of redundancy if the contract is renewed before the end of his employment under the previous contract and the renewal takes effect within four weeks of the termination of the original contract: s138(1) ERA 1996. An employee under a fixed-term contract will however be regarded as having been dismissed by reason of redundancy if he is offered a new contract which is substantially different in terms of capacity, location or terms and conditions from the old contract.

A person who worked under a fixed-term contract could, until recently, surrender his right to a redundancy payment. However, the Fixed-term Employees (Prevention of Less Favourable Treatment) Regulations 2002 repeal the provisions enabling fixed-term employees to waive their right to a redundancy payment. The effect of the Regulations is that any waivers inserted into contracts agreed, renewed or extended after 1 October 2002 will not be valid, and fixed-term employees will have a right to statutory redundancy payments if they have been continuously employed for two years or more. If an employee on a fixed-term contract signed a waiver clause before 1 October 2002, the waiver will still apply and they will not be entitled to statutory redundancy payments if their contract expires and is not renewed. However, if the contract is renewed or extended after 1 October, any waiver clause will not be effective.

Fixed-term employees should not be selected for redundancy purely because they are on fixed-term contracts, unless the employer can objectively justify the redundancy. However, where fixed-term employees have been engaged to complete specific tasks or to cover for a peak in demand, it is likely that an employer could objectively justify selecting them for redundancy at the end of their contracts.

2.6 Vicarious liability

The distinction between an employee and an independent contractor becomes extremely important in the event of a worker committing a tort during the course of his employment. A potential litigant who has suffered harm may pursue a claim for compensation against the tortfeasor. However, under the doctrine of vicarious liability if he can establish that a tort was committed during the course of employment he may also bring a claim against the employer of the tortfeasor.

One of the reasons behind this doctrine is that it is argued that the employer derives a benefit from the work of his employees and therefore he should also accept associated risks. Furthermore, if an employer knows that he may be pursued in the event of negligence on the part of his staff he will take more care in the selection and training of those he employs.

However, the most compelling argument behind the doctrine is that in the event of liability being imposed it is more likely that an employer will be in a better financial position to satisfy the claim than his employees.

An employer may also be vicariously liable for acts done by one employee to another. In *Waters* v *Commissioner of Police of the Metropolis* [1997] IRLR 589 the House of Lords held that the Commissioner was liable in respect of sexual assaults upon Ms Waters by a fellow officer. A similar outcome can also be seen in the case of *Jones* v *Tower Boot Co Ltd* [1997] 2 All ER 406 where the Court of Appeal held an employer was liable for the racial harassment suffered by Mr Jones as a result of the conduct of fellow employees.

3

The Contract of Employment

3.1 Introduction

3.2 Written particulars of terms

3.3 Express terms

3.4 Implied terms

3.5 Collective agreements

3.6 Company handbook/rule book

3.7 Variation of contractual terms

3.8 Post-termination obligations

3.9 Whistle-blowing

3.1 Introduction

The contract of employment is the foundation stone of the legal relationship between employer and employee. Terms of a contract such as pay and conditions may be agreed between the employer and the employee or through collective bargaining. In some respects the employment contract is the same as any other contract and normal contractual principles will apply.

Offer and acceptance

An offer of employment may be made to a prospective employee formally in writing or informally by word of mouth. Whether an offer is formal or informal, in order for there to be a valid contract there must be an unconditional offer by an employer which is accepted by an employee. However, many job offers are made subject to certain conditions, such as satisfactory references or the passing of a medical examination, and they would appear to conflict with general contractual principles. The matter was considered by the Court of Appeal in *Wishart* v *National Association of Citizens Advice Bureau* [1990] IRLR 393 where the defendant withdrew an offer of employment after receiving a reference from a previous employer which showed that the employee had taken considerable sick leave. The Court held that the employer was entitled to employ a person who was not likely to take time off work and the claim was dismissed.

In *Stubbs* v *Trower, Still & Keeling* [1987] IRLR 321 the Court of Appeal considered whether an offer of a position as an articled clerk contained the implied condition that the offer was conditional upon the applicant passing the necessary professional examinations. It was held that the firm of solicitors was in breach of contract when it withdrew the offer of articles after Mr Stubbs failed all but one of his examinations. The Court considered that the passing of the examinations was not necessary to give efficacy to the contract.

Illegality

It is a fundamental general contractual principle based on public policy that a party to litigation cannot rely upon a contract to enforce their rights under that contract if it is tainted with illegality. In *Hall* v *Woolston Hall Leisure Ltd* [2001] ICR 99 Peter Gibson LJ said:

> 'There can be no doubt but that under English law a claim, whether in contract or in tort, may be defeated on the ground of illegality or, in the Latin phrase, ex turpi causa non oritur actio.'

The classic statement of the principle was by Lord Mansfield CJ in *Holman* v *Johnson* (1775) 1 Cowp 341:

> 'No court will lend its aid to a man who founds his cause of action upon an immoral or an illegal act. If, from the plaintiff's own stating or otherwise, the cause of action appears to arise ex turpi causa, or the transgression of a positive law of this country, there the court says he has no right to be assisted.'

Thus an employee who knowingly conspires with his employer to avoid payment of tax and national insurance would, in the event that he was dismissed, be unable to present a claim to the employment tribunal because clearly the avoidance of such payments is unlawful. In *Cole* v *Fred Stacey Ltd* [1974] IRLR 73 the applicant knowingly received additional tax-free pay. The contract was void for illegality and he therefore lost the right to redundancy pay. There are, however, some exceptions to this general principle. If an employee is completely unaware of the illegality then it would be manifestly unfair to consider the contract and his rights unenforceable. The test that is applied is whether the employee did in fact know that the contract was illegal, as opposed to whether he ought to have known of the illegality.

An employee who does not gain any advantage from an illegal contract may be entitled to rely upon the contract. In *Hewcastle Catering Ltd* v *Ahmed and Elkamah* [1991] IRLR 473 two employees had knowingly participated in a scheme with their employer to evade VAT. The Court of Appeal held that they could make a claim for unfair dismissal because, although they had known that their actions were unlawful, they had not benefited from the illegality. Furthermore, on the ground of public policy, if the employees were denied the right to rely upon their contract it could have the effect of deterring others from disclosing any illegal act on the part of an employer.

In the event that a contract is lawful at its inception but, because of the way it is carried out, it becomes tainted with illegality, this will not necessarily mean that the contract becomes unenforceable. In *Coral Leisure Group Ltd* v *Barnett* [1981] IRLR 204 a distinction was drawn between a contract which is for the performance of an illegal act and one which can be carried out lawfully but was in fact carried out by unlawful means. In this case the hiring of prostitutes by an employee to keep rich punters happy was held not to be a part of his terms and conditions, but merely a way in which he performed his duties.

If an employee wishes to claim a statutory right, such as the right not to be unfairly dismissed, he will have to show that he has been continuously employed for one year under a legal contract of employment. If at any time an employee has been working under an illegal contract, the period during which the contract was illegal cannot be relied upon with respect to continuity of employment. Furthermore, continuity will only be calculated from the date that the contract became legal and not from the date that the employment began.

If an employer wants to defend a claim on the grounds of illegality the burden of proof is firmly on the employer to establish the illegality; it is not on the employee to establish that he is entitled to bring a claim. This was restated by the Court of Appeal in *Colen & Another* v *Cebrian (UK) Ltd* [2003] EWCA Civ 1676.

Whether or not a claimant is entitled to rely upon an illegal contract may depend upon to what extend the employee was aware of the illegality. This was considered by the Court of Appeal in *Wheeler* v *Quality Deep Ltd t/a Thai Royale Restaurant* [2004] EWCA Civ 1085. This case concerned a Thai national with limited English who worked as a cook at the respondent's restaurant for three years without receiving a pay slip. She did not pay tax and national insurance. When she was dismissed she claimed unfair dismissal but at tribunal her claim was dismissed on the grounds that the contract was illegal. The tribunal considered that despite Mrs Wheeler's poor understanding of English and the British tax system, her husband was aware of the failure to pay tax or national insurance and that Mrs Wheeler should also have been aware of the illegality. However, the tribunal did say that but for the illegality they would have made a finding of unfair dismissal, and the EAT also held that Mrs Wheeler could not rely upon the contract. On appeal, the Court of Appeal considered the principles set out in *Hall* v *Woolston Hall Leisure Ltd* [2001] 1 WLR 225 and the dictum of Peter Gibson LJ:

'In cases where the contract of employment is neither entered into for an illegal purpose nor prohibited by statute, the illegal performance of the contract will not render the contract unenforceable unless in addition to knowledge of the facts which make the performance illegal the employee actively participates in the illegal performance. It is a question of fact in each case whether there has been a sufficient degree of participation by the employee.'

The Court of Appeal considered that Mrs. Wheeler's lack of understanding of English was such that she did not actively participate in the illegality and the matter was referred back to the EAT to consider the merits of the unfair dismissal claim.

Sources of terms of the contract

There are many potential sources of the terms of an employment contract. It may be that they are contained within a job advertisement to which a prospective employee responds or they may be detailed in a job application form. It is also possible that further details of terms are given verbally at a job interview and these too may form part of the contract. Another potential source is a letter of appointment which will generally outline the basic terms upon which the employer is offering the position.

It may be that an employee is given a formal contract when he commences his employment which details the terms of his engagement, further details of which may be found in a staff handbook or organisational rule book. Other employment terms may be found in union negotiated collective agreements or may be implied by national and local custom and practice. Changes to contractual terms such as pay increases or a change in working hours may be found in letters detailing the new arrangement. Additionally, the tribunals and courts are prepared to imply terms into an employment contract and these will be considered below.

It is therefore clear that there is not always one particular document detailing all the terms of a contract and reference may be had to one or more source to determine contractual terms.

3.2 Written particulars of terms

We have already seen that a contract of employment may be either formal or informal. In the case of an informal contract, if there is a dispute between the employer and employee it is difficult to determine the precise terms of the agreement. To alleviate such problems, s1 Employment Rights Act (ERA) 1996 provides that where an employee begins employment with an employer, the employer shall give to the employee a written statement of particulars of his employment within two months of the commencement of employment. Section 1(3) ERA 1996 provides that the statement shall contain particulars of:

'(a) the names of the employer and employee,
(b) the date when the employment began, and
(c) the date on which the employee's period of continuous employment began (taking into account any employment with a previous employer which counts towards that period).'

The statement should also contain particulars, as at a specified date which should not be more than seven days before the statement is issued to the employee, relating to:

1. the scale or rate of remuneration or the method of calculating remuneration;
2. the intervals at which remuneration is paid;
3. any terms and conditions relating to hours of work;
4. any terms and conditions relating to any of the following:
   - entitlement to holidays, including public holidays, and holiday pay;
   - incapacity for work due to sickness or injury, including any provision for sick pay;
   - pensions and pension schemes;
5. the length of notice which the employee is obliged to give and entitled to receive to terminate his contract of employment;
6. the title of the job which the employee is employed to do or a brief description of the work for which he is employed;
7. where the employment is not intended to be permanent, the period for which it is expected to continue or, if it is for a fixed term, the date when it is to end;
8. the place of work or, where the employee is required or permitted to work at various places, an indication of that and of the address of the employer;
9. any collective agreements which directly affect the terms and conditions of the employment including, where the employer is not a party, the persons by whom they were made; and
10. where the employee is required to work outside the United Kingdom for a period of more than one month:
    - the period for which he is to work outside the United Kingdom;
    - the currency in which remuneration is to be paid while he is working outside the United Kingdom;
    - any additional remuneration payable to him, and any benefits to be provided to or in respect of him, by reason of his being required to work outside the United Kingdom; and
    - any terms and conditions relating to his return to the United Kingdom.

The statement must also include details of the employer's disciplinary and grievance procedures. The statement should either set out the rules or make reference to a document (normally the company handbook) where the rules may be easily accessible to the employee.

Particulars of entitlement to sick leave, pay and pensions may also be given by reference to some other document – such as an employee's handbook – which the employee has a reasonable opportunity of reading in the course of his employment or is reasonably accessible to the employee.

Particulars of the entitlement of both the employee and the employer to notice of termination of the contract may be given in the written statement by reference to the relevant statute or to the provisions of any collective agreement directly affecting the terms and conditions of the employment which is reasonably accessible to the employee.

All employees who are employed under a contract of service, work wholly or mainly in Great Britain and have worked for more than one month are entitled to a written statement of terms. Employees who were employed before 30 November 1993 must request a statement before they have such an entitlement.

If a qualifying employee does not receive a written statement of terms within two months he is entitled to enforce his rights by making an application to the employment tribunal, although it should be noted that the tribunal can only include those terms which have been agreed between the parties and has no power to rewrite the contract of employment: *Mears* v *Safecar Security* [1982] IRLR 183. However, in *Mears*, Stephenson LJ suggested obiter that, in the event that a tribunal, when looking at a contract of employment, does not have enough material to determine what would have been agreed, they must determine what would have been agreed between the parties. This approach would lead to a tribunal inventing terms and was rejected by the Court of Appeal in *Eagland* v *British Telecommunications* [1992] IRLR 323. In many cases recourse through management, the company grievance procedure, or the relevant trade union or staff association will resolve the issue without the need to make an application to an employment tribunal.

The legal status of the statement of terms was considered by the Court of Appeal in *Gascol Conversions Ltd* v *Mercer* [1974] IRLR 155 where there was an agreed variation in contractual terms between the employer and the employees. Pursuant to the Industrial Relations Act 1971 the employers sent a new contract of employment to each of their workers which required them to sign a document stating 'I confirm receipt of a new contract of employment dated 25 February 1972, which sets out, as required under the Industrial Relations Act 1971, the terms and conditions of my employment'. The Court of Appeal held that the document constituted a binding written contract.

However, the EAT has held that the statement of terms is not necessarily a contract of employment. In *System Floors (UK) Ltd* v *Daniel* [1982] ICR 54 Mr Daniel started work as an agency worker and was then offered permanent employment with the respondents to commence on the 26 November. Mr Daniel was given, and signed for, a statement of terms stating that he commenced permanent employment on 19 November. Later when Mr Daniel claimed that he had been unfairly dismissed the issue arose as to when his employment commenced. The EAT held that a statutory statement of terms does not constitute a contract of employment between an employer and an employee and therefore the date of commencement was 26 November. The fact that Mr Daniel had signed the statement did not alter the legal status because he signed simply to acknowledge that he had received it rather than to confirm the terms of the statement.

Where there is a difference between a contract and the statement of terms the contractual terms will apply: *Robertson* v *British Gas Corporation* [1983] ICR 351.

3.3 Express terms

The terms of an employment contract may be either express or implied. In the event of a dispute between an employer and his employee it is essential that the terms of the contract are clearly expressed in order to facilitate an early resolution of the dispute. Some terms are expressly stated whilst others may be implied into the contract: see section 3.4.

Express terms will generally be found in the documentary sources already referred to above, such as a job advertisement or letter of appointment. Express terms usually state, inter alia, the position and duties of the employee, the rate that he will be paid, the number of hours he is required to work, holiday entitlements etc. Express terms are important to both employees and employers alike because they allow for certainty within the working relationship, with each party knowing the extent of their rights and obligations.

An employer has the opportunity when drawing up a contract of employment to protect his legitimate business interests and he can do so by inserting a clause to protect confidential information and restrain his new employee from entering into business with competitors in the future. An employer can also insert a mobility clause to allow him the flexibility to move his employee should the need arise, and any such clause will be subject to the test of reasonableness.

There may also be company rules which are express contractual terms. These will generally be found in a company rule book or handbook. The employer can only vary these rules with the consent of the employee, otherwise any variation may be deemed to be a unilateral variation of terms and render the employer in breach of the contract.

3.4 Implied terms

An implied term is one which has not been expressly incorporated into the written or verbal contract but has been incorporated by implication. It is a term which the courts consider is so obvious that the parties did not consider it necessary to expressly state it. In *Courtaulds Northern Spinning* v *Sibson* [1988] IRLR 305, in a case where the contract of employment had been silent with respect to the location of the employees' work, Slade LJ in the Court of Appeal said that in cases where it is essential to imply some term into the contract of employment as to place of work:

'... the court does not have to be satisfied that the parties, if asked, would in fact have agreed the term before entering into the contract. The court merely has to be satisfied that the implied term is one which the parties would probably have agreed if they were being reasonable.'

This case can be contrased with *United Bank* v *Akhtar* [1989] IRLR 507 where the contract of employment contained a mobility clause. The Court of Appeal implied the term of reasonableness and held that even where a contract included a mobility clause an employer would not be entitled to force an employee to move some considerable distance without notice.

Implied terms play a significant role in employment matters, not only filling in gaps in express terms and conditions but also as a guide to interpreting the express terms. Implied terms may therefore be of assistance in giving business efficacy to an employment contract or to protect employees' rights. In *Scally & Others* v *Southern Health & Social Services Board* [1991] IRLR 478 the House of Lords held that if an employee is entitled to exercise rights under his contract of employment, but cannot do so unless he is aware of such rights, there is an implied term that the employer will advise an employee of any such entitlement.

It will not however be the case that the courts will always be prepared to incorporate terms into a contract of employment even though the absence of such terms may be detrimental to the employee.

In *Ali & Others* v *Christian Salvesen Food Services Ltd* [1995] IRLR 624 following negotiations with the union Mr Ali and his fellow workers were employed on an annual hours contract. The contract provided that the employees were to work 1,824 hours a year which is equivalent to 40 hours per week. In the event that at the end of the year the employees had worked more than 1,824 hours they would be entitled to overtime for the additional hours. Six months into the working year Mr Ali and four others were made redundant and although they had worked in excess of 40 hours a week they had not reached the overtime threshold of 1,824 hours. They claimed that the refusal of the employer to pay them for the additional hours worked amounted to an unlawful deduction of wages. It was held by the Court of Appeal that there was no implied term that in the event that the contract ended before 12 months the employees would be entitled to payment at the standard rate for any hours in excess of 40 hours per week.

Whilst this decision appears harsh the Court of Appeal said that the importation of an implied term depends upon the intention of the parties as evidenced from the wording of the contract and the surrounding circumstances. In this case the contract was negotiated by the union and that the failure to make some provision for the early termination of the contract was due in part to the fact that it is difficult to provide for every eventuality. The Court also considered that because of the failure of the parties to address this issue it would be impossible to incorporate a term that it could be said with confidence the parties would have agreed to had they directed their minds to the issue.

There are two types of implied term that may be implied into the contract of employment.

1. A term implied as a matter of law into all contracts of employment.
2. A term implied as a matter of fact into a particular contract of employment, ie common law terms.

Terms implied as a matter of law

These are contractual obligations which are imposed on employers or employees by either common law principles or legislation. The test used to determine whether a term is to be implied into the contract is the 'officious bystander' test. This test was applied by the Court of Appeal in *Shirlaw* v *Southern Founderies Ltd* [1939] 2 KB 206 where MacKinnon LJ described the test, saying 'if, while the parties were making their bargain, an officious bystander were to suggest some express provision for it in their agreement, they would testily suppress him with a common: "Oh, of course".' In other words, the term is so obvious it does not need expressly stating.

The approach of the courts in determining whether a term will be implied into the contract appears to have shifted so that the courts will not only look at what is obvious, but also what is reasonable. The concept of reasonableness was considered by Lord Denning in *Shell UK Ltd* v *Lostock Garages Ltd* [1977] 1 All ER 481 and has more recently been applied in *BG plc* v *O'Brien* [2001] IRLR 496 where the EAT said that when an employer acts without reasonable cause, it is a breach of what Lord Steyn in *Johnson* v *Unisys* [2001] IRLR 279 referred to as the 'employer's obligation of fair dealing'. In *BG plc* v *O'Brien* the employer failed to offer Mr O'Brien a revised contract of employment which provided for enhanced redundancy payments. The tribunal and the EAT held that the fact that the employer had offered the new contract to an entire class of employees with the exception of the applicant was a breach of the implied term of trust and confidence.

In *O'Brien* v *Associated Fire Alarms Ltd* [1988] 1 All ER 93 Lord Denning considered the status of implied terms and said 'I have always understood that the question whether a term is to be implied in a contract is a question of law for the court and not a question of fact'.

Common law implied terms

These are terms which the courts and tribunals will impose upon any employment relationship and they operate as implied general duties of both the employer and the employee.

Duty of obedience

An employee will be deemed to have impliedly agreed to obey his employer in respect of all reasonable orders. In *Ottoman Bank* v *Chakarian* [1930] AC 277 the Privy Council held that where an employee leaves his place of work because of fears for his own personal safety this will not amount to disobedience. In considering the reasonableness of an order the courts will take into consideration good industrial relations practice: *Payne* v *Spook Erection Ltd* [1984] IRLR 219. The courts will also consider the status of the employee: *Cole* v *Midland Display Ltd* [1973] IRLR 62.

The order given by the employer must be lawful. If the order is unlawful, as in the case of *Morrish* v *Henleys Ltd* [1973] IRLR 61 where an employee was ordered to falsify accounts, a refusal to follow the order will not amount to a breach of contract.

An employee's implied duty to obey orders may be offset by the employer's implied duty to treat employees with proper respect and reasonable consideration: *United Bank Ltd* v *Akhtar* [1989] IRLR 507. However, this does not mean that the employer must treat an employee reasonably, only that he should not be treated unreasonably: *Courtaulds Northern Spinning* v *Sibson* [1988] IRLR 305.

A breach of the implied duty of obedience may constitute a repudiation of the employment contract and give the employer grounds for dismissal.

Duty of skill and care
There is an implied term that the employee is reasonably competent to carry out his work and that he will use all reasonable care and skill when carrying out his duties. A breach of this term will render an employee liable to dismissal. In *Taylor* v *Alidair* [1978] IRLR 82 a pilot was dismissed after a particularly bumpy landing. The dismissal was held to be fair even though it was an isolated incident. The scope of this implied duty has been given a broad interpretation.

In *Lister* v *Romford Ice and Cold Storage Co* [1957] 1 All ER 125 a father and son were employed by the respondents. Whilst reversing a lorry one day the son negligently ran over his father. The father claimed against the employer on the grounds that they were vicariously liable. The respondent's insurance company sought to recover damages paid to the father by the company from the son, who in turn claimed that there was an implied term in his contract of employment that he would be indemnified. It was held by the House of Lords on a three to two majority that there was no term implied into a contract of employment that employees would be indemnified against all claims arising our of acts of negligence during the course of their employment. Lord Tucker considered that to imply such a term would 'result in completely nullifying the effect of the duty of care which the servant owes to his master and give him licence to be as negligent as he liked'. However, this decision is not without criticism and could in some circumstances produce harsh results. In order to overcome this there is an agreement amongst insurance companies not to pursue such claims against employees unless there is evidence that an employee has acted fraudulently.

Duty of good faith
There are several duties owed by the employer and employee under this common law duty.

Trust and loyalty. There is an implied term that an employee will be loyal to his employer. In *Hivac Ltd* v *Park Royal Scientific Instruments* [1946] Ch 169 the Court of Appeal held that employees who had worked for a competitor during their spare time had breached the implied term of good faith and fidelity to their employer. However, the courts will not automatically consider that work for a competitor is a breach of the duty of fidelity. In *Nova Plastics Ltd v Froggatt* [1982] IRLR 146 the EAT considered whether an employee who had been 'moonlighting' had breached the implied term. It was held that not all moonlighting would amount to a breach but it all depended upon the circumstances of the case. In this case the employee was an odd job man and his working for a competitor did not amount to a serious breach or assist the rival company in any significant way. It may therefore be argued that the decision in *Hivac Ltd* is limited to cases where an employee can cause significant harm to his employer by working for a competitor. However, the courts will consider each case on the facts.

There is also an implied term that an employer will not act in a manner that is likely to seriously damage the relationship of trust and confidence between the employer and employee. This implied term may be breached even though the employer did not intend to repudiate the contract; it is sufficient that the conduct of the employer results in the employee considering that the situation is no longer tenable. This implied term affords some protection for employees against underhand methods of employers which, whilst not amounting to a breach of an express term of the contract, will give rise to a claim for a breach of implied terms. A good example is where an employer persistently attempts to vary an employee's conditions of service with a view to getting rid of the employee. In *Woods v W M Car Services Ltd* [1982] IRLR 413 it was held by the EAT that the employer had breached this implied term when he had tried to alter the employee's working hours, pay and job title, although in the event the applicant was unsuccessful in her claim.

In *Lewis v Motorworld Garages Ltd* [1985] IRLR 465 the Court of Appeal held that where an employer breaches express terms of the employment contract the cumulative effect of such breaches may amount to a breach of the implied term of trust and confidence even though the breaches were waived by the employee.

In *Malik v Bank of Credit and Commerce International SA (In Liquidation)* [1997] IRLR 462 the House of Lords widened the ambit given to the implied term of trust and confidence. In this case Mr Malik claimed 'stigma' damages from the liquidator in respect of financial losses which he suffered due to his being unable to find alternative employment after the bank went into liquidation following alleged fraudulent practices. He alleged that although he was entirely innocent, his reputation had been tainted by the activities of his employer, and that the bank had been in breach of the implied term of trust and confidence. The House of Lords held that damages for loss of reputation can be recovered provided that a relevant breach of contract can be established. In this case the bank had been operating its business in a corrupt manner and this was a breach of the implied term of trust and confidence.

Following the case of *Malik* there have been a number of cases which have explored further the implied term of mutual trust and confidence. One of the issues that has been considered is the distinction between a breach of the implied term of trust and confidence during the currency of the employment relationship which would entitle a claimant to commence proceedings in the civil courts for psychiatric injury which is caused as a result of the manner of dismissal. In *McCabe* v *Cornwall County Council* [2004] IRLR 733 Mr McCabe, a teacher, was suspended in May 1993 after allegations of inappropriate sexual behavior were made by girls at the school where he taught. No details of the allegations were given to Mr McCabe at the time of his suspension and indeed he was not interviewed until one week after his suspension. In September 1993 the allegations made by the girls were put to Mr McCabe for the first time. Mr McCabe alleged that the conduct of his employer caused him to suffer psychiatric illness; he was finally dismissed in March 1994. The applicant successfully pursued a claim for unfair dismissal and also commenced proceedings in the High Court alleging a breach of the implied term of trust and confidence because of the way that he was treated at the time of his suspension. The High Court agreed to an application by the employer to strike out the claim because it was tied up with the claimant's dismissal and therefore Mr McCabe was limited to the statutory claim for unfair dismissal. This decision was reversed by the Court of Appeal which held that the claim should not have been struck out. The council appealed in a case which was heard by the House of Lords together with *Eastwood and Another* v *Magnox Electric plc*.

The House of Lords held that where there has been a breach of the implied term of trust and confidence prior to a dismissal an employee will be able to claim for breach of contract claiming damages in the courts for psychiatric injury or any other losses that have been incurred. However, there does have to be a clear distinction between the breach of the implied term prior to a dismissal and a breach which is part of the dismissal. The former will be actionable in the ordinary courts, whereas in the latter case an employee will be limited to bringing a claim in the employment tribunal for unfair dismissal.

In *McCabe* Lord Nicholls highlighted some of the difficulties that may arise in cases where a cause of action accrues prior to a dismissal. He said that whilst it may be relatively easy to identify the boundary lines between the common law rights and remedies and the statutory rights and remedies, the practical consequences may lead to the courts and tribunals hearing substantially the same claims. Lord Nicholls suggested that one way around the problem was for the cap on unfair dismissal claims to be lifted saying that the issue 'merits urgent attention by the government.'

The implied contractual term of trust and confidence has been subject to a great deal of discussion over the last few years. However, the Court of Appeal has recently dealt with the issue of the extent to which an employer is under a duty of trust and confidence not to cause economic harm to an employee.

Although the expansion of the implied term of trust and confidence has been embraced by the courts and tribunals some limitation has been placed on its expansion. In *Crossley* v *Faithful & Gould Holdings Ltd* [2004] IRLR 377 the Court of Appeal held that to extend the implied term so as to impose upon an employer a duty not to cause economic harm to an employee would place too much of a burden on employers. Furthermore, in the cases of *Scally* v *Southern Health and Social Services Board* [1991] IRLR 478 and *Spring* v *Guardian Assurance plc* [1995] 2 AC

296 the House of Lords had declined to introduce such an implied term into all contracts of employment. Although in *Scally* the House of Lords held that if an employee is entitled to exercise his rights under his contract of employment but cannot do so unless he is aware of those rights, there is an implied term that the employer will advise the employee of his entitlement.

It is becoming increasingly common for employers who wish to bring the employment relationship to an end to offer an employee the choice between being dismissed and resigning on a generous resignation package. This approach may amount to a breach of the implied term of trust and confidence and any employer should exercise a great deal of caution in the way in which they broach the subject with an employee: *Billington v Michael Hunter & Sons Ltd* [2003] EAT/05780/03.

The principle laid down in *Malik* was applied by the Court of Appeal in *Gogay v Hertfordshire County Council* [2000] IRLR 703, where an employee was awarded damages for clinical depression which she suffered as a result of being suspended from work. The Court of Appeal considered that the failure of the employer to properly investigate the circumstances surrounding the suspension amounted to a breach of the implied term. The Court awarded damages even though the suspension of the employee did not lead to a dismissal.

If there is an express or implied term in a contract of employment an employer may require an employee to submit to a medical examination if the employer has reasonable grounds for believing that the employee is suffering from some mental or physical disability. In *Bliss v South East Thames Regional Health Authority* [1985] IRLR 308, where the Health Authority suspended an orthopaedic surgeon for his failure to undergo a psychiatric examination, the Court of Appeal held that to require to an employee to submit to such an examination without reasonable grounds for believing that he was suffering from a psychiatric illness was a fundamental breach of contract, and that in this particular case it was almost certain to destroy the relationship of confidence and trust which ought to exist between employer and employee.

Dishonesty on the part of an employee or an employer can also amount to a breach of contract. In *Boston Deep Sea Fishing & Ice Co v Ansell* (1888) Ch D 339 the Court of Appeal held that the receipt of secret commissions by the managing director of the respondent company from suppliers constituted a breach of confidence and good faith between an employee and employer.

There is no general duty upon employees to disclose misconduct by other employees. However, in certain circumstances such a duty may exist and in determining whether there is such a duty it is necessary to consider various factors, particularly the seniority of the employee. In *Sybron Corporation v Rochem Ltd & Others* [1983] IRLR 253 the Court of Appeal held that whilst the employee was not under a duty to disclose his own misconduct, because of his position as a senior executive he was under a duty to disclose the misconduct of others even though such disclosure would have the effect of incriminating him. It could also be argued that an employee who understands that misconduct by a fellow worker could lead to personal injury or the death of any individual is also under an obligation to advise his employer.

Faithful service. An employee is under an implied duty to faithfully serve his master. In *Secretary of State for Employment* v *ASLEF & Others* [1972] 2 All ER 949 the Court of Appeal held that a work to rule which disrupted the business of the employer was a breach of the implied term to serve the employer faithfully and the implied term 'to perform the contract in such a way as not to frustrate the commercial objective': per Lord Buckley.

Co-operation and flexibility. This aspect of the implied duty of good faith extends the duty of obedience beyond narrowly defined contractual obligations found in the job description, such as duties, location hours of work etc. In *Cresswell* v *Board of Inland Revenue* [1984] IRLR 190 the Inland Revenue introduced a new computer system which replaced a manual operation involving pen, paper and pocket calculator to work out new tax codes. The employees claimed that the change in the method of working constituted such a change in the nature of the job that the Inland Revenue were requiring them to work under new contracts of employment. It was held by the High Court that the employees were under an implied duty to adapt to new working methods provided that the employer gave sufficient training to enable them to acquire the necessary skills to undertake the work. In such a situation it is necessary to consider what was the employee employed to do and in the instant case it was held that the same job was done, albeit that a different method was to be used.

There is authority for the proposition that a greater degree of flexibility is required from professional and senior personnel than other members of the workforce. In *Sim* v *Rotherham Borough Council* [1986] IRLR 391, a case concerning the refusal of teachers to cover for absent colleagues, Scott J considered that teachers were professional persons who are employed to carry out a particular service to 'proper professional standards' and that in doing so flexibility on the part of teachers was an essential requirement.

Duty to inform. The Court of Appeal has held that if an employer intends to depart from a normal practice there is an implied term to inform employees of the departure. In *Glendale Managed Services* v *Graham & Others* [2003] IRLR 465 Mr Graham and his colleagues were employed by Southend-on-Sea Council at a leisure centre. Their contracts provided that pay would be in accordance with the National Joint Council for Local Government. Following a TUPE transfer the new employer (Glendale Managed Services) failed to honour NJC agreed pay increases. Mr Graham successfully brought a claim for unauthorised deduction from wages in respect of the non-payment of the NJC agreed increase. The employer's appeal to the EAT failed and a further appeal was made to the Court of Appeal which found in favour of Mr Graham and his colleagues. The Court of Appeal took a robust view of the implied terms of employment contracts. Keene LJ referred to the dictum of Phillips in *FC Gardner Ltd* v *Beresford* [1978] IRLR 63 where he said that there will normally be an implied term in contracts of employment that an employer will not treat his employees arbitrarily, capriciously or inequitably in respect of matters of pay. Keene LJ went on to say:

> 'I see that as being simply one part of the general obligation not to destroy the mutual trust and confidence between employer and employee.'

Common practice
The courts may imply terms into a contract of employment in accordance with common practice within a particular industry or by reference to national agreements. In *Stevenson* v *Teeside Bridge and Engineering Ltd* [1971] 1 All ER 296 the High Court implied a mobility clause into the contract of employment of a steel erector. The court took into consideration the nature of the industry in which he worked, where it was quite normal to have to work all over the country, and the fact that the contract provided for travelling and subsistence allowances.

In *Sagar* v *Ridehalgh* [1931] 1 Ch 310 the Court of Appeal held that a custom within the cotton industry to deduct money from the wages of weavers for bad workmanship that had been in existence for over 30 years could be implied into the contract even though the employee was unaware of the custom and not all employees within the industry adopted the practice.

When considering the application of custom and practice, the EAT in *Quinn & Others* v *Calder Industrial Materials Ltd* [1996] IRLR 126 was not prepared to accept that an employer was in breach of contract when he failed to pay enhanced redundancy payments even though there was a policy containing guidelines on such payments and that enhanced payments had been paid since the formulation of the policy. It was argued that there was an implied term in the contract of employment that the employer would pay enhanced redundancy payments by reason of the employer's established custom and practice. However, the EAT held that there was no evidence that the employer intended to become contractually bound by the policy guidelines, particularly as these guidelines had not been communicated to the employees.

Duty to care for the safety of employees
All employers must take reasonable steps to ensure the safety of employees. In *Wilsons and Clyde Coal Co Ltd* v *English* [1938] AC 57 the House of Lords laid down three requirements.

1. An employer must take reasonable care to provide safe equipment and materials.
2. He must provide a safe workplace and a safe system of work.
3. He must employ competent staff.

An employer must be covered by insurance so that in the event of an accident at work resulting from the failure of an employer to abide by the implied terms above an employee will be compensated for his injuries and consequential losses by virtue of the Employers' Liability (Compulsory Insurance) Act 1969.

An employer is also under an implied duty not to knowingly expose employees to anything which may cause or increase the risk of health problems.

In *Walker* v *Northumberland County Council* [1995] IRLR 35 Mr Walker worked for the respondents as an area social services officer. As a result of an increase in the number of child abuse cases his work load substantially increased. However, no additional assistance was provided to help with the extra workload. As a result Mr Walker suffered a nervous breakdown. Following assurances from the council that he would be provided with assistance Mr Walker returned to work, but the support that had been promised was not provided and he suffered a further breakdown. He was dismissed by the council on health grounds but argued that the council was in breach of its implied duty of care by failing to take reasonable steps to avoid exposing him to a workload that was likely to endanger his health. It was held by the High Court that the council was liable for the applicant's second nervous breakdown as it was reasonably foreseeable that if the council failed to reduce Mr Walker's workload, he was likely to suffer from further mental illness.

Smoking

In *Dryden* v *Greater Glasgow Health Board* [1992] IRLR 469 Ms Dryden, a heavy smoker, had worked for the respondents for 12 years when a no-smoking ban was introduced. Ms Dryden was unable to carry out her eight-and-a-half hour shift without smoking and so she resigned and claimed constructive dismissal. It was held by the EAT that the tribunal had been correct in holding that there was no implied term in her contract of employment entitling her to smoke at work.

Duty to provide work

There is no general duty for an employer to provide work for an employee: *Collier* v *Sunday Referee Publishing Co Ltd* [1940] 4 All ER 234. However, such a term may be implied if it is necessary for an employee to continue to work to maintain his skill. Thus, it may be that a surgeon should be provided with work because if he is unable to carry out surgical operations for a period of time he may lose his skills. Indeed, in *Collier* v *Sunday Referee Publishing Co Ltd* [1940] 4 All ER 234 the High Court held that the employer was in breach of contract because although the employee, a chief sub-editor of the *Sunday Referee*, had been paid his salary after the paper had been sold his skill was one which fell into the category of those who rely on work to give them publicity.

It should be noted that in *Langsten* v *AEUW* [1974] 1 All ER 980 Lord Denning in the Court of Appeal argued that there should be a general right to work on the basis that there is a benefit to be derived by actually doing a particular job, in other words job satisfaction. However, this argument no longer represents the current state of law.

Duty to provide pay

Under normal circumstances an employer is under a duty to pay wages to an employee. If a contract is silent with respect to the rate of remuneration the courts will imply a term that a reasonable amount should be paid. In *Way* v *Latilla* [1937] 3 All ER 759 the House of Lords held that an agreement between two parties that if the plaintiff secured certain gold-mining concessions the defendant would 'look after his interests' was sufficient to imply a term that he would be paid and this was calculated on a quantum meruit basis.

Notice period

If there is express provision in a contract for the amount of time that must be given by either the employer or employee as notice of termination of the contract that notice period will apply unless it is less than that provided by s86 Employment Rights Act 1996 (discussed in more detail in Chapter 4, section 4.11). In the event that the contract is silent as to the notice period there will be implied into the contract a period of reasonable length. What is reasonable will depend upon the circumstances of the case, although it will the same as, or greater than, the statutory minimum. In *Hill* v *C A Parsons & Co Ltd* [1972] 1 Ch 305 the Court of Appeal considered that a senior engineer would have been entitled to a period of notice between six and 12 months.

3.5 Collective agreements

Certain express and implied contractual terms may be found in collective agreements. These are agreements between either a single employer and a union or an employers' federation and a union and will be considered in more detail in Chapter 11.

Collective agreements are not normally legally binding and the common law authority for this proposition can be found in *Ford Motor Co* v *AUEFW* [1969] IRLR 67 where the High Court held that a collective agreement would only be enforceable at law (subject to other legal requirements being satisfied) if the parties intended it to be so. In the absence of such an intention any agreement would be binding in honour only. However, if an agreement is expressly stated as being binding in honour only but is incorporated into the contract of employment it will become a term of the contract and will be legally binding.

If as a result of a collective agreement between an employer and a union certain working conditions or terms are agreed, an employee may become bound by those terms if his contract expressly incorporates the collective agreement, even though he may not be aware of the precise details. If there is express reference in the employee's contract to the collective agreement then it will be deemed to be incorporated into the contract.

In *NCB* v *Galley* [1958] 1 All ER 91 Mr Galley worked for the NCB as a pit deputy. An agreement between the NCB and the union who represented Mr Galley provided by cl 12 that 'deputies shall work such days or part days in each week as may reasonably be required'. Mr Galley and other pit deputies refused to work on Saturdays and the NCB sued for breach of contract. Mr Galley argued that cl 12 was not enforceable because it was vague and uncertain. The Court of Appeal held that cl 12 was enforceable. The collective agreement was intended to have legally binding effect and had been incorporated into Mr Galley's contract and therefore Mr Galley was in breach of his contract of employment.

If an employee's contract incorporates a collective agreement there is no need to amend each individual's contract every time negotiations between employers and unions result in some change.

Some terms of a collective agreement may become incorporated into a contract of employment if the parties observe the terms over a period of time even though they are not expressly incorporated into the contract: however, strong evidence to support observance would be required.

In *Hamilton* v *Futura Floors Ltd* [1990] IRLR 478 the Court of Session held that an employer who had joined an employers' association which had entered into a collective agreement with the applicant's union was not necessarily bound by the terms of the collective agreement nor were the terms incorporated into the employee's contract of employment. There was no evidence of custom and practice to show that the collective agreement would become incorporated into the contract.

The terms of a collective agreement will also apply to employees who are not members of a union if there is express reference to the collective agreement in the contract. If, however, there is no express reference in the contract the position is less certain.

Not all terms of a collective agreement are suitable for incorporation into the contract of employment and in determining whether incorporation is appropriate the courts and tribunals will look at the purpose and subject matter of the agreement. In *Young* v *Canadian Northern Railway Co* [1931] AC 83 it was held by the Privy Council that an agreement consisting of some 188 rules by which the employer undertook to observe the rules for the benefit of the workforce was not intended to create any binding contractual obligation between employer and employee. Similarly, in *British Leyland* v *McQuilken* [1978] IRLR 245 a planned reorganisation which had been agreed between the employer and the union was held by the EAT to be a 'long-term plan dealing with policy' and was not to be incorporated into the contract of employment. The subsequent failure of the employer to implement the reorganisation was therefore not a breach of contract.

Once a clause of a collective agreement has been incorporated into the contract of employment it will become binding even though the agreement between the employer and the union may be terminated.

In *Robertson* v *British Gas Corporation* [1983] ICR 351 Mr Robertson was employed as a meter reader by the respondents. The letter of appointment provided that a bonus scheme would apply to meter readers. In June 1981 British Gas gave notice to the union that the bonus scheme would no longer apply and when bonus payments were no longer paid Mr Robertson and others claimed against the respondents for unlawful deduction of wages. It was held by the Court of Appeal that the terms of the collective agreement providing for the payment of a bonus had been incorporated into the contract of employment and British Gas could not unilaterally withdraw from the scheme.

3.6 Company handbook/rule book

Many companies will issue a company handbook or rule book to employees which may include provision for sick pay, holiday entitlements, health and safety issues, maternity and paternity leave, disciplinary and grievance procedures etc. These rules or provisions will not necessarily be contractual terms; it may be that some provisions are too ambiguous or uncertain to be considered to be binding contractual terms.

In *Secretary of State for Employment* v *ASLEF & Others* [1972] 2 All ER 949 a union representing railway workers which imposed a work to rule argued that the employees were not in breach of contract because they were merely following to the letter the rules as laid down in the company rule book. It was held by the Court of Appeal that not all the rules were contractually binding and therefore the employees were in breach of the implied term to faithfully serve the employer and not to wilfully disrupt the employer's business.

If an employee accepts as part of his contract any rules which are set out in a company handbook (for example by signing a document to that effect) these rules will be incorporated into the contract of employment.

An employer may also notify employees of company rules by posting them on a notice board or publishing them on a company intranet, and whether such rules are contractually binding will be a question of fact to be determined by looking at the surrounding circumstances. In *Petrie* v *MacFisheries* [1940] 1 KB 258 the High Court held that a note on a factory notice board, stating that employees who were off sick would receive half pay for three weeks as a concession but not as of right, was contractually binding even though the notice had not been drawn to the employee's attention.

3.7 Variation of contractual terms

Having established how certain terms are incorporated into a contract of employment it is now necessary to consider the position if either an employer or indeed an employee wishes to change those terms.

Within the context of employment, matters do not stay still for very long and companies evolve and grow; they change their organisational structures in response to, and in anticipation of, changes within the market in which they operate. In order to put necessary changes into effect an employer may need to alter the terms and conditions of some or all of his employees.

An employer cannot unilaterally vary contractual terms and change must be done with the agreement of the employee. In *Rigby* v *Ferodo Ltd* [1987] IRLR 516 the House of Lords held that the employer had breached the contract of employment when, in a time of financial difficulty, he unilaterally imposed a wage cut on Mr Rigby.

If an employer imposes new terms and conditions upon an employee, the employee is not obliged to accept the new terms and may protest against them.

In *Marriott* v *Oxford & District Co-operative Society* [1970] 1 QB 186 Mr Marriott had been employed by the respondents as a supervisor. The respondents found that there was not sufficient work for him and so they offered him alternative employment but at a reduced rate of pay. Mr Marriott accepted the job under protest and later resigned with notice and claimed that he had been made redundant. It was held by the Court of Appeal that the imposition of a new rate of pay amounted to a unilateral variation of contract, and although Mr Marriott had worked under the new terms for four weeks his protests made it clear that he did not agree to the new terms. He was therefore entitled to redundancy payments.

If an employee continues to work under unilaterally varied terms without protest then it may be argued that the variation has been accepted by conduct and any rights to damages in respect of the breach have been waived. This contractual principle is, however, limited in its application.

In *Jones* v *Associated Tunnelling Co Ltd* [1981] IRLR 477 Mr Jones had worked at a NCB colliery for 11 years for an independent contractor. The contract at this particular colliery came to an end but he was offered work at another location which he refused. He was, however, offered work by the NCB at the original site which he accepted. His original employer rejected a claim by the applicant for redundancy arguing that the original contract included a mobility clause, although on the facts the exact scope of this was unclear. Furthermore, argued the employer, a revised statement had been issued to Mr Jones which included a mobility clause, although in different terms, which entitled the employer to move the applicant to another location. Mr Jones did not protest against the new clause and therefore the respondents argued that they were not liable to pay him redundancy payments.

In the EAT Browne-Wilkinson J said that a distinction should be drawn between unilateral variation by an employer of employment terms which have an immediate impact upon an employee (such as a variation in wages), and terms such as mobility clauses which in this case did not have any affect upon Mr Jones at the time of variation. His lack of protest was therefore attributed to the fact that the variation had no immediate effect and he was therefore entitled to refuse the alternative employment.

An employer can effect a variation in terms and conditions by lawfully dismissing employees with appropriate notice and then re-engaging the employees on new terms and conditions. The employer does, however, take the risk of the employees claiming unfair dismissal. If an employer chooses to adopt this approach he must make it absolutely clear in the letter of termination that he is terminating the contract. In *Burdett-Coutts* v *Hertfordshire County Council* [1984] IRLR 91 the High Court held that it was not possible to interpret a letter headed 'Amendments of Contract of Service' as a notice of termination and an offer of re-employment on new terms.

Another way to effect a change in terms is for an employer to 'buy out' certain contractual rights. If an employee agrees to the variation in return for a sum of money or other benefit the variation will be by mutual agreement and enforceable.

The contract of employment may provide for a variation of terms – such as a change in location or duties – and if this is the case both parties are bound by any variation. It is also possible that a contract may be varied by implication. In *Armstrong Whitworth Rolls* v *Mustard* [1971] 1 All ER 598 the High Court held that where an employee had worked longer shifts than provided for in his contract of employment for a period of six years, a variation of contract could be implied by conduct.

It is essential that any clauses in a contract of employment are clear and unequivocal; if there is any ambiguity the contra proferentum rule will operate against the employer. It is also important that where the contract of employment provides for the variation of a particular term of the contract any actual variation is communicated to the employee.

In *Bainbridge* v *Circuit Foil UK Ltd* [1997] IRLR 305 Mr Bainbridge was employed by the defendants and in November 1985 he commenced sick leave. The applicant's contract of employment provided that he was entitled to sick pay under the employers' long-term sickness benefit scheme after six months in employment. The scheme was supported by a health insurance policy. The rules were contained in the applicant's contract and included, inter alia, that if the applicant was dismissed while receiving sick pay the insurers would continue to pay the benefits due to him until he reached the age of 65 and that the employers reserved the right to amend or terminate the scheme at any time 'without prior notice'.

The applicant received sick pay from November 1985 until March 1993 when his employment was terminated on grounds of redundancy. He was then told that his health insurance policy had been terminated in 1982 prior to his illness. When the payments ceased the applicant complained to a county court that his employers had breached his contract by failing to notify him that the policy had been cancelled and that in effect they were still bound by the terms of the scheme.

The county court found for the employers. The judge formed the view that the employers were only bound to continue with the scheme for those already in receipt of long-term benefits before the termination of the scheme. In the applicant's case his long-term sickness commenced after the termination of the policy. Mr Bainbridge appealed to the Court of Appeal.

The Court of Appeal held that the judge at first instance had erred in holding that the employee's right to benefit had automatically terminated even though there was an express provision reserving the employers' right to amend or terminate. They further held that the termination clause in the rules did not end the employee's right to sickness benefit under the contract until he was given notice that his contract of employment was being varied. In the absence of such notice his entitlement continued. Aldous LJ considered the effectiveness of the words 'without prior notice' but still held that notice must be given to effect variation under a contract of employment. The words referred to the scheme and even though they were ambiguous they did not affect the contract which offered sickness benefit.

Flexible working

The Employment Act 2002 further implements the 'family-friendly' policies of the government and provides a statutory right for employees to request a variation of their contract so that they may alter their working arrangements to enable them to look after their children. Section 47 of the 2002 Act provides for the implementation, by means of Regulations, for a provision to enable parents of children under the age of six or, if the child is disabled, under the age of 18, to apply to their employer for more flexible working arrangements. The employer is under no duty to accede to any such request, but must consider the application, hold a meeting with the employee if it intends to refuse, and put its reasons for refusal in writing. See Chapter 8 for detailed consideration of the Regulations.

3.8 Post-termination obligations

The termination of a contract of employment does not necessarily bring all the rights and obligations created by the contract to an end. During the course of employment the parties to a contract are bound by the implied terms of trust, confidence and fidelity and in certain circumstances such duties will survive the termination of the contract. An employer who wishes to protect his legitimate business interest may rely solely upon the implied terms of the contract or he may depend upon an express term or covenant.

Restraint of trade

During the course of his employment with a particular company an employee will generally become more skilled and knowledgeable with respect to his employer's business. The employer may have spent considerable sums of money training an employee with a view to not only improving the skills of the worker but to benefit the long-term interests of the company.

When an employer is drafting a contract of employment he may rely solely on the implied term of fidelity to protect his business interests. However, an employer may consider it prudent to include a covenant in the contract of employment which will come into operation in the event that an employee leaves the company at some time in the future. A covenant which prevents an employee from using commercial or trade secrets which he has gained as a result of his employment with a former employer is called a covenant in restraint of trade.

The common law doctrine of restraint of trade is based on public policy considerations. In the case of *Nordenfelt* v *Maxim Nordenfelt Guns & Ammunition Co* [1894] AC 535 Lord MacNaghten said:

> 'The public have an interest in every person's carrying on his trade freely; so has the individual. All interference with individual liberty of action in trading, and all restraints of trade themselves, if there is nothing more, are contrary to public policy.'

This view has been echoed in a later case by Lord Morris of Borth-y-Gest in *Esso Petroleum Co Ltd* v *Harper's Garage (Stourport) Ltd* [1968] AC 269.

It is clear that there are two competing interests – an ex-employee should be allowed to use his skill and knowledge to further his employment prospects, even if such skills were gained during the course of his employment with an ex-employer, whilst an employer must be allowed to protect his legitimate business interests.

The question as to whether a covenant in restraint of trade is enforceable generally only arises when an employee leaves a company to work for a competitor. If an employee leaves to work in an entirely different industry there is no legitimate business interest to protect.

In determining whether a covenant in restraint of trade is enforceable it is necessary for the courts to look at various factors such as time, geographical area and the position of the employee to determine whether the clause is reasonable.

Time

If a covenant is too wide in terms of the length of time it is to operate after an employee's termination with the company it is unlikely that the clause will be considered to be reasonable. A restriction that is wider than is reasonably necessary for an employer's protection will be unenforceable.

In *Mason* v *Provident Clothing and Supply Co Ltd* [1913] AC 724 a clause in Mr Mason's contract provided that he should not be engaged in any similar business within 25 miles of London within three years of the termination of his engagement with the company. After Mr Mason was dismissed he went to work for a competitor and his former employer sought to rely upon the restraint of trade clause. The House of Lords held that the restriction imposed was far wider than was necessary to protect the company's legitimate interests and was therefore unenforceable.

A similar conclusion was reached in the House of Lords in the case of *Herbert Morris Ltd* v *Saxelby* [1916] 1 AC 688 where the employer sought to rely upon a covenant which prevented an employee from working for a competitor anywhere in the UK for a period of seven years following termination of employment. The

House of Lords held that a restraint which amounts simply to a protection against competition will be unenforceable.

Seniority

When determining the enforceability of a restraint of trade clause the courts and tribunals will consider the seniority of the employee. The more senior the status of an employee the more likely the employee is to have knowledge that may threaten the employer's business. The courts will therefore be more inclined to enforce such a clause to protect the employer's interest, subject of course to the test of reasonableness.

In *Littlewoods Organisation Ltd* v *Harris* [1978] 1 WLR 1472 a covenant restraining a director of a mail-order company from working for a competitor within the UK for 12 months after his contract ended was considered by the Court of Appeal to be reasonable. The Court took into account the extensive personal contacts of the director and his knowledge of the company's commercial strategy.

The issue of seniority was also taken into account by the Court of Appeal in *Dentmaster (UK) Ltd* v *Kent* [1997] IRLR 636. In this case Mr Kent was employed as a dental repair technician by Dentmaster (UK) and was the exclusive manager in the Thames Valley. His contract of employment contained a restraint clause that prevented solicitation for a period of six months following termination of employment of 'any person or business who was a client of his employer during the six months preceding the termination of employment'.

The non-solicitation clause applied to the whole of England. After Mr Kent left his employment with Dentmaster his employers discovered that he was working in breach of the restraint clause and applied to the High Court for an interlocutory injunction to restrain Mr Kent from breaching the covenant; this was refused and the employers appealed. It was held by the Court of Appeal held that the non-solicitation clause was enforceable. The six-month period was reasonable as it was a short one and limited to persons and businesses who had been customers of the employers within the six months preceding termination of employment.

Geographical area

A restrictive covenant will only be enforceable if it is necessary for the protection of the employer's legitimate business. If a small accountancy company in Liverpool attempted to restrict ex-employees from working for any competitor within the UK, quite clearly this would be unenforceable. A similar covenant restricting ex-employees from working for a competitor within Liverpool may be enforceable.

In the case of *Fitch* v *Dewes* [1921] 2 AC 158 the House of Lords held that a covenant restraining a solicitors' clerk from working for another solicitor within a seven-mile radius of Tamworh was enforceable because the area of restriction was quite small and another position could be relatively easily found outside the restricted area.

In the later case of *Office Angels Ltd* v *Rainer-Thomas and O'Connor* [1991] IRLR 214 the Court of Appeal restated the general principle that a court must be satisfied that the covenant is no greater than necessary for the protection of the employer's legitimate interest and went on to say that in considering the reasonableness of a restrictive covenant, the court can examine whether a covenant drawn in narrower terms would have been sufficient.

In *Office Angels* v *Rainer-Thomas and O'Connor* the employer carried on a business as an employment agency. Two employees had accepted as being incorporated into their contract of employment the following clauses.

1. Employees would not, for six months after the termination of their employment, solicit custom from any person who had been a company client during his/her employment.
2. Employees would not, within six months after termination of the employment relationship, engage in or undertake the trade or business of an employment agency within a one-kilometre radius the branch or branches at which the employee had worked during a period of six months prior to the employment relationship ceasing.

The two employees subsequently left to set up their own employment agency and the employer sought to rely upon the covenant. The Court of Appeal held that in order for a covenant to be enforceable the employer must demonstrate that there is some asset or knowledge which can be regarded as the property of the employer which requires protection and that the restriction imposed is no greater than is necessary to protect the company. In this case, although the Court held that the company was entitled to protect itself, the covenant in the employees' contract would do little to protect the employer because, although there was a geographical limitation, orders from customers were taken by telephone and therefore there was no connection between the area covered by the covenant and the area worked.

Previous customers

During the course of employment a worker may build up close business relationships with clients so that once the worker moves on clients may follow. This frequently happens with hairdressers – clients may be happy to travel considerable distances to have their hair 'done' by someone they know and trust. Quite clearly an employer who believes that the loss of an employee will also mean the loss of business may try to protect his interests by means of a restrictive covenant.

Alterations to covenants

We have already seen that if a covenant is more restrictive than is necessary to protect a company's legitimate business the courts will not enforce such a covenant. However, the courts may be prepared, in exceptional circumstances, to consider altering the covenant under the well established contractual device known as the 'blue pencil' rule.

Where a contract contains a covenant in restraint of trade that is valid and one that is not valid, the invalid restraint can be severed and the other enforced: *T Lucas & Co Ltd* v *Mitchell* [1972] 3 All ER 689. Russell LJ in the Court of Appeal said that if there are two restraints within a contract which are to be separate and severable the restraint that is invalid may be severed provided that there would be no further addition or modification required to give the contract efficacy.

In the later case of *Marshall* v *N M Financial Management Ltd* [1997] IRLR 449 Mr Marshall was employed as a self-employed sales agent by N M Financial Management Ltd (N M Ltd) from 1980 to 1992 selling life, term and pension policies. These investment agreements generated commissions that were payable to Mr Marshall. His agreement with the company with reference to payments were split into 'initial commission' (payable during the early stages of an investment agreement) and 'renewal commission' (which was any other commission earned subsequently). His agency agreement also provided that entitlement to commission ceased with termination of the agreement, but there was a clause in the agency agreement stating that he would be entitled to renewal commission after termination of agency provided that he had five years' continuous service. The renewal commission due to him would be payable throughout his employment, after retirement at the age of 65 and after ceasing employment with N M Ltd provided he did not work as a representative for a competitor for one year after termination, in which case the payments would cease immediately.

In 1992 Marshall resigned and joined another firm of independent financial advisers. N M Ltd refused to pay him any further initial or renewal commissions and Mr Marshall commenced proceedings for breach of contract in the High Court.

The plaintiff claimed that the company's refusal to pay him was because he had commenced work with a competitor and was void for being an unlawful restraint of trade. The question arose as to whether it was possible to sever the first part of the proviso and leave the second part, although that would have meant that the plaintiff was ineligible for renewal commission as he was not 65 years old. The plaintiff contended that the best course would be to sever both parts, thereby leaving him entitled to renewal commission. The court accepted the plaintiff's arguments and ruled that the clause be severed as an unlawful restraint of trade. N M Ltd appealed.

The Court of Appeal dismissed the appeal, holding that Mr Marshall was entitled to commission after termination of the contract. They placed the emphasis on the reality of the situation. Mr Marshall had earned his commission whilst procuring business for a company during the time he was their agent; he had already provided sufficient consideration to receive the commissions even though the company argued that by severing the proviso the entire contractual provision became void for lack of valuable consideration.

Trade secrets

During the course of employment an employee may have sight of extremely sensitive confidential information or trade secrets. A company may wish to protect itself from such confidential information being disclosed to its competitors. For example, Coca Cola would certainly not want the secret 'coke' formula to be disclosed to other soft drinks' manufacturers, nor would Ferrari want its technical secrets to be disclosed to any of its Formula One rivals.

In the absence of an express term in the contract of employment an employer who wishes to protect trade secrets may try to rely upon the duty of fidelity owed by an employee to his employer. However, to what extent this duty survives the termination will depend upon the circumstances of the case. The leading authority on the protection of confidential information is *Faccenda Chicken Ltd* v *Fowler & Others* [1985] IRLR 69 where the Court of Appeal gave useful guidance as to the factors that would be taken into account in determining whether the duty not disclose confidential information survived the termination of employment.

In *Faccenda Chicken Ltd* v *Fowler & Others* the plaintiffs, who owned a chicken farm, sold their chickens to wholesalers and retailers. Following a dispute Mr Fowler, who was the sales manager for the company, left and set up a similar business in competition with the plaintiffs, taking with him five of the plaintiffs' staff. There was no express stipulation in their contracts with Faccenda Chicken Ltd against disclosure of confidential information after leaving their employment.

Faccenda Chicken Ltd claimed that Mr Fowler and the others had breached the implied terms in their contracts that they would not use confidential information, including trade secrets, that they had gained during their employment to the detriment of their former employer. The information which was the subject matter of the claim included:

1. names and addresses of customers;
2. prices charged to individual customers;
3. requirements of individual customers both as to quantity and quality;
4. days and times of deliveries;
5. most convenient routes to be taken to reach the individual customers.

The High Court rejected the company's claim for damages and the employer appealed to the Court of Appeal. The Court drew a distinction between the duty owed to an employer during the course of his employment and the duty owed after that employment has ended. It is established law that whilst an employment contract subsists an employer can rely upon the implied term imposing a duty of good faith and fidelity on employees. However, when the employment has terminated, the obligation not to use or disclose information covers only information that is of a sufficiently high degree of confidentiality as to amount to a trade secret. The duty does not extend to other information which, if disclosed during the course of employment, would be a breach of the duty of good faith. On the facts there was no evidence that Faccenda had ever given any express instructions that the sales information or information about prices was to be treated as confidential. Furthermore, such information was generally known among van drivers who were employees at quite a junior level and therefore this was not a case where the relevant information was restricted to senior management.

The Court of Appeal concluded that neither the sales information as a whole nor the information about prices in particular fell into a category of confidential information which was capable of amounting to a trade secret and therefore there was no breach of the implied terms in the contracts of the defendants.

In *Faccenda Chicken* the Court identified three different categories of information which employees may have access to during the course of their employment.

1. General information available to all categories of staff – there is no implied term preventing an employee from disclosing such information.
2. Information which is given specifically for the purpose of carrying out the job – there is an implied term that this information should not be disclosed by an employee during the course of his employment.
3. Trade secrets – these should not be disclosed during the course of employment, nor should they be disclosed after the employment relationship has terminated.

In *Lancashire Fires Ltd* v *S A Lyons & Co Ltd and Others* [1997] IRLR 113 the Court of Appeal considered the nature of information that would amount to a trade secret and whether it was necessary for an employer to state that such information was to remain confidential. In this case the plaintiff and defendant companies were owned by brothers. The plaintiffs used a licensed process to produce artificial coals for fires but had altered the process in certain respects to enable mass production. The second defendant (brother of the owner of the plaintiff company) worked for the plaintiffs but had started to put in place plans to open up his own company, SA Lyons Ltd, in competition with the plaintiffs.

The plaintiffs issued a writ against the defendants claiming that the defendants had breached the duty of confidence which they continued to owe because the process that the plaintiffs had developed was a trade secret. A further claim was brought about in respect of the second defendant in respect of a breach of fidelity which he had owed to the plaintiffs during his employment with them.

At first instance it was held that the second defendant (the brother) had breached the implied duty of fidelity by setting up his own business whilst still in the employment of the plaintiffs, but because it had not been made clear to him that the new manufacturing process was a trade secret there had been no breach of confidence by the second defendant. The plaintiffs succesfully appealed.

The Court of Appeal considered that the manufacturing process was a trade secret within the third category set out by Goulding J in *Faccenda Chicken* v *Fowler* which cannot be used or disclosed by an employee even after leaving his employment. The Court further held that it is not necessary for an employer to expressly state that such information is a trade secret.

Where an injunction is granted restraining a former employee from using confidential information the injunction should be limited to a period of time when the court considers that any unfair advantage may be expected to continue: *Bullivant Ltd v Ellis* [1986] IRLR 491.

A distinction has also been drawn between trade connections and trade secrets. In order to prevent an ex-employee from doing business with clients of his former employer such a prohibition should be in the form of a covenant in restraint of trade. In *Wallace Bogan & Co v Cove & Others* [1997] IRLR 453 Cove and two other employees were employed by Wallace Bogan & Co as practising solicitors. They decided to set up their own practice and all three gave notice to their employer. Following the termination of their employment they set up a new practice and wrote to former clients informing them that Wallace Bogan & Co Ltd would continue in practice, but that if the client wanted the new firm to take over the client's case they would be happy to do so. In the event many of Wallace Bogan's clients transferred their business to the new firm.

The contracts of employment of Cove and the other defendants did not contain a restraint of trade clause and so Wallace Bogan applied to the High Court for an injunction claiming that there was an implied term that a solicitor would not solicit former clients for a period of time after the termination of his employment. A High Court judge granted an interlocutory injunction against the individual solicitors and the new firm. The solicitors appealed to the Court of Appeal.

The Court of Appeal held that the High Court judge had erred in granting the injunction. The Court had established in *Faccenda Chicken Ltd v Fowler* (above) that the implied duty not to misuse confidential information ceased upon termination of employment unless such information amounted to a trade secret. In the case of a solicitor and his client, the relationship is of a confidential nature and the Court held it is to be considered as a trade connection rather than a trade secret. The only way a company could prevent solicitation by former employees would be by means of an express covenant in the contract of employment.

Garden leave

Normally when a contract is terminated by either party the contractual notice period will be given and worked. However, in some situations an employer may request that the employee stay at home during the period of notice – this is commonly referred to as 'garden leave'. Employers do not generally like to pay employees to stay at home and do nothing and therefore employers will generally only resort to using garden leave in the case of a senior employee who is likely to work for a competitor. During the period of notice the employee will be paid and is therefore bound by the terms of his contract, including the implied term of fidelity not to disclose confidential information to competitors.

One of the questions that has arisen is whether garden leave is a breach of contract because it deprives the employee the opportunity to carry out his skills. We have already seen that there is no implied duty upon an employer to provide work, although in certain circumstances there may be such an obligation.

An employer who wishes to impose garden leave may only do so if there is an express clause in the contract of employment. In *William Hill Organisation Ltd* v *Tucker* [1998] IRLR 313 Mr Tucker was a senior dealer with William Hill. His contract was lawfully varied, whereby he had to give six months' notice of leaving. In February 1998 he gave one month's notice to leave in order to join a competitor. His personnel manager wrote to him stating that six months' notice was required and that he did not have to attend work but would be paid in full. There was, however, no express clause in the contract in relation to garden leave. In order to ensure that the employee did not work the employer applied to the court for an order restraining him from working for the competitor for the relevant period. The application was refused and the employer appealed to the Court of Appeal.

The Court of Appeal dismissed the appeal. Morritt LJ, in examining the implications of whether garden leave could be enforced without an express term, said that there were two issues to be considered. First, the employee's 'right to work' and, second, the employee's 'right to wages'. If the issue was the employee's right to work then the employer does not have any inherent right to prevent an employee from working elsewhere unless he is contractually bound not to do so. If the issue only concerns the right to wages then an employer can restrain the employee from working provided the employer pays him.

What was significant about this case was that Morritt LJ said that even if the garden leave was enforceable he would have only enforced it for three months and not six months. The Court of Appeal also stated that more employers were relying upon garden leave clauses instead of restraint of trade clauses because of the belief that the courts treated garden leave clauses with greater flexibility. They went on to state that decided cases showed that the courts should be careful not to grant interlocutory relief to enforce a garden leave clause to any greater extent than would be covered by a justifiable covenant in restraint of trade entered into by an employee. The accent is on reasonableness.

A clause in the contract of employment providing for garden leave may still only afford an employer minimum protection, particularly when an employee commences work for a competitor during the period of leave. In *Hutchings* v *Coinseed Ltd* [1998] IRLR 190 Miss Hutchings was employed by Coinseed Ltd and under the terms of her contract of employment she was required to give one month's notice should she wish to terminate her employment. There was also a provision in the contract that 'during any period on notice the company is under no obligation to provide you with work and may ... require you to stay at home and do no work for the company or for anyone else'.

On 29 March 1996 Miss Hutchings terminated her employment in writing, giving one month's notice. On 2 April her employer accepted her resignation and responded by stating that she was not required to work out her notice and that they would pay her in lieu of notice, the payment to be credited to her bank account at the end of the month on the same day Miss Hutchings commenced new employment at a higher salary. When the previous employer discovered that not only was she working but was working for a competitor they refused to pay her the promised salary.

Miss Hutchings claimed her arrears in the small claims court. A district judge dismissed her claim by holding that the plaintiff had repudiated her contract by securing another job during the notice period. She appealed unsuccessfully to the county court and then to the Court of Appeal. She claimed that the employment ended by exchange of letters dated 29 March and 2 April and that she was entitled to the promised payment. For the defendants it was argued that the contract of employment continued in spite of the exchange of letters and that the appellant had repudiated her contract by working for a competitor. Furthermore, they contended that the appellant had suffered no real loss.

The Court of Appeal, in allowing the appeal by Miss Hutchings, held that the district judge had erred in holding that she had repudiated her contract. The appellant was entitled to her salary, and further stated that the submission by the defendants that the appellant had suffered no real loss was irrelevant because she was under no obligation to mitigate as her claim was for monies actually owed under her contract of employment. The Court also held that in working for a competitor she had not breached the confidentiality clause as there had been no allegation that she had acted in bad faith. Therefore, in the circumstances, there was no express or implied obligation that Miss Hutchings should not secure new employment.

A more robust approach has been taken by the Court of Appeal in the later case of *Symbian Ltd* v *Christensen* [2001] IRLR 77 where an executive vice president of a company carrying out research into new generation mobile phones gave his employers one week's notice and attempted to start work for a competitor. His contract provided for six months' garden leave and also contained a restraint of trade clause which restricted him from working for a competitor for a period of six months following the termination of his employment. In granting an injunction preventing the employee from immediately working for the new employer the Court of Appeal agreed that the approach taken in *Willliam Hill Organisation Ltd* v *Tucker* (above) was correct and that the garden leave clause should only be enforced to the extent that it is necessary to protect the business. This particular clause had been modified in the High Court so that the employee was only prevented from working for one particular competitor during the garden leave.

3.9 Whistle-blowing

The Public Interest Disclosure Act 1998 inserted provisions into Pt IVA and Pt X of the Employment Rights Act (ERA) 1996 to protect employees from unfair treatment for raising concerns about wrongdoing in the workplace – this is commonly referred to as whistle-blowing. The 1998 Act seeks to balance two competing interests:

1. the interests of the public which are served by workers exposing misconduct and potential dangers; and
2. the protection of the interests of employees and employers.

Section 103A ERA 1996 provides:

> 'An employee who is dismissed is automatically regarded as unfairly dismissed, if the reason (or, if more than one, the principal reason) for the dismissal is that the employee made a protected disclosure.'

Section 47B ERA 1996 provides:

> 'An employee has the right not to be subjected to any detriment by any act, or any deliberate failure to act, by his employer, done on the ground that the worker has made a protected disclosure.'

An employee who believes that he has suffered a detriment or been unfairly dismissed may present a claim to the employment tribunal. There is no qualification period: therefore an employee can present a claim regardless of the length of time that he has been employed by the employer.

Section 43B ERA 1996 provides that a disclosure of information only qualifies for protection if, in the reasonable belief of the worker making the disclosure, it tends to show one or more of the following:

1. that a criminal offence has been committed, is being committed or is likely to be committed;
2. that a person has failed, is failing or is likely to fail to comply with any legal obligation to which he is subject;
3. that a miscarriage of justice has occurred, is occurring or is likely to occur;
4. that the health or safety of any individual has been, is being or is likely to be endangered;
5. that the environment has been, is being or is likely to be damaged; or
6. that information tending to show any matter falling within any one of the preceding paragraphs has been, is being or is likely to be deliberately concealed.

The test for determining whether the worker had a reasonable belief is subjective, which means that the worker only has to show that he reasonably believed one of the above requirements. The disclosure can relate to conduct outside the UK but will not be a qualifying disclosure if the person making the disclosure commits an offence by doing so.

In order for a worker to be afforded protection, the disclosure must be in accordance with the requirements laid down in s43 ERA 1996 which provide that the disclosure must be made to certain persons or bodies which include the employer, a legal advisor and, in relevant circumstances, a Minister of the Crown.

In the case of *ALM Medical Services Ltd* v *Bladon* [2002] IRLR 807 ALM appealed against a decision of the EAT on the grounds that at the hearing before the employment tribunal the company had not been allowed to call all the evidence it wanted to admit to show that the reason for the dismissal of Mr Bladon was for a reason other than his having made a protected disclosure. The EAT held that the evidence should have been heard and the case was remitted to be heard by a differently constituted tribunal. Mummery LJ said that in protected disclosure cases there should be directions hearings to identify the issues and determine the evidence upon which each party intended to rely.

4
Dismissal

4.1 Introduction
4.2 Termination by agreement or operation of law
4.3 Dismissal: definition and language of termination
4.4 Wrongful dismissal
4.5 Constructive dismissal
4.6 Automatically fair reasons for dismissal
4.7 Automatically unfair reasons for dismissal
4.8 Potentially fair/unfair reasons for dismissal
4.9 Excluded categories
4.10 Reasonableness and the importance of procedure
4.11 Notice
4.12 Time limits
4.13 Remedies

4.1 Introduction

The relationship between an employer and employee will inevitably at some point come to an end, either as a result of mutual agreement, resignation, frustration or dismissal. The major focus in this chapter will be dismissal which, in 2003–2004 accounted for 37,644 applications to the employment tribunals – more than any other single category of applications. The dismissal of an employee by an employer may be deemed to be wrongful, fair or unfair.

If an employee is dismissed he may be able to seek a remedy under the common law in respect of a wrongful dismissal. He may also, in certain circumstances, be protected by statute in respect of an unfair dismissal by virtue of s94 Employment Rights Act (ERA) 1996 which provides that an employee shall not be unfairly dismissed.

64 *Dismissal*

If the employer unilaterally terminates the employees contract of employment the employee may wish to make an application to an employment tribunal claiming that he was either wrongfully or unfairly dismissed. An application must be submitted within three months of the date of the termination of the contract. If the employee is successful the tribunal may order the employer to compensate him, reinstate him or re-engage him.

Under s93 ERA 1996 an employee is entitled to ask for the reason for his dismissal to be in writing and if the employer refuses, and the employee makes an application to a tribunal, the tribunal may award the employee two weeks' pay.

This chapter will initially consider termination of contracts of employment by operation of law or agreement and then discuss whether a termination amounts to a dismissal. Consideration will then be given to the different types of dismissal, including whether a dismissal was wrongful, fair or unfair. We will also look at those persons who are excluded from statutory protection, the importance of procedure and the remedies available for successful applicants.

4.2 Termination by agreement or operation of law

Termination by agreement

Parties to an employment contract may agree that the contract is to be discharged, in other words it will come to an end by mutual agreement. It may be that the contract was for a specific purpose which has now come to an end or it may be that a parting of the ways is in the interests of both parties. The parties may come to an agreement that an employee will resign in return for a sum of money – this is known as a 'golden handshake' and is usually only applicable to senior employees or directors.

Whenever there is an agreement to terminate a contract of employment there is no dismissal either at common law or by operation of statute. However, the courts and tribunals have been keen to ensure that any agreement is mutual and that pressure is not put upon employees to resign.

In *McAlwane* v *Boughton Estates Ltd* [1973] 2 All ER 299 Sir John Donaldson highlighted the need for a complete understanding on the part of the employee of the implications of an agreement to terminate a contract. In this case the employee was under notice of dismissal. He asked if he could leave a week early to start a new job and the employer agreed; he then claimed that he had been dismissed and the employer argued that the termination had been by agreement. The employer's argument was rejected; any request to leave before the end of the notice period only varies the notice period and does not affect the dismissal which remains effective. The court considered that the employee was unlikely to have agreed to the termination because of the detrimental financial consequences that would have resulted.

In *Sheffield* v *Oxford Controls Company Ltd* [1979] ICR 208 Mr Sheffield was employed as a director of a small business and his wife was also employed by the company. Following an argument between Mrs Sheffield and the wife of another director Mr Sheffield was told that if he did not resign he would be dismissed. Discussions took place as to what would be an appropriate severance pay and the sum of £10,000 was agreed. Mr Sheffield left the company and claimed unfair dismissal. This was rejected by the tribunal and Mr Sheffield appealed.

The EAT held that if an employee resigns because he is faced with a threat of dismissal then in such circumstances the contract is terminated by dismissal. If however the threat no longer operates because the parties have agreed terms for the ending of the contract the contract will be deemed to have been terminated by agreement. In this case Mr Sheffield had agreed to the terms and therefore the termination was by mutual agreement.

The termination of a contract of employment which results from an application for early retirement is a termination by mutual agreement and is not a dismissal. In *Birch and Humber* v *University of Liverpool* [1985] IRLR 165 the Court of Appeal considered that the fact that the agreement was conditional upon the University's acceptance of each individual's application did not change the mutual nature of the agreement reached.

Another question that has vexed the courts is whether there is a termination by agreement when an employee, who takes extended leave, gives an undertaking to return on a certain date in the full knowledge that a failure to do so will mean that the employment has come to an end, and then fails to return to work on the stated date.

In *British Leyland* v *Ashraf* [1978] ICR 979 an employee took extended leave and signed a form stating that he would return to work on a certain date and that if he failed to do so the contract of employment would come to an end. The EAT considered that this was a subsidiary contract and the failure to return on the agreed date was an agreed termination.

A less restrictive approach was taken by the Court of Appeal in similar circumstances in the case of *Igbo* v *Johnson Matthey Chemicals Ltd* [1986] IRLR 215. In this case the employee had taken extended leave but did not return on the agreed date because of illness. The EAT followed the approach taken in *British Leyland* v *Ashraf* but the Court of Appeal disagreed and considered that such an approach could limit the protection afforded by the Employment Protection (Consolidation) Act 1978 for employees. Parker LJ said that if the defendant's argument was accepted 'it must follow that the whole object of the Act can be easily defeated by the inclusion of a term in a contract of employment that if the employee is late for work on the first Monday in any month, or indeed on any day, no matter for what reason, the contract shall automatically terminate'.

If both the employer and employee wish to bring the relationship to an end because one or other party has a particular complaint, one of the best ways to do this is to enter into a 'compromise agreement'. In essence the employer will agree to pay a sum of money to the employee in return for which the employee agrees not to pursue a claim against the employer. The compromise agreement sets out the financial and other terms on which the employment relationship will end. In order for the compromise agreement to be legally binding on both parties, the requirements of s203 ERA 1996 must be satisfied. These include the requirement that the agreement must be in writing and that the employee must receive advice from a relevant independent advisor. A relevant advisor includes a solicitor, a trade union official or advice centre worker who is certified as competent to give advice or a legal executive. Interestingly, barristers are excluded! The employer is required to pay a sum of money (currently a minimum of £250) towards legal costs incurred by the employee.

The compromise agreement is legally enforceable and under the Employment Tribunals Extension of Jurisdiction (England and Wales) Order 1994 an employee may bring a claim for payment under the agreement in the employment tribunal. The agreement will generally include an extensive list of claims that an employee agrees that he will no longer pursue, including unfair dismissal, sex discrimination, race discrimination, disability discrimination etc. In *University of East London* v *Hinton* [2005] ICR 1260 the EAT held that all potential claims did not have to be specified – the list was illustrative, not exhaustive – and the whistle-blowing claim in this case which was not on the list was barred by the compromise agreement. However, this decision was reversed by the Court of Appeal which held that because a strict construction of s203(3)(b) requires that 'particular proceedings' which are being compromised need to be identified and particularised. In this case the compromise agreement did not expressly state that the applicant would not bring a complaint of detrimental treatment as a result of making a protected disclosure and therefore was entitled to do so.

Death

If an employee dies this will clearly terminate the employment contract. If an employer dies then the position with respect to the employment contract will largely depend upon the nature and size of the enterprise. If it is a small family business it is likely that the contract will automatically come to an end. However, in large businesses this is less likely because a corporation cannot 'die', and therefore the death of a chief executive will not impact upon the contract of employment.

Frustration

This is a common law concept that has crept into employment law. It occurs when, without fault of either party, the contract becomes either impossible to perform or becomes fundamentally different from what the parties intended. If a contract of employment is frustrated there is no dismissal at law: *Poussard* v *Spiers* (1876) 1 QBD 410.

The common law doctrine of frustration provides that if an event occurs which was not reasonably foreseeable when the contract was made, and is not under the direct control of either party, which makes continued performance impossible in the way originally intended, the contract is discharged by operation of law.

The guidelines set out above were taken into account by the EAT in *Hogan v Cambridgeshire CC* [2001] IDS B699/10 when a legal executive claimed that she had been unfairly dismissed. Her claim was rejected on the grounds that her contract had been 'frustrated' as a result of her continued absence through ill health.

Illness
In the context of incapacity due to illness the question of whether or not the employment relationship has come to an end because of frustration is far more difficult to assess. Consideration should be given as to whether the employee's incapacity was likely to continue for such a period that further performance of his obligations in the future would either be impossible or would be something radically different from that originally undertaken by him. Further consideration should be given to the following:

1. provision for sick pay – when the contract provides for sick pay an employee cannot be dismissed within the period during which sick pay is payable;
2. period for which the employment can be kept open – the role of the employee concerned will be a significant factor in determining how long the absence can be tolerated. If he holds a key position the employer may be able to justify treating the contract as frustrated: *Hart v A R Marshall & Sons* [1977] IRLR 51.

Further guidance as to when the employee's incapacity will be taken to frustrate the contract was given by the EAT in *Egg Stores v Leibovici* [1977] ICR 260. The case concerned a long-standing employee of the defendants who was unfit to work for five months following an injury he sustained due to a road accident. When he asked to return to work his employers told him that he could not do so as they had found a replacement for him. He claimed unfair dismissal but the employers argued that the contract had been frustrated. The EAT said the basic question that should be asked was 'Has the time arrived when the employer can no longer reasonably be expected to keep the absent employee's post open for him?'. The EAT also said that consideration should be given to other factors such as:

1. length of service of employee;
2. how long the employment had been expected to continue;
3. nature of the job;
4. nature length and effect of disabling event;
5. can there be a temporary replacement;
6. whether wages have continued to be paid.

The case was remitted back to the employment tribunal so that the above factors could be taken into account.

Imprisonment

An employee who has been absent due to imprisonment may be dismissed under the doctrine of frustration even though this does not fall within the strict definition of the doctrine because in this instance one party may be considered to be at fault.

If the employee through his conduct has brought the contract to an end it may be preferable to use the term repudiation instead of frustration as it is the employee who is no longer in a position to continue with his contract of employment. This was considered in *Hare v Murphy Brothers Ltd* [1974] ICR 603 by the Court of Appeal. Lord Denning took the novel approach that a sentence of imprisonment for 12 months operated to frustrate the contract because it was the action of the court and not the unlawful conduct of the employee which actually brought about the imprisonment. This was, not surprisingly, the minority view of the Court of Appeal. The majority considered that further performance of the contract was impossible and therefore there was termination by the employee.

The length of the period away from work will be relevant in determining whether the contract has been terminated by frustration.

In *Shepherd v Jerrom* [1986] IRLR 358 the Court of Appeal, moving away from the approach taken by the majority in *Hare v Murphy Brothers Ltd*, held that a prison sentence of between six months and two years was capable of frustrating an apprenticeship contract which had been due to last for four years.

Resignation

An employee may decide to terminate his employment contract by means of resignation. Provided that the resignation is given freely and the employee gives the requisite period of notice there will be no breach of contract. However, there may be problems when an employee claims that he was forced to resign. Whether an employee has resigned or has been dismissed is a matter of fact to be determined by the tribunal.

In *Martin v MBS Fastenings (Glynwed) Distribution Ltd* [1983] IRLR 49 Mr Martin was a warehouse manager. He drove a company minibus to work each day and was allowed to give lifts to other workers. One weekend he drove the minibus and passengers to a company football match; after the match he had six or seven pints of beer and then on the way home had an accident and wrote off the minibus. The employers, not being best pleased, advised him that this would be a disciplinary matter that would probably end in his dismissal and that he should think about resigning. After giving the matter some thought Mr Martin offered his resignation the next day. Mr Martin then presented an application to the tribunal claiming unfair dismissal.

The tribunal found that there had been a voluntary resignation. However, Mr Martin appealed to the EAT which allowed his appeal. The company appealed to the Court of Appeal. The Court held that the question before the tribunal was one of fact and once they had determined that the employee had voluntarily resigned the decision was not open to review on appeal.

4.3 Dismissal: definition and language of termination

An employee is dismissed when his employer unilaterally terminates his employment. If the dismissal is in breach of the terms of the contract this will be a wrongful dismissal. Alternatively, a dismissal may accord with contractual obligations but contravene statutory protection, in which case it may be an unfair dismissal. However, before the issue of whether a dismissal is wrongful, fair or unfair can be discussed it is necessary to determine that an employee has been dismissed.

The meaning of dismissal

In any claim for dismissal, the first issue to consider is whether in fact there has been a dismissal within the three-fold definition of dismissal found in s95 ERA 1996, namely:

1. the employee's contract is terminated by the employer with or without notice;
2. the employee has a fixed-term contract and that term expires without being renewed; or
3. the employee terminates his contract with or without notice in circumstances in which he is entitled to terminate due to the employer's conduct.

An employer may terminate an employee's contract at any time provided he complies with the notice period stated in the contract of employment, the disciplinary procedure and any other relevant contractual terms but the reasons must be justifiable. He may also terminate an employee's contract without notice but the reasons must be such that continuance of employment is untenable. Normally such termination arises from gross misconduct.

A dismissal will not generally take effect until the dismissal has been communicated to the employee. In *Brown v Southall & Knight* [1980] IRLR 130 the EAT held that the effective date of termination (EDT) is the date upon which the employee becomes aware of the dismissal or, as in this case, the date upon which the employee has a reasonable opportunity of reading a letter of dismissal.

To be effective, a dismissal, whether with or without notice, must take place on a specific date. In *Morton Sundour Fabrics v Shaw* [1967] 2 ITR 84 an employee, having been told of impending redundancies, found alternative work and claimed that he was entitled to his redundancy payment: his claim failed because there was no actual dismissal. Parker CJ said 'As a matter of law you cannot dismiss an employee by saying "I intend to dispense with your services in the coming months"'. A similar situation arose in *Doble v Firestone Tyre and Rubber Co* [1981] IRLR 300 where the respondents announced that they would be closing their factory in Brentford. They said that they would keep the situation under review: however, termination notices would be issued 'as they became due'. Mr Doble found alternative employment and tried to claim that he had been made redundant and unfairly dismissed. Relying on *Morton Sundour Fabrics* v *Shaw*, the EAT held that he had not been dismissed and therefore was not entitled to redundancy payments or a claim of unfair dismissal.

There may also be a dismissal if an employer unilaterally alters terms in the employment contract. However, whether or not a variation amounts to a dismissal will depend upon the extent of any change. In *Alcan Extrusions* v *Yates* [1996] IRLR 327 the employers tried to radically alter a shift system, which meant that employees would be working longer and more unsociable hours and would have their holiday entitlement reduced. The employees started to work the new shift pattern under protest and claimed that the unilateral variation by the employer amounted to a breach of contract entitling them to claim compensation for unfair dismissal. The employer argued that their claim must fail because there was no actual dismissal. The EAT, in upholding the decision of the tribunal, held that because of the radical nature of the changes, the effect was to withdraw the previous contract and therefore there had been a dismissal.

Where an employee has been disciplined by an employer and dismissed but still retains the right to appeal against the decision to dismiss him, that will not amount to a dismissal for the purposes of s95 ERA 1996. In *Roberts* v *West Coast Trains Ltd* [2004] IRLR 788 Mr Roberts was dismissed for alleged gross misconduct. However, the company disciplinary procedure allowed him to appeal against his dismissal. Before the appeal was heard Mr Roberts submitted a claim to the employment tribunal alleging unfair dismissal. Following the appeal the company advised Mr Roberts by telephone that the company had decided to reduce the punishment from dismissal to demotion. Mr Roberts remained off work due to ill health, submitting sick notes to the company. In August 2002, having failed to return to work, the appellant was treated as having resigned. Mr Roberts continued with his claim for unfair dismissal and at tribunal a preliminary issue arose as to whether or not he had in fact been dismissed. The tribunal and the EAT held that there had been no dismissal and this was upheld by the Court of Appeal.

The decision of the Court of Appeal further encourages employees to exhaust internal remedies before submitting an application to the employment tribunal. This accords with the objectives behind the Employment Act 2002 (Dispute Resolution) Regulations 2004 discussed below.

Language of termination

There can be no successful claim for wrongful or unfair dismissal unless there has actually been a dismissal. As we have seen, dismissal arises where the employer terminates the contract with or without notice, however once given it is not open for the employer to retract it unilaterally. Similarly, an employee who has given notice of termination cannot unilaterally withdraw his resignation, although the courts have accepted that if an employee is dismissed or resigns in the heat of the moment then an instant retraction should be accepted by the other party.

It is sometimes difficult to determine whether the language used by either the employer or the employee actually amounts to a dismissal or resignation. An employer may argue that the words spoken which an employee assumes to be a dismissal should be interpreted more as a rebuke than as a dismissal. If there is difficulty in construing what the words used by the employer actually meant, it is up to the tribunal to decide. If the tribunal finds that the employer was merely using abusive language there may be no dismissal, but it should be noted that this may give rise to a claim for constructive dismissal if the language used by the employer was of such a serious nature that it amounted to a breach of the implied term of trust and confidence.

In determining whether the language used amounted to a dismissal or resignation the employment tribunal may adopt one of the following solutions.

1. To concentrate on the intention of the speaker. Did he intend to dismiss or resign when he uttered the relevant words? If the words were uttered in a fit of pique, time is of the essence because if the words were withdrawn immediately there may be no dismissal or resignation.
2. To concentrate on the way in which the words were in fact understood by the listener. Did he genuinely believe that the speaker was intending to dismiss or resign?
3. To consider how a reasonable listener would have understood the words uttered. If the words are ambiguous then the test is how the words would have been understood by a reasonable listener.

In *Tanner* v *Kean* [1978] IRLR 110 Mr Tanner had been loaned money by his employer, Mr Kean, to purchase a car so that he would not use the company van for his own purposes. One day Mr Kean visited a night club where Mr Tanner worked in the evenings and noticed the company van parked outside. Being understandably annoyed Mr Kean asked Mr Tanner 'What is my fucking van doing outside; you're a tight bastard; I've lent you £275 to buy a car and you're too tight to put juice in it. That's it; you're finished with me!'

Mr Tanner claimed the employer's outburst constituted a dismissal, but the tribunal held that the employer had used the language by way of a reprimand and not by way of dismissal and had he thought about it Mr Tanner ought to have realised that no dismissal was intended. Mr Tanner appealed to the EAT who dismissed his appeal, pointing out that they would have arrived at the same conclusion as the tribunal and in any event there was no appealable point of law.

At first sight the language used should give rise to a dismissal. But there are other factors that may fall to be considered, such as the tone of the language and the place where the words were uttered.

In *Martin* v *Yeoman Aggregates Ltd* [1983] IRLR 49 an employee obtained a wrong spare part for a car. He refused to collect the correct part and there was an angry exchange between him and a director who then dismissed him. A few minutes later the director realising that he was in breach of the company's disciplinary procedure told the employee that he was being suspended for two days without pay. The employee walked out and claimed that he had been summarily dismissed.

The EAT held that there had been no dismissal and said that as a matter of common sense, which is essential to good employment practice, the employer should be given the opportunity of withdrawing words uttered in the heat of the moment. A prudent employer should always give an employee who has resigned in the heat of the moment a reasonable amount of time to retract a resignation before accepting the decision to resign: *Kwik-Fit* v *Lineham* [1992] ICR 183.

4.4 Wrongful dismissal

A wrongful dismissal occurs when an employer dismisses an employee in breach of the employee's contract of employment. This will generally arise when the employer dismisses the employee either without any notice or with a notice period which is shorter than that provided in the contract of employment. There will also be a wrongful dismissal if an employer terminates a person's employment without following either the minimum statutory disciplinary procedure as set out in the Employment Act 2002 (Dispute Resolution) Regulations 2004 or any procedure set out in the employee's contract.

If an employer dismisses an employee without notice this will be a summary dismissal and will ordinarily give rise to a claim for breach of contract. However, the employer may have a defence if he can satisfy the tribunal that the applicant was himself guilty of conduct which amounted to a serious breach of contract.

In *Sinclair* v *Neighbour* [1967] 2 QB 279 a manager of a betting shop borrowed money from the till and replaced the money with an IOU, knowing full well that such behaviour was forbidden by his employers. His summary dismissal was upheld. Davies LJ said that 'It was conduct of such a grave and weighty character as to amount to a breach of the confidential relationship between master and servant'.

An employer may be justified in dismissing an employee summarily where there is wilful disobedience on the part of the employee. In *Pepper* v *Webb* [1969] 2 All ER 216 a gardener was dismissed when he refused to plant some geraniums shortly before he was due to finish for the day. His employer urged him to carry out the task, whereupon he told the employer 'I couldn't care less about your bloody greenhouse and your sodding garden'. The Court of Appeal held that the dismissal was reasonable, particularly when other incidences of disobedience were taken into account.

Any person who believes that he has been wrongfully dismissed may present a claim to the employment tribunal regardless of the length of time that he has worked for the employer.

An employee who has been employed for less than one year at the time of dismissal will generally only be able to claim wrongful dismissal unless of course the reason is related to pregnancy, trade union membership or any of the automatically unfair reasons for dismissal discussed later in the chapter. Once an employee satisfied the one-year qualification period s94 ERA 1996 provides that the employee has the right not to be unfairly dismissed by his employer. However, the question arises as to whether an employer who wrongfully dismisses an employee who has worked just less than a year, by failing to give the full contractual notice period with the result that the employee is denied the opportunity to gain the requisite 12 months, had wrongfully or unfairly dismissed that employee. This issue was considered by the Court of Appeal in *Virgin Net* v *Harper* [2004] IRLR 390 where an employee was summarily dismissed for reasons which the tribunal considered would have been regarded as unfair. If Ms Harper had been given her three-month contractual notice period she would have achieved in excess of 12 months' employment and could have claimed unfair dismissal. Ms Harper presented a claim for wrongful dismissal and the tribunal awarded her a sum of £40,000, made up of £9,500 in respect of three months' notice pay and the balance representing the full award she would have received had she been permitted to bring a claim of unfair dismissal. The total sum assessed was then netted down by the tribunal to an award of £25,000, being the maximum recoverable in the tribunal: art 10 of the Employment Tribunals Extension of Jurisdiction (England and Wales) Order 1994. The employer successfully appealed to the EAT which set aside the part of the tribunal's award which exceeded the three-month payment in lieu of notice. An appeal by Ms Harper to the Court of Appeal failed. The Court of Appeal held that an employee could not lose the opportunity to claim unfair dismissal if they were employed for less than one year as this right was only secured after one year's continuous service. The decision of the Court of Appeal was one of policy. The effective date of termination (EDT) in such situations has consistently been held to be the date of dismissal plus the statutory minimum notice period and not the contractual notice period. The Court of Appeal reflected the views of the EAT and said that Parliament could choose to allow the date of termination to be extended by reference to the contractual notice period but has not done so.

The most common remedy for an employee who believes that he has been wrongfully dismissed is an action for damages for breach of contract. Damages will normally equate to the amount that an employee would have been entitled to if he had been paid in lieu of notice. However, where an employee is given some notice, but not the period stated in the contract, he will be entitled to a sum representing the difference between the notice period that he has worked and the period of notice that he should have received.

If an employer has breached a contract by failing to follow disciplinary procedures an employee will be awarded damages which represent the time that he would have been employed if the correct procedures had been followed.

In *Dietman* v *London Borough of Brent* [1987] IRLR 259 the plaintiff, a senior social worker, was dismissed following the publication of a report into the death of Jasmine Beckford, a little girl who had been murdered by her stepfather some 17 months earlier. The plaintiff claimed that she had been wrongfully dismissed because the defendants had not followed the disciplinary procedures which were provided for in her contract of employment. The employers argued that she had been dismissed for gross misconduct and therefore her dismissal was not wrongful. It was held by the High Court that the plaintiff had been dismissed for gross negligence and that in this case, taking into account the fact that the plaintiff had continued to work for the council for 17 months following the child's death, this did not amount to gross misconduct justifying summary dismissal. The plaintiff was therefore entitled to compensation, which represented the time it would have taken to hold the correct disciplinary proceedings and her notice period.

At common law a wrongfully dismissed employee was unable to recover damages for injury to feelings which resulted from the manner of his dismissal: *Addis* v *Gramophone Company Ltd* [1909] AC 488. However, in *Malik* v *Bank of Credit and Commerce International SA (In Liquidation)* [1997] IRLR 462 the House of Lords held that there is an implied term in the employment contract requiring both employers and employees not to conduct themselves in a manner which is likely to destroy or seriously damage the relationship of trust and confidence. The effect of the decision in *Malik* appeared to suggest that if the manner in which a person was wrongfully dismissed was in breach of the implied term of trust and confidence, the employee could claim compensation for injury to feelings. In *Malik* Lord Nicholls explained the departure from *Addis* by stating that *Addis* was decided before the implied term of trust and confidence was adumbrated and that today damages should be awarded in the event of a breach of the term. However, following the case of *Dunnachie* v *Kingston-upon-Hull City Council* [2004] IRLR 727, where the House of Lords held that an award for injury to feelings for unfair dismissal was not recoverable, it is questionable as to whether damages for injury to feelings will be awarded in wrongful dismissal claims.

Since the Extension of Jurisdiction Order 1994 employment tribunals have had jurisdiction to hear claims for wrongful dismissal. However, there is a three-month limitation period. If an employee fails to bring the claim within three months he may bring the claim in the county court where the limitation period is six years. Certain claims still cannot be determined by employment tribunals, including employment contracts providing accommodation and breaches concerning intellectual property.

Statute imposes a limit for compensation in respect of unfair dismissal claims and therefore certain employees may benefit from bringing a claim of wrongful dismissal in the ordinary courts where there is no limit to the compensation that may be awarded. These employees will include those who are highly paid and those whose contracts provide for a long period of notice.

Other possible remedies for wrongful dismissal are the equitable remedies of injunctive relief or specific performance. However, because an employment contract is a contract for personal services, under common law such a contract cannot be enforced. Furthermore, s236 of the Trade Union and Labour Relations (Consolidation) Act 1992 provides that a court cannot make an order for specific performance compelling an employee to work. Nevertheless in *Hill* v *C A Parsons & Co Ltd* [1972] 1 Ch 305, where pressure was put upon an employer to dismiss an employee because he was not a member of a trade union, an interlocutory injunction was granted restraining the employer from dismissing the employee. The reason for this decision was that first, there was no breakdown in the mutual trust and confidence between the employer and employee, and second, there was the impending introduction of legislation that would give protection to Mr Hill. In *Irani* v *Southampton and South-West Hampshire Health Authority* [1985] IRLR 203 the plaintiff was an opthamologist who was dismissed with notice by his employers following a conflict between the plaintiff and a senior consultant. The plaintiff sought an injunction preventing his employers from dismissing him until contractual disciplinary procedures had been carried out. The High Court granted the injunction. However, Warner J quoted Lane LJ from the earlier case of *Chappell* v *Times Newspapers Ltd* [1975] IRLR 90 where he said:

> 'Very rarely indeed will a court enforce, either by specific performance or by injunction, a contract for services, either at the behest of the employers or of the employee. The reason for this is obvious: if one party has no faith in the honesty or integrity or the loyalty of the other, to force him to serve or to employ that other is a plain recipe for disaster.'

It is clear, therefore, that injunctions or orders for specific performance will only be granted in exceptional circumstances. In *Wishart* v *National Association of Citizens Advice Bureaux* [1990] IRLR 393 an employee, whose offer of a job was revoked by the defendants following an unsatisfactory reference, sought an interlocutory injunction preventing the defendants from employing someone else until her case came to trial. An injunction granted by the High Court was discharged by the Court of Appeal on the grounds that there was no employment relationship between the employer and employee and it would be wrong to force upon them an employee who they had regarded as unsuitable.

In deciding whether or not to grant equitable relief the courts will look at whether the order sought is 'workable': *Robb* v *London Borough of Hammersmith and Fulham* [1991] IRLR 72.

4.5 Constructive dismissal

This arises when an employee terminates his contract of employment with or without notice due to the conduct of the employer. Such conduct may be either express or implied. It reflects the common law position that a person may be entitled to resign in reaction to his employer's unreasonable conduct yet claim to be dismissed. A claim for constructive dismissal is governed both by statute (s95(1)(c) ERA 1996) and by common law.

Section 95(1)(c) provides that there is a dismissal if:

> 'the employee terminates the contract under which he is employed (with or without notice) in circumstances in which he is entitled to terminate it without notice by reason of the employer's conduct.'

To successfully claim constructive dismissal the employee must prove the following:

1. the nature of the contractual obligation that has been breached by the employer;
2. the actual breach;
3. that the term or the breach is fundamental to the employment relationship;
4. that the employer has actually broken the contract;
5. that the employee has accepted the repudiation and terminated the contract;
6. that the employee has neither affirmed the breach nor delayed before acting.

An employee can only claim constructive dismissal when his employer's conduct constitutes a significant breach of contract which goes to the root of that contract or where an employer shows an intention to no longer be bound by an essential term of the contract. The employer's conduct must be serious enough to entitle the employee to resign without notice. Where an employee is entitled to claim constructive dismissal, he must leave soon after the conduct which has given rise to his complaint occurred. Failure to do so will imply that he has decided to affirm the contract.

In determining whether an employee has been constructively dismissed the tribunal must adopt a contractual approach rather than considering the reasonableness of the employer.

In *Western Excavating* v *Sharp* [1978] IRLR 27 Mr Sharp had originally been suspended for taking the afternoon off to play cards. He subsequently found himself in financial difficulties and requested his accrued holiday pay or a loan. The company refused and he resigned. He claimed constructive dismissal and both the industrial tribunal and the EAT, albeit for different reasons, held that he had been constructively dismissed. The employer successfully appealed to the Court of Appeal where it was said that it was not the reasonable conduct of the employer that had to be questioned but whether the company had breached the contract.

The Court of Appeal in *Western Excavating* v *Sharp* made it clear that a strictly contractual approach should be adopted and that any test based on the reasonableness of the employer's behaviour is wrong in law. Although it may appear that Sharp may have been unreasonably treated, the company was well within its rights to refuse him accrued holiday pay or a loan and therefore there was in fact no breach of the contract of employment.

The employee must be able to demonstrate that the employer's conduct was a fundamental breach of contract that made continuance of employment untenable. This would include non-payment of wages by the employer to the employee, a deliberate reduction in pay and a refusal to increase pay in line with a contractual entitlement.

The conduct of the employer which would amount to a repudiation of the contract, or the extent of the breach, is a matter of degree. In some circumstances one single act by an employer may not on its own be sufficiently serious for the employee to resign and claim constructive dismissal. However, if an employer persists in unfairly treating the employee, he may be able to resign under the 'last straw' doctrine and claim constructive dismissal on the basis that the cumulative effects of such incidents destroyed the implied contractual term of mutual trust and confidence.

In *Lewis v Motorworld Garages Ltd* [1985] IRLR 465 the employee was demoted without warning, lost his office and his pay structure was altered. All this constituted a fundamental breach of contract but the employee chose to affirm the contract by continuing to work. The employee was then subjected to persistent and unfair criticisms and was also threatened with dismissal. The employee left and claimed unfair dismissal under the 'last straw' doctrine. The industrial tribunal decided that the demotion and change in pay structure could not be relied upon as the employer had affirmed the contract. The tribunal further decided that the subsequent criticisms did not amount to a repudiation and the application failed. The employee appealed to the Court of Appeal which held that the demotion and alteration of the pay structure may be relied upon to demonstrate the continuing conduct of the employer to support a claim for constructive dismissal. The Court of Appeal ordered that the case be reheard by a differently constituted tribunal.

The 'last straw' doctrine and the seriousness of the 'final act' of the employer which causes an employee to resign has been considered recently by the Court of Appeal in *London Borough of Waltham Forest v Omilaju* [2004] EWCA Civ 1493. The Court considered the test as applied by Glidewell LJ in *Lewis v Motorworld Garages Ltd* that the final act of the employer does not itself have to be a breach of contract to amount to the 'final straw', but went on to consider that although the final straw may be insignificant it must be something more than trivial. The Court rejected a submission that the final act had to be something blameworthy or unreasonable but held that 'the last straw must contribute, however slightly, to the breach of the implied term of trust and confidence': per Dyson LJ.

Temporary changes to a contract of employment by the employer are treated less severely and are less likely to give rise to a successful claim of constructive dismissal. However, the employee must be advised of the temporary nature of any such change and a failure to do so may give rise to a successful claim for constructive dismissal. In *Millbrook Furnishing Industries Ltd v McIntosh* [1981] IRLR 309 the transfer of a highly skilled sewing machinist to unskilled work in another section was held to be a breach of contract because the transfer was to last until work picked up in the former section and therefore could not be accurately assessed.

The Court of Appeal in *Western Excavating v Sharp* said that unreasonable conduct by the employer on its own would not be sufficient to constitute a successful claim of constructive dismissal. However, it appears that this has now managed to creep in by the back door. This is based on the fact that if an employer behaves badly the essential elements of the implied term of mutual trust and confidence may have been destroyed. The courts will also consider if an employer had acted reasonably where the business needs of his company are concerned.

In *Savoia* v *Chiltern Herb Farms Ltd* [1982] IRLR 166 the employers decided to reorganise their business operation after the death of one of their employees. Having received complaints about the applicant from fellow employees they moved him to the position previously held by the deceased. The new position was termed a promotion and offered a higher salary, but the applicant refused claiming that because of the new working environment he would be exposed to the risk of conjunctivitis. He refused to undergo a medical so that the employer could judge whether he would in fact be exposed to such a risk. The employee subsequently resigned and claimed that he had been constructively dismissed. The EAT held that in spite of the employers' conduct the constructive dismissal was fair because the reorganisation was necessary and that the employee had refused to undergo a medical. Even if the court determines that an employee has been constructively dismissed it will not necessarily mean that the dismissal is unfair.

In *Woods* v *W M Car Services Ltd* [1981] IRLR 413 the appellant was employed as chief secretary and accounts clerk. Following a take-over of the business she was pressurised to take a drop in salary and then required to work long hours but she refused. The employer then dropped the word 'chief' from her title. She subsequently left and claimed constructive dismissal. The Court of Appeal dismissed her appeal and Browne-Wilkinson J said that 'the tribunal's function is to look at the employer's conduct as a whole and determine whether it is such that its effect, judged reasonably and sensibly, is such that the employee cannot be expected to put up with it'.

The issue of when an alleged breach of the implied term of mutual trust and confidence would entitle an employee to resign and claim constructive dismissal has been considered more recently by the High Court in *Cantor Fitzgerald International* v *Bird and Others* [2002] IRLR 867. In this case three employees worked for the claimants as brokers. Their contracts of employment provided that they would receive a fixed annual salary plus a discretionary bonus, which was to be of a minimum fixed percentage of their commission revenue. In 2001 the claimants decided to change the way in which the employees were to be paid so that they were to be remunerated on a commission only basis. The employees were advised of the proposed change and senior executives tried to persuade the employees to accept the new arrangement. One of the employees was advised of the new scheme by a senior executive, who although friendly, nevertheless gave information which was thought to be misleading. The other two employees were dealt with in a much more aggressive manner and were threatened with the non-payment of their bonus. All the employees decided to reject the new proposals and advised the company accordingly. Another competing company approached the employees with an offer of employment which, despite a restrictive covenant, the employees decided to accept. The employees claimed that the action of the employers amounted to a breach of the implied term of trust and confidence that entitled them to treat the contract as being repudiated by the employer. The claimants sought an injunction restraining the employees from working for the new company.

It was held by the High Court that the two employees who had been treated in an aggressive manner were entitled to treat the behaviour of the employer as a breach of the implied term of trust and confidence. The manner in which they had been advised of the new contractual arrangements was misleading, and the use of swearing and other obscenities was so unacceptable that it was likely to damage or destroy the employment relationship. On the other hand, the third employee was not treated in such a way that entitled him to resign and therefore he was in repudiatory breach of his contract of employment. The distinction lay in the manner in which the first two employees and the third employee were dealt with: it was only where an employer behaved in such a way that his conduct was so serious that the inevitable conclusion was that the employment relationship had broken down where the implied term of trust and confidence would be breached. The High Court considered that the loss of confidence in management was not sufficient in itself to lead to a breach of the implied term.

In *Morrow* v *Safeway Stores plc* [2002] IRLR 9 the applicant, a bakery production controller, claimed that she had been unfairly and constructively dismissed following an incident when her store manager had seriously rebuked her in front of other members of staff and at least one customer for failing to have sufficient bread on the supermarket shelves. The tribunal held that although there had been a breach of the implied term of trust and confidence, it was not sufficiently serious as to amount to a repudiatory breach and therefore did not give rise to a claim of constructive dismissal. The applicant appealed against the decision of the tribunal. The EAT considered that the approach of the tribunal had been incorrect and that a finding of a breach of the implied term of mutual trust and confidence will almost certainly give rise to a repudiatory breach. The EAT remitted the case to a freshly constituted tribunal to determine whether the conduct of the store manager, both in terms of what was said and the circumstances giving rise to the rebuke, did amount to a breach of the implied term of trust and confidence.

It appears therefore that the courts are taking a much more robust approach in cases where there has been a breach of the implied term of trust and confidence, and take the view that a breach of this implied term may entitle an employee to consider himself to be constructively dismissed.

The breach by the employer must be fundamental, that is, it must go to the root of the contract. However, in *Adams* v *Charles Zub Associates Ltd* [1978] IRLR 551 failure to pay the employee on the due date because of cash-flow problems was held not to be a fundamental breach because the employee was assured that there would be full settlement in the near future and the employer did not intend to break the contract. In *Spafax* v *Harrison* [1980] IRLR 443, a case which mainly concerned the effectiveness of a restrictive covenant, the question arose as to whether a unilateral reduction in pay by the employer amounted to a fundamental breach of contract. It was held by the Court of Appeal that, although the employer had imposed a new method of working upon the employee which resulted in a loss of pay, because the employee was paid on a commission basis and there was provision within the contract which anticipated that this may go up or down, the unilateral variation did not amount to a fundamental breach of contract.

The EAT has recently held that if an employer imposes a disciplinary sanction on an employee which is out of all proportion to the alleged conduct such an action on the part of the employer could amount to a repudiatory breach of contract. In *Stanley Cole (Wainfleet) Ltd v Sheridan* [2003] IRLR 52 an employee was issued with a final written warning after she had taken half an hour unauthorised leave from work. The reason that Mrs Sheridan gave for her conduct was that she was distressed after an altercation with another employee. Mrs Sheridan left her employment and submitted an application to the employment tribunal claiming constructive dismissal. The tribunal considered that the penalty was disproportionate and that the subsequent constructive dismissal was unfair.

Any delay between the alleged breach of contract by the employer and the resignation by the employee may amount to a waiver of the breach unless there is good reason for the delay. In *Western Excavating v Sharp* Lord Denning MR said 'Moreover he (the employee) must make up his mind soon after the conduct of which he complains: for, if he continues for any length of time without leaving, he will lose his right to treat himself as discharged. He will be regarded as having elected to affirm the contract.'

In *Stanley Cole* the EAT also considered whether a delay of one month was too long for an employee to claim constructive dismissal. The EAT considered that the application of the principles laid down in *Western Excavating v Sharp* should not be 'mechanistic' and that it is a question of fact for the tribunal, which should take into account all the circumstances of each case. A person who is sick or suffering from some psychological disorder may take longer to consider himself to be constructively dismissed and any such delay should not be regarded as a waiver of the right to claim constructive dismissal. In *El-Hoshi v Pizza Express Restaurants Ltd* [2004] IDS 768 a two-month delay in claiming constructive dismissal was regarded by the EAT as 'understandable' given that the employee had been off work due to sickness which was itself related to the employer's breach of contract.

The test as to whether the conduct of a supervisory employee can be considered the conduct of the employer was clarified in *Hilton Hotels v Protopapa* [1990] IRLR 316. If the supervisory employee was acting in the course of employment he could bind the employer – as in vicarious liability in tort.

Constructive resignation

It has been argued that where an employee repudiates his contract an employer is entitled to consider that there has been a 'constructive resignation'. This issue was considered by the Court of Appeal in *London Transport Executive v Clarke* [1981]

ICR 355. In this case, Mr Clarke asked his employers if he could have extended unpaid leave. However, because the employee had already exhausted his holiday entitlement his request was refused. Nevertheless he went on holiday in the full knowledge that this would result in dismissal. When he returned from his vacation he claimed that he had been unfairly dismissed. The question for consideration was: did the employee repudiate the contract by taking his holiday, or did the employer repudiate the contract by dismissing him? The Court of Appeal (Lord Denning dissenting) rejected the argument put forward by the employers that he had resigned. It was held that there had been a dismissal, although in the circumstances the dismissal was fair.

4.6 Automatically fair reasons for dismissal

There are certain circumstances whereby an employer can dismiss an employee and the dismissal will be automatically regarded as fair, but the reasons for dismissal must be approached with caution.

National security

In *Council of Civil Service Unions* v *Minister for the Civil Service* [1985] IRLR 28, which concerned the removal of employment protection rights and rights to trade union membership at GCHQ Cheltenham, the House of Lords held that although ministers acting under a prerogative power might be under a duty to act fairly it was for the government and not the courts to decide whether questions of fairness were outweighed by national security.

Dismissal during strike or lock-out

An employee has no right to complain of unfair dismissal if, at the time of the dismissal, he was taking part in an unofficial strike or other unofficial industrial action: s237(1) Trade Union and Labour Relations (Consolidation) Act (TULR(C)A) 1992. However, withdrawal of labour does not necessarily constitute an automatically fair reason for dismissal. In *Wilkins* v *Cantrell and Cochrane (GB) Ltd* [1978] IRLR 483 Kilner-Brown J said that 'the whole point of men withdrawing their labour is so that existing contracts can be put right, so that grievances can be remedied, so that after a period in which they are on strike, management will agree to their demands'.

An employment tribunal will not determine whether a dismissal is fair or unfair where at the date of the dismissal:

1. the employer was conducting or instituting a lock-out; or
2. the complainant was taking part in a strike or other industrial action, unless it can be shown that one or more of the relevant employees of the same employer

have not been dismissed or that a relevant employee has been offered re-engagement within three months of his dismissal and the complainant has not been offered re-engagement: s238 TULR(C)A 1992.

Tribunals have been reluctant to put a time limit on activities which might constitute industrial action for the purposes of s238. Although industrial action is not defined, tribunals have held that it will include a go-slow, work to rule, concerted non-co-operation and probably a picket at the employer's workplace.

The test for the purposes of s238 is merely whether the employee was dismissed in the course of industrial action. It does not make any difference whether the employer deliberately engineered or provoked a dispute.

In *Heath* v *Longman (Meat Salesmen)* [1973] IRLR 214 the employer said that if employees continued their dispute about overtime payments for working on Saturdays he would dismiss them. The applicant and two of his workmates went on strike in response to the employer's ultimatum. Later one of the employees, having seen their union representative, informed the employer that the strike was at an end but the employer dismissed the three strikers. It was held by the Industrial Relations Court that the dismissals were unfair.

There has been difficulty in establishing whether an employee was actively participating in industrial action and is a 'relevant employee' for the purposes of s238(3). In *Coates* v *Modern Methods and Materials* [1982] ICR 763 the 'relevant employee' refused to cross a picket line on the first day of a strike because she was afraid that the pickets may be abusive. The following day she became ill and was unable to return until the strike action was over. The others who were dismissed for participating claimed that she too should have been dismissed as she was a relevant employee.

The Court of Appeal held that by failing to cross the picket line she was indeed a relevant employee, that her motive for not crossing the picket line on the first day was irrelevant and that the test applied should be objective rather than subjective.

If a strike has already begun and an employee who is off-duty states a clear intention to strike as soon as his shift starts he is treated as participating from the time he signals his intention.

Whether an employee is taking part in industrial action is not to be determined by whether or not the employer knew that he was so engaged. A genuine belief by the employer that the employee took part in the strike is not enough; it is for the employer to prove that the employee took part in the strike. The employee must be taking part in industrial action at the time of the dismissal for an employer to remain immune from an unfair dismissal claim.

If the employer was not aware that the employee he had recently appointed had been previously dismissed the mistake will not protect the employer. The employee would be considered to have been re-engaged for the purposes of s238.

4.7 Automatically unfair reasons for dismissal

An employee can claim that he or she has been automatically unfairly dismissed regardless of the time that the employee has worked for the employer if it can be established that the reason for dismissal fell within one or more of the following categories:

Pregnancy and connected reasons

Section 99 ERA 1996 provides that a dismissal will be automatically unfair if the reason for the dismissal is related to a woman's pregnancy. The provision provides that if a woman can show that her dismissal was in any way connected with her being pregnant she will be regarded as having been automatically unfairly dismissed. In *Brown* v *Stockton-on-Tees Borough Council* [1988] IRLR 263 the House of Lords held that a woman who had been selected for redundancy because she was pregnant had been unfairly dismissed.

Spent offences

The Rehabilitation of Offenders Act 1974 allows previous offenders to live down their past and move on. Section 4(3)(b) of the 1974 Act provides that a conviction which has become spent, or any failure to disclose a spent conviction, shall not be a proper ground for dismissing a person from employment. The effect is limited by certain regulations in the case of a number of sensitive professions, including medical practitioners, lawyers, accountants, dentists, nurses, police, social service workers and those wishing to work in educational establishments. The Act does not apply to any person who has received a prison sentence of two-and-a-half years or more.

Dismissal on transfer of undertakings

The Transfer of Undertakings (Protection of Employment) Regulations (TUPE) 1981 render a dismissal automatically unfair if the transfer or the reason connected with it is the principle reason for dismissal. The employer may be able to rely on the defence that dismissal was necessary because of economic, technical or organisational reasons. This defence is broad and vague and will be closely examined by an employment tribunal.

In *Berriman* v *Delabole Slate Ltd* [1984] ICR 636 the employee refused to accept the disadvantageous terms of the transferee employer and resigned, claiming constructive dismissal. The transferee employer claimed that economic and organisational reasons demanded a change of contractual terms especially to bring it into line with other employees.

The Court of Appeal held that the employee was constructively dismissed. The employer's intention to alter the applicant's contract to bring into line with other employees was not enough to show an economic, technical or organisational reason: it must also be shown that the reason entailed a change in the workforce as an objective rather than simply as a consequence of it.

Matters arising out of the transfer of an undertaking will be considered in more detail in Chapter 5.

Dismissal for union membership/non membership

The dismissal of an employee, including selection for redundancy, because of a reason related to trade union membership, will be regarded as automatically unfair. Section 152(1) TULR(C)A 1992 provides that the dismissal of an employee shall be regarded as unfair if the reason for it (or if more than one, the principal reason) was that the employee was, or proposed to become, a member of a trade union, or had taken part in activities of an independent trade union.

The Employment Relations Act 2004 strengthens the protections provided to trade union members from interference by employers in relation to union membership and activity. Section 29, which came into effect on 1 October 2004, inserts new ss145A–145F into TULR(C)A 1992 to protect workers from being persuaded by an employer not to join a trade union, take part in the activities of the trade union or to take advantage of its services by some inducement or bribe. This is considered in more detail in Chapter 11. If an employee is dismissed for a reason relating to trade union membership there is a minimum basic award which is currently £3,800 regardless of the length of time that the employee had been employed with the employer prior to the dismissal.

Dismissal for assertion of a statutory right

Section 104 ERA 1996 provides that an employee has been unfairly dismissed if the reason for the dismissal is that he has brought proceedings against the employer to enforce a right of his which is a relevant statutory right, or if the employer has infringed a relevant statutory right such as the non-provision of particulars of employment within the prescribed time.

Dismissal for reasons of health and safety

An employee who is dismissed under this category can claim that he has been unfairly dismissed if he can show that the reason for dismissal was for having made his employer aware that the health and safety of himself or his colleagues were at risk.

Section 100 ERA 1996, which implements the EC Health and Safety Framework Directive 89/391, provides that it will be automatically unfair to dismiss an employee in the following situations:

1. The employee was carrying out, or proposed to carry out, activities in connection with prevention of health and safety risks at work, having been designated to do so by the employer: s100(1)(a). In the event of a dismissal there is a minimum basic award which is currently £3,800.
2. The employee, being a representative of workers on matters of health and safety at work or a member of a safety committee, performed (or proposed to perform) any functions as such a representative or a member of such a committee: s100(1)(b). Contravention of this provision also provides for a basic minimum award which is currently £3,800.
3. The employee, being at a place where there was no health and safety representative or safety committee, or there was such a representative or safety committee but it was not reasonably practicable for the employee to raise the matter by those means, brought to the employer's attention matters which he reasonably believed were harmful or potentially harmful to health or safety: s100(1)(c).
4. The employee left or proposed to leave his place of work because he reasonably believed there was serious and imminent danger which he could not reasonably be expected to avert: s100(1)(d)).
5. The employee took or proposed to take appropriate steps to protect himself or others from danger which he reasonably believed to be serious and imminent: s100(1)(e)).

Failure to carry out disciplinary procedure

The Employment Act 2002 provided a framework for the introduction of minimum disciplinary and grievance procedures. These have been set out in the Employment Act 2002 (Dispute Resolution) Regulations 2004 (SI 2004/752) and are discussed in more detail in section 4.10. The Employment Act 2002 has also amended the ERA 1996 with a new s98A which provides that any dismissal will be regarded as automatically unfair if the employer dismisses an employee without going through the statutory disciplinary procedure. A failure by an employer to follow a disciplinary procedure will result in the employment tribunal increasing the basic award by four weeks pay: s120(1A) ERA 1996.

Fixed term contracts

Regulation 6 of the Fixed-Term Employees (Prevention of Less Favourable Treatment) Regulations 2002 (SI 2002/2034) provides that a dismissal will be regarded as being automatically unfair if the reason is one set out in reg 6(3), including situations where a fixed-term employee exercises or attempts to exercise any of the new rights provided for in the Regulations. The Regulations are discussed in more detail in Chapter 2, section 2.5.

Whistle-blowing

Section 5 of the Public Interest Disclosure Act 1998, commonly referred to as the Whistleblowing Act, inserts s103A into the ERA 1996 and provides that if an employer dismisses a worker for making a protected disclosure that dismissal will be regarded as being automatically unfair. To provide even greater protection there is no limit on the compensatory award. More consideration of the Public Interest Disclosure Act can be found in Chapter 3.

Family friendly policies

We have already seen that a dismissal on the grounds of pregnancy will be automatically unfair. However, in the last few years several 'family friendly' policies have been introduced to help working parents balance their work and family life. These include parental leave, adoption leave, paternity leave, flexible working and leave for domestic reasons. These are considered more fully in Chapter 8, but it is important to note that a dismissal in connection with these rights will generally be regarded as being automatically unfair.

Working time cases/sunday working

Employees working in the retail and betting industry will, by virtue of s101 ERA 1996, be regarded as having been unfairly dismissed if the reason for their dismissal was for refusing or proposing to refuse to work on a Sunday. Section 101A ERA 1996 provides that an employee who is dismissed for refusing to comply with a requirement of the employer when the requirement is a contravention of the Working Time Regulations will be regarded as being unfairly dismissed. A worker who is dismissed for refusal to waive his rights to protection under the Regulations will also be regarded as having been unfairly dismissed.

National minimum wage

An employee who is dismissed for asserting or proposing to assert his rights under the National Minimum Wage Act 1998 will also be regarded as being unfairly dismissed.

Jury service

Although there is no statutory provision which requires an employer to give an employee time off work to undertake jury service, an employee will be regarded as being automatically unfairly dismissed if the reason for the dismissal is that the employee took time off work to serve on a jury: s98B ERA 1996. This new provision, which came into effect on 6 April 2005, was introduced into the ERA

1996 by the Employment Relations Act 2004. There is no qualification period for the purposes of s98B.

Unfair selection for redundancy

A person who has been selected for redundancy can claim that he was unfairly selected if he can prove that his selection was due either to health and safety issues, union membership, pregnancy or asserting a statutory right.

4.8 Potentially fair/unfair reasons for dismissal

Section 94 ERA 1996 provides that an employee shall not be unfairly dismissed. If an ex-employee is claiming that he has been dismissed unfairly it will be for the employer to establish that he had a justifiable reason and that the reason was fair and satisfies one or more of the reasons contained in s98.

Section 98 ERA 1996 provides:

> '(1) In determining for the purposes of this Part whether the dismissal of an employee is fair or unfair, it is for the employer to show –
> (a) the reason (or, if more than one, the principal reason) for the dismissal, and
> (b) that it is either a reason falling within subsection (2) or some other substantial reason of a kind such as to justify the dismissal of an employee holding the position which the employee held.
> (2) A reason falls within this subsection if it –
> (a) relates to the capability or qualifications of the employee for performing work of the kind which he was employed by the employer to do,
> (b) relates to the conduct of the employee,
> (c) is that the employee was redundant, or
> (d) is that the employee could not continue to work in the position which he held without contravention (either on his part or on that of his employer) of a duty or restriction imposed by or under an enactment.'

It can be seen therefore that the employer has to satisfy the tribunal on a balance of probabilities that the reason for dismissal was due to at least one of the following:

1. capability;
2. qualification;
3. conduct;
4. redundancy;
5. continued employment would be in breach of statute;
6. some other substantial reason of a kind to justify dismissal.

In *Yates* v *British Leyland* [1974] IRLR 367 the applicant's foreman alleged that the applicant had been seen urinating on the factory floor. There was no evidence to justify this conclusion, which included examination of scrapings of the relevant area.

It was held that the employer had not established a reason to justify dismissing the applicant.

Once the employer has established that the reason for the dismissal falls with s94 ERA 1996, s98(4) provides that in order to determine if a dismissal is fair or unfair a tribunal should take into consideration matters such as the conduct, size and administrative resources of the employer and disciplinary and appeal procedures. If the tribunal does not consider s98(4) an applicant may appeal against the decision of the tribunal.

Before we consider the issue of whether a dismissal is fair or unfair it is necessary to look at the justifiable reasons in s98(2) in more detail.

Capability

Section 98(2)(a) ERA 1996 provides that a dismissal may be fair if the reason relates to the capability of the employee. Capability is defined by s98(3)(a) and may be assessed by reference to skill, aptitude, health or any other physical or mental requirement.

Prior to dismissing an employee on grounds of incapability, an employer has to consider the following.

Warnings

It is important that an employee is warned that his performance is unsatisfactory. The difficulty for the employer arises if an employee has completed a probationary period where his capability was not questioned. If an employer fails to give a warning this is not always fatal to his case, for in some circumstances a tribunal may consider that a warning will not remove the honest belief that had been formed by the employer about the capability of the employee.

In *Alidair* v *Taylor* [1978] ICR 445 a pilot landed his plane very badly, not only damaging the aircraft but frightening the passengers on board. He was dismissed by his employer. Mr Taylor claimed that he had not been warned and hence unfairly dismissed. The Court of Appeal held that his dismissal was fair and it was reasonable for the employer to form a reasonable belief that the pilot had lost his ability to land a plane safely.

Counselling

The employee must not only be warned about his underperformance but also be told what aspect of his job is unsatisfactory and what is expected of him to improve himself.

Training

In order to avoid a complaint of unfair dismissal, a prudent employer who is considering dismissing an employee because of lack of capability should also consider whether the employee has been given sufficient and relevant training and a reasonable time-scale within which to improve. The employer should monitor the employee taking care not to harass or pressurise him.

In *Davison* v *Kent Meters* [1975] IRLR 145 a woman was dismissed for assembling 471 out of 500 components incorrectly. She claimed that this was the way that she had been show to assemble them by the chargehand who denied that he had ever shown her how to assemble the parts and insisted that it was all her fault. The tribunal held that the chargehand should have shown the employee how to assemble the parts, should have checked on her performance and should have supervised her properly. The dismissal was held to be unfair.

Incompetence

Prior to dismissing an employee for incompetence a reasonable employer should assess the employee's capability, appraise him accordingly and discuss any criticisms openly with the employee. He should also warn the employee of the consequences of non-improvement and allow him a reasonable period and opportunity to improve.

In *Lewis Shops Group* v *Wiggins* [1973] IRLR 205 a shop manageress was dismissed when she left her shop dirty and untidy, with stock not put away and cash registers which failed to operate properly. She was dismissed for incompetence and the tribunal held that the dismissal was fair.

If an employee is considered to be incompetent, and has not responded to training, a reasonable employer should look elsewhere within his business to see if he can accommodate the employee according to the employee's capabilities. If the employee is dismissed the tribunal will take into account, inter alia, the length of service of the employee and the size of the organisation. It should however be noted that the employer is not under an obligation to create a new position.

Qualifications

Section 98(2)(a) also provides that a dismissal may be deemed to be fair if the applicant lacked the necessary qualifications to perform the tasks for which he was employed. Section 98(3)(b) defines qualifications as any degree, diploma or other academic, technical or professional qualification relevant to the position which the employee held. The employer can dismiss an employee should he discover that the employee had falsified his application form with qualifications that he does not actually possess.

In *Blackman* v *Post Office* [1974] ICR 151 the employee was required to pass an aptitude test that was agreed between the union and the employer to gain further employment. He was allowed to take the test three times but failed on each occasion. The court eventually found that his dismissal was fair on the grounds of lack of qualifications.

Conduct

This is the most common ground put forward by employers to justify a dismissal and the onus is upon the employer to show that he acted reasonably in dismissing the employee. In assessing whether the employer discharges this burden certain factors are taken into consideration, including the employer's own disciplinary procedures and whether the employer gave regard to the ACAS Code of Practice on Disciplinary and Grievances Procedures.

In addition to the Code, ACAS published an advisory handbook, *Discipline and Grievances at Work* which amplifies the recommendations of the Code of Practice. All disciplinary rules should be stated clearly, preferably in writing, and given to every employee before the commencement of their employment. If the employee is unable to understand the language in which the rules are written the employer must take such steps to have the rules interpreted.

Where there is a disciplinary rule and it is breached a tribunal may still find a dismissal unfair if, for example, the rule breached is of no relevance to the employment and where the punishment does not fit the alleged offence.

In determining whether a dismissal for a reason which falls within s98 ERA 1996 is fair or unfair another factor that the tribunals will consider is whether the punishment is proportionate to the alleged misconduct.

In *Ladbroke Racing Ltd* v *Arnott* [1983] IRLR 154 three betting-shop employees were summarily dismissed for placing bets on behalf of relatives in breach of a clearly stated rule. The tribunal's finding of unfairness was upheld by the Employment Appeal Tribunal (EAT) on the grounds that the dismissal was an unreasonable response to the misconduct. The full extent of the misconduct was that one employee had placed just one bet for his brother, the second occasionally for two pensioners and the third was the office manager who had apparently condoned the practice. In *Boychuk* v *H J Symons Holdings Ltd* [1977] IRLR 395 an employee was dismissed for wearing badges proclaiming her lesbianism. In determining that the dismissal was fair the tribunal considered that an employer can take into account what may be offensive to customers and other employees.

It is rare for an employee to be dismissed for a single act of misconduct unless the misconduct is of such a serious nature that it is considered to be gross misconduct warranting dismissal without notice or money in lieu of notice. Any other form of misconduct should normally be dealt with in accordance with the minimum statutory disciplinary procedure or the contractual disciplinary procedure if this is more favourable to the employee.

Conduct amounting to gross misconduct

Insubordination. When an employee refuses to obey a lawful request or order he could be dismissed for gross misconduct, but it is often necessary to take into consideration why he had refused to comply. If the reason given is justifiable he should be warned that further refusal could result in dismissal.

In *Retarded Children's Aid Society* v *Day* [1978] 1 WLR 763 an employee made it clear that he would not follow the policy laid down by his employers for the treatment of children. He was dismissed and when he complained to an industrial tribunal the employer successfully argued that the employee had made it abundantly clear that he would not adhere to the employer's instructions and, as such, a warning would have served no purpose.

If an employer requires an employee to follow instructions that are unlawful or unreasonable an employee may be justified in refusing to comply.

Breach of discipline. There are numerous offences which fall under this category and are normally brought to the attention of the employee when he receives his written statement of particulars of employment. The particulars must make reference to 'any disciplinary rules that apply'. The list of offences is not exhaustive but will generally include such matters as fighting, theft, drunkenness, drug-taking, use of offensive language, lateness and bringing the company into disrepute.

There may be instances when an employer has formed a suspicion that an employee is guilty of gross misconduct. However, before the employer dismisses the employee he must follow the rules proposed by Arnold J in the case of *British Home Stores* v *Burchell*. These are now commonly referred to as the *Burchell* principles and set out a three-stage process which employers must follow.

The facts of *British Home Stores* v *Burchell* [1980] IRLR 379 were really quite straightforward. The applicant was dismissed following an allegation that she had misused the Company staff-discount purchase scheme. She claimed that she had been unfairly dismissed and presented her claim to the employment tribunal. At the hearing the tribunal correctly stated it should not be 'concerned with whether the employee was guilty or innocent of the offences charged against her but whether the employers had reasonable grounds for believing that she had committed the offences when they dismissed her'. The tribunal found that Miss Burchell had been unfairly dismissed. When the employers appealed to the EAT Arnold J laid down a set of guidelines which should be followed in cases concerning suspected misconduct. These are as follows:

1. the employer must form a reasonable belief that the employee has committed an act of gross misconduct;
2. that he had reasonable grounds upon which to sustain that belief; and
3. that he formed that belief after having carried out as much investigation into the matter as was reasonably possible in all the circumstances of the case.

In this case the EAT considered that the employer satisfied all three requirements and therefore the dismissal was fair in all the circumstances.

If an employer follows the three-stage process a tribunal may hold the dismissal to be fair, even though at a later date relevant facts emerge which indicate that the employee may not have been guilty of the gross misconduct.

A recent application of the *Burchell* principles can be seen in the case of *Porter* v *Oakbank School* (2004) 19 March Case No XA52/03 (Court of Session), where it was held that even if an employer has a genuine belief that an employee has committed an act of serious misconduct that will not be sufficient to justify dismissal. For a dismissal to be regarded as being fair the employer must have reasonable grounds upon which the belief has been formed. In *Porter v Oakbank School* Mr Porter was a teacher at a special needs school. A 15-year-old male pupil left his classroom without permission and met Mr Porter in the corridor. An incident occurred which resulted in the pupil being taken to hospital with a broken elbow. An investigation was carried out and a disciplinary hearing was held at which Mr Porter was accompanied by a trade union representative. Following the meeting Mr Porter was summarily dismissed for gross misconduct because it was alleged that he had used unnecessary force and inappropriate physical intervention techniques. Following an unsuccessful appeal Mr Porter made a complaint to the employment tribunal alleging unfair dismissal. The tribunal held that the investigation into the matter was flawed and that important findings on the injury were made without medical evidence and that accordingly the dismissal was unfair. The decision was overturned on appeal to the EAT and Mr Porter appealed to the Court of Session where it was held that a genuine belief that misconduct has occurred is not enough to justify dismissal. In this case the crucial issue was whether Mr Porter had used 'unnecessary' force in restraining the boy and, in the absence of other evidence, the fractured elbow was not on its own a sufficient ground upon which to base a genuine belief that the force was unnecessary.

If an employer suspects that an employee is guilty of gross misconduct, but is experiencing difficulty in ascertaining which employee is the guilty party, he may be justified in dismissing more than one employee.

In *Monie v Coral Racing Ltd* [1980] IRLR 464 the appellant was employed by the respondent as an area manager with control over 19 betting shops. While Mr Monie was away on holiday, his assistant discovered that £1,750 was missing from the safe at the company headquarters. There was no indication that the safe or the premises had been forcibly entered into. The respondents' security officer concluded that either Mr Monie or the assistant must have broken into the safe and both were dismissed.

The EAT held that by applying the *Burchell* principles the dismissals would be unfair on the basis that the employer could not have had a reasonable belief in the employees' guilt as more than one employee was under suspicion. However, the Court of Appeal held that the requirement was that the employer must reasonably suspect one or more employees to be guilty of misconduct but cannot identify which employee, and in these circumstances he may be justified in dismissing both although he has no reasonable grounds for believing that both are guilty. The Court of Appeal further held that the *Burchell* principles should be confined to cases where only one employee was to be dismissed.

Where there are a number of workers who could have committed an offence an employer may be justified in retaining some staff and dismissing others. However, the employer must be able to demonstrate that he has good grounds for differentiating between the workers: *Frames Snooker Centre v Boyce* [1992] IRLR 472.

There is no 'all or none' principle applicable to group dismissals for suspected dishonesty. Therefore, where any one of a group of employees could have committed a particular offence, the fact that one or more members of that group are not dismissed does not render dismissal of the remainder unfair, provided that the employer is able to show solid and sensible grounds (which do not have to be related to the relevant offence) for differentiating between members of the suspected group.

Conduct outside work
The ACAS Code of Practice recommends that a conviction for a criminal offence should not be treated as an automatic reason for dismissal. The main considerations should be whether the nature of the offence and its consequential relevance is one which makes the employee unsuitable for his employment or unacceptable to other employees. An employment tribunal will also take into consideration whether the conduct of the employee has brought the employer into disrepute.

In *Moore v C & A Modes* [1981] IRLR 71 a section leader was dismissed after being convicted of shoplifting from another store. The offence was clearly relevant to her position and the dismissal was held to be fair.

Redundancy

Dismissal by reason of redundancy is usually a fair dismissal and the employee will be compensated accordingly for the loss of his employment. However, the employee may feel that he has either been unfairly selected for redundancy or that there was no genuine redundancy situation justifying dismissal. In these circumstances he may present an application to an employment tribunal within three months of the effective date of termination claiming unfair dismissal. An employee can also claim unfair dismissal if he becomes aware that his position has been advertised within six months of the date of his dismissal.

Redundancy will be considered more fully in Chapter 5.

Statutory prohibition

A dismissal may be deemed to be fair if the reason for the dismissal is that the employee is statutorily prohibited from undertaking the duties for which he was employed. The most obvious example would be where a delivery driver was banned by a court from driving, although even in such circumstances an employer would be advised to exercise caution. An employer would be expected to have taken into account the period of time that the employee is prevented from driving, the length of the employee's service, the previous disciplinary record of the employee and other relevant matters. He will also have to consider whether the employee can be redeployed. However, in assessing whether the dismissal was fair a tribunal will take into account the size and resources of the business. The employer is under no obligation to create a new position.

Some other substantial reason

An employer can claim that the reason for dismissing the employee was for some other substantial reason. This has been criticised for being too wide and sometimes for being vague, but the employer has to satisfy a tribunal that the reason for dismissal was fair.

In *Ely* v *YKK Fasteners (UK)* [1994] ICR 164 an employee had indicated that he was planning to resign and emigrate to Australia but he subsequently changed his mind. He did not formally resign but his employer nonetheless treated his employment as at an end. The employee claimed that he had been unfairly dismissed, whilst the employer claimed that there was no dismissal at all since it had merely acted upon the employee's stated intention to leave. The Court of Appeal held that the dismissal came within the ambit of some other substantial reason and was fair.

Normally there are two common categories under this heading that are canvassed by an employer, first that a dismissal is necessary for the continued operating of the business and, second, pressure from third parties.

Business needs
In determining whether a dismissal is fair or unfair a tribunal will take into account the needs of a business.

In *RS Components* v *Irwin* [1973] 1 All ER 41 the employer found he was losing business because sales staff were leaving to join a competitor. The employer unilaterally sought to vary his employees' contracts by inserting a restraint of trade clause which would prevent them from working for a competitor. The employee refused to sign the new covenant and was dismissed. The dismissal was held to be fair on the grounds of 'some other substantial reason'.

In redundancy cases an employer would also plead s98(1)(b) ERA 1996 in the alternative where he has difficulty in satisfying the detailed requirements of s139 ERA 1996. Under s98(1)(b) the employer will usually say that due to economic reasons he had either to reorganise or to rationalise his workforce which resulted in redundancies.

Even if the employer was following his own policy on reorganisation he still has to show that the dismissal was fair.

In *Banerjee* v *City and East London AHA* [1979] IRLR 147 a consultancy had been held by two part-time employees. One consultant left and the authority decided to create a full-time appointment, resulting in the applicant Dr Banerjee being dismissed. At the tribunal hearing the employers relied upon their policy of rationalisation and their practice of amalgamating part-time posts. However, the employers were unable to satisfy the tribunal on how the policy had been formulated and the dismissal was held to be unfair by the tribunal and the EAT.

Pressure from third parties

In *Treganowan* v *Knee* [1974] ICR 405 a woman who upset other office staff by boasting of her affair with a much younger man was deemed to have been fairly dismissed.

In *Dobie* v *Burns International Security Services* [1984] IRLR 329 a company provided the security at Liverpool Airport and the applicant was a security officer at the site. Following a couple of incidents, which the Court of Appeal were prepared to assume were not the fault of the applicant, the airport authority refused to have him at the airport. The only alternative position that the employer could offer him was at a lower rate of pay which he refused. The Court of Appeal found that his dismissal was fair because the employer had no other alternative work for the applicant.

However, the employer cannot argue as a defence, nor in mitigation of compensation, that he was forced to dismiss because of the threat of a strike, whether the pressure was explicit or implicit.

In *Colwyn Borough Council* v *Dutton* [1980] IRLR 420 the applicant was a dustcart driver. The applicant's trade union branch refused to act when the applicant's workmates were unwilling to work with him, complaining that he was a dangerous driver. He was consequently dismissed. The dismissal was unfair but his driving contributed to the dismissal, resulting in a reduction of compensation.

If an employer bows to pressure from third parties and dismisses an employee, any decision by a tribunal that the dismissal was fair could lead to inconsistencies because a person could be dismissed for a reason which, if it had been the sole reason for a dismissal by the employer, may be deemed to be unfair.

4.9 Excluded categories

Even if a person is in employment it does not necessarily mean that he can present a claim for unfair dismissal. Certain categories of workers are excluded from the right to claim.

1. Persons who do not have the requisite one-year qualifying period: s108 ERA 1996.
2. Persons past retirement age: s109 ERA 1996.
3. Persons dismissed in connection with an unlawful dispute or strike, unless they can show that they have been discriminated against.
4. Persons employed under an illegal contract.
5. Some Crown employees.
6. Employees not employed in Great Britain.

Age

Section 109 ERA 1996 excludes an applicant who, on or before the effective date of termination, has attained the 'normal retiring age' for an employee holding the position which he held, or has attained the age of 65. It is the relationship between the normal retiring age and 65 which causes most concern.

A tribunal should apply the normal retiring age contained in the contract of employment, if there is one. If none is stipulated only then should the tribunal apply the age of 65. The Court of Appeal has emphasised that it is the construction of the contract, not what actually happens in practice, that is important. These can differ widely when an employer has discretion.

In *Waite* v *Government Communication Headquarters* [1983] IRLR 341 the House of Lords established the principle that 'normal retiring age' is the age at which a group of employees can reasonably be expected to be compelled to retire. However, if there is evidence to show that employees are allowed to retire at a variety of ages then the age of 65 will be applied.

The test is clear enough, but what is interesting is that in this case the House of Lords held that the fact that one-quarter of the relevant group of employees had not retired at the 'normal retiring age' was not sufficient to show that it had been displaced and ought to be replaced by the age of 65.

The Court of Appeal in *Brooks* v *BT* [1992] IRLR 66 held that if an employer wished to alter the 'normal retiring age' he could do so providing that this did not breach the employee's contract of employment. He could do so even if this did not accord with the expectation of the employee.

According to the EAT in *Swaine* v *Health & Safety Executive* [1986] IRLR 205 a normal retiring age must be a definite cut-off point and not range within a band.

The strict application of s109 has recently been thrown into doubt as European law has once again been relied upon to challenge UK legislation.

In *Nash* v *Mash Roe Group plc* [1998] IRLR 168 the applicant was successful in his claim for unfair dismissal even though he was aged 69. The employment tribunal decided that s109 was discriminatory because in the UK more men than women are economically active after they reach the age of 65.

The same issue arose in the cases of *Rutherford and Another* v *Secretary of State for Trade and Industry* [2004] IRLR 892.

In this case the Court of Appeal considered the position where two male employees had exceeded the age limit of 65 at the time of their dismissals. There was no 'normal retiring age' in the case of either man. Mr Rutherford, who was dismissed when he was aged 67, presented a claim for unfair dismissal and redundancy pay. Mr Bentley, the second appellant, who was aged 73 when he was made redundant, claimed redundancy pay. The insolvency of the employers of both men led to the joinder of the Secretary of State for Trade and Industry as a party.

In both cases different employment tribunals considered that the upper age limit of 65 for bringing a claim (it was previously 60 for women, but following the decision of the ECJ in *Marshall* v *Southampton and South-West Hampshire Area Health Authority* [1986] ICR 335 it is now 65) had a greater adverse impact on men than on women. The tribunal considered that the relevant pool of comparators was those in the workforce who would be affected by the upper qualifying age – this was assessed as people aged over 55 and it was found that far more men than women fell into this group. Thus the upper qualifying age had an adverse impact on men. The tribunals considered that the indirect discrimination could not be objectively justified and they therefore had jurisdiction to hear the claims.

In joined cases the Secretary of State successfully appealed to the EAT following which the appellants appealed to the Court of Appeal. The Court of Appeal dismissed the appeal on the grounds that the employment tribunal had not given sufficient consideration to the decision of the House of Lords in the case of *R* v *Secretary of State for Employment, ex parte Seymour-Smith* [2000] IRLR 263, where it was held that the whole workforce must be used as a pool when determining whether there was an adverse impact on one gender compared with the other. When the statistics for the entire workforce were applied the difference between the number of men affected by the upper qualifying age limit and the number of women affected was so negligible that it did not amount to discrimination.

Illegality

Generally an employee cannot claim employment protection rights if his contract is tinged with illegality.

The classic statement of the general principle was by Lord Mansfield in *Holman* v *Johnson* (1775) 1 Cowp 341:

> 'No court will lend its aid to a man who founds his cause of action upon an immoral or illegal act. If, from the plaintiff's own stating or otherwise, the cause of action appears to arise ex turpi causa, or the transgression of a positive law of this country then the court says he has no right to be assisted.'

A more recent application of the general principle can be found in the case of *Napier* v *National Business Agency* [1951] 2 All ER 264 where a secretary was employed on a wage of £18 per week. Her pay included £5 per week as expenses to avoid having to pay tax on the full amount. The Court of Appeal held that this was an illegal contract and hence unenforceable. In *Hannen* v *Ryman* [1979] EAT/478/79 a contract was declared invalid even though the tax evaded amounted to only £4 in a four-year period.

However, more recently this principle has not been so strictly applied where an illegal act by an employer would deny the employee protection under s94 ERA 1996.

In *Newland* v *Simmons & Willer (Hairdressers) Ltd* [1981] IRLR 359 the EAT held that whether or not a contract was void for illegality, thus denying the employee protection, would depend upon whether the employee was aware of the illegality.

In *Wilkinson* v *Lugg* [1990] ICR 599 the EAT reaffirmed that an innocent party will not be affected by the illegality and can still proceed to make an application to an employment tribunal. In *Hewcastle Catering Ltd* v *Ahmed and Elkamah* [1991] IRLR 473 the Court of Appeal held that if employees participated in some form of illegality, but did not gain any personal advantage, they can still rely on s94 and make an application to an employment tribunal.

There are also instances where the courts may apply the 'blue pencil' rule but this is only applied if the contract is severable. A severable contract is one where the clauses are independent of one another.

Incidental illegality does not necessarily preclude an employment tribunal from hearing a case. In *Coral Leisure Group Ltd* v *Barnett* [1981] IRLR 204 Barnett complained of unfair dismissal. He alleged that in his job as public relations executive he was, inter alia, expected to procure prostitutes for the company's customers. The company denied the allegation but stated that should the contract of employment be what Barnett claimed then the contract should be void as it was contrary to public policy. The EAT held the alleged illegality should not be a bar to the proceedings and that the tribunal should hear the merits of the case.

In *Hall* v *Woolston Hall Leisure Ltd* [2001] 1 WLR 225, a case concerning alleged sex discrimination and fraud on the Inland Revenue, Peter Gibson LJ said:

> 'In cases where the contract of employment is neither entered into for an illegal purpose nor prohibited by statute, the illegal performance of the contract will not render the contract unenforceable unless in addition to knowledge of the facts which make the performance illegal the employee actively participates in the illegal performance. It is a question of fact in each case whether there has been a sufficient degree of participation by the employee.'

This dictum was recently relied upon in the case of *Wheeler* v *Quality Deep Ltd t/a Thai Royale Restaurant* [2004] EWCA Civ 1085. In this case Mrs Wheeler, a Thai national, had worked as a cook at the respondent's restaurant for three years. She was married to an English man but her English was limited. During her employment Mrs Wheeler had consistently taken home £220 per week despite her basic pay being £220. She repeatedly asked for pay-slips and a tax code but never received them. Mrs Wheeler was dismissed and she claimed unfair dismissal. At the employment tribunal her claim was dismissed on the grounds that the contract was illegal because of the failure to pay tax and national insurance. The tribunal considered that despite Mrs Wheeler's poor understanding of English and the British tax system, her husband was aware of the failure to pay tax or NI and that Mrs Wheeler should also have been aware of the illegality.

Persons employed outside Great Britain

Employees who work overseas have generally been excluded from the protection afforded by s94 ERA 1996, the right not to be unfairly dismissed. The rules contained in s196 ERA 1996 were complex and were repealed by s32(3) of the

Employment Relations Act 1999. Following the repeal of s196 there is no longer any specific statutory requirement that an employee must ordinarily work in Great Britain in order to qualify for protection under the ERA 1996. Nevertheless the position of workers who worked overseas was unclear. A recent decision of the Court of Appeal in *Lawson* v *Serco* [2004] IRLR 206 has helped to remove some of the uncertainty

In *Lawson* the respondent, Mr Lawson, was a British national who was appointed a security supervisor with the appellants who provided support services for the RAF and civilian police on Ascension Island. The contract of employment made no mention of any other governing law other than English law. The respondent was interviewed and appointed in England and paid in pounds sterling. The Ascension Islands are a dependency of St Helena which is an overseas territory of the United Kingdom in the South Atlantic. Mr Lawson objected to the number of additional working hours that he was being asked to perform and on 6 April 2001 he resigned, claiming unfair dismissal. Mr Lawson did not have the requisite qualifying period to bring a claim of unfair dismissal and so brought his claim under the Working Time Regulations 1998. The employment tribunal held that it had no jurisdiction to hear the claim because Mr. Lawson did not work in Great Britain. However, the EAT reversed that decision and Serco appealed.

The Court of Appeal, in allowing the appeal, held that the respondent was not employed in Great Britain despite his strong connections with the country. It is not sufficient that an employer is incorporated or carries on business in England and Wales. The issue is whether the employer is employed in Great Britain. The Court of Appeal briefly considered some of the tests that have been applied, including the 'substantial connection' test as suggested by the EAT in *Jackson* v *Ghost Ltd* [2003] IRLR 824 and the base test advocated by Lord Denning MR in *Todd* v *British Midland Airways* [1978] ICR 959. However, the Court held that whilst the country in which a company carried out its business and the base of the employee may be relevant, nevertheless the determining factor is where the employment itself is carried out.

Despite some clarification on the issue from the Court of Appeal the judgment did not lay down clear guidelines and continues the dichotomy of rights contained within discrimination legislation which protect employees who work outside Great Britain and the lack of rights in respect of unfair dismissal and overseas workers.

Exclusion by agreement

As a general rule any agreement by an employee to waive his right to make an application to an employment tribunal is void. However, some agreements are valid and they are as follows.

1. Settlements reached as a result of the intervention by a conciliation officer from ACAS.

100 *Dismissal*

2. Compromise agreements wherein the parties agree to refrain from instituting or continuing any proceedings. Section 203 ERA provides that the agreement must be in writing, must be specific and the employee must seek independent legal advice from a qualified barrister or solicitor.

In *Livingstone* v *Hepworth Refractories* [1992] IRLR 63 the EAT held that an agreement reached under the auspices of a conciliation officer does not prevent the employee from bringing a claim under the discrimination legislation.

Under the Trade Union Reform and Employment Rights Act 1993 certain agreements not to take proceedings before employment tribunals are for the first time to be exempted from the general rule that such agreements are void. Section 203 of the 1993 Act also extends to collective agreements provided:

1. the agreement must be in writing;
2. the agreement must relate to a particular complaint;
3. the employee must have received independent advice.

4.10 Reasonableness and the importance of procedure

Once an employer has established that he had a fair reason for dismissing an employee a tribunal will then consider the fairness of the decision to dismiss the employee. Section 98(4) ERA 1996 provides that:

> '... the determination of the question whether the dismissal was fair or unfair (having regard to the reason shown by the employer) –
> (a) depends on whether in the circumstances (including the size and administrative resources of the employer's undertaking) the employer acted reasonably or unreasonably in treating it as a sufficient reason for dismissing the employee, and
> (b) shall be determined in accordance with equity and the substantial merits of the case.'

In applying the section the tribunal has to consider the reasonableness of the employer's decision to dismiss the employee. In most cases there is a band of reasonable responses to the employee's conduct, within which one employer might reasonably take one view, and a different employer quite reasonably take another. The tribunal's function is not to substitute its decision for that of the employer but to decide whether, in the particular circumstances of the case, the decision fell within the band of reasonable responses which a reasonable employer might have adopted: *Iceland Frozen Foods* v *Jones* [1983] ICR 17. A dismissal will not be unfair if it falls within this band of reasonable responses: *British Leyland* v *Swift* [1981] IRLR 91.

Once a tribunal has determined that the conduct of an employer falls within the band of reasonable responses it should conclude that the dismissal was fair. In *Thomas* v *Hillingdon London Borough Council* (2002) The Times 4 October, the applicant was dismissed for gross misconduct after using an office computer to visit hard core pornographic web sites. The tribunal held that the applicant had been unfairly dismissed because, after holding that the dismissal was within the band of reasonable responses, the tribunal considered that the conduct of the applicant was no more than misconduct and the dismissal was unfair. The respondent's appealed to the EAT. It was held by the EAT that having come to the conclusion that the response of the employer was within the band of reasonable responses that should be the end of the matter and no further consideration was required. Accordingly the decision of the tribunal that the dismissal was unfair was perverse and the appeal was allowed.

If a dismissal falls within the band of reasonable responses the dismissal is fair; if a dismissal falls outside the band it is unfair. The band of reasonable responses test adopted by tribunals has recently been reviewed by the EAT and the Court of Appeal. In *Haddon* v *Van Den Burgh Foods Ltd* [1999] IRLR 672 the EAT purported to abolish the test. However, in *Midland Bank* v *Madden* [2000] IRLR 827 the EAT overturned its decision in *Haddon* and restored the range of reasonable responses test. The Court of Appeal in *Midland Bank* made it clear that no court below that of the Court of Appeal could abolish such an established test.

The employer must follow his own company's disciplinary procedure, but a failure to do so is not necessarily fatal to his case. In *Bailey* v *BP Oil (Kent Refinery) Ltd* [1979] IRLR 287 the employee notified his employer that he was sick when he was in fact holidaying in Majorca. Unfortunately for him so was one of the company's directors! The company's procedure included a clause which stated that a full-time union official should be consulted prior to any dismissal. The company failed to do so. It was held that this failure was not sufficient to render the dismissal unfair.

In determining whether the conduct of an employer falls within the band of reasonable responses the tribunal should take into account all the circumstances, including whether the employer has advised employees as to what type of conduct is acceptable and what is unacceptable in the workplace. In *Bournemouth Borough Council* v *Meredith* [2003] ELR 1 Mr Meredith was employed as a music teacher by Bournemouth Borough Council. He was dismissed for gross misconduct following an incident when he took a disruptive 12-year-old girl by the wrist and dragged her outside the classroom during an examination. The girl had refused several instructions to leave the examination room. Mr Meredith appeared before a disciplinary panel, who concluded that Mr Meredith was guilty of gross misconduct, stating, inter alia, 'that as an experienced professional person it was incumbent upon you to keep yourself abreast of the legislation and published guidance on classroom management including that relating to disruptive students': Mr Meredith was dismissed and claimed that the dismissal was unfair. He was successful at the employment tribunal and the employers appealed.

The appeal was dismissed. The conclusion of the tribunal that the disciplinary panel 'had no reasonable basis upon which to conclude that [Mr Meredith] knew or ought reasonably to have known that what he did amounted to misconduct' was correct, and because the contract of employment did not define 'misconduct' or 'gross misconduct', it was incumbent upon the employer to satisfy the disciplinary panel that Mr Meredith knew or ought reasonably to have known that his conduct was prohibited. The conduct of the employers was not within the band of reasonable responses, taking into account the slightness of the injury to the student, the fact that Mr Meredith had nine years service, the quality of his teaching, the absence of any previous incident of this nature, the lack of clear guidance and the lack of any definition of gross misconduct.

The employer may sometimes wish to introduce as evidence matters that came to his attention after the employee had been dismissed and the admissibility of such evidence was examined by Viscount Dilhorne in *Devis v Atkins* [1977] IRLR 314. In this case the respondent had been employed as a manager at the company's abattoir. Despite repeated instructions to buy animals directly from farmers, he persisted in buying from dealers. He was dismissed with pay in lieu of notice and given an ex-gratia payment of £6,000. He then claimed that his dismissal was unfair.

At the tribunal hearing the employer tried to introduce allegations that the employee had been taking commission from the dealers, but they had not discovered this until after his dismissal. The tribunal refused to admit this evidence and held the dismissal unfair for lack of warning. The decision of the tribunal was upheld by the House of Lords who said that whilst evidence that had been discovered after the dismissal could be adduced to show that the dismissal was fair for the reason given, evidence discovered after the dismissal could not be adduced if its only purpose was to show another reason why the employee could be dismissed. Evidence discovered after the dismissal may be used to reduce the award to a successful applicant.

The proposition that a dismissal that may be deemed unfair at the time of dismissal but could become fair by virtue of after-acquired evidence was again considered by the Court of Appeal in *British Labour Pump v Byrne* [1979] IRLR 94. The principle that emerged was a 'no-difference rule' and the effect of that rule was that even if the employer had not acted reasonably at the time of the dismissal as a result of a failure to follow correct procedure, the dismissal could still be found to be fair if the employment tribunal considered that on the facts the employer would still have reached the same decision if they had carried out the correct procedure. This rule was severely criticised on the grounds that this was using after-acquired knowledge to justify an earlier decision to dismiss. This rule was later expressly overruled by the House of Lords in *Polkey v A E Dayton Services* [1988] IRLR 503.

In *Polkey v Dayton Services Ltd* the company employed four van drivers, including the applicant. It was decided to replace the four drivers with three van salespeople. Only one of the existing four drivers was considered capable of carrying out the selling function as well as driving, so the other three were made redundant.

The first Mr Polkey knew of this was when he was called into the office, told he was redundant and sent home. There was no warning, consultation or discussion before-hand. However, the tribunal held that in accordance with the *British Labour Pump* principle any such consultation would have made no difference to the decision to dismiss. They found the dismissal fair and Mr Polkey appealed ultimately to the House of Lords.

The House of Lords allowed the appeal and the case was remitted to be heard by another tribunal. The Law Lords stressed that a tribunal should concentrate on what the employer did and not what he might have done. Unless the employer has reasonable grounds for concluding that consultation would be useless, the lack of a fair procedure could lead to a finding of unfair dismissal.

The effect of this ruling has been a renewed emphasis on the importance of using correct procedures in relation to all kinds of dismissals. The test has also reverted more closely to the wording of the statute which requires the tribunal to examine whether or not there has been an injustice done to the employee.

In *West Midland Co-operative Society* v *Tipton* [1986] IRLR 112 the employee was continually taking time off work and was told that if his attendance record did not improve he would be dismissed. The warnings were made clear to him but there was no improvement. He was summarily dismissed. He appealed against his dismissal but the employer refused to entertain his appeal, even though they were in breach of an agreed contractual procedure.

The industrial tribunal found the dismissal to be unfair because of the employer's refusal to hear his appeal. The employer appealed to the EAT which dismissed his appeal. He further appealed to the Court of Appeal which reversed the original decision. The matter then progressed to the House of Lords which held that an appeal hearing was an integral part of the dismissal process and that if an employer denies that right to an employee the dismissal may be construed to be unfair. A failure by an employer to follow strictly the rules of natural justice will not necessarily render an appeal process unfair: *Rowe* v *Radio Rentals* [1982] IRLR 177.

Disciplinary and grievance procedures

The position regarding disciplinary procedures and appeals is now governed by the Employment Act 2002 (Dispute Resolution) Regulations 2004 (SI 2004/752) which came into effect on 1 October 2004. The Regulations provide that all employers, regardless of the number of employees employed by a company, must provide and follow minimum statutory disciplinary and grievance procedures.

The Regulations enhance the statutory disciplinary and grievance procedures introduced by the Employment Rights Act 1996. However, the procedures introduced by the ERA 1996 only applied to companies employing more than 20 employees. This exemption has now been removed which means that all employers must ensure that their contracts of employment and disciplinary and grievance policies meet the requisite minimum standard. A failure to comply with the statutory minimum procedures will result in a dismissal being classed as automatically unfair. In essence the Regulations provide for the following:

1. Introduce minimum internal disciplinary and grievance procedures; most

employees will need to raise grievances with their employer before applying to tribunal.

There is a minimum three-stage process:

a) a letter must be written explaining the issues;
b) a meeting must be held to discuss the issues;
c) the employer must provide for an appeal process.

2. Provide limited extension to time limits for lodging a tribunal complaint to allow appeal against a decision to be completed.

A failure to comply with the new Regulations may result in tribunals altering any awards made – an employer will pay more if he has failed to introduce grievance and disciplinary procedures and employees will have any award reduced if they have failed to invoke the grievance procedure.

If an employee is facing a disciplinary hearing he has the right to be accompanied by a work colleague or a trade union representative of a recognised trade union. Section 37 Employment Relations Act 2004 (replacing s10 Employment Relations Act 1999) extends the role of representatives at disciplinary or grievance hearings. A representative accompanying an employee was previously limited to addressing the meeting and conferring with the worker. The new rights provide that representatives will now have the right to sum up and respond on the worker's behalf to any view expressed at the hearing. The representative will not have the right to answer questions on behalf of the employee.

The Advisory, Conciliation and Arbitration Service (ACAS) has produced a Code of Practice called *Disciplinary and Grievance Procedures*. This Code is issued under s199 Trade Union and Labour Relations (Consolidation) Act 1992 and also came into effect on 1 October 2004. Employers should, as a matter of best practice, follow the Code, although a failure to follow it will not automatically lead to a finding against an employer. Nevertheless, any breach of the Code will be taken into account by a tribunal at any subsequent hearing. ACAS have also produced an advisory handbook entitled *Discipline and Grievances at Work*.

If an employer has a more comprehensive contractual disciplinary procedure he must follow that procedure. A failure to do so would amount to a breach of contract and any subsequent dismissal would be a wrongful dismissal.

If an employee appeals against dismissal but his appeal is unsuccessful, for the purposes of determining the effective date of termination (EDT) the operative date is the date of dismissal and not the date when the appeal was heard: *Sainsbury* v *Savage* [1981] IRLR 109. This approach was approved by the House of Lords in *West Midland Co-operative Society* v *Tipton* (above). The House of Lords also approved the decision of the EAT in *National Heart and Chest Hospital* v *Nambiar* [1981] IRLR 196 which stated that an employer would not be able to use any new evidence at the appeal hearing in order to validate his original reason to dismiss. They added that the proper course would be for the employer to allow the employee's appeal and then, if need be, dismiss the employee for the newly discovered reason.

The importance of the EDT is that the time limit for presenting a claim of unfair or wrongful dismissal to the employment tribunal is three months from the EDT. However the Employment Act 2002 (Dispute Resolution) Regulations 2004 do give the tribunal discretion to extend the three-month limitation period to allow for further discussion to take place between the employer and employee. This accords with the philosophy of the Employment Act 2002 of providing as much opportunity to resolve disputes in the workplace as possible, with a view to reducing the number of claims to the tribunal. See further section 4.12 (below).

The employer must be consistent in following the company's procedure in either disciplining his staff or dismissing them. If a dismissed employee alleges that he has been treated differently to other employees due to the employer's inconsistent approach a tribunal may be persuaded to find in the applicant's favour, though this will not always be the case. In *Hadjioannous* v *Coral Casinos* [1981] IRLR 352 an employee at a casino was dismissed for socialising with customers contrary to company policy. Mr Hadjioannous argued that the dismissal was unfair because other employees who had broken the rule in the past had not been dismissed. The EAT, in upholding the decision of the tribunal that the dismissal was fair, said that employers must be allowed a little flexibility when looking at misconduct.

In *Post Office* v *Fennell* [1981] IRLR 221 the employee was summarily dismissed after assaulting a fellow employee in the works canteen. He argued that his dismissal was inconsistent with the way fellow workers who had committed similar offences had been treated. The Court of Appeal upheld the decision that the dismissal was unfair because of the inconsistency of treatment by the employer, although it was pointed out that this would generally only be so if the circumstances were strongly similar in two cases which had been treated differently. The date at which the reasonableness of the employer is taken into account is, according to Sir Ian Glidewell in *Parkinson* v *March Consulting Ltd* [1997] IRLR 308, the date that the contract comes to an end, not the date at which the decision was made to dismiss the employee.

Human rights and unfair dismissal

An employee who has been dismissed may claim that the dismissal is unfair because his rights under the Human Rights Act (HRA) 1998 have been violated. The HRA 1998 does not make the European Convention on Human Rights (ECHR) part of UK domestic law but it does enable employees to enforce Convention rights against public authorities through the domestic courts. However, so far the courts have taken a fairly cautious approach when considering the application of the HRA 1998 to dismissals, particularly in respect of art 8 ECHR – the right to privacy and family life.

In *Pay* v *Lancashire Probation Service* (2003) The Times 27 November Mr Pay, a probation officer, was dismissed by his employer because of activities that he carried out when not in work. In his spare time, he ran a company selling bondage, domination and sado-masochism merchandise through a website and was also involved with a club called 'Club Lash'. He was dismissed on the grounds that such activities, which were advertised in the public domain, were inconsistent with his duties as a probation officer, particularly as he was responsible for dealing with sex offenders and their victims, and because his conduct could bring the probation service into disrepute. Mr Pay brought a claim for unfair dismissal. However, the tribunal found the dismissal was fair and did not offend Mr Pay's rights under art 8 ECHR. Mr Pay appealed to the EAT.

The EAT upheld the finding of a fair dismissal. There was no breach of art 8 as it was not engaged because Mr Pay's activities had been brought into the public domain by advertising on the internet.

A similar approach has been taken by the Court of Appeal in the case of X v Y [2004] IRLR 625. In this case the applicant (X) was employed as a development officer and worked with young people who were either at risk of offending or on probation. He was dismissed following an incident whilst off duty which had resulted in his arrest and a caution for gross indecency. The incident had involved consensual sexual activity with a man who he had never met before in the toilet of a transport café. He did not reveal to police that he worked with young people and sought to withhold the matter from his employers. He presented a claim for unfair dismissal. However, the employer argued that the reason for the dismissal was because the incident had damaged the working relationship, first because of his involvement with young people and, second, by placing the employer, a charity, at risk of embarrassing publicity. The tribunal found the dismissal was fair. The applicant appealed on the ground that the tribunal had failed to take into account art 8 ECHR. At the EAT it was held that because the incident took place in a public toilet the activities in which the applicant engaged were not private and accordingly did not fall within the ambit of art 8. X appealed to the Court of Appeal

The appeal failed for the reasons stated by the EAT – the conduct for which the appellant was dismissed did not take place in private and therefore art 8 was not engaged. However, the Court of Appeal also considered the relationship between the HRA 1998 and the ERA 1996, particularly s98 ERA 1996. Under s3 HRA 1998 an employment tribunal must, so far as is reasonably possible, give effect to s98 ERA 1996 and other relevant provisions of the 1996 Act in accordance with Convention rights. Section 3 HRA 1998 does not distinguish between private and public sector employers. The Court considered how s3 HRA 1998 affects the interpretation of s98 ERA 1996 and said that an employment tribunal, in discharging its duty under s3 HRA 1998, must 'read and give effect to s98 of the ERA in a way which is, so far as possible, compatible with art 8': per Mummery LJ.

Warnings

If an employer is dissatisfied with an employee for any reason whatsoever it is good employment practice to warn him and give him the opportunity to improve. An employer may only dispense with this requirement should the warning make no difference: *Retarded Children's Aid Society* v *Day* [1978] ICR 437. Certain conduct may be treated as gross misconduct thereby allowing the employer to dismiss without a warning, but it still remains ultimately for the tribunal to decide whether the conduct was sufficiently serious to warrant summary dismissal in the circumstances.

In *Law Stores Ltd* v *Oliphant* [1978] IRLR 251 the employee was dismissed for one lapse in operating the till. He was aware that such conduct could lead to summary dismissal as it fell within the definition of gross misconduct in the company's rules. The dismissal was held to be unfair.

It is possible that a warning may be dispensed with where the disciplinary rules are so clear as to constitute a warning of dismissal in themselves. This principle islimited in its application, so that in *Meridian Ltd* v *Gomersall* [1977] IRLR 425 a notice that 'anyone found clocking cards on behalf of other personnel will render themselves liable to instant dismissal' was held to be insufficiently specific since it did not necessarily mean that the employee would be sacked for one offence.

4.11 Notice

At common law the parties are free to incorporate any period of notice into the contract of employment but the period of notice should not be excessively long. The statutory right to a minimum period of notice is found in s86 ERA 1996 which provides that a person who has been continuously employed for one month or more should receive at least one week's notice. If the period of continuous employment exceeds two years then he should receive not less than one week's notice for each year of continuous employment up to a maximum of 12 weeks.

The employer may wish to terminate the employment without requiring the employee to continue in employment. The employee will then be entitled to money in lieu for the relevant period of notice.

Withdrawal of notice during the relevant period

Once an employer has given notice of termination of employment he cannot unilaterally withdraw his notice. The employee similarly cannot withdraw his resignation once given without the agreement of the employer.

4.12 Time limits

A person who wishes to bring a claim for wrongful or unfair dismissal must do so within three months of the effective date of termination (EDT), including the first day – ie the day of termination. The EDT is normally the last day the employee has worked, unless the termination letter stipulates another date.

A claim is deemed to have been presented when it is received by the regional office of the employment tribunals. The employment tribunals will also register facsimiles of the application. The three-month rule is strictly applied. In *Dedman v British Building & Engineering Appliances Ltd* [1974] ICR 53 Lord Denning said 'If an application arrives a minute after midnight on the last day the clerks must throw it out'.

However, s111(2) ERA 1996 provides that a tribunal may allow a further reasonable period 'in a case where it is satisfied that it is not reasonably practicable for the complaint to be presented before the end of that period of three months'. The tribunals, however, take a strict approach and the onus is on the applicant or his representative to prove to the satisfaction of the tribunal why the application could not have been presented within the limitation period.

The Court of Appeal in *Palmer v Southend-on-Sea Borough Council* [1984] IRLR 119 held that it was a question of fact for the tribunal to decide whether it was 'reasonably feasible to present the complaint to the industrial tribunal within the relevant three months'.

Circumstances under which the tribunal may accept an application that has been made out of time are as follows:

1. illness;
2. misleading advice from Department of Employment officials;
3. misleading advice from an employment tribunal official;
4. ignorance of fact.

In *Defer-Wyatt v Williams* [2003] EAT/0270/03 the applicant resigned from her position with her employer and presented a claim for constructive unfair dismissal. The tribunal held that her claim was out of time because it was presented one day after the three-month limitation period had expired. Mrs Defer-Wyatt appealed. The EAT held that if an employee reasonably holds a mistaken belief as to the correct effective date of termination (EDT), it is not reasonably practicable for the employee to present a claim for unfair dismissal within time. In this case there was confusion over the EDT, confusion that had partly been caused by a letter to Mrs Defer-Wyatt by the employer and therefore the EAT held that an extension of time should be granted.

Ignorance of the law or awaiting criminal proceedings will not be acceptable reasons for submitting an application out of time.

If an applicant has received negligent advice from someone who acts in an advisory capacity such as a citizens advice bureau adviser, a consultant, a solicitor or a trade union official he may be able to bring proceedings in the tort of professional negligence.

Regulation 15 of the Employment Act 2002 (Dispute Resolution) Regulations 2004 provides that where a complaint of unfair dismissal is presented to an employment tribunal and either the statutory disciplinary or grievance procedures are ongoing, the normal time limit of three months will be extended for a further three months, beginning with the day after the day on which the original three months would have expired.

The concept of the EDT is a very important particularly with respect to unfair dismissal.

1. It establishes the end of the employee's period of continuous employment. This is important both for establishing that the employee has the relevant qualifying period and for determining the amount of the basic award for compensation.
2. The relevant age of the employee for the purposes of qualification and calculation of any compensation is the age he has reached at this date.
3. An employee is entitled to request a written statement of reasons for his dismissal after the EDT.

The EDT is strictly construed. Indeed, the courts have gone further and have considered the time of day at which the employee was dismissed as being relevant, even where this has been to the detriment of the employee.

In *Octavius Atkinson & Sons Ltd* v *Morris* [1989] IRLR 158 an employee who was a steel erector was informed at lunch time that no more work was available for him. He left the site at 2 pm and arrived home at about 4 pm. His contract of employment included payment for travelling time. At about the time he arrived home his employers received an urgent message requiring work to be done. The employee claimed unfair dismissal for not having been offered alternative employment.

The industrial tribunal held that he was to be treated as employed until midnight on the day in question and hence the dismissal had been unfair. The EAT, although taking a slightly different route, deemed the dismissal to be unfair as the alternative employment had become available before the contract ended. The Court of Appeal in reversing the decision of the EAT held that the dismissal took effect from the moment the employee was dismissed, ie at lunch time. Accordingly, the alternative employment did not become available until after the dismissal which therefore rendered the dismissal to be fair.

Section 111(3) ERA 1996 provides that where a dismissal takes place with notice an employee may make an application during that notice period.

Discovery

In employment matters, as in any other civil dispute, there may be documentary evidence relating to a disputed issue which is in the possession of one party which the other side wants disclosed to strengthen its case. The party seeking disclosure should make an informal request of the other side for copies of the documents: however, in the event that the documents are not forthcoming it may be necessary for the tribunal to make an order for discovery. In determining whether an order should be made the tribunal will take into account any issues of confidentiality contained within the documents requested. This issue was recently considered by the EAT in *Asda Stores Ltd* v *Thompson* [2002] IRLR 245, where the applicants were dismissed following an investigation into illegal drug-taking at company events. The respondents had carried out an investigation into the allegations, but statements that were taken from other employees were not disclosed to the applicants prior to their dismissal on the grounds that it would breach a promise of confidentiality made to those employees who had made the statements. The applicants applied for discovery of the documents and, at a preliminary hearing, the tribunal found that the documents were both relevant and necessary and should therefore be disclosed in totality. The respondents appealed against the order for disclosure. The EAT held that whilst the tribunal had erred in ordering the documents to be disclosed in full, a tribunal does have the power to order disclosure of documents in anonymised or edited form, which will then preserve the identity of the maker of a statement. Furthermore, the applicants did not need to know the identities of those persons who had made statements with respect to the allegations in order for there to be a fair hearing.

The powers of the tribunal chairman to order disclosure and discovery of documents are now set out in the Employment Tribunals (Constitution and Rules of Procedure) Regulations 2004 (SI 2004/1861), Sch 1.

4.13 Remedies

When an employment tribunal finds that a complaint of unfair dismissal has been established it may then make an order for the applicant to be either reinstated, re-engaged or compensated.

Reinstatement

Where a tribunal considers that it would be practical and appropriate to do so it may issue an order requiring the employer to reinstate the employee.

Section 114 ERA 1996 states that the employer shall treat the complainant in all respects as if he had not been dismissed. In other words, he returns to the same position that he held prior to dismissal and is entitled to all the benefits rights and privileges that may have accrued between the period of dismissal and reinstatement. He is also entitled to retain the seniority that he may have held.

The tribunal must consider whether the employee wishes to be reinstated and whether it is practicable for the employer to comply with an order for reinstatement.

It is not very often that a tribunal orders reinstatement principally because the mutual trust and confidence that should exist between an employer and an employee may have suffered a serious setback.

Re-engagement

Section 115 ERA defines re-engagement as an order on such terms as the tribunal may decide that the complainant be engaged by the employer or by a successor of the employer or by an associated employer in employment comparable to that from which he was dismissed or other suitable employment.

On making an order for re-engagement the tribunal shall specify the terms on which re-engagement is to take place.

Orders for reinstatement or re-engagement are rare and are only occasionally made by employment tribunals. If an employer fails to comply with either of these orders the employee can make a further complaint to the employment tribunal. The tribunal can make an 'additional award' under s117 ERA 1996 and this will be in addition to any other award of compensation for unfair dismissal. The additional award is not less than 26 times, nor more than 52 times, a 'week's pay' as defined in s227(1)(b), which is subject to change each February.

Compensation

Section 112(4) ERA 1996 provides that if the tribunal does not order reinstatement or re-engagement it may allow compensation that will be calculated in accordance with ss118–127A ERA 1996. The compensation generally comprises the basic award, the compensatory award and an amount for loss of statutory rights.

Basic award

The formula for calculating this is the same as for statutory redundancy and takes into consideration the age of the complainant and the complete number of years of service at the EDT. The formula is as follows.

1. Half a week's pay for each year of employment during which the employee was between the ages of 18 and 21.
2. One week's pay for each year of employment during which the employee was between the ages of 22 and 40.
3. One-and-a-half week's pay for each year of employment during which the employee was between the ages of 41 and 65.
4. From the age of 64 to 65 the award will reduce by one-twelfth for every complete month until he reaches the age of 65.

Regardless of the salary earned by the applicant there is a current statutory limit of £280 per week up to a maximum of 20 years. The amount of a 'week's pay' is changed each February by the Secretary of State for the Department of Works and

Pensions. Section 34 of the Employment Relations Act 1999 provides that the Secretary of State must make annual orders to index-link most maximum limits, including a 'week's pay', by reference to changes in the retail prices index (RPI). The maximum that can currently be awarded is £8,400. One interesting question that has arisen recently is whether a tribunal, in calculating the basic award, is entitled to calculate the award on the basis of an hourly rate which is below the national minimum wage. In *Paggetti* v *Cobb* (2002) The Times 12 April (EAT) the applicant, who was a groom, was dismissed from his employment by the respondent. He presented a claim of unfair dismissal which was successful. In determining compensation the tribunal took into consideration the weekly wage received by the applicant, which was below the national minimum wage. Mr Paggetti appealed to the EAT on the grounds that the tribunal, in determining a week's pay, should have taken the national minimum wage into account. The EAT held that in a case of unfair dismissal, an employment tribunal is under a duty to consider the national minimum wage when determining a week's pay for the purpose of calculating the basic award and when calculating the net rate of pay for the loss of earnings element of a compensatory award, even if the applicant has not raised the matter.

Should the applicant be successful in a claim for unfair dismissal arising out of a redundancy situation any statutory redundancy payment made will either reduce or off-set the basic award: s122(4) ERA 1996.

The tribunal may reduce the award if it considers the employee's conduct contributed to his dismissal.

Compensatory award

In addition to the basic award s123 ERA 1996 provides that a tribunal may make a compensatory award up to a maximum of £56,800. This award compensates the applicant for the losses he has suffered due to having been unfairly dismissed. The losses also include any quantifiable fringe benefits such as pension, company car and health care.

The tribunal calculates the compensatory award by taking into consideration: loss of net wages from the date of dismissal to the date of hearing; future loss of net wages until the applicant achieves a comparable rate of pay in new employment; and loss of statutory rights.

This award will also be reduced accordingly if the tribunal deems it just and equitable that the conduct of the applicant contributed to the dismissal.

The applicant will also have to satisfy the tribunal that he has made all reasonable efforts to secure alternative employment; in other words, he is under a duty to mitigate his losses.

The tribunal may sometimes declare that some state benefits should be returned to the state under a recoupment notice.

Any ex-gratia payment made by the employer will be deducted from the compensatory award but the deduction must be made before the statutory maximum is applied.

Injury to feelings
Over the last few years there has been considerable debate as to whether an employment tribunal can make an additional award to an employee who has been unfairly dismissed, to compensate him for injury to feelings which result from the manner of his dismissal.

The general principle which was established in *Norton Tool Co Ltd* v *Tewson* [1972] IRLR 86 provides that in unfair dismissal claims damages can only be awarded for financial loss. This principle was upheld by the House of Lords in *Johnson* v *Unisys Ltd* [2001] IRLR 279 where a claim for compensation in respect of psychiatric injury caused by the manner of the employee's dismissal was dismissed. The majority of the House of Lords considered that because an employee has a statutory right to compensation in the event of an unfair dismissal, it was most unlikely that Parliament intended that there would be a co-existing right to bring the same claim in tort or contract. However, Lord Hoffmann considered obiter that this view was too narrow because a tribunal may award such damages as it considers just an equitable and therefore, in the view of Lord Hoffmann, a tribunal could award damages for distress.

The position has now been clarified by the House of Lords in the case of *Dunnachie* v *Kingston-upon-Hull City Council* [2004] IRLR 727. In this case the applicant, who had been employed as an environmental health officer, claimed that the conduct of his employer was such that he had been constructively unfairly dismissed. He alleged that he had been bullied and harassed by one of his colleagues and that his employer had failed to address his complaints. The tribunal, relying upon the views of Lord Hoffmann in *Johnson*, awarded him £10,000 for injury to feelings. The employer appealed against the decision. The EAT held that non-pecuniary losses are not recoverable in employment tribunals in unfair dismissal claims because such claims were not recoverable prior to *Johnson*, and that Lord Hoffmann's views in *Johnson* were obiter and therefore *Johnson* did not change the position. An appeal by Mr Dunnachie led to a reversal by the Court of Appeal. The Court of Appeal accepted that Lord Hoffmann's views were obiter but held that compensation for injury to feelings was recoverable. The Council appealed further to the House of Lords where it was held that compensation for non-economic loss is not recoverable because s123(1) ERA 1996 does not provide for the recovery of non-economic loss. Lord Steyn considered that the view of Lord Hoffmann was obiter and therefore did not present any obstacle to the House of Lords in coming to its decision.

5

Redundancy

5.1 Introduction

5.2 Dismissal

5.3 Rationalisation or restructuring

5.4 Alternative employment

5.5 Misconduct

5.6 Lay-off and short-time working

5.7 Redundancy payments

5.8 Consultation

5.9 Selection criteria

5.10 Role of the employment tribunal

5.11 Transfer of undertakings

5.1 Introduction

Redundancy is concerned with the dismissal of an employee with or without notice, if the reason for that dismissal falls within s139 ERA 1996, that is, that the employer has ceased or intends to cease the business for which the employee was employed, or to carry on that business in the place where the employee was so employed. A person will also be considered to be redundant if the requirements of a business for employees to carry out work of a particular kind, or for employees to carry out work of a particular kind in the place where the employee was employed by the employer, have ceased, diminished or are expected to cease or diminish.

Dismissed employees, subject to certain exceptions, are entitled to receive a lump-sum payment if the reason for their dismissal is by reason of redundancy or the employee is eligible for a redundancy payment by reason of being laid off or kept on short time: s135 ERA 1996. The payment is calculated according to an employee's age, length of service and pay. The payment is considered to be compensation for the loss of a job and is not intended just to tide a person over until he finds alternative employment. Therefore, an employee who is dismissed by reason of redundancy will be entitled to a lump-sum payment even if he secured alternative employment immediately following his dismissal. Although the word dismissal is used it must be noted that redundancy is a reason for the dismissal and is not a dismissal in the same sense as unfair or wrongful dismissal. An employee who has been made redundant will also be entitled to the Job Seekers' Allowance.

5.2 Dismissal

In order to claim redundancy entitlements an employee must show that he has been dismissed by reason of redundancy. Section 136 ERA 1996 provides that a dismissal takes place if:

1. the employer terminates the contract with or without notice;
2. the fixed-term contract expires without being renewed under the same contract; and
3. the employee terminates the contract with or without notice in circumstances which are such that he is entitled to do so by reason by reason of the employer's conduct: *Marriott* v *Oxford & District Co-operative Society* [1970] 1 QB 186.

A unilateral variation in a contract imposed by an employer upon an employee may amount to a dismissal.

Any person who is employed at the time that a redundancy situation arises but is not working or being paid, perhaps due to sickness, will, provided that he is dismissed, be entitled to redundancy payments: *Marshall* v *Harland & Wolff Ltd* [1972] IRLR 90. There will be no dismissal in the following situations.

1. If there is an agreement on the part of the employer and the employee that the contract should be terminated: *Burton Allton & Johnson Ltd* v *Peck* [1975] IRLR 87 and *Birch* v *University of Liverpool* [1986] ICR 470.
2. If a person secures alternative employment as a result of being told that there may be a redundancy situation but has not actually been made redundant there will be no dismissal: *Morton Sundour Fabrics* v *Shaw* [1967] 2 ITR 84.
3. If there is a clause in the employment contract specifically providing for a variation of contractual terms, and the employer varies the terms, an employee who does not agree with the new terms may not claim that he has been dismissed: *McCaffrey* v *Jeavons & Co Ltd* [1967] 2 ITR 636.

Leaving early

When an employer has given a certain date for termination it is possible for an employee to leave before that date in order to take up alternative employment and yet still preserve his right to a redundancy payment. This may be done by either of the following means.

1. By consensual variation of notice period – the employer and employee may come to an arrangement whereby the employer agrees to the employee leaving before the original date of termination.
2. By s136 ERA 1996 an employee, who has received notice from his employer, can serve a counter-notice, which must be in writing and within the obligatory notice period, stating that he intends to leave before the expiry of the notice period.

An employer is not bound to accept a counter-notice and may, in writing, inform the employee that he requires the employee to serve out his original notice period. If an employee fails to comply he may find that his entitlement to redundancy payments is contested and indeed an employment tribunal may, after hearing representations from both employee and employer, reduce the redundancy payment as it considers just and equitable in the circumstances.

Constructive redundancy

A redundancy can be 'constructive' and this operates in the same way as constructive unfair dismissal. A unilateral variation of the employee's contract such as an enforced change in duties or location, which is caused by a redundancy situation affecting the employee causing him to resign, may amount to a constructive redundancy giving rise to an entitlement to redundancy payments: *Marriott* v *Oxford & District Co-operative Society* [1970] 1 QB 186.

Dismissal for reason of redundancy

An employee will only be entitled to redundancy payments if the dismissal was as a result of a redundancy situation. Section 163(2) ERA 1996 provides that if an employee is dismissed it is presumed to have been by reason of redundancy unless the employer proves otherwise.

Section 139 ERA 1996 provides that an employee shall be taken to be dismissed by reason of redundancy if the dismissal is wholly or mainly attributable to:

1. *Business redundancy* – the fact that his employer has ceased, or intends to cease, to carry on the business for the purposes for which the employee was employed by him.
2. *Location redundancy* – the employer has ceased or intends to cease to carry on that business in the place where the employee was so employed.
3. *Job redundancy* – the fact that the requirements of that business for employees to carry out work of a particular kind, or for employees to carry out that work in the place where they were employed, have ceased or diminished or are expected to cease or diminish.

Business redundancy

This situation arises where an employer closes down the part of the business in which the employee works. It is not necessary for the whole business to be closed down, although in order to be eligible for redundancy payment an employee will have to show that his duties are confined to that part of the business that has been closed down: *Nelson* v *BBC* [1977] IRLR 148. Section 139(6) ERA 1996 provides that the closure does not have to be permanent.

In *Gemmell* v *Darngavil Brickworks Ltd* [1967] 2 ITR 20 the applicant was dismissed by his employer whilst machines in the respondents' brickworks were repaired. The works were closed for 13 weeks, but after 11 weeks the applicant secured alternative employment and applied for a redundancy payment. The Scottish employment tribunal held that Mr Gemmell's dismissal was as a result of the closure of the brickworks, albeit temporarily, and he was therefore entitled to redundancy pay.

For the purposes of s139 ERA 1996 a person carries on in business if he has control of it and it is not necessary to prove that the employer owns the business: *Thomas* v *Jones* [1978] ICR 274.

Location redundancy

This form of redundancy arises when the activities for which the employee was employed cease to be performed at his present location. If an employer relocates his business the question arises as to whether the move creates a redundancy situation. This will be a question of fact and will depend upon the distance between the old and new locations and upon the effect of the new location upon employees.

In *Managers (Holborn) Ltd* v *Hohne* [1977] IRLR 230 the company moved its business from Holborn to Regent Street in London, a distance of less than one mile. The applicant, who was a manageress, claimed that she was entitled to redundancy payments because her contract provided that her place of work was in Holborn. There was no implied term in her contract that she would only be required to work in Holborn. She was, however, entitled to a redundancy payment on other grounds.

The location of work is normally incorporated into the contract of employment but difficulties arise when a contract contains a mobility clause and an employer ceases operation at one location but continues to operate from another. In order to determine where an employee works it is necessary to apply the geographical factual test as opposed to the contractual test. This test was applied by the EAT in *Bass Leisure* v *Thomas* [1994] IRLR 104, and approved by the Court of Appeal in *High Table Ltd* v *Horst* [1997] IRLR 513 where three employees who were employed as waitresses by the respondent catering company claimed that they had been unfairly dismissed. Their claim was that although there had been a diminution in need for their services at their place of work, their contracts contained a mobility clause and they claimed that they should have been redeployed elsewhere. The Court of Appeal held that the dismissals on grounds of redundancy were fair, stating that the place of work should be where the employees actually performed their duties prior to dismissal.

Job redundancy
This situation arises when an employer decides that he requires less employees to carry out existing work, or there is less work for existing employees to carry out. Such a situation may arise in a variety of circumstances.

1. There is less work so fewer employees are needed, such as where there is a fall in orders or where work is contracted out: *Chapman v Goonvean and Rostowrack China Clay Co Ltd* [1973] 2 All ER 1063. In this case the employer provided a free bus service to work for ten of its employees. Three of the employees were made redundant and the employer decided to discontinue the service. The remaining seven employees could no longer get to work and gave in their notice. They claimed constructive redundancy. The Court of Appeal held that the employees had been constructively dismissed but not on the grounds of redundancy because there was no diminution in the requirement of the business for the employees to do work of a particular kind.
2. Technological changes which may result in a change or reduction in particular labour requirements: *Murphy v Epsom College* [1985] IRLR 271. In this case Mr Murphy was employed as an assistant plumber to an existing plumber at the College and about 18 months after he started the College modified the heating-installation system. Following a review of staffing levels it was decided by the College that it would be better to employ a heating engineer to look after all heating installations and assist the existing plumber. It was held by the Court of Appeal that a redundancy situation arises when there is a diminution in the requirement of the business for employees to carry out work of a particular kind, and a reorganisation which creates a substantial change in the kind of work required by the employer can amount to a redundancy situation even though the overall requirements of the employer for work or employees is the same.

5.3 Rationalisation or restructuring

It is recognised that in the commercial and highly competitive market in which most companies operate there is a need to constantly review the structure of an organisation, its branding or its image so that a company can remain competitive within its field.

In *Vaux Breweries v Ward* [1968] 3 ITR 385, following a relaunch of one of their hotels, the brewery dismissed an older barmaid who was replaced by younger 'bunny girl'. The barmaid claimed that she had been made redundant. The High Court stated that the barmaid was not entitled to redundancy payments because the work that was to be done in the altered premises was the same as the work before the relaunch, even though the type of person required to undertake that work was different.

It can be seen therefore that the essential issue for consideration is whether the requirement for the particular type of work that the employee was contracted to perform has ceased or diminished. In *Archibald v Rossleigh Commercials Ltd* [1975] IRLR 231 it was held that the work of an unsupervised emergency night mechanic was of a different type of work to that of an ordinary mechanic who was supervised during the day.

In *Nelson v BBC* [1977] IRLR 148 the Court of Appeal held that in considering whether there is a redundancy situation the correct approach for the tribunals to take is to adopt the 'contractual approach' and consider whether the work that an employee is employed to carry out under his contract of employment to do has ceased or diminished. This approach was affirmed by the Court of Appeal in *Haden v Cowan* [1982] IRLR 314.

The question as to whether a change in hours amounts to work of a particular kind has also been considered. In *Johnson v Nottinghamshire Combined Police Authority* [1974] IRLR 20 in order to maximise efficiency the police authority restructured a shift system so that two clerks who had previously worked from 9.30 am to 5.00 pm would work from 8.30 am to 3 pm and from 1 pm to 8 pm on alternate weeks. The two clerks refused to work the new shift system and were dismissed. They claimed that they were entitled to redundancy payments. It was held by the Court of Appeal that if the only variation in the contract is the hours of work, and there is no change in the actual tasks performed, there cannot be said to be a redundancy within the statutory definition because there has been no change in 'work of a particular kind'.

The matter came under further review in *Lesney Products Ltd v Nolan* [1977] IRLR 77 where a shift system was reorganised resulting in the reduced opportunity for overtime for employees, and those employees who were dismissed for refusing to work the new system claimed that they had been made redundant. The Court of Appeal applied the principles laid down in *Johnson v Nottinghamshire Combined Police Authority* and stated that a reorganisation done in the interest of efficiency and not as a result of a diminution of work required to be carried out by employees does not, of itself, create a redundancy situation.

Section 136(1)(b) ERA 1996 provides that a failure to renew a fixed-term contract is a dismissal for redundancy purposes. Further, an employer who fails to renew a temporary contract, even though it was known by both parties at the outset that there may not be sufficient work at the end of the contract period to justify renewal, may find himself in a redundancy situation.

Transferred redundancy

This situation which is commonly called 'bumping' arises when a redundant employee is moved into another position within an organisation to replace an existing employee. The 'bumped' employee can claim a redundancy payment even though there has been no diminution of his work. This was considered by the Court of Appeal in *North Yorkshire County Council* v *Fay* [1986] IRLR 247, where it was held that provided there was a diminution of someone's work it does not matter that it is not the employer's requirements for the work of the dismissed employee that have ceased or diminished.

However, in *Church* v *West Lancashire NHS Trust* [1998] ICR 423, the EAT expressly cast doubt on this approach. But in the more recent case of *Murray* v *Foyle Meats Ltd* [1999] ICR 827 the House of Lords appeared to restore the previously accepted view that provided that a 'bumped' employee could claim to be redundant even though the job itself had not become redundant. It should be noted, however, that the case of *Murray* was concerned with the issue of selection of employees for redundancy, and therefore because the House of Lords did not specifically reject the view of the EAT this may not be the end of the matter.

5.4 Alternative employment

If, before the end of an employment contract, an employer makes an offer of a new position to a redundant employee, then, provided that the new job commences immediately upon the termination of the old contract or within four weeks of termination, the employee is deemed not to have been dismissed and will no longer be entitled to redundancy payments: s138 ERA 1996. This applies if the offer of alternative employment is made by an associated employer or as a result of a transfer of the business. The offer of alternative employment should be substantially equivalent to the employee's previous employment and an employer will only be able to claim that an employee is not entitled to redundancy payments if one of the following applies.

1. The offer of alternative employment is identical to that from which the employee has been dismissed and the employee turns it down.
2. The new employment contract has different terms and conditions to the original contract but is a suitable offer and the employee has acted unreasonably in rejecting the new position.
3. The new job varies in terms and conditions but the employee accepts it and remains in the new job for the agreed trial period.
4. The new job varies in terms and conditions and the employee accepts it but leaves before the end of the agreed trial period and the job was suitable and the employee has acted unreasonable in rejecting it.
5. The new job varies in terms and conditions and the employee accepts the job but is dismissed for a reason not connected with the change of job, eg misconduct.

The issue of whether work of a lower status is suitable alternative employment was considered in *Taylor* v *Kent County Council* [1969] 2 All ER 1080 where a headmaster who was made redundant was offered alternative employment as one of a pool of mobile teachers. Although his salary was maintained at the previous level he refused the offer of alternative employment, arguing that the drop in status and responsibility made it unsuitable. The High Court held that suitable employment meant employment which was substantially equivalent in status to the redundant position and that in this case the drop in status made the alternative employment unsuitable.

In *Cambridge and District Co-operative Society* v *Ruse* [1993] IRLR 156 it was held that even though the offer of an alternative position was suitable when viewed objectively the fact that the employee felt that it was not, because of the perceived drop in status, did not mean that his refusal to accept was unreasonable. When considering the suitability of alternative employment, pay and conditions will obviously be major factors although the fact that pay and associated benefits remain the same will not automatically render the alternative position suitable.

If an employer fails unreasonably to consider the possibility of alternative employment for a redundant employee this may render the dismissal unfair: *Vokes Ltd* v *Bear* [1974] ICR 1. In determining what is reasonable a tribunal will take into account the size and structure of the employer's business. An employer also has a duty to offer alternative work to employees even where this may involve a demotion: *Avonmouth Construction Ltd* v *Shipway* [1979] IRLR 14, where the EAT held that it is primarily for an employee to determine whether the alternative job is a demotion and not for the employer. An employee who unreasonably refuses an offer of suitable alternative employment will not be entitled to statutory redundancy pay: s141 ERA 1996.

Trial period

An employee who accepts alternative employment is entitled to a trial period to see if the position is a suitable alternative to his previous employment.

In *Elliott* v *Richard Stump Ltd* [1987] IRLR 215 Mr Eliot was employed by the respondents as a cutting-room manager at one of the respondents' factories. The company decided on economic grounds to close the factory which employed Mr Eliot and transfer some of the staff to another factory. The factory to which Mr Eliot was transferred already had a cutting-room manager so the company offered Mr Eliot a job working under the existing manager, but they refused his request for a trial period. Because of this refusal Mr Eliot refused the alternative employment and was dismissed. The EAT held that the refusal of the company to allow a trial period was 'insensitive and unreasonable' and rendered the dismissal unfair.

Section 138(3) ERA 1996 provides that the statutory minimum for a trial period is four weeks and according to the Court of Appeal in *Benton* v *Sanderson Keyser* [1989] IRLR 19 these are calendar weeks. In *Benton* v *Sanderson Kayser* Mr Benton was dismissed prior to Christmas and he began a trial period for a new job which expired on 18 January. He resigned from the new position on 19 January. The employer argued that he was no longer entitled to his redundancy payment because he had resigned after the four-week trial period. Mr Benton argued that the Christmas holiday period of one week should be excluded. It was held by the Court of Appeal that the holiday period should be included and therefore he had lost his right to his redundancy.

Parties may agree a longer trial period provided that the agreement is in writing and is made before the employee commences the new employment.

In the case of a constructive redundancy an employee may have the benefit of a longer trial period without formally agreeing this with his employer. It was held in *Air Canada* v *Lee* [1978] IRLR 392 by the EAT that in a situation where an employer unilaterally alters an employee's terms and conditions, the employee is entitled to a reasonable amount of time in which to decide whether he accepts his employer's breach or not.

In *Turvey* v *C W Cheyney & Sons Ltd* [1979] IRLR 105, following a diminution in work for polishers, the employer offered the employees in that department alternative work. The employees agreed to try the new work but decided after six weeks that the work was not suitable and resigned. The EAT, following the decision in *Air Canada* v *Lee*, held that the four-week statutory trial period did not apply to constructive redundancy and that an employee should be allowed a reasonable period of time in which to decide whether or not a job is suitable. However, after a reasonable period has expired an employee will no longer be able to resign and claim constructive dismissal.

5.5 Misconduct

If, during his notice period, an employee commits an act of misconduct which would entitle an employer to dismiss him without notice, the employee will no longer be entitled to redundancy payments: s140 ERA 1996.

In *Bonner* v *Gilbert Ltd* [1989] IRLR 475 a employee was summarily dismissed during his notice period for alleged theft. The EAT held that where an employer relies upon a reasonable belief of the misconduct of the employee the burden is upon the employer to show that the conduct of the employee was such that it amounted to a significant breach which went to the root of the contract.

Section 140 also operates with respect to employees who are on strike and are then made redundant. Strike action is a breach of the contract of employment which entitles an employer to terminate the contract: *Simmons* v *Hoover Ltd* [1977] IRLR 266. However, where an employee who has been given notice by his employer of a redundancy dismissal subsequently goes on strike, he will not automatically lose his entitlement to all of his redundancy payment. Where an employee goes on strike after being given notice that he is to be made redundant the employer can require the employee to return to work for the period of time that was lost by the strike: s143 ERA 1996. If an employee refuses to comply he will no longer be entitled to redundancy payments, unless he can show that he was unable to comply with the request or it was reasonable in the circumstances for him not to comply: s143(5) ERA 1996.

5.6 Lay-off and short-time working

We have already seen that in order for there to be an entitlement to redundancy payments there normally has to be a dismissal. However, an employer may find that because of short term economic difficulties with a business he has to lay off employees temporarily or reduce the number of hours employees work by putting them on short time. Unless there is an express or implied term in an employee's contract of employment, laying-off or putting employees on short-time work may amount to a repudiatory breach of contract giving rise to a claim for redundancy payments based on a constructive dismissal.

Section 147 ERA 1996 provides that an employee shall be taken to be laid off for a week if he is not provided with work of the type that he is contracted to perform and does not receive any pay. A person will be deemed to have been kept on short time for a week if by reason of the reduction of work provided the employee's pay for the week is less than half a week's pay: s147(2).

An employee who is laid off or on short time will become eligible for a redundancy payment if:

1. the lay-off or short-time working has lasted for more than four consecutive weeks (s148(2)(a)); or
2. the lay-off or short-time working has lasted for a series of six weeks or more within a period of thirteen weeks: s148(2)(b).

The employee must give notice in writing to the employer terminating the contract and indicating his intention to claim redundancy. If the contract of employment contains a notice period the notice period will be the minimum period which the employer is required to give, if not the period of notice will be one week.

Upon receipt of a 'notice of intention to claim' an employer may either agree to pay the redundancy entitlement or may serve a 'counter-notice' stating that he will contest any liability to pay to the employee a redundancy payment. A counter-notice must be in writing and served within seven days of receipt of the 'notice of intention'.

An employee who has served a 'notice of intention' will not be entitled to a redundancy payment if the employer has served a 'counter-notice' and on the date of service of the 'notice of intention' it was reasonably foreseeable that in the next four weeks the employer would be able to provide at least 13 weeks continuous employment, during which time the employee would not be laid-off or put on short-time working.

In some industries, such as the building industry, it is common practice to include a contractual term allowing an employer to lay off employees for an indefinite period if there is a downturn in available work. In *Kenneth McRae & Co Ltd* v *Dawson* [1984] IRLR 5 the EAT held that if there is such a term in a contract of employment it is not subject to the test of reasonableness and therefore an employee cannot claim that he has been constructively dismissed. If an employee considers that he has been laid off for too long, his remedy is to invoke s148 ERA 1996 and claim redundancy.

5.7 Redundancy payments

Entitlement to redundancy payments

An employee who is dismissed on grounds of redundancy will be entitled to a statutory redundancy payment provided that he or she has completed a minimum two years' service with the employer or an associated employer. Continuous service is not broken by periods of lay-off or strike action. However, continuity of employment will be broken if there is no subsisting contract between the employer and employee: *Curr* v *Marks & Spencer plc* [2003] IRLR 75. Any service prior to the employee's eighteenth birthday does not count.

Local authority, health and education service workers have the continuity of employment protection even though they may move from one authority to another.

Many employers provide their employees with an enhanced contractual redundancy payment which is generally significantly more than the statutory minimum. If an employee has a contractual right to an enhanced payment he should receive a payment which is in accordance with his contract. In the absence of such a term in the contract of employment an employee will be solely reliant upon statutory redundancy pay.

Making a claim for redundancy payments

If an employee wishes to make a claim for redundancy payments he must do so by making a written request to the employer for such payments or have commenced proceedings in the employment tribunal in respect of either a claim for redundancy payments or unfair dismissal. A claim for redundancy must be made within six months of the 'relevant date'. This date will depend upon the method by which the employment contract was terminated.

1. If the contract was terminated by notice the 'relevant date' will be the date the notice expired.
2. If the contract was terminated without notice the 'relevant date' will be the date upon which the termination took effect.
3. In the case of the non-renewal of a fixed-term contract it is the date the contract expired.

Non-eligibility

Certain categories of workers are not eligible to receive redundancy payments. These include:

1. share fishermen and certain public office holders;
2. domestic servants in private household who are close relations of their employers;
3. apprentices who have not completed their training;
4. an employee who, on the relevant date, is outside the UK unless the contract of employment stipulates that he ordinarily worked in the UK;
5. employees over the age of 65 if 65 is the normal retiring age in the business in which the employee is employed.

Computation

The amount of a statutory redundancy payment is regulated by statute and will depend upon the age of the employee and the length of time that he has worked for the employer. Section 162 ERA 1996 sets down the appropriate calculations for computing a redundancy payment.

It is necessary first of all to determine the length of time the employee has been employed ending with the 'relevant date' and then to multiply the number of complete years of service by an appropriate amount. The appropriate amount is calculated as follows:

1. one-half of a week's pay for every year of employment in which the employee was under 22 but aged 18 or over;
2. one week's pay for every year of employment in which the employee was over 22 and under 41;
3. one-and-a-half weeks' pay for every year of employment in which the employee was not below the age of 41.

The maximum number of years that will be used for the calculation is 20 working backwards from the 'relevant date', in other words it will be the most recent 20 years that are taken into account. This is particularly important for employees over the age of 41.

Pay

A week's pay will be a normal week's pay subject to the current statutory maximum of £280 which will be increased to £290 from 1 February 2006. Overtime is not generally included unless the employer is legally bound to provide it and the employee is equally bound to work such overtime. Expenses will not be used in the calculation but 'perks' may be taken into consideration by the tribunals.

Written statement

When an employer makes a redundancy payment to an employee he must give a written statement showing how the payment was calculated and a failure to do so will render the employer liable on summary conviction to a fine not exceeding level 1 on the standard scale: s165 ERA 1996.

If an employer fails to give a written statement detailing the calculation of a redundancy payment an employee can request in writing that the employer do so, and a failure to accede to such a request will render an employer liable on summary conviction to a fine not exceeding level three on the standard scale.

5.8 Consultation

The concept of redundancy is sometimes difficult to comprehend. Employees who have worked for an employer for many years with loyalty and fidelity find dismissal by reason of redundancy traumatic. Therefore, to ameliorate this feeling certain procedures have to be followed, failing which a finding of unfair dismissal may result.

The Employment Protection Act 1975 extended collective bargaining to cover consultation over redundancies. Such consultation is now governed by s188 Trade Union and Labour Relations (Consolidation) Act (TULR(C)A) 1992 which has been amended by the Trade Union Reform and Employment Rights Act 1993 and by the Collective Redundancies and Transfer of Undertakings (Protection of Employment) (Amendment) Regulations 1995. These amendments were necessary because in *EC Commission* v *United Kingdom* Case C–373/92 [1994] IRLR 142 it was held by the ECJ that the original provisions of TULR(C)A 1992 did not correctly implement art 2 of EC Directive on Collective Redundancies (75/129/EEC) with respect to consultation with employees' representatives.

Nevertheless, despite the amendment, it still appeared that art 2 of the EC Directive on Collective Redundancies had not been fully implemented because there was no mechanism for the election of employee representatives. To remedy this the Collective Redundancies and Transfer of Undertakings (Protection of Employment) (Amendment) Regulations 1999 were passed to provide for the election of representatives by inserting s188A into TULR(C)A 1992.

Section 195 TULR(C)A 1992 provides that for the purposes of consultation a redundancy is a 'dimissal for a reason not related to the individual concerned or a number of reasons all of which are not so related'.

Duty of employers to consult with representatives

An employer proposing to dismiss 20 or more employees at one establishment within a period of 90 days or less shall consult about the dismissals with all the persons who are appropriate representatives of any of the employees who may be dismissed: s188 TULR(C)A 1992.

An employer must begin consultation at the earliest opportunity and s188(1A) TULR(C)A 1992 provides that:

1. where the employer is proposing to dismiss as redundant 100 or more employees at one establishment consultation should take place at least 90 days before the dismissals take effect;
2. if the employer is proposing to make less than 100 employees redundant consultation should take place at least 30 days before the first dismissal takes effect.

'Proposing'

In *Hough* v *Leyland DAF Ltd* [1991] IRLR 194 the EAT held that before an employer can be said to be proposing redundancies matters must have reached a stage where a specific proposal has been formulated. This would appear to be out of line with the purpose of Council Directive 75/129/EEC which requires that consultation should take place with the objective of avoiding large-scale redundancies although the EAT considered that on a matter of linguistic construction their decision was not in conflict with the Directive. However, a prudent employer will enter into a period of consultation at the earliest opportunity, bearing in mind the need to balance the requirements of openness and consultation with business efficacy, confidence and motivation.

'Establishment'

It is important to consider the meaning of 'establishment' because s188 only applies if those persons who are being dismissed are at the same establishment. If there are several associated businesses at the same establishment, but they are separate distinct trading units, then the numbers of employees will not be aggregated. Conversely, it may be the case that an employer has several sites which may be considered to be one establishment if each site is lacking a degree of permanence or its own administrative structure: *Barratt Developments Ltd* v *UCATT* [1978] IRLR 403.

Appropriate representatives

The representatives with whom an employer has an obligation to consult will be those representatives elected by the employees either as union representatives or those specifically elected for the purpose of redundancy consultation. If employees who may be affected by redundancy are represented by an independent trade union recognised for collective bargaining purposes, that union has an automatic right to be informed and consulted over collective redundancies. An employer cannot bypass the union in favour of other employee representatives.

Section 188(1B) TULR(C)A 1992 details who are the appropriate representatives of any affected employees. If the employees are of a description in respect of which an independent trade union is recognised by their employer, those representatives are representatives of the trade union. In any other case, the appropriate representatives are employee representatives.

Consultation process

When consulting with the appropriate representatives the following matters should be considered:

1. any ways in which the dismissals can be avoided;
2. the possibilities of reducing the numbers of employees to be dismissed;
3. the ways in which the consequences of dismissals can be mitigated.

In order to facilitate the consultation process between employers and representatives s188(4) TULR(C)A 1992 provides that the employer should state in writing to the representatives the numbers and descriptions of employees that he is proposing to dismiss and the total number of employees of that description at the establishment in question. The employer must also outline the method of selecting those employees to be made redundant, the proposed method of carrying out the dismissals and, if the redundancy payments are to be more favourable than the statutory minimum, the proposed method of calculating the payments. The consultation process should be meaningful and not just a paper exercise.

The nature of consultation which may be regarded as meaningful was discussed by the EAT in *Securicor Omega Express Ltd* v *GMB* [2004] IRLR 9, where the EAT considered that consultation within the meaning of s188 must be fair and meaningful. In this case a meeting was held with union representatives after a decision to make employees redundant had been made. Nevertheless, the EAT considered that the meeting was meaningful because the consultation included discussions on reducing the number of redundancies which were in fact successful. This decision of the EAT appears to limit the scope of what will amount to 'meaningful' consultation. It is questionable just how meaningful consultation can be if the decision to dismiss has already been made and is surely limited, as in this case, to reducing the number of redundancies and possible redeployment.

To avoid unfairness, consultation with potential redundant individual employees is particularly likely to be necessary if:

1. they are not members of a recognised union so that, although the union has to be consulted about the proposed redundancies, the presumption is that the union will not keep non-union members informed about the consultation;
2. there is no recognised union for the employment group to which the employees belong;
3. the employee is in a senior position.

The EAT in *Freud* v *Bentalls Ltd* [1982] IRLR 443 stated:

'... in the particular sphere of redundancy, good industrial relations practice in the ordinary case requires consultation with the redundant employee so that the employer may find out whether the needs of the business can be met in some other way than by dismissal and, if not, what other steps the employer can take to ameliorate the blow to the employee.'

The importance of consultation was affirmed by the House of Lords in *Polkey* v *A E Dayton Services* [1988] AC 344. Mr Polkey was one of four van drivers. The employer decided to cut costs by reducing the number of van drivers to three and adding salesman duties to the remaining drivers. The employer took the view that Mr Polkey was the least suitable person to take on the new role and dismissed him without any consultation or warning. At the employment tribunal, the EAT and the Court of Appeal the employers successfully pursued a line of argument given force by the EAT in the earlier case of *British Labour Pump* v *Byrne* [1979] IRLR 94 that lack of procedure would have made no difference to the outcome. However, the House of Lords in allowing the appeal by Mr Polkey rejected the argument. Lord Bridge suggested that:

'... in the case of redundancy, the employer will normally not act reasonably unless he warns and consults with any employees affected or their representatives, adopts a fair basis on which to select for redundancy and takes such steps as may be reasonable to avoid or minimise redundancy by redeployment within his organisation ... the one question the industrial tribunal is not permitted to ask in applying the test of reasonableness by s57(3) EP(C)A 1978 [now s98 ERA 1996] is the hypothetical question whether it would have made any difference to the outcome if the appropriate procedural step had been taken. On the true construction this question is simply irrelevant.'

In *Mugford* v *Midland Bank* [1997] IRLR 208 Mr Mugford was a bank manager with Midland Bank plc with over 20 years' service. In 1995 Midland Bank planned a reorganisation involving some 3,000 redundancies of which 858 were from the ranks of managers. The bank had an agreement with BIFU (the Banking Union) on the procedures to be adopted in the event of potential redundancies. The procedures underlined consultation with the union but made no reference to consultation with individual employees. From March 1995 Mr Mugford underwent a series of briefings which included redundancy selection criteria. Mr Mugford's employers eventually made him redundant because according to the employers he did not meet the required standard in credit skills and risk management. Efforts were made to find alternative employment but to no avail and he was dismissed on 30 September 1995. Mr Mugford claimed that he had been unfairly dismissed on the grounds, inter alia, that there had been no consultation or inadequate consultation.

An employment tribunal held that Mr Mugford had been selected fairly as the employers had exercised an objective criteria and that proper consideration had been given to find alternative employment. The tribunal also concluded that the employers' consultation with the union was sufficient to fulfil the obligation to consult. Mr Mugford appealed to the EAT stating that the finding of the tribunal that there had been adequate consultation was perverse. The EAT held that the tribunal had not erred in law as the employers had fulfilled their duty to consult by doing so with the union of which the employee was a member and dismissed the appeal.

The employers in *Mugford* relied upon Lord Bridge's comment in the House of Lords' decision in *Polkey* v *A E Dayton Services* [1988] AC 344 that an employer will not normally be acting reasonably 'unless he warns and consults any employees affected or their representatives'. The employers therefore argued that they had fulfilled the obligation by consulting the union. Whether an employer has acted reasonably is a question of fact for a tribunal to decide. Following *Polkey* there is no obligation for an employer to consult with an employee if there is a union involved. However, there was extensive discussion of this matter in *Mugford* and there was support for the proposition that individual employees should also be consulted to enable them to evaluate the criteria and put forward proposals of their own.

In *John Brown Engineering Ltd* v *Brown & Others* [1997] IRLR 90 John Brown Engineering Ltd (JBE) were faced with a redundancy situation. Four unions represented the workforce and JBE entered into consultation and agreed redundancy selection criteria to be applied to the workforce. Redundancy was based on a marking system and Brown and a few others were selected. They complained to an employment tribunal that they had been unfairly dismissed. The basis of their complaint was that as they had no access to their individual marks they could not challenge the fairness of their selection and any internal appeal that was held was therefore a 'sham'.

The tribunal, in upholding the employees' claim, agreed that the internal appeal hearings were a sham and held that there had been no fair consultation. The employers had refused to disclose the marks not only to the individuals but also to their unions. That refusal breached fairness under s98(4) ERA 1996. The employers appealed to the EAT, contending that there was no requirement to consult individuals affected by redundancy provided they had followed agreed criteria and had implemented the criteria fairly and cited as authorities, inter alia, *British Aerospace plc* v *Green & Others* [1995] IRLR 433 (CA). The EAT held that the tribunal had not erred in holding that the employees had been unfairly dismissed. Individual consultation is not a requirement but if employers withheld markings in a redundancy selection process, thus depriving redundant employees the opportunity to challenge dismissal, the employers could be acting unfairly. The tribunal only had to consider the issue of whether the employers had treated the employees in a fair manner and were correct in concluding that the internal appeals were a sham for the lack of disclosure of the marks.

Failure to consult

If an employer has dismissed as redundant, or is proposing to dismiss as redundant, any of his employees and fails to comply with the requirements of s188 TULR(C)A 1992 then either the representative trade union or the individual concerned may present a complaint to an employment tribunal. If the tribunal finds the complaint well-founded it can make a declaration to that effect and may also make a protective award. A protective award is an award ordering the employer to pay remuneration for the protected period. The protected period begins with the date on which the first of the dismissals to which the complaint relates takes effect, or the date of the award, whichever is the earlier, and will be of such length as the tribunal determines to be just and equitable in all the circumstances, taking into account the seriousness of the employer's failure to comply with any requirement of s188. The protective period shall not exceed 90 days. The purpose of the protective award is to punish an employer who has not engaged in consultation or has not adaquatley consulted representatives. In *Susie Radin Ltd* v *GMB and Others* [2004] IRLR 400 the Court of Appeal dismissed an argument that the award was compensatory and restated that the award was most definitely a penalty.

Where a tribunal makes a protective award every employee to whom the award relates is entitled to be paid remuneration by his employer for the protected period. The rate of remuneration payable is one week's pay for each week of the period: in the event that the protected period is less than one week the remuneration will be calculated by reducing proportionately the amount of a week's pay. In *Susie Radin Ltd* the employer paid a protective award of 90 days' salary to each affected employee which amounted to approximately £250,000.

The approach that has generally been taken is that an employee who has been made redundant would be entitled to a sum which represents any additional time he would have been employed if consultation had taken place. However, recently the EAT has adopted a broader approach in the case of *Elkouil* v *Coney Island Ltd* [2002] IRLR 174, where the applicant was made redundant without any warning or consultation even though the employers had known for some weeks that he would be dismissed. At the employment tribunal it was held that the dismissal was unfair, although the tribunal accepted that the employee would have been dismissed even if consultation had taken place. In determining compensation the tribunal adopted the conventional method of awarding compensation for the period of time that the employee would have been employed if consultation had taken place. The tribunal awarded the applicant two weeks' pay, which represented the additional time the applicant would have had in work if consultation had taken place. The EAT held that the tribunal had failed to take into account the fact that the employers knew of the applicant's impending redundancy about ten weeks before he was dismissed. If the employers had warned the applicant at an earlier stage he would have had more opportunity to find alternative employment. The EAT considered that because the applicant had lost the chance of being re-employed earlier than he was, he should be awarded ten weeks' pay rather than the two awarded by the tribunal.

5.9 Selection criteria

When an employer is proposing to make some members of the workforce redundant he will want to select which employees will be retained and which employees to make redundant. In order for a redundancy to be regarded as a fair redundancy the selection criteria used by the employer must be carefully and exactly defined so that they can be fairly and consistently applied to each affected employee. The selection criteria must also be agreed by the employees' representatives.

An employer's duty is to be fair both to the employee and to the business in all circumstances. An employer must ensure that he acts reasonably in treating redundancy 'as a sufficient reason for dismissing the employee': s98(4) ERA 1996. Furthermore, an employer who has warned of impending redundancies may invite voluntary redundancies. In *British Aerospace plc* v *Green* [1995] ICR 1006 the Court of Appeal stated:

> 'It has been accepted from the outset of the unfair dismissal jurisdiction that the concept of fairness, when applied to the selection process for redundancy, is capable of being expressed in absolute terms. There are no cut and dried formulae and no short cuts ...'

An employer who is proposing redundancies must ensure that the selction criteria are fair and aconsistently applied.

The following are examples of selection criteria:

1. length of service;
2. appraisals;
3. skills;
4. sickness/absence records;
5. disciplinary records;
6. qualifications;
7. aptitude.

In the past employers relied on the principles of last in first out (LIFO) to select for redundancy but practices have changed and business needs form the basis of employment matters. The above criteria can be applied singly or cumulatively. The employer may be under an obligation to disclose the selection criteria to the dismissed employees to enable any challenge of the decision.

The following selection criteria would be regarded as unfair and could give rise to claims of unfair dismissal or discrimination:

1. trade union reasons;
2. carrying out duties relating to redundancy, as an elected representative of the employees;
3. maternity;
4. sex, race, disability, sexual orientation or religious belief.

5.10 Role of the employment tribunal

In the event that a claim is presented to an employment tribunal, the tribunal must establish that the real reason for dismissal was redundancy. The tribunal itself has to decide whether or not in the circumstances, including the size and administrative resources of the employer's undertaking, the employer acted reasonably when dismissing the employee: s98(4) ERA 1996. Tribunals will also have to consider well established principles, even though they have not been expressly pleaded by the parties or raised at the hearing: *Langston* v *Cranfield University* [1998] IRLR 172.

5.11 Transfer of undertakings

In today's commercial climate businesses may transfer from one owner to another several times during the course of an employee's working life. Historically, if the owner of a business enterprise wanted to sell his business to another neither he nor the new owner were under any legal duty to the employees. In order to protect workers in the event of a transfer of a business from one owner to another the Acquired Rights Directive (77/187/EEC) was passed to safeguard the rights of workers in the event of a change of employer. The Acquired Rights Directive provided that an employee of a business that was sold would continue to work for the new employer under the same terms and conditions as agreed with their previous employer.

The Acquired Rights Directive was implemented in the UK by means of the Transfer of Undertakings (Protection of Employment) Regulations 1981 (SI 1981/1794), more commonly referred to as TUPE. The original regulations did not fully implement the Directive and had to be amended. More surprisingly, at the time the House of Lords in *Litster* v *Forth Dry Dock & Engineering Co Ltd* [1989] ICR 341 said that TUPE should be interpreted purposively to give effect to the European Court's interpretation of the provisions of the Acquired Rights Directive. The Acquired Rights Directive and the 1998 amending directive (98/50/EC) were repealed in 2001 and replaced by a new consolidating directive – the Acquired Rights Directive (2001/23/EC) – which changed some numbering but nothing else of substance.

In order to afford protection to employees in the event of a transfer of a business the concept of automatic transfer of employees was adopted. TUPE aims to provide for automatic transfer of employees by adopting the following measures:

1. Automatically transferring to the new employer most of the relevant employees' contractual rights and obligations.
2. Imposing on the parties to the transfer an obligation to inform and consult with employee representatives (originally only trade union representatives) before the transfer takes effect.

3. Ensuring that certain collective trade union agreements are observed for a period of at least one year after the transfer.
4. Providing that any dismissals for a reason connected with the transfer will be automatically unfair, subject to certain exceptions which are of an economic, technical or organisational nature.

TUPE does not apply to the following:

1. Transfers of a business solely through a transfer of shares – there is no transfer of the business and the same company continues to be the employer: *Brookes* v *Borough Care Services Ltd* [1998] IRLR 636.
2. Transfers of assets only – the sale of equipment alone would not be covered, but the sale of a going concern including equipment would be covered.
3. Transfers of a contract to provide goods or services where this does not involve the transfer of a business or part of a business.
4. Transfers of undertakings situated outside the United Kingdom.

Meaning of undertaking

Article 1(1) of the Directive provides that the Directive shall apply to the transfer of an undertaking, business or part of a business to another employer as a result of the legal transfer or merger. The aim of the Directive is therefore to ensure continuity of employment within a business irrespective of any change of ownership. However, problems have arisen in defining an undertaking for the purpose of the Directive and reg 3 of TUPE. In *Spijkers* v *Gebroeders Benedik Abbatoir CV* Case 24/85 [1986] 3 ECR 1119 a slaughterhouse business became insolvent. However, assets such as buildings and stock were purchased by another company and used to continue a similar operation. The question for determination was whether there had been a transfer within the meaning of art 1(1) Acquired Rights Directive. It was established by the European Court of Justice (ECJ) that the decisive criterion is whether the business in question retains its identity and that the mere sale of assets is not sufficient to constitute a transfer. Factors that will be taken into consideration by the courts will include the nature of the undertaking, any transfer of tangible assets, the value of intangible assets, the number of staff transferred, the transfer of customers and the degree of similarity between the entity before and after transfer.

Contracting-out

In its original form TUPE did not apply to the transfer of contractual arrangements such as franchises and the contracting out of public services such as hospital cleaning contracts. The approach adopted by the ECJ in its interpretation of the Acquired Rights Directive was much more broad and in *Rask & Christensen* v *ISS Kantineservice* [1993] IRLR 133 the ECJ held that the contracting-out of a catering service which was only ancillary to the transferors's business to another company in return for a management fee did constitute a transfer for the purposes of the Directive. The fact that the contractor (the transferee) would be using the same premises, equipment and maintenance services of the transferor did not preclude the operation of the Directive. In *Schmidt* v *Spar* [1995] ICR 237 the ECJ went so far as to hold that one cleaning lady using a mop and bucket provided by the contractor was a distinct unit of activity and was subject to the protection afforded by the Directive.

The TUPE Regulations were amended by Trade Union Reform and Employment Rights Act 1993 to provide that the Regulations apply to the contracting-out of services, franchising and licensing arrangements. Following the amendments to TUPE the courts and tribunals adopted the broad approach much favoured by the ECJ when considering 'contracting-out cases'. Where an economic entity was substantially the same after it was sold by the transferor to the transferee any employees affected by the transfer would receive the protection afforded by TUPE. However, in a surprising decision of the ECJ it appears that such a broad approach may be limited.

In *Suzen* v *Zehnacker Gebaudereinigung GmbH Krankenhaus Service and Lefarth GmbH* [1997] IRLR 255 Mrs Suzen had worked for a contractor in a secondary school in Germany but was dismissed when her employers lost the cleaning contract. She claimed that her contract ought to have been transferred to the new contractor. It was held by the ECJ, following the opinion of the Advocate-General, that the Directive does not apply in a situation where one contract is terminated and another contract awarded for the performance of similar work if there is no concomitant transfer from one undertaking to the other of significant tangible or intangible assets or taking over by the new employer of a major part of the workforce in terms of their numbers and skills. The Court also considered that the lack of a contractual link between the two undertakings successively charged with the contract may point to an absence of a transfer but is one factor to be considered and is not conclusive.

This decision of the ECJ represented a significant change of emphasis. The Court considered the established factors but then went on to say that there is no automatic transfer of an economic entity merely because the service provided by the old and new contractors is similar.

This decision gave rise to a great deal of uncertainty as to whether TUPE applies to a change of contractors. Whilst the Court considered that the transfer of assets is one criteria to be taken into account it clearly stated that the absence of the transfer of such assets does not preclude the existence of such a transfer.

Initially the tribunals applied the decision in *Suzen* rigorously. In *Connick Tree Care* v *Chapman* (1997) (unreported) it was held that there was no transfer when a contract passed from one business to another because the transferee only took on one of two employees, did not purchase or take on any of the equipment of the transferor and the organisation and administration of the new entity was different to the business prior to transfer.

In *Betts & Others* v *Brintel Helicopters Ltd (Defendants) and KLM ERA*

Helicopters (UK) Ltd (Defendants/Appellants) [1997] IRLR 361 the applicants had worked for Brintel Helicopters who had a contract with Shell (UK) Ltd transporting men and goods to North Sea oil rigs. When the contract was due to expire Shell awarded KLM the new contract. KLM did not take over any staff or equipment. nor did they use the same helicopter base. Seven employees who had worked for Brintel claimed that there had been a transfer within TUPE of the undertaking to provide helicopter services to Shell, a claim that was upheld by the High Court.

However, the Court of Appeal adopted the approach taken by the ECJ in *Suzen* and held that the first of all it was necessary to consider the nature of Brintel's operation and then to look at whether that undertaking had been transferred so that it retained its identity in the hands of KLM. On the facts Kennedy LJ considered that whilst there was an undertaking or economic entity such were the differences in the operation upon transfer it could not be considered to be a transfer under TUPE.

The similarity of an enterprise before and after transfer is no longer a crucial factor in determining whether TUPE applies but just one factor to be taken into consideration. In *Betts* Kennedy LJ also drew a distinction between labour-intensive undertakings where the activity continues with substantially the same staff after the transfer so that it retains its identity and is therefore more likely to be a relevant transfer, and other less labour-intensive undertakings where a more wide-ranging inquiry is necessary to decide whether there has been a transfer for the purpose of TUPE.

However, in *ECM (Vehicle Delivery Service)* v *Cox and Others* [1999] IRLR 559 the Court of Appeal questioned the strict application of the decision of the ECJ in *Suzen*. In *ECM* the applicants were employed by Axial Ltd who had a contract to collect imported cars at Grimsby and Folkestone and deliver the vehicles to dealers. Axial Ltd lost the contract for collection from Grimsby to ECM. The Axial employees consulted with their union on the possibility of claiming unfair dismissal if they were not employed by ECM and for this reason ECM did not take on any of Axial's workforce.

The employees pursued their claim for unfair dismissal and succeeded at the employment tribunal. The tribunal found that the new contractor did not take on the men precisely because they were asserting that TUPE applied. Not surprisingly ECM appealed. The EAT held that the tribunal was correct in holding that there had been a transfer of undertaking. ECM further appealed to the Court of Appeal.

The Court of Appeal dismissed the appeal. The decision in *Suzen* did not require there to be a transfer of employees for there to be a transfer of undertaking otherwise the purpose of the Directive would be subverted. The essential elements to consider following *Suzen* were whether there was an economic activity as distinct from a mere activity, and whether the economic activity retained its identity after the transfer. In this case both requirements were satisfied.

Thus, in *Francisco Hernandez Vidal SA* v *Gomez Perez & Others* [1999] IRLR 132 the ECJ attempted to clarify the issues raised as a result of their decision in *Suzen* and provided further guidance. In this case a cleaning contract was brought to an end and the cleaning work taken back in-house. The two applicant cleaners were dismissed. The ECJ said that in determining whether there has been a transfer of an economic entity several factors should be considered:

1. the entity must be stable;
2. the entity must not be limited to performing one specific works contract;
3. it must be an organised grouping of persons and assets.

It would appear that there can be a transfer of an undertaking even though there is no significant transfer of assets or a majority of the workforce. All the facts characterising the transaction in question must be taken into account and the decisive criterion is whether the business in question retains its identity: *RCO Support Services Ltd* v *Unison & Others* [2002] ICR 751.

The DTI has recently issued a consultation paper on the draft Transfer of Undertakings (Protection of Employment) Regulations 2005 which it is proposed will come into effect in late 2005. The new Regulations will extend TUPE to service contracting operations such as cleaning services and increase the transparency of the transfer process by introducing a requirement on the old employer to notify the new employer of any employment liabilities. Helpfully the new Regulations will clarify the circumstances in which an employers can lawfully make transfer-related dismissals and negotiate transfer-related changes to terms and conditions of employment for 'economic, technical or organisational' reasons. The new Regulations will also be more flexible to encourage rescue operations and the transfer of insolvent businesses.

Non-commercial undertakings

Originally TUPE did not apply to non-profit-making undertakings. In *Dr Sophie Redmond Stichting* v *Bartol* [1992] IRLR 366 the ECJ held that the concept of a 'legal transfer' in art 1(1) of the Acquired Rights Directive must be interpreted broadly and held that it applied where a local authority who had been funding a drug-rehabilitation foundation transferred the grant to another foundation carrying out similar work. TUPE was subsequently amended so that the Regulations now apply to the transfer of any 'trade or business' and include charitable activities.

Employee protection

The TUPE Regulations provide that an employee will be protected in the event of a transfer if he is employed at the time of the transfer. In order for an employee to come within the protection afforded by the Regulations:

1. he should be employed under a contract of employment;
2. he should be employed by the transferor (ie the company selling the business);
3. he should be employed in the undertaking or part of the undertaking to be transferred;

4. he must be employed immediately before the transfer;
5. his employment contract would otherwise have been terminated as a result of the transfer.

Employed under a contract of employment
Regulation 2(1) TUPE defines an 'employee' as:

> 'Any individual who works for another person whether under a contract of service or apprenticeship or otherwise but does not include anyone who provides services under a contract for services ...'

Thus, any employee who is working under a contract of service will come within the class of persons who are protected by the Regulations. Whether a person is an employee is a question of fact, albeit in some circumstances a difficult question of fact, to be determined taking into account all the factors previously discussed in Chapter 2.

Transfers and part transfers
The TUPE Regulations only apply to a transfer of undertaking or part of an undertaking by the transferor to the transferee so that the economic entity after the transfer is substantially the same as it was prior to the transfer. Where a whole organisation is transferred the question of transfer will be one of fact. However, it becomes more difficult to determine if there has been a 'relevant transfer' for the purposes of TUPE where the undertaking transferred is part of a larger business or a more complicated company structure. Difficulties may also arise where an employee has a wide job description which provides that he carries out duties for different parts of an organisation and it is not therefore clear whether he is employed in the part of the undertaking that is being transferred.

To overcome these difficulties the tribunals and courts have devised two tests. The first considers the organisational framework of the economic entity to be transferred and whether the particular employee or employees were assigned to work within this part of the group. The second test considers whether affected employees were located within the particular entity that has been transferred. In practice courts will generally use an amalgamation of the two tests to determine whether or not an employee works for the part of an organisation that is to be transferred.

In *Duncan Web Offset (Maidstone) Ltd* v *Cooper* [1995] IRLR 633 Mr Cooper, a purchasing manager, had carried out duties for several subsidiary companies owned by a parent company. Part of the group went into receivership and the question was whether Mr Cooper was assigned to the business of the group transferred. The EAT said that where a person in assigned to a particular group, but carries out duties elsewhere within the organisation, it would take persuasive evidence to show that he was not a part of the group to which he was originally assigned if that group was transferred. In this case the EAT held that Mr Cooper was an employee of the part of the company transferred and was therefore entitled to the protection afforded by

TUPE. The EAT stressed that tribunals will be keen to ensure that the protection of TUPE is not evaded by the use of service companies or complex group structures which may conceal reality.

If an employee is employed by a holding company, or has a job description which gives him responsibility for various organisations within a group, the question of whether he is employed by the transferor can also be difficult to determine. This question was considered by the EAT in *Michael Peters Ltd* v *Farnfield* [1995] IRLR 190 where Mr Farnfield was employed as the chief executive of a holding company. The company and its subsidiaries ran into financial difficulties and receivers were appointed. Interest was expressed in some of the subsidiary companies which were sold. Mr Farnfield was not transferred as a result of the sale and claimed that he had been unfairly dismissed. The tribunal considered that the parent company and its subsidiaries could be regarded as a single economic unit for the purposes of TUPE. However, the EAT rejected this and held that because Mr Fairfield was not employed in any of the undertakings transferred TUPE did not apply.

Employed immediately before the transfer
The requirement of reg 5(3) that an employee must be employed by the transferor immediately before the transfer has caused some difficulties. The Directive states that it is the date upon which the transfer takes place that should be taken into account. However, the ECJ and national courts have referred to both the date and the time of transfer.

In *Secretary of State for Employment* v *Spence* [1987] QB 179 the Court of Appeal took the view that a literal interpretation meant that an employee had to be employed by the transferor moments before the transfer. In this case employees were dismissed three hours before the business was transferred. They were taken on by the transferee but nevertheless claimed that they were entitled to redundancy payments from the state because the transferor had gone into liquidation. The Court of Appeal held that reg 5(1) and (2) relates only to contracts of employment that subsist at the moment of transfer, and the words 'employed immediately before the transfer' in reg 5(3) must be interpreted in that sense.

The decision of the Court of Appeal in *Spence* was reviewed by the House of Lords in *Litster* v *Forth Dry Dock & Engineering Co Ltd* [1989] IRLR 161 where employees were dismissed just one hour before the undertaking was transferred. The House of Lords considered that in order to conform with the Acquired Rights Directive they should adopt a purposive interpretation of reg 5 and it was held that the employees were still employed at the time of the transfer. The decision of the Court of Appeal in *Spence* was distinguished because in *Litster* the employees were dismissed an hour before the transfer in an attempt to avoid the operation of the TU(PE) Regulations.

The effect of the decision of the House of Lords in *Litster* is that if an employee is dismissed before or after the transfer of an undertaking for a reason connected with the transfer then any such dismissal will be automatically unfair.

Consideration was also given to the question of whether a dismissal connected to a transfer is in effect a nullity. Lord Oliver in *Litster* said that 'it follows from the construction that I attach to reg 5(3) that where an employee is dismissed before and by reason of the transfer, the employment is statutorily continued with the transferee by virtue of the Regulations'. This approach was adopted by the Court of Appeal in *Wilson & Others* v *St Helens Borough Council* [1997] IRLR 505, but on appeal to the House of Lords ([1998] IRLR 706) it was said that the Court of Appeal had erred in its view that a dismissal is a nullity. In *Wilson* Lord Slynn of Hadley said that when the view of Lord Oliver in *Litster* was read as whole it did not support the contention that a dismissal either prior to a transfer or following a transfer is a nullity. The decision of the House of Lords in *Wilson* has therefore clarified this issue and thus if an employee is dismissed the dismissal will be effective. However, if the employee wishes to pursue a claim for wrongful or unfair dismissal he may bring the claim against the transferor if the entity in which he worked prior to the dismissal has been transferred.

Another issue which has caused concern is the point at which a transfer actually takes effect. In *Celtec Ltd* v *Ashley* Case C–478/03 [2005] IRLR 647 the ECJ held that a TUPE transfer occurs at a specific point in time and cannot be postponed by the parties. In this case civil servants were temporarily seconded from the Department of Education to Training and Enterprise Councils which were privatised bodies. When the employees were subsequently dismissed or threatened with dismissal the issue of continuity of employment arose with respect to the calculation of redundancy payments. Celtec Ltd rejected the proposition that the date for continuity of employment should run from the day when the employees had joined the civil service and argued that art 3(1) of the Acquired Rights Directive which provides that the 'transferor's rights and obligations arising from a contract of employment or from an employment relationship existing on the date of a transfer … shall, by reason of such transfer, be transferred to the transferee' did not apply where a transfer had taken place over a period of time. The Court of Appeal held that art 3(1) did apply to the transfer of an undertaking which took place over several years. However, the House of Lords referred the matter to the ECJ which ruled that the 'date of a transfer' within art 3(1) was the date on which responsibility as employer for carrying on the business of the unit transferred moved from the transferor to the transferee.

Automatic transfer

We have already seen that the effect of TUPE is to provide for the automatic transfer of all rights and obligations from the transferor to the transferee. Consideration has been given as to whether TUPE applies where affected employees are unaware of the transfer or the identity of their new employer. In *Photostatic Copiers (Southern) Ltd* v *Okuda and Japan Office Equipment Ltd* [1995] IRLR 11 the EAT held that employees should be aware of the transfer because not only do employees have the right to know the identity of their employer, they also have the right to object to a transfer and if they are unaware of the transfer they cannot exercise this right.

The issue of automatic transfer was considered by the ECJ in *Rotsart de Hertaing v J Benoidt SA and IGC Housing Services SA* [1997] IRLR 127. In this case Mrs Rotsart was employed as a receptionist by a company calling itself Housing Services. On 19 November 1993 the company changed its name to Benoidt and went into liquidation. Its activities were subsequently carried out by a newly formed company IGC Housing Services. On the 23 November 1993 Mrs Rotsart was given six months notice of dismissal to run from 1 December. However on 22 December she was dismissed with immediate effect by the liquidator on the grounds of gross misconduct.

She brought proceedings against Benoidt in liquidation and IGC Housing Services. IGC Housing Services argued that they had never been her employers and therefore could not have dismissed her. In the Brussels tribunal it was held that there had been a transfer of an undertaking but that Mrs Rotsart's contract had not been transferred. The matter was referred to the ECJ where it was held that art 3 of the Directive is to be interpreted as meaning that all employment contracts existing at the time of the transfer and concerning all staff employed in the undertaking are to be transferred without any option on the part of the transferee. Staff are to be transferred regardless of any refusal by the transferee to comply with this obligation. They are transferred on the date of the transfer and neither the transferee or the transferor may fix a later date.

The principles laid down by the ECJ in *Rotsart* were followed by the EAT in *Secretary of State for Trade and Industry v Cook* [1997] IRLR 150 where three employees were told that they were being made redundant and that the business they worked for was being taken over. Their employer was insolvent and the employees applied to the Secretary of State for payment of debts. The employment tribunal found that there had been a transfer of undertakings but that the obligation to pay the former employees had not been transferred. The tribunal considered that it was bound by *Photostatic Copiers (Southern) Ltd v Okuda* (above) that reg 5 does not take effect in relation to an employee's contract of employment 'unless and until the employee is given notice of the fact of the transfer and the identity of the transferee'. And that in this case the employees had not been told of the identity of the purchaser and therefore liability for the for the relevant payments remained with the transferor.

However, on appeal to the EAT it was held that *Okuda* was not a correct interpretation of the Directive and that there is no precondition that a TUPE transfer cannot be effective unless the employee knew of the transfer and the identity of the transferee.

The question of automatic transfer as provided by TUPE must also be considered in respect of employees who object to the transfer. The well established principle laid down in *Nokes v Doncaster Amalgamated Collieries Ltd* [1940] AC 1014 that an employee cannot be transferred from one employer to another against his will would appear to conflict with the principles of TUPE. This dilemma has been resolved by an amendment to TUPE which gives effect to a decision of the ECJ in *Katsikas* v *Konstantinidis* [1993] IRLR 179 where it was held that the Acquired Rights Directive does not prevent an employee employed on the date of the transfer from objecting to the automatic transfer of his employment contract.

Regulation 5(4A) as inserted by Trade Union Reform and Employment Rights Act 1993 provides that:

> 'Paragraphs (1) and (2) above shall not operate to transfer his contract of employment ... if the employee informs the transferor or the transferee that he objects to becoming employed by the transferee.'

Furthermore, reg 5(4B) states that:

> 'Where an employee so objects the transfer of the undertaking or part in which he is employed shall operate so as to terminate the contract of employment with the transferor but he shall not be treated, for any purpose, as having been dismissed by the transferor.'

Dismissals

Regulation 8(1) of TUPE provides that an employee who is dismissed either before or after a transfer of an undertaking will be treated as being unfairly dismissed if the transfer or a reason connected with it is the reason or the principle reason for his dismissal. In *Berriman* v *Delabole Slate Ltd* [1984] IRLR 394 an employee successfully claimed constructive dismissal when the transferee reduced his rate of pay in order to bring him in line with other employees with the transferee's organisation.

Provided an employee can show that there is a causal connection between his dismissal and the transfer he will come within the protection afforded by TUPE. Although there is no time limit on the application of reg 8, the longer the period of time between the dismissal and the transfer the more difficult it will be to establish the causal connection.

However, TUPE also recognises that many transfers are brought about as a result of economic difficulties and therefore it may be necessary to dismiss employees in order to sell a company as a going concern. A prospective purchaser of a business is unlikely to want to purchase an undertaking if one of the reasons that the business is in trouble is because there are too many employees for the amount of work to be done.

An employer may therefore be required to dismiss employees prior to the transfer simply to make the business more attractive to potential purchasers. This economic reality is recognised by reg 8(2), which provides that where an economic, technical or organisational reason entailing changes in the workforce of either the transferor or the transferee before or after a relevant transfer is the reason or principal reason for dismissing an employee the dismissal shall be treated as having been of a kind such as to justify the dismissal of an employee holding the position which that employee held.

It can be seen therefore that reg 8(2) provides a defence to a claim of unfair dismissal – this defence is commonly referred to as an 'ETO' defence. An ETO defence will generally be successful if an employer can show that there is either some *economic* factor (such as a loss in profits), a requirement for *technical* change (for example the requirement of persons with different skills) or an *organisational* reason which justifies a dismissal.

If an employee is dismissed for an ETO reason then the dismissal is deemed to be for a 'substantial reason' for the purposes of unfair dismissal.

The operation of reg 8(1) and (2) can be seen in the case of *Warner* v *Adnet Ltd* [1998] ICR 1056. Mr Warner was employed by Microsystems as an accountant. Following financial difficulties the bank appointed receivers on 22 July 1994 and on 27 July the receivers dismissed Mr Warner and all other members of staff. On the 3 August the business was sold to the defendants and on 4 August the defendants re-engaged the dismissed staff with the exception of four employees, including Mr Warner. Mr Warner submitted an application to the employment tribunal claiming that he had been unfairly dismissed. At the tribunal hearing it was considered that the principal reason for the applicant's dismissal fell within reg 8(1) of TUPE – the transfer of the undertaking or a reason connected with it. However, the tribunal also found that the dismissal was not unfair because it fell within the reg 8(2) defence – it was for an economic, technical or organisational reason. The applicant appealed to the EAT where his appeal was dismissed and then to the Court of Appeal, arguing that reg 8(1) and (2) were mutually exclusive.

The Court of Appeal held that reg 8(1) and (2) are not mutually exclusive and that the correct approach to adopt is to consider if the dismissal is as a result of the transfer under reg 8(1) and then to consider whether the dismissal is for an ETO reason, in which case the dismissal is not unfair. Therefore, the employment tribunal and the EAT had correctly concluded that the dismissal was fair.

However, the relationship between reg 8(1) and (2) has come under further scrutiny by the Court of Appeal in *Whitehouse* v *Chas A Blatchford & Sons* [1999] IRLR 492. In this case Mr Whitehouse was employed as an artificial limb maker by James Stubbs & Co. Stubbs secured a contract to supply prosthetic appliances to the Northern General Hospital in Sheffield. The contract was due for renewal in April 1997 and although Stubbs put in a bid the contract was awarded to the defendants. At the time the number of technicians working on the contract was 13. However, the award of the contract was conditional upon certain cost-cutting measures, one of which was to reduce the number of technicians to 12. After the transfer the defendants carried out an assessment to see which of the technicians was to made redundant and Mr Whitehouse was the unfortunate employee. He presented a claim to the employment tribunal, arguing that the reason for his dismissal was because of the transfer and therefore in breach of the TUPE Regulations. It was held by the tribunal and the EAT that the reason for the dismissal fell within reg 8(2) and thus provided the respondents with the ETO defence. Mr Whitehouse further appealed to the Court of Appeal.

The Court of Appeal dismissed the appeal. The transfer of the undertaking was the occasion for the dismissal and not the cause of the dismissal. The requirement that the number of technicians be reduced to 12 was the same regardless of who was awarded the contract and therefore reg 8(1) did not apply.

Variation of contractual terms

One of the essential features of TUPE is that it operates to preserve the terms and conditions of employees when a business is transferred. If, therefore, a transferee attempts to alter terms and conditions, any such variation will be ineffective unless the reason for variation is economic, technical or organisational. The operation of the ETO defence was considered in the case of *Wilson & Others* v *St Helens Borough Council* [1998] IRLR 706.

The employees in this case were employed by Lancashire County Council at a home for boys with behavioural problems. The council decided that they could no longer afford to manage the home due to funding problems and it was agreed that St Helens Borough Council would take over the management with effect from 1 October 1992. Prior to the transfer, negotiations took place with the recognised union NASUWT to reduce the staff from 162 to 72 and, because it was not considered to be a TUPE transfer, these 72 staff were made redundant and then re-employed on less favourable terms by St Helens Council. Nine of the staff concerned later claimed that their reduction in wages was unlawful by virtue of the Wages Act 1986 and TUPE.

It was agreed by both parties at the employment tribunal that this was a TUPE transfer; however, the applicants' claim was dismissed on the basis that they had agreed to the variation in terms and conditions following the transfer. On appeal to the EAT it was held that the employees could not be bound by their new terms and conditions if the only reason for the variation was the transfer of the undertaking. In the Court of Appeal the Court concentrated on the issue of the dismissal of the employees and the application of reg 8(2), the ETO defence, and held that there was an economic or organisational reason for the variation in terms and the appeal by the council was allowed. The Court of Appeal also said that any purported dismissal because of a transfer of an undertaking is a nullity and therefore the contract of employment continues unless there is an ETO defence.

The House of Lords held that the Court of Appeal had erred in saying that a dismissal resulting from a transfer is a nullity. Such a dismissal is legally effective and the only remedy for a dismissed employee is to pursue a claim for unfair or wrongful dismissal. The House of Lords also considered that the reason for the variation in terms was the financial difficulties being experienced by the Lancashire County Council, and that such a variation would have been likely whether the transfer took place or not, and therefore the reason for the variation was 'economic and organisational' and the appeal by the employees was dismissed.

Transfer of liabilities

The effect of reg 5 TUPE is to transfer to the transferee all the obligations of the transferor. We have already seen that liability for unfair dismissal may be transferred to the new owner of a company; however, other liabilities will also be transferred. In the case of *DJM International* v *Nicholas* [1995] IRLR 76 the EAT held that a transferee was liable for sex discrimination committed by the transferor because reg 5(2)(b) TUPE is so widely worded that anything done before the transfer in respect of an employee in an undertaking is deemed to have been done by the transferee. In *Wilson & Others* v *West Cumbria Healthcare NHS Trust* [1995] PIQR 38 a transferee was held to be liable for personal injuries sustained by employees as a result of the negligence of the transferor.

There are, however, exceptions to the automatic transfer of all liabilities and these include any liability for the criminal acts of the transferor and occupational pension schemes: reg 7. It would appear that a failure on the part of TUPE to require the transfer of occupational pension schemes is contrary to the purpose of the Directive.

However, in *Walden Engineering Co Ltd* v *Warrener* [1993] IRLR 420 the EAT held that occupational pension schemes are supplementary schemes within the meaning of art 3(3) of the Acquired Rights Directive and are therefore excluded from the protection afforded by the Directive and TUPE. If, however, a transferor has failed to fulfil his obligation in terms of a contractual obligation to contribute to an occupational pension scheme, then this liability would be transferred to the transferee.

In *Hagen* v *ICI Chemicals and Polymers Ltd* [2002] IRLR 31 the High Court considered whether any liability relating to pensions would be transferred to the transferee. In this case the claimants worked for ICI at a central engineering resource centre. As part of a restructuring, it was decided that engineering resources should be transferred to Redpath Engineering Services (RES). The claimants were concerned about the transfer, not least because they feared a loss of benefits, including pensions. The company was aware that without the support of the workforce the transfer was unlikely to proceed and therefore efforts were made to keep employees informed on the way the transfer was progressing. Representations were made to the employees by the defendants to the effect that their terms and conditions would be the same following transfer and that they would be offered a broadly similar pension scheme. It was also made clear that if the transfer did not go ahead there would be job losses. The claimants reluctantly accepted the transfer but then discovered that the representations that had been made with respect to the pension scheme were false. The claimants brought a claim alleging negligent misrepresentation and a breach of the implied terms of mutual trust and confidence.

It was held by the High Court that the first defendants owed a duty of care to their employees to ensure the accuracy of information given to them. The court further held that the representations made by the first defendants with respect to pension provision were false and therefore there was a breach of the duty of care. However, because the incorrect information that had been given related to pension benefits, liability would not pass to the second defendants because reg 7 of TUPE provides that no liabilities transfer to the transferee when they are in connection with occupational pensions.

Consultation

An employer who is contemplating the sale or transfer of his undertaking is required by reg 10 TUPE to consult all appropriate representatives of any employees who may be affected by the transfer. Representatives should be advised in respect of the following matters:

1. the fact of the transfer;
2. when, approximately the transfer should take place;
3. the reasons for the transfer;
4. the legal, economic and social implications of the transfer for those affected;
5. any measures that the transferor believes the transferee may make in connection with the transfer.

During the course of consultation a prudent employer should not only advise representatives of measure he proposes to take but should also seek their agreement on such measures. An employer is also under a duty to consider any representations made by the representatives, and if he rejects any proposals he must respond to the representations stating the reasons for rejection. The employer must also allow representatives access to all affected employees and provide accommodation and other appropriate facilities for their discussions.

If there is insufficient time or other special circumstances which mean that it is not reasonably practicable for an employer to engage in consultation with representatives, the employer must take such steps as are reasonable in the circumstances to carry out some consultation.

Regulation 11 provides that where an employer has failed to comply with the requirements of reg 10 any affected employees or representatives may present a complaint to an employment tribunal. If the employer claims that it was not reasonably practicable to engage in consultation because of special circumstances the burden of proof will rest upon him to provide evidence of such circumstances and to show that he took all steps that were reasonably practicable in those circumstances.

If a tribunal finds that an employer has failed to carry out appropriate consultation the tribunal may order the employer to pay appropriate compensation to affected employees. Any award of compensation will not exceed the equivalent of four weeks' pay. Any failure to engage in consultation by the transferor will result in potential liability to the transferor. In *Alamo Group* v *Tucker* [2003] IRLR 266 the transferor failed to consult with employee representatives as required to do so by reg 10 TUPE. It was accepted that the transferee, Alamo Group, had done all that they were required to do. However, the employment tribunal awarded one week's gross wages to employees who were affected by the failure to consult. Alamo appealed against the decision of the tribunal on the grounds that liability under regs 10 and 11 should not transfer to the transferee. It was held by the EAT that the obligation to consult with employees and the award of compensation in default of compensation are in 'connection with' the contract of employment and therefore under reg 5 are transferred to the transferee. This decision has resolved the controversy that arose over two conflicting decisions of the EAT. In *Kerry Foods* v *Creber* [2000] IRLR 10 the EAT held that that liability for a failure to consult did transfer to the transferee. However, in *TGWU* v *McKinnon* [2001] IRLR 597, another division of the EAT declined to follow *Kerry* and held that such liability does not transfer.

Collective agreements

Regulation 6 provides that where at the time of a transfer of an undertaking there is in existence a collective agreement made by the transferor with a recognised trade union which concerns any employees that are to be transferred then the agreement will be transferred in respect of those employees.

6

Discrimination in Employment

6.1 Sex discrimination

6.2 Race discrimination

6.3 Disability discrimination

6.1 Sex discrimination

Introduction

Discrimination by an employer on the grounds of a person's sex is prima facie unlawful.

The modern approach towards sex discrimination law began with the Equal Pay Act 1970, which came into effect in 1975, along with the Sex Discrimination Act (SDA) 1975. In order to comply with the Equal Treatment Directive (76/207/EEC) it was necessary to pass a further piece of legislation – the Sex Discrimination Act 1986 – which amended the Act of 1975.

Although it was considered that women were in greater need of protection, the SDA 1975 as amended applies to both men and women which means that it is unlawful for an employer to discriminate against a man or a women on the grounds of that person's sex. Further amendments have been made to the SDA 175 with the implementation of the Sex Discrimination Act 1975 (Amendment) Regulations 2003 (SI 2003/1657) which came into force in July 2003.

The SDA 1975 as amended will be considered in particular detail. However, reference will be made to the Employment Act 1989 (which further removed statutory restrictions on women working in certain occupations such as mines and factories) and the Social Security Act 1989 which implemented the Equal Treatment in Occupational Pension Schemes Directive (providing for equal treatment with respect to occupational pension schemes).

The SDA 1975 defines discrimination in terms of direct and indirect discrimination.

Effect of EC law

An article of the EC Treaty may be of direct effect and therefore give rights to individuals if it is sufficiently clear, precise, unconditional and does not require any further implementation. Article 141 EC provides that men and women should receive equal pay for equal work and is of direct effect. However, the European Court of Justice (ECJ) originally held that art 141 EC could only be relied upon with respect to direct discrimination: in subsequent cases the ECJ has adopted a broader interpretation and has held that art 141 EC is also applicable to indirect discrimination.

A directive may also give rights to employees if a Member State fails to implement the directive correctly or within the stipulated time limit: however, only employees who are employed by emanations of the state may invoke the rights conferred by a directive (in other words persons employed in the public service, or a nationalised industry or a body which is in the control of the state). In *Marshall* v *Southampton and South-West Hampshire Area Health Authority* [1986] ECR 723 Miss Marshall, a dietician, was dismissed by the Health Authority at the age of 62 on the ground that she was two years past the normal retirement age for women. Miss Marshall claimed that she had been discriminated against contrary to Council Directive (76/207/EEC) (which is commonly referred to as the Equal Treatment Directive), because the retirement age for men was 65. The ECJ held that the dismissal of Miss Marshall was contrary to the Directive, which is sufficiently clear and unconditional to have direct effect. Furthermore, the Court held that the Health Authority was a public authority and therefore an emanation of the state. The effect of the decision of the ECJ in this case was the implementation of s2 Sex Discrimination Act 1986 which amends s6(4) of the 1975 Act of the same name rendering discrimination with respect to retirement, promotion, demotion, training, transfer and dismissal unlawful.

Although a directive cannot be directly relied upon by an employee who works for a private enterprise, in *Dekker* v *Stichting Vormingscentrum voor Jong Volwassenen* [1991] IRLR 27, a case concerning a woman who was refused employment because she was pregnant, the ECJ held that it was possible to rely upon rights conferred in a directive (in this case Directive 76/207/EC) when interpreting national legislation. In *Dekker* the refusal to offer the applicant a job was because of her sex and therefore contrary to the Equal Treatment Directive. In *Webb* v *EMO Air Cargo (UK) Ltd* [1993] IRLR 27, Ms Webb was employed to cover for an employee who was to take maternity leave. Shortly after starting her training Ms Webb announced to her employers that she too was pregnant and would also need maternity leave which would coincide with the person for whom she was covering. Her employers dismissed her and she claimed that this was discriminatory. The employers argued that it was not discrimination because they would have dismissed a male employee if he had been unavailable for a similar amount of time. The ECJ held that the dismissal was contrary to the Equal Treatment Directive, even though a man would have been treated in the same way.

The implementation of the Pregnant Workers Directive (92/85/EEC) gives further protection to women and provides that it is unlawful to dismiss a woman on the grounds of pregnancy, regardless of the length of time that she has been employed or whether the contract is permanent or for a fixed term. This position is now reflected in s99 ERA 1996 and reg 20(7) of the Maternity and Parental Leave etc Regulations 1999 which provide that dismissal is automatically unfair if the reason for the dismissal is connected with pregnancy, childbirth, maternity leave or parental leave.

Direct discrimination

This is the most obvious form of discrimination. An example would be a situation whereby a person of either sex was refused a job or promotion solely on the ground of his or her sex.

Section 1 SDA 1975 provides:

'(1) ... a person discriminates against a woman if –
(a) on the ground of her sex he treats her less favourably than he treats or would treat a man ...'

One of the leading cases illustrating direct discrimination – *James* v *Eastleigh Borough Council* [1990] IRLR 288 – does not concern an employment issue but was a test case brought with the backing of the Equal Opportunities Commission as part of their duties under the SDA 1975. Mr James claimed that he had been discriminated against on the grounds of his sex because when he and his wife, who were both aged 61, visited a local municipal swimming pool, his wife was able to get in free of charge but he was required to pay an entrance fee. The council had adopted a policy of allowing free entry to those persons who had reached statutory retirement age, which was 60 for women and 65 for men. The question considered by the House of Lords was whether men would be treated differently but for their sex and it was held that women were being treated more favourably than men because they qualified for free admission five years earlier than men. Another example of direct discrimination can be found in the case *Batisha* v *Say* [1977] IRLR 13, where a female applicant was refused a job as a cave guide on the ground that it was 'a man's job'.

Motive

When an employment tribunal considers a case of direct discrimination it must establish that the applicant has been treated less favourably than a person of a different sex. It must then go on to consider whether that treatment was due to the sex of the applicant.

In *Peake* v *Automotive Products Ltd* [1978] ICR 968 a male applicant claimed that he had been unfairly treated because female shop-floor staff were allowed to leave the factory at 4.25 pm whereas male employees were not allowed to leave until 4.30 pm. The respondent employer claimed that the reason for the difference was his concern for the safety of workers as they left the factory and this was accepted by Lord Denning in the Court of Appeal as a justification for the discrimination. It was also considered that the complaint was de minimis – too trivial to constitute a detriment.

As a result of this decision it appeared that provided any discriminatory act was carried out with good intention this would not constitute discrimination. Indeed, Shaw LJ considered that the motive of an employer was a central issue. This provoked academic criticism on the ground that such consideration would severely limit the scope of the SDA 1975.

This criticism was partly answered in the decision of the Court of Appeal in *Ministry of Defence* v *Jeremiah* [1980] IRLR 436 where it was held that the only sound reason for the decision in the *Peake* case was the application of the de minimis principle. In *Ministry of Defence* v *Jeremiah* men were required to work in dirty conditions making shells which exploded in red or orange for artillery practice. Women were not required to do this work because they did not want to take showers afterwards, and it was also considered that the conditions in the 'colour-bursting shell shop' may affect their hair.

The Court of Appeal upheld the applicants' claim of discrimination, even though the men had been given small additional payments to compensate them for such dirty work. Lord Denning said 'An employer cannot buy a right to discriminate by making an extra payment to the men. If he could, it would drive a gaping hole in the statute. All the men would pass through it.'

The motive for the discrimination would therefore appear to be irrelevant. In *Greig* v *Community Industry* [1979] IRLR 158 the female applicant claimed that she had been discriminated against purely on the grounds of her sex. The respondent employer claimed that he had not employed her as a painter and decorator because she would have been the only female within a group and he had learnt from experience that to employ a female in such circumstances would be unwise. However, the EAT found that he had unfairly discriminated against the woman.

While the good intentions of an employer do not remove the fact of discrimination, they may well be relevant in assessing any compensation to be awarded to an employee.

The motive for discrimination would therefore appear to be irrelevant, although some consideration must be given to the decision by the EAT in *Barclays Bank plc* v *James* [1990] IRLR 90 where it appears to have been suggested that the correct approach is to establish the alleged discriminator's reason and not the cause of treatment, and therefore not to enquire whether that reason itself is sexually neutral.

In *Bullock* v *Alice Ottley School* [1992] IRLR 564 it was held that differences in retirement ages for two groups of workers, one consisting of men and the other mainly women, was not discriminatory because the reason for the difference was a result of recruitment difficulties for the jobs which just happened to be carried out by men. The Court of Appeal acknowledged that the effect of the different retirement ages for different jobs did, in practice, have a disparate effect between the sexes, but the policy was not based on gender but rather on recruitment difficulties.

Treatment

In order to establish that there has been discrimination s1(1) SDA 1975 requires that an employer treats a woman less favourably and therefore it is necessary to consider what is meant by treatment. Treatment can include a brief remark, as in the case of *Insitu Cleaning Co Ltd* v *Heads* [1995] IRLR 4 where the EAT considered that a single offensive comment made by the son of the boss to a much older woman about the size of her breasts amounted to treatment for the purposes of the SDA 1975.

'Treatment' can also include the way in which something is done, and according to the Court of Session in *Porcelli* v *Strathclyde Regional Council* [1986] ICR 564 includes sexual harassment even though this is not specifically provided for in the SDA 1975. In this case the female applicant, who worked as a laboratory technician in a school, claimed that two male colleagues had subjected her to sexual harassment in order to force her to apply for a transfer to another school. The employer argued that such conduct did not fall within the provisions of the SDA 1975 because the men would have treated a male colleague that they disliked in a similar way. The Court held that the treatment of the woman had involved sexual innuendo and treatment of a sexual nature and this was done purely on the grounds of her sex and therefore fell within the meaning of s1(1)(a).

Treatment does not necessarily have to comprise one single act but can be a continuing state of affairs: *Owusu* v *London Fire & Civil Defence Authority* [1995] IRLR 574.

'Less favourably'

When an employment tribunal considers whether an applicant has been treated less favourably it must take an objective approach, and the fact that the employee considers that he or she has been treated less favourably is irrelevant. In *Schmidt* v *Austicks Bookshops* [1977] IRLR 360 a female employee refused to comply with a dress code prohibiting the wearing of trousers and was dismissed. She claimed that she had been treated less favourably than her male colleagues. However, it was held that because male employees were also subject to a dress code (albeit a different one!) the appellant had not been treated less favourably. Philips J also held that the prohibition did not amount to a detriment within the meaning of s6(2)(b) SDA 1975 since it 'must have something serious or important about it'.

The question as to whether the approach adopted in *Schmidt* was correct was considered by the Court of Appeal in *Smith* v *Safeway* [1995] IRLR 132 where a male employee who was dismissed by the employer because of the length of his hair which he wore in a ponytail brought a claim of sex discrimination. The company dress code required 'conventional' hairstyles for both men and women but did differentiate between men and women with respect to the length of hair. The Court of Appeal held that the employer did not unlawfully discriminate against the employee because although the prohibition on hair length applied only to male employees, it did not, when viewed in the context of the employer's dress code as a whole, constitute less favourable treatment within the meaning of s1(1)(a) SDA

1975. The requirement for a conventional appearance was applied to the same standard for both male and female employees.

The Court of Appeal restated the principle set out in *Schmidt* that it is not discriminatory for an employer to insist upon the conventional appearance of their staff, provided that the same standard of conventionality is applied to both sexes. Leggat LJ said:

> 'Provided that an employer's rules, taken as a whole, do not result in men being treated less favourably than women, or vice versa, there is room for current conventions to operate.'

However, in *Owen v Professional Golfers' Association* (2000) (unreported) a training manager was succesful in claiming that the dress code of the PGA was in fact discriminatory because they refused to allow woment to wear trousers for work.

The issue over whether the requirement for employees to conform to a dress code was considered by the EAT in the case of *Thompson v Department for Work and Pensions* [2004] IRLR 348. Mr Thompson complained that the introduction of a new business dress code, which required men to wear a collar and tie and women to wear clothes of a smilar standard, was discriminatory against men. The employment tribunal found for Mr Thompson and the respondent appealed against that finding. The EAT acknowledged that the effect of their judgment would be important because 6,950 cases were pending awaiting the oucome of the appeal.

The EAT considered the approach taken in *Safeway* and particularly the 'package approach' adopted by Phillips LJ in the Court of Appeal. Phillips LJ considered that when looking at the requirements of a business dress code the 'package approach was the correct test' because whilst individual requirements (such as the wearing of a tie) may be discriminatory, it is necessary to look at the overall dress code. The EAT stated that the issue of less favourable treatment 'is not resolved by asking whether the requirement on men to wear a collar and ties meant that a higher level of smartness is being required of men rather than women'. That issue is to be resolved, says the EAT, by asking 'whether an equivalent level of smartness to that required of the female members of staff could only be achieved in the case of men, by requiring them to wear a collar and tie'.

The EAT also found that the tribunal had misapplied the decision of the House of Lords in *James v Eastleigh Borough Council* [1990] IRLR 288. The tribunal decided that, but for the fact that he was a man, Mr Thompson would not have been asked to wear a collar and tie, and that there was therefore less favourable treatment. However, the 'but for' test in *James* should only be applied once less favourable treatment has been demonstrated. The EAT remitted the case back to the employment tribunal.

In *Stewart v Cleveland Guest (Engineering) Ltd* [1994] IRLR 440 the EAT considered that an employment tribunal had not erred in dismissing the sex-discrimination claim of a woman who found the display of pictures of naked women in her workplace offensive. The question to be considered was whether there has been less favourable treatment on the grounds of sex and the EAT considered that this will depend upon the facts of each case. In the instant case the tribunal were entitled to hold that a male employee might have found the pictures equally offensive and therefore the woman had not been treated less favourably than a man.

A similar point was made in the case of *Bahl* v *Law Society* [2004] IRLR 799 where the appellant Ms Bahl failed in her claim of sex and race discrimination. Whilst it was accepted that her employer had been antagonistic towards her, Ms Bahl failed to establish that it was on the grounds of her sex or race. It is clear that any unfavourable treatment has to be directly referable to a person's sex and that unreasonable treatment alone is not sufficient to successfully establish a claim of sex discrimination.

However a broad view of what does amount to unfavourable treatment was adopted in *Moonsar* v *Fiveway Express Transpor Ltd* [2004] EAT/0476/04. The EAT held that downloading pornographic material onto a monitor in an office where the appellant was working as a cleaner amounted to less favourable treatment, even though it was not clear whether the appellant had seen the images or not. Being aware of what was going on was held to be sufficient.

Discrimination against married persons and civil partners

Under the SDA 1975 it is unlawful to treat a married person or civil partner less favourably than an unmarried person on the ground of his or her marital/partnership status. It is not, however, unlawful to discriminate against a single person on the ground of his unmarried status. Section 3(1) as amended by the Civil Partnership Act 2004 provides:

> 'In any circumstances relevant for the purposes of any provision of Part II, a person discriminates against a person ("A") who fulfils the condition in subsection (2) if –
> (a) on the ground of the fulfilment of the condition, he treats A less favourably than he treats or would treat a person who does not fulfil the condition, or
> (b) he applies to A a provision, criterion or practice which he applies or would apply equally to a person who does not fulfil the condition, but –
> (i) which puts or would put persons fulfilling the condition at a particular disadvantage when compared with persons not fulfilling the condition, and
> (ii) which puts A at that advantage, and
> (iii) which he cannot show to be a proportionate means of achieving a legitimate aim.'

In *Horsey* v *Dyfed County Council* [1982] IRLR 395 it was held that an employer who had treated an employee in a particular way based on an assumption that being a married woman she would leave to join her husband discriminated against the employee. Similarly, in *Skyrail Oceanic Ltd* v *Coleman* [1981] IRLR 226 the Court of Appeal held that an employer who dismissed a female employee who had recently married an employee of a rival company based on the assumption that the husband would be the breadwinner of the family had unlawfully discriminated against the woman. The employer argued that the reason for the dismissal was to protect confidential information, but admitted that the reason the two rival employers had discussed the matter and decided to dismiss Mrs Coleman was based on the assumption that Mr Coleman was the breadwinner. However, Shaw LJ in a strong dissenting judgment, considered that there was no tenable basis for an allegation of sex discrimination because once the competing employers had decided that they were not going to dismiss the husband, the employer was entitled to dismiss Mrs Coleman in order to protect the legitimate interests of the company.

Comparator

Section 5 SDA 1975 requires that a person claiming sex discrimination must have an appropriate actual or hypothetical comparator with whom they can compare their case to show that they have been treated less favourably. A comparator must have relevant circumstances which are the same or not materially different as the claimant. In *Bullock* v *Alice Ottley School* [1992] IRLR 564 the claimant, who was a member of the domestic staff, used as her comparator a member of the garden and maintenance staff in an attempt to establish discrimination. It was held by the Court of Appeal that there were differences between the two groups of workers, the latter being more difficult to recruit, which not only justified the difference in retiring ages but meant that the chosen comparator did not have relevant circumstances that were materially the same.

In *Shamoon* v *Chief Constable of the Royal Ulster Constabulary* [2003] IRLR 285 the House of Lords has given further consideration as to who is the correct comparator for the purposes of s5 SDA 1975. In this case Ms Shamoon was employed by the RUC as a chief inspector and worked in the traffic division which was split into three geographic regions. She worked with two other chief inspectors, each having responsibility for one of the three regions. Part of their duties involved appraisals of junior police officers. A complaint by an officer was made and upheld over the manner in which Ms Shamoon had conducted his appraisal. The matter was referred to the Police Federation who asked Ms Shamoon's superior officer, the superintendent, to remove appraisal responsibilities from Ms Shamoon. This request was acceded to and Ms Shamoon no longer carried out appraisals. Ms Shamoon presented a claim of sex discrimination, claiming that she had been discriminated against because the right to carry our appraisals had been removed. At tribunal it was accepted that she had been treated less favourably than her male comparators – the other two chief inspectors. An appeal to the Northern Ireland Court of Appeal by the RUC was successful. The Court of Appeal held that the tribunal had erred in two respects. First, the applicant had not suffered a 'detriment' within the meaning adopted by the EAT in *Lord Chancellor* v *Coker* [2001] IRLR 116 and, second, the other two chief inspectors could not be correctly regarded as comparators.

The House of Lords held that the Court of Appeal had erred in accepting the meaning of detriment as set out by the EAT in *Coker*. A detriment should be regarded as a situation where a reasonable employee may consider that he is at a disadvantage in the circumstances in which he has to work – there is no requirement for some physical or economic consequence.

However, the House of Lords went on to consider whether the other two male chief inspectors could properly be regarded as suitable comparators and held that the decision of the Court of Appeal had been correct. The House of Lords made it clear that when selecting a comparator it is insufficient to simply select a person of the opposite sex. The comparator must, according to their Lordships, comply with s5(3) SDA 1975 and be a person for whom 'the relevant circumstances in the one case are the same, or not materially different, in the other'. In this case the male chief inspectors were not appropriate comparators within the meaning of the legislation because there were material differences. First, no complaints had been made against the other chief inspectors and, second, the superintendent did not have direct line responsibility for them.

It would appear that such a strict approach would make it impossible to bring a successful sex discrimination claim in many cases because there is rarely a comparator in exactly the same circumstances as the complainant. However, the House of Lords confirmed that if there is no actual comparator, a 'hypothetical comparator' should be used.

Indirect discrimination

Inequality of treatment can result from an act which is not overtly discriminatory but which operates to discriminate by more subtle means. An employer may apply some sort of provision, criterion or practice which applies to both men and women but which in reality has the effect of discriminating against one or the other.

Section 1 SDA 1975, as amended by the Sex Discrimination (Indirect Discrimination and Burden of Proof) Regulations 2001, provides:

> '(2) In any circumstances relevant for the purposes of a provision to which this subsection applies, a person discriminates against a woman if –
> (a) on the ground of her sex, he treats her less favourably than he treats or would treat a man, or
> (b) he applies to her a provision, criterion or practice which he applies or would apply equally to a man, but –
> (i) which is such that it would be to the detriment of a considerably larger proportion of women than of men, and
> (ii) which he cannot show to be justifiable irrespective of the sex of the person to whom it is applied, and
> (iii) which is to her detriment.'

This section as originally worded caused considerable difficulties for applicants and employment tribunals. For employees to successfully pursue a claim it was necessary to show that an employer had imposed a requirement or condition which women found more difficult to comply with than men, and this is discussed in more detail below. However, the new wording of s1 is broader and in cases of indirect discrimination an employee will no longer be required to show a strict rule or policy was in place: she will merely have to show that the employer engages in some sort of practice which is indirectly discriminatory. Nevertheless it is important to consider how the courts interpreted the old wording to gain an understanding of the general principles.

Requirement or condition

In *Price* v *Civil Service Commission* [1977] IRLR 3 the EAT said that it is necessary to define with some precision the requirement or condition which is called in question and that a person should not be taken as being able to comply with a condition or requirement just because it is theoretically possible. In *Price* a woman aged 35 replied to an advertisement for Civil Service executive officers and discovered that there was an upper age limit of 28 for the position. She claimed that she was being indirectly discriminated against because the number of women who could comply with that condition was less than men because many women in their twenties were having children and involved in child care. At tribunal it was considered that that requirement or condition should be interpreted strictly and her application was dismissed. It was held that a strict interpretation was contrary to the spirit of the SDA 1975 and it is necessary to look at the reality of the situation rather than looking at what is theoretically possible. Her appeal was therefore successful and the case was remitted to a fresh tribunal to find out whether on a proper analysis of the statistical evidence the number of women who could comply with the condition was smaller than the number of men.

A similar approach was taken by the EAT in *Clarke* v *Eley (IMI) Kynoch Ltd* [1982] IRLR 482 where a part-time worker was made redundant following a selection process which provided that part-time workers were to be made redundant before full-time workers. The EAT rejected the decision of the tribunal that the applicant could have complied with the condition for being retained in a redundancy situation by becoming a full-time worker before the redundancy situation arose. The EAT said that when considering whether an employee can or cannot comply with a requirement or condition the relevant time is the date upon which she suffers a detriment. In *Home Office* v *Holmes* [1984] IRLR 299 the EAT held that the requirement by an employer that a woman who had requested to work part-time following the birth of her child work full time was a 'requirement or condition' and was thus indirectly discriminatory. The approach taken by Waite J in this case, which gives the words 'requirement' and 'condition' a broad meaning, was adopted by the Northern Ireland Court of Appeal in *Briggs* v *North Eastern Education and Library Board* [1990] IRLR 181, where it was held that the requirement of an employer for the employee to teach badminton classes after school fell within the old wording of the SDA 1975, although in this case the requirement was held to be justified.

Training or management experience can also be a 'requirement or condition' according to the EAT in *Falkirk Council* v *White & Others* [1997] IRLR 560. Ms White and two of her colleagues applied for a managerial post at a prison which was run by the Central Regional Council in Scotland but were unsuccessful. They complained to an employment tribunal that the requirement of management training and supervisory experience was indirect discrimination contrary to the SDA 1975 as the women who were mostly on basic grade posts would be unable to fulfil this requirement or condition. In finding for the applicants the employment tribunal held that, although management training and supervisory experience had been stated to be desirable, in reality they were the decisive factors in the selection of the candidate and therefore the requirement had an unfair impact upon these women. On appeal the EAT upheld the decision of the employment tribunal, holding that management training and supervisory experience was a 'requirement or condition' within the meaning of the SDA 1975.

An employee may be both directly discriminated against and suffer from indirect discrimination. In *Hurley* v *Mustoe* [1981] ICR 490 a woman with four young children applied for a job as a waitress, but when the owner of the restaurant discovered she had children the offer of the job was revoked. The EAT, Browne-Wilkinson J presiding, held that the employee had been directly discriminated against contrary to s1(1)(a) and that she had suffered indirect discrimination.

'Considerably smaller'

In order to establish that there has been indirect discrimination it is necessary to make a comparison between those who can comply with a requirement or condition and those who cannot. Difficulties can arise with respect to identifying the appropriate group with whom comparison should be made. A case that has been subject to heavy criticism is *Kidd* v *DRG (UK) Ltd* [1984] IRLR 190 where the EAT held that in considering whether, in an all-female workforce, a redundancy scheme which provided that part-time workers would be made redundant before full-time workers was discriminatory as against married persons with child-care responsibilities, the choice of the section of the population for the purpose of comparison was a question of fact for the tribunal. Further, the tribunal could limit the range of comparison to that section of the population for whom full-time work is not possible because of the need to care for children and refuse to rely on generalised assumptions about working patterns without evidential support.

In *Greater Manchester Police Authority* v *Lea* [1990] IRLR 372 statistics which showed that 95.3 per cent of men compared to 99.4 per cent of women could not comply with a condition that applicants should not be in receipt of an occupational pension scheme were sufficient to prove a claim of indirect discrimination. The EAT held that in determining whether a considerably smaller proportion of men could comply with the condition compared to the proportion of women the tribunal was entitled to consider the entire economically active population as the appropriate pool for comparison. The appropriate pool does not have to be statistically a perfect match of the persons who would be interested and capable of applying for the post.

The issue of the use of statistics and the correct group for comparison was considered more recently in *London Underground* v *Edwards* [1997] IRLR 157 where the Morison J in the EAT was prepared to look beyond the statistics produced to see if a smaller proportion of women than men could comply with a new requirement. Mrs Edwards, a single parent with a young child, complained that she was unable to conform to a new flexible shift pattern that her employers, London Underground, had introduced. The basis of her case was that only a very small proportion of female single parents could comply with the new rostering system compared with male single parents. The employment tribunal upheld her claim. London Underground's appeal was allowed by the EAT on the grounds that the correct pool for consideration must comprise of all train drivers and not those operators who were single parents and the matter was remitted to a new tribunal. At the new hearing the employment tribunal again held that there had been indirect discrimination on the grounds that 100 per cent of the 2,000 male train operators could comply with the new shift system, whilst only 95.2 per cent of the 21 female train operators could comply. London Underground again appealed and in *London Underground* v *Edwards (No 2)* [1998] IRLR 364 the EAT upheld the decision. London Underground then appealed to the Court of Appeal.

The Court of Appeal held that the employment tribunal was correct in concluding that the proportion of female operators who could comply with the new requirement was considerably smaller than the proportion of male operators and therefore the new roster arrangements indirectly discriminated against the woman. It was a question of fact and for the purposes of the SDA 1975 a 5 per cent difference between the respective proportions of men and women who could comply constituted a significant difference.

'Detriment'

The requirement or condition imposed must be to the detriment of the complainant; the employee who believes that he or she has been discriminated against must suffer some disadvantage as a consequence. This will normally be the loss of opportunity to obtain employment or gain promotion or dismissal. In *London Underground* v *Edwards (No 2)* (above) the detriment was the inability to comply with the new roster system without incurring difficulties with respect to child care.

'Justification'

If an employer can show that his indirect discrimination is justified then this may afford a defence to a claim of sex discrimination. When considering whether the actions of an employer are justifiable the tribunal must distinguish between a requirement or condition which is necessary and one which is merely convenient. In *Steel* v *Union of Post Office Workers* [1977] IRLR 288 the EAT laid down guidelines for determining whether a requirement or condition is justified.

1. The burden of proof lies upon the party wishing to justify a requirement or condition.
2. The burden will not lightly be discharged. The tribunal must be satisfied that the requirement or condition is necessary.

3. In deciding whether the employer has discharged the burden the tribunal should take into account all the circumstances, including the discriminatory effect of the requirement or condition if it is permitted to continue.
4. It is necessary to weigh the need for the requirement or condition against that effect.
5. It is essential to distinguish between a requirement or condition which is necessary, and one which is merely convenient, and for this purpose it is relevant to consider whether the employer can find some other and non-discriminatory method of achieving his object.

However, these broader tests must now be considered with more recent narrower tests that have been adopted bringing into line the law on indirect discrimination with the defence of material defence in the Equal Pay Act 1970. In *Bilka-Kaufhaus GmbH* v *Weber von Hartz* [1986] IRLR 317 the European Court of Justice held that a breach of art 119 EC Treaty (now art 141 EC) is unlawful unless it can be justified objectively on grounds unrelated to sex discrimination. In *Bilka-Kaufhaus GmbH* the ECJ stated:

'If the national court finds that that the measures chosen by [the employer] correspond to a real need on the part of the undertaking, are appropriate with a view to achieving the objectives pursued and are necessary to that end, the fact that the measures affect a far greater number of women than men is not sufficient to show that they constitute an infringement of [what was then] art 119.'

In subsequent cases such as *Barry* v *Midland Bank* [1998] IRLR 138 the Court of Appeal considered that the tripartite test set out in the citation in *Bilka* should be adopted with the gloss that the word 'necessary' is to be taken to mean reasonably necessary. This approach was more recently taken by the EAT in *Health and Safety Executive* v *Cadman* [2004] IRLR 29. In *Rainey* v *Greater Glasgow Health Board Eastern District* [1987] IRLR 26 the House of Lords said obiter that there seems to be 'no significant difference in principle' between the burden of justifying a pay differential under s1(3) Equal Pay Act 1970 and a discriminatory requirement under the SDA 1975. The requirements for justification of *Bilka-Kaufhaus GmbH* and the Equal Treatment Directive are that there has to be a real need on the part of the employer and that the practice must be appropriate to meet this necessity. In *Hampson* v *Department of Education & Science* [1989] IRLR 302, a case decided under the Race Relations Act 1976, the Court of Appeal said that the appropriate test for justifying an act of discrimination requires an objective balancing of the discriminatory effect of a requirement or condition against the reasonable needs of the employer for that requirement or condition to be applied – a test which was subsequently approved by the House of Lords in *Webb* v *EMO Air Cargo (UK) Ltd* [1993] IRLR 27.

In order to justify a requirement or condition an employer must show that there is a real need for the requirement, and that reason may be economic, administrative or some other justifiable reason. In *Jones* v *University of Manchester* [1993] IRLR

218, where a female graduate applied for a job with the university but was rejected because the university required a younger person, the employer was able to show that there was a real need for a younger person and that the requirement could be objectively justified. The department in question was staffed by a large number of employees approaching retirement age and the university was concerned that if they did not employ a younger person the department would not operate effectively. In this case the Court of Appeal found that the requirement was not a general requirement of the university but a need in the particular department for a younger person because of the possibility of other employees applying for early retirement.

In order for an employer to sucessfuly argue that a reqirement or condition is justified the test is objective. It will not therefore be a defence to show that the employer considered that the requirement was justified if, when viewed objectively by a tribunal, there is no sufficient justification.

In *R* v *Secretary of State for Employment, ex parte Equal Opportunities Commission* [1994] IRLR 176 the House of Lords held that the Secretary of State for Employment had failed to show any objective justification for indirect discrimination against women. The indirect discrimination was brought about by the requirement that in order to receive employment protection under the Employment Protection (Consolidation) Act 1978 a part-time worker had to have five years' qualifying employment, whereas a full-time worker only had to have two years' employment. The argument put forward by the govenment to justify the difference was that to remove the five-year qualifying period would be onerous for employers and lead to fewer jobs for part-time workers. This was rejected by their Lordships.

The decision of the House of Lords was followed by the swift implementation of the the Employment Protection (Part-Time Employees) Regulations 1995 (SI 1995/31), which came into force in February 1995 and which reduced the qualifying period from five years to two years. This has now been amended by the Part-Time Workers (Prevention of Less Favourable Treatment) Regulations 2000 (SI 2000/1551) which provides that part-time workers are to be treated no less favourably than full-time employees unless any such treatment is objectively justified.

Victimisation

Section 4(1) SDA 1975 makes it unlawful to treat an employee less favourably because the employee has brought proceedings or given evidence in respect of an alleged breach of the SDA 1975, the Equal Pay Act 1970 or under ss62–65 Pensions Act 1995. Section 41(1) SDA 1975 provides that 'Anything done by a person in the course of his employment shall be treated for the purposes of this Act as done by his employer as well as by him, whether or not it was done with the employer's knowledge or approval.' The relationship between s4(1) and s41 was considered by the Court of Appeal in *Waters* v *Commissioner of Police of the Metropolis* [1997] IRLR 589. Ms Waters was employed as a WPC. In February 1988 she complained that she had been sexually assaulted by a fellow officer while both were off duty. After an initial inquiry the Commissioner of Police decided that her complaint was unsubstantiated. She was transferred to another police station and prior to July 1991 she was successful in anti-terrorist training. Her name was placed on the 'POLSA2 list' – a list comprising of specially trained officers in terrorist matters. In July 1991 her name was removed from the list on medical grounds. Ms Waters, believing that her removal from the list was due to her earlier allegation of sexual assault, applied to an employment tribunal claiming that she had been the subject of victimisation contrary to s4(1) SDA 1975.

The tribunal had to determine as a preliminary issue whether the respondent was vicariously liable for the act of the fellow officer under s41(1) SDA 1975. It considered that because the officers were off duty at the time the alleged assault took place the respondent was not vicariously liable and therefore her employer could not have victimised her for making the complaint. The decision of the tribunal was upheld by the EAT. However, the applicant was granted leave to appeal to the Court of Appeal in the light of the decision in *Jones* v *Tower Boot Co Ltd* [1997] IRLR 168 which had broadened the scope of vicarious liability and conduct during the course of employment. The Court of Appeal held that s4(1) SDA 1975 only applied if the appellant was able to establish that the act committed by the fellow officer was an act for which the Commissioner could be held vicariously liable under s41(1). On the facts the alleged incident occurred whilst both officers were off duty and the appellant failed to establish vicarious liability and therefore her appeal failed.

An employee who claims victimisation is required to show: first, that he or she was treated less favourably; second, that the cause of that less favourable treatment was as a result of bringing or supporting proceedings under the SDA 1975; and, third, that the conduct for which proceedings are brought would amount to a contravention of the SDA 1975 within the meaning of s4(1). This places employees in a difficult position because before making a complaint in respect of the racial or sexual misconduct of a fellow employee the employee must consider whether in fact the employer would be vicariously liable for the misconduct.

In *Chief Constable of Bedfordshire* v *Liversidge* [2002] IRLR 651 the Court of Appeal held that a chief constable would not be liable for sexual or racial harassment committed by officers under his command. However, this position has now been remedied by reg 2 of the Sex Discrimination Act 1975 (Amendment) Regulations 2003 (SI 2003/1657) which provides that chief constables of police forces will be vicariously liable for sex discrimination committed by one police officer against another.

If an employee brings a claim under the SDA 1975 but that claim is settled under the auspices of an ACAS conciliation officer the settlement is detailed in a compromise agreement, which is known as COT 3 agreement. Difficulties may arise if an employee brings subsequent victimisation proceedings against the same employer, because the employer may argue that the matter and anything arising from it has been settled. This issue was considered by the EAT in *Royal National*

Orthopaedic Hospital Trust v *Howard* [2002] IRLR 849 where the applicant, Mrs Howard, had worked for the National Orthopaedic Hospital Trust for 18 years. She brought an unfair dismissal and sex discrimination claim against her employers and in 1998 the claims were compromised in a COT 3 agreement, which compromised 'these proceedings and all claims which the Applicant has or may have against the Respondent'. Two years later, she was asked by a surgeon to assist at an operation for one day but the hospital refused to authorise a temporary appointment – she claimed that this was because of her previous sex discrimination claim. Mrs Howard submitted a claim for victimisation to the employment tribunal. The hospital applied to have her claim dismissed on the grounds that the COT 3 agreement precluded Mrs Howard's further claim for victimisation: however, the tribunal found for the applicant. The EAT upheld the decision of the employment tribunal. The compromise agreement did not prevent Mrs Howard from bringing the later claim of victimisation.

Scope of the Sex Discrimination Act 1975

To ensure that employees recieve maximum protection the SDA 1975 applies to every stage of employment from recruitment to dismissal.

Interviews

Section 6 SDA 1975 provides that it is unlawful for a person, in relation to employment by him at an establishment in Great Britain, to discriminate against a woman 'in the arrangements he makes for the purpose of determining who should be offered that employment': s6(1)(a). In *Saunders* v *Richmond-upon-Thames London Borough Council* [1977] IRLR 362 the question arose as to whether questions came within the term 'arrangements' for the purposes of s6(1)(a). The EAT held that the asking of questions may constitute arrangements, but the question to ask is whether by asking such questions a person is treated less favourably on the grounds of sex and that this would be a question of fact in each case.

In *Brennan* v *J H Dewhurst Ltd* [1983] IRLR 357 the conduct of an interview was held to be discriminatory because during the course of the interview the manager of the shop indicated his unwillingness to recruit a woman.

In *Woodhead* v *Chief Constable of West Yorkshire Police* (1990) (unreported) it was held that questions relating to child care and domestic arrangements were not discriminatory arrangements for the purposes of s6(1)(a) because they were an enquiry as to how children were going to be cared for to determine whether the applicant had fully thought through the implications of taking on the office of a police officer. Questions about child-care arrangements put to the applicant in the form of practical considerations with respect to how the children were going to be cared for carried with them no implication that it was the applicant's sole responsibility to involve herself in child care.

Advertisements

It is also unlawful to discriminate against one sex when advertising a vacancy. Section 38 SDA 1975 provides that it is 'unlawful to publish or cause to be published an advertisement which indicates, or might reasonably be understood as indicating, an intention by a person to do any act which is or might be unlawful by virtue of Part II or III [of the SDA 1975]'.

Proceedings in respect of alleged discriminatory advertisements can only be brought by the Equal Opportunities Commission, as in the case of *Equal Opportunities Commission v Robertson* [1980] IRLR 44 where an advertisement for a 'bloke or blokess' was held to be discriminatory. However, in *Brindley v Tayside Health Board* [1976] IRLR 364 it was held by an employment tribunal that an individual is entitled to bring a discrimination claim on the basis that a job advertisement may form part of the 'arrangements' under s6(1)(a) and, although the EAT has cast doubt upon this entitlement, the case has not been expressly overruled.

Discrimination in employment

Any discrimination during the course of employment may also be unlawful. There must be equal opportunities for men and women with respect to training, access to promotion, facilities and transfers. In *Sloan v Strathclyde Regional Council* (1978), an unreported case from the Scottish employment tribunal, it was held to be discriminatory to put men rather than women in temporary jobs which had a better chance of becoming permanent, even though there was no guarantee of permanency. In *Baxter v Glostal Architectural Anodising Ltd* (1976) (unreported) it was held to be unlawful to offer the opportunity for overtime to male employees but not to females.

Difficulties may arise with respect to the terms and conditions of an employment contract. If there is any alleged discrimination in terms and conditions between male and female employees then a claim can be brought under the Equal Pay Act 1970 and this will be considered further in Chapter 7. If, however, a prospective employee has been offered employment but has not yet accepted and believes that there may be discrimination, then such a claim can be brought under s6(6) SDA 1975.

Sexual harassment

The SDA 1975 as originally enacted did not specifically provide protection from sexual harassment, although we have already seen in *Porcelli v Strathclyde Regional Council* [1986] ICR 564 'treatment' has been interpreted to include sexual harassment.

In *Bracebridge Engineering v Darby* [1990] IRLR 3 it was held that a single act of sexual harrassment can amount to 'treatment' for the purpose of s1(1)(a) SDA 1975 and a 'detriment' within the meaning of s6(2)(b).

However, in October 2005 the Employment Equality (Sex Discrimination) Regulations 2005 (SI 2005/2467) were introduced to comply with the amending

Equal Treatment Directive 2002/73/EC. The Regulations amend the Sex Discrimination Act 1975 to include for the first time a statutory definition of harassment. Regulation 5 inserts a new section 4A into the Sex Discrimination Act 1975 which provides that a person subjects a woman to harassment if, on the grounds of her sex, he engages in unwanted conduct which violates her dignity or creates an intimidating, hostile, degrading, humiliating or offensive environment. Furthermore, a person will be regarded as having committed sexual harassment if he engages in unwanted verbal, non-verbal or physical conduct of a sexual nature that affects a person's dignity or creates an intimidating, hostile, degrading, humiliating or offensive environment. The effect of this is that we now have a much more broad definition of sexual harassment which can include non-verbal, non-physical conduct. The practical effect of this is that employers need to be particularly careful with respect to less obvious conduct by employees. The Christmas lucky dip which may contain suggestive items which could cause offence could be a potential minefield for employers may become a thing of the past!

An employer will not be automatically liable for acts of harassment committed by his employees, even though s41 SDA 1975 states that anything done by a person in the course of his employment shall be treated as done by his employer, whether or not it was done with the employer's knowledge or approval. In *Balgobin* v *Tower Hamlets London Borough Council* [1987] IRLR 401 the EAT held that an employer who could show that he was unaware of sexual harassment, had provided staff with proper supervision and had in place a well known equal-opportunities' policy could escape liability.

An employer will not be liable under the SDA 1975 if he can show that a man would have been subject to the same treatment: *Balgobin* v *Tower Hamlets London Borough Council* (above) where, following an inconclusive investigation, an employee was allowed to return to work. It was held that the women who had complained of sexual harassment were in the position as a hypothetical man who had been subjected to homosexual advances and the position they were in was because of the inconclusive investigation not because of their sex.

Gender reassignment
The Equal Treatment Directive (76/207/EEC) also applies to employees who have suffered discrimination or harassment as a result of gender reassignment. In *P* v *S and Cornwall County Council* [1996] IRLR 347 the European Court of Justice held that a woman who was dismissed because she was to have surgery for gender reassignment had suffered discrimination. The Court considered that the principle of equality is one of the fundamental principles of community law and that art 5(1) of the Equal Treatment Directive, which provides that the principles of equal treatment also include conditions governing dismissal, precludes the dismissal of a transexual because of gender reassignment.

The decision of the ECJ was followed by the EAT in *Chessington World of Adventures Ltd* v *Reed* [1997] IRLR 556 to include protection for harassment. The applicant changed her gender identity from male to female, she changed her name to Niki and her work colleagues became aware of her change. The applicant claimed that since her change she had been subjected to continued harassment from her male colleagues and that she had been unlawfully discriminated against. The employment tribunal held that the applicant had been subject to unlawfuly discrimination. The EAT held that the tribunal was correct to interpret the SDA 1975 to include those who have suffered discrimination on the grounds of gender reassignment. It was also held that where harassment is sex-based there is no requirement for any comparison to be made with someone of the opposite sex subjected to the same treatment. The applicant has merely to satisfy a tribunal that his or her employers, aware of the harassment, did nothing to stop it.

Protection for employees undergoing gender reassignment was given statutory force in 1999 with the implementation of the Sex Discrimination (Gender Reassignment) Regulations 1999 (SI 1999/1102).

In *Chief Constable of West Yorkshire Police* v *A* [2004] ICR 806 the House of Lords held that it is unlawful sex discrimination for a police force to refuse to accept a person as a police constable because he or she had had a sex change, unless justified by for example public interest considerations. See below, *Genuine occupational qualification*.

Sexual orientation
Whilst the European Court considered that the right not to be discriminated against on grounds of sex is one of the fundamental human rights, it did not extend such rights to those who were discriminated against on the grounds of their sexual orientation. In the case of *Grant* v *South West Trains Ltd* [1998] IRLR 206 the employer refused to grant travel concessions to the partner of an employee because they were of the same sex, even though such concessions were available for the partners of heterosexual employees. The ECJ held that the refusal by the employer was not discrimination under either art 119 EC Treaty (now art 141 EC) or the Equal Treatment Directive. The ECJ added that European Community law did not recognise stable relationships between persons of the same sex in the same was as stable relationships between two persons of the opposite sex. The decision of the ECJ was contrary to the opinion of the Advocate-General, who had stated, inter alia, that it would be unjustifiable for an employer to confer benefits on heterosexual couples as opposed to homosexual couples and escape the discriminatory provisions under art 119.

The decision of the ECJ was followed by the House of Lords in the joined cases of *MacDonald* v *Advocate General for Scotland* and *Pearce* v *Mayfield School* [2003] IRLR 512. In the first case Mr MacDonald was in the RAF and applied for a transfer to Air Traffic Control. He declared his homosexuality and was subsequently subjected to a vetting process about his sexual activities. He compulsory resigned in 1997 and claimed unlawful discrimination on the grounds of his sex. In the second case Ms Pearce, a science teacher at a secondary school, was subjected to taunts from children because she was a lesbian. She advised the headmaster that the abuse was causing her stress which, at times, rendered her unfit to work. The headmaster advised her to 'grit your teeth'. Eventually Ms Pearce took early retirement on health grounds and claimed that she had been discriminated against on the grounds of her sex. The crucial question for consideration was whether the Sex Discrimination Act 1975 covered alleged discrimination on the grounds of sexual orientation.

There were two competing arguments. The argument in favour of the application of the Sex Discrimination Act 1975 was that if an employer dismisses a homosexual male who is sexually attracted to men, but would not dismiss a female who is sexually attracted to men, the man has been treated less favourably than the woman and so has been discriminated against on grounds of gender. However, the contrary argument was that the two employees are not in the same position and therefore the correct comparator is an employee who is attracted to a person of the same gender rather than a person who is attracted to a person of the opposite gender.

It was held by the House of Lords held that the SDA 1975 does not protect persons from discrimination on the grounds of their sexual orientation. If an employee is dismissed because he is homosexual this can be regarded as gender-neutral treatment by the employer provided it applies to both homosexual men and lesbian women. This position has now been remedied by the Employment Equality (Sexual Orientation) Regulations 2003 (SI 2003/1661) has largely rectified the position.

Employment Equality (Sexual Orientation) Regulations 2003. These Regulations prohibit discrimination on the grounds of sexual orientation. The Regulations apply to all employment and vocational training and include recruitment, terms and conditions, transfers, dismissals and training.

Regulation 3 provides that it is unlawful to directly discriminate against any person, that is to treat them less favourably than others because of their actual or perceived sexual orientation. Furthermore, reg 3 protects employees from indirect discrimination by providing that it is unlawful to apply a criterion provision or practice which disadvantages people of a particular sexual orientation unless it can be objectively justified.

Regulation 4 makes it unlawful to victimise a person because they have made, or intend to make, a complaint or allegation in relation to a complaint of discrimination on the grounds of sexual orientation. This provision extends to persons who have given, or intend to give, evidence in relation to a complaint of discrimination on the grounds of sexual orientation.

Regulation 5 protects employees from harassment. Harassment is unwanted conduct that violates a person's dignity or creates an intimidating, hostile, degrading, humiliating or offensive environment for them having regard to all the circumstances, including the perception of the employee.

Regulation 21 provides that it is unlawful to discriminate against a person after the working relationship has ended where the discrimination or harassment arises out of, and is closely connected to, that relationship.

References
The European Court of Justice held in the case of *Coote* v *Granada Hospitality Ltd* [1998] IRLR 656 that the SDA 1975 is in breach of European law. Council Directive 76/207/EEC applies to victimisation which takes place after the termination of employment, whilst the SDA 1975 only provides protection during the period of employment. In this case Ms Coote, who had been employed by the respondents from December 1992 until September 1993, complained to an employment tribunal that she had been dismissed because of her pregnancy contrary to the SDA 1975. The matter was settled but Ms Coote made a further application to the tribunal claiming that the respondents had failed to provide an employment reference because of her earlier complaint to the tribunal in respect of her dismissal and that this amounted to unlawful victimisation contrary to s4(1) SDA 1975. The tribunal considered that the 1975 Act only applied to discrimination during the course of employment and therefore it did not have jurisdiction to hear the application. Ms Coote appealed to the EAT who referred to the ECJ in respect of whether UK legislation was contrary to Council Directive 76/207/EEC in that the SDA 1975 applies only to discrimination within the employment relationship.

Post-termination
It has been established that an employer may still be liable to an employee for victimisation after the employment relationship has ended. The extent of any liability was considered by the House of Lords in the case of *Relaxion Group* v *Rhys-Harper; D'Souza* v *London Borough of Lambeth; Jones* v *3M Healthcare* [2003] IRLR 484. These three joined cases involved claims brought under the Sex Discrimination Act 1975, the Race Relations Act 1976 and the Disability Discrimination Act 1995, and were all concerned with whether acts done after the termination of the employment relationship could be regarded as being within the scope of the three anti-discrimination statutes. The House of Lords held that discriminatory acts committed by an employer after the termination of the employment relationship would be regarded as being covered by the three statutes if there is a substantive connection between the employment relationship and the discriminatory conduct.

Regulations 3 and 4 of the Sex Discrimination Act 1975 (Amendment) Regulations 2003 (SI 2003/1657) partly implement the decision of the House of Lords in *Relaxion Group* v *Rhys-Harper* and prohibit discrimination where the act of discrimination arises out of, and is closely connected with, the employment relationship even though the employment relationship has come to an end.

The test to be applied to alleged acts of post-employment discrimination is whether there is a substantive connection between the employment relationship and the discriminatory conduct. The practical effect will be that an ex-employee will no longer have to establish victimisation and will be able to bring a claim if there is discrimination in the way he or she is treated during the process of dismissal or after the employment relationship has ended.

The burden of proof

The burden of proof in sex discrimination cases under the SDA 1975 was changed in October 2001 by the Sex Discrimination (Indirect Discrimination and Burden of Proof) Regulations 2001. These Regulations insert s63A into the SDA 1975 which provides as follows:

> '63A(2) Where, on the hearing of the complaint, the complainant proves facts from which the tribunal could, apart from this section, conclude in the absence of an adequate explanation that the respondent –
> (a) has committed an act of discrimination against the complainant which is unlawful under Part 2 [the employment field], or
> (b) is by virtue of section 41 or 42 [of the SDA 1975: liability of employers and aiding unlawful acts] to be treated as having committed such an act of discrimination against the complainant,
> the tribunal shall uphold the complaint unless the respondent proves that he did not commit, or, as the case may be, is not to be treated as having committed, that act.'

In *Barton* v *Investec Henderson Crosthwaite Securities Ltd* [2003] IRLR 332 the EAT gave guidance on how the burden of proof and the application of s63A should be approached.

In *Igen* v *Wong* [2005] IRLR 258 the Court of Appeal restated these guidelines, subject to a few minor changes. The guidance given by the Court of Appeal is stated in terms of sex discrimination but can be regarded as applying equally to disability discrimination. The guidance is as follows:

1. Pursuant to s63A SDA 1975, it is for the claimant who complains of sex discrimination to prove on the balance of probabilities facts from which the tribunal could conclude, in the absence of an adequate explanation, that the respondent has committed an act of discrimination against the claimant which is unlawful by virtue of Part 2 or which by virtue of s41 or s42 SDA 1975 is to be treated as having been committed against the claimant. These are referred to below as 'such facts'.
2. If the claimant does not prove such facts the claim must fail.
3. It is important to bear in mind in deciding whether the claimant has proved such facts that it is difficult and unusual to find direct evidence of sex discrimination. Generally employers are reluctant to admit to such discrimination, even to themselves. In some cases the discrimination will not be an intention but merely based on the assumption that 'he or she would not have fitted in'.
4. In deciding whether the claimant has proved such facts, the analysis by the tribunal will usually depend on what inferences it is proper to draw from the primary facts found by the tribunal.
5. It is important to bear in mind the word 'could' in s63A(2). At this stage the

tribunal does not have to determine that such facts would lead it to the conclusion that there was an act of unlawful discrimination. At this point a tribunal is looking at the primary facts before it to see what inferences of secondary fact could be drawn from them.
6. In considering what inferences or conclusions can be drawn from the primary facts, the tribunal must assume that there is no adequate explanation for those facts.
7. These inferences can include, in appropriate cases, that it is just and equitable to draw in accordance with s74(2)(b) SDA 1975 an unfavourable inference from an evasive or equivocal reply to a questionnaire or any other questions that fall within s74(2) SDA 1975.
8. The tribunal must also decide whether any provision of any relevant code of practice is relevant in drawing an inference and, if so, take it into account in determining such facts pursuant to s56A(10) SDA 1975. This means that inferences may also be drawn from any failure to comply with any relevant code of practice.
9. Where the claimant has proved facts from which conclusions could be drawn that the respondent has treated the claimant less favourably on the ground of sex, then the burden of proof moves to the respondent.
10. It is then for the respondent to prove that he did not commit an act of unlawful discrimination.
11. To discharge that burden the respondent must prove, on the balance of probabilities, that the treatment was in no sense whatsoever on the grounds of sex, since 'no discrimination whatsoever' is compatible with the Burden of Proof Directive.
12 The tribunal must assess not merely whether the respondent has provided an explanation for the facts from which such inferences can be drawn, but further that it is adequate to discharge the burden of proof on the balance of probabilities that sex was not a ground for the treatment in question.
13. Cogent evidence will be required to discharge the burden of proof because any explanation for the unfavourable treatment would normally be in the possession of the respondent. The tribunal will therefore need to examine carefully explanations for failure to deal with the questionnaire procedure and/or code of practice.

The requirement that the treatment by the respondent was in 'no sense whatsoever on the grounds of sex' was further clarified be the EAT in *Chamberlin Solicitors* v *Emokpae* [2004] IRLR 592, where it was said that in *Barton* the EAT was not saying that the respondent had to show that gender had no effect whatsoever on they way they treated an applicant; what was required was for the employer to show on the balance of probabilities that the less favourable treatment was not significantly influenced by gender.

The weight of evidence necessary to satisfy the burden of proof was considered by the Court of Appeal in *Nelson* v *Carillion Services Ltd* [2003] IRLR 428. The applicant was claiming indirect pay discrimination but failed to provide statistics in support of her argument that the employer's pay practice had a disproportionate effect on women. The Court of Appeal said that the burden of 'proving on the balance of probabilities facts from which the tribunal could conclude, in the absence of an adequate explanation, that the respondents had committed an act of discrimination' could not be satisfied by only raising a 'credible suggestion' that, were relevant statistics provided, they might establish a disproportionate impact on women.

Defences
Genuine occupational qualification. We have already seen that s6(1)(a) provides that it is unlawful to discriminate in the arrangements for determining who shall be offered employment, that s6(1)(c) provides that it is discriminatory to refuse to offer that employment on the grounds of sex and that s6(2)(a) provides that there may be discrimination in respect of opportunities for promotion, transfer or training, or to any other benefits, facilities or services, or by refusing or deliberately omitting to afford access to them.

If an employer faces a claim under these subsections he may try to invoke the defence of genuine occupational qualification.

Section 7 provides as follows:

'(1) In relation to sex discrimination –
(a) section 6(1)(a) or (c) does not apply to any employment where being a man is a genuine occupational qualification for the job, and
(b) section 6(2)(a) does not apply to opportunities for promotion or transfer to, or training for, such employment.'

Section 7(2) provides that an employer may discriminate on the grounds and claim a defence of genuine occupational qualification if he can prove any of the following.

1. The nature of the job calls for a man for reasons of physiology (excluding physical strength or stamina) or, in dramatic performances or other entertainment, for reasons of authenticity, so that the essential nature of the job would be materially different if carried out by a woman.
2. The job needs to be held by a man to preserve decency or privacy because it is likely to involve physical contact with men in circumstances where they might reasonably object to its being carried out by a woman, or the holder of the job is likely to do his work in circumstances where men might reasonably object to the presence of a woman because they are in a state of undress or are using sanitary facilities.
3. The job is likely to involve the holder of the job carrying out duties, or living, in a private home and needs to be held by a person of one sex rather than the other because objection might reasonably be taken to one particular sex.
4. The nature or location of the establishment makes it impracticable for the holder

of the job to live elsewhere other than in premises provided by the employer and the only premises are not reasonably equipped with separate sleeping accommodation.
5. The nature of the establishment, or of the part of it within which the work is done, requires the job to be held by a particular sex because it is, or is part of, a hospital, prison or other establishment for persons requiring special care, supervision or attention by a person of a particular sex.
6. The holder of the job provides individuals with personal services promoting their welfare or education, or similar personal services, and those services can most effectively be provided by a person of a particular sex.
7. The job needs to be held by a man because it is likely to involve the performance of duties outside the United Kingdom in a country whose laws or customs are such that the duties could not, or could not effectively, be performed by a woman.
8. The Employment Act 1989 provides that discrimination may be lawful if it is necessary to protect women at work to comply with a statutory requirement prior to the SDA 1975 with respect to pregnacy, maternity or other risks concerning women or to comply with the Health and Safety at Work etc Act 1974.

In *Lasertop Ltd* v *Webster* [1997] IRLR 498 Mr Webster applied for a position as a sales manager with the respondents who operated ladies-only health clubs. He was informed by telephone that the jobs were for women only. He complained to an employment tribunal that he had been unlawfully discriminated against on the grounds of sex. The tribunal upheld his complaint even though the employer claimed genuine occupational qualification as their defence: s7(2)(b)(ii) SDA 1975 – that the job should be held by a woman to preserve 'decency or privacy' because duties included showing prospective members around the changing rooms and other places where women might reasonably object to the presence of a man.

The tribunal, however, rejected this defence and considered that s7(4) applied, which provides that the genuine occupational qualification defence under s7(2)(b) could not be relied upon because there would be sufficient women in the employment of the respondent who could carry out any duties that concerned the protection of decency without undue inconvenience to the employer. The employer appealed, stating that s7(4) was not relevant because at the time of advertising the position the club was not open and as such there were no female employees capable of performing the said duties.

The EAT allowed the employer's appeal and held that the employer could rely upon a defence of genuine occupational qualification. The EAT further held that the true construction of s7(4) requires consideration of the time when the purported discrimination took place and, in the instant case, at that time the employer did not have sufficient female employees capable of carrying out the prohibited duties.

If, however there are other employees of the appropriate sex to carry out duties which are of a personal nature the the defence may not operate. In *Wylie* v *Dee &*

Co (Menswear) Ltd [1978] IRLR 103 a woman who may have been required to take the inside leg measurements of gentlemen was refused a job in a gentleman's outfitters and claimed that she had been unlawfully discriminated against. The employer's claim of genuine occupational qualification failed on the basis that when it was necessary to take personal measurements there were plenty of other staff to undertake the job.

The genuine occupational qualification defence is only applicable to claims brought under s6(1)(a) or (c) or s6(2)(a) and therefore if an employee claims that he has been dismissed on the grounds of sex and brings his claim under the SDA 1975 the employer will not be able to raise a defence of genuine occupational qualification.

In *Timex Corporation* v *Hodgson* [1981] IRLR 522 a man was selected for redundancy and a female employee retained even though she had less service than her male colleague. The company argued genuine occupational qualification, stating that it was necessary to keep on a woman supervisor to deal with women's issues. The male employee complained that he had been discriminated against contrary to the SDA 1975 in that he had been selected for redundancy on the grounds of his sex. The tribunal found in his favour and rejected the genuine occupational defence put forward by the respondents because the defence did not apply to a dismissal situation. The company appealed.

It was held by the EAT that the discrimination against the male employee had taken place in the form of failing to transfer him or omitting to offer him an alternative job, and in either case the defence of genuine occupational qualification was a permissible one. The case was remitted to the employment tribunal to determine whether the requirement for a woman did amount to such a defence.

In *A* v *Chief Constable of West Yorkshire Police* [2004] IRLR 573 the House of Lords rejected a defence of genuine occupational qualification relied upon by the respondents who argued that the claimant could not perform the full duties required of her. In 1998 the Chief Constable of the West Yorkshire Police refused Ms A's job application on the basis that she was a male-female transsexual and could not perform the full 'searching' duties required of a police officer. The issue was whether Ms A has been subjected to unlawful sex discrimination. The Chief Constable admitted that the refusal to offer the position was prima facie discriminatory, but defended the claim on the basis that the requirement to be able to carry out a search was a 'genuine occupational qualification'.

The House of Lords held that this was an act of sex discrimination and that the requirement of a specific gender was not a genuine occupational qualification. The House of Lords considered that it would have been within the operational control of the Chief Constable to assign search duties to another officer. The refusal to employ Ms A was not, in the view of the Court, a proportional response to the situation.

This judgment is very interesting and complex, however it has been largely overtaken by the introduction of the Gender Reassignment Regulations.

National security. Another possible defence is provided by s52 SDA 1975 which provides that any discrimination shall not be unlawful if it is done for the purpose of safeguarding national security. In order to prove this defence the employer would have to provide a certificate purporting to be signed by, or on behalf of, a minister of the Crown certifying that the act specified in the certificate was done for the purpose of safeguarding national security.

Other exceptions. Section 43 SDA 1975 provides that charitable trusts are exempted from the application of the Act and an example of this can be seen in the case of *Hugh-Jones* v *St John's College, Cambridge* [1979] ICR 848 where a female graduate, who was refused a research fellowship because such fellowships were not open to women, was unsuccesful in her claim because the college had charitable status.

Further exceptions can be found in s17 SDA 1975 which provides that in respect of police officers discrimination may be permissible when considering requirements relating to height, uniform or equipment, or allowances in lieu of uniform or equipment, or in so far as special treatment is accorded to women in connection with pregnancy or childbirth. Section 18 provides that discrimination will not be unlawful with respect to male and female prison officers as to requirements relating to height and s19 states that in respect of an organised religion, where the employment is limited to one sex so as to comply with the doctrines of the religion or avoid offending the religious susceptibilities of a significant number of its followers, there will be an exemption from the provisions of the Act.

Positive discrimination

Positive discrimination is contrary to both the Equal Treatment Directive (76/207/EEC) and the SDA 1975. In *Kalanke* v *Freie Hansestadt Bremen* [1996] ICR 314 the European Court of Justice ruled strongly against positive discrimination where a man who was equally qualified for a job was passed over for promotion in favour of a woman because of a law which favoured female candidates. However, in the later case of *Marschall* v *Land Nordrhein-Westfalen* [1998] IRLR 39 the ECJ, contrary to the opinion of the Advocate-General, appears to have allowed limited positive discrimination. In this case Mr Marschall was a German school teacher in North Rhine Westphalia. In that region there was provision applicable to civil servants which provided for positive discrimination in favour of women if it could be shown that there were fewer women or men in a particular grade. In 1994 Marschall applied for a promotion but was told that the position was to be offered to a woman because of the policy of positive discrimination if women were under-represented. Mr Marschall brought legal proceedings and the German court referred the matter to the ECJ to determine whether the provision in question was contrary to the Equal Treatment Directive.

The ECJ held that because the provision which gave preference to women in the event of under-representation was subject to the rider 'unless reasons specific to the individual (male) candidate tilt the balance in his favour' such a provision was not contrary to the Equal Treatment Directive. It was considered that there was an objective assessment which took into account criteria which were specific to male candidates and that this objective assessment saved the provision from falling foul of the Directive.

Whilst it can be seen that because there was some objective assessment in *Marschall* it can be distinguished from *Kalanke*, it is also necessary to bear in mind that the decision of the Court is in accordance with the amendment to art 119 (now art 141 EC) by the Treaty of Amsterdam 1997 which provides for positive discrimination and addresses some of the criticisms of the decision in *Kalanke*.

Questionnaires

With a view to helping a person who considers he may have been discriminated against s74 SDA 1975 provides for a questionnaire procedure to help the claimant to decide whether to institute proceedings and, if he does, to help him formulate and present his case.

A person considering bringing a complaint under the 1975 Act is generally well advised to use the questionnaire procedure. The forms consist of a questionnaire which the applicant or potential applicant may send to the respondent to ask questions about the reasons for doing an act which has given rise to the applicant's complaint. The use of the questionnaire is of particular benefit in cases involving complaints of indirect discrimination because the answers given by the respondent may give statistical information about his workforce which will assist the complainant to assess the prospects of success.

The time limit for presenting a questionnaire is three months beginning with the date of the act complained of or, if the applicant has already presented an originating application, 21 days from the day of presentation. Answers given in the questionaire may be used in evidence at the tribunal hearing, although it must be noted that in *Rendell* v *University of London Institute of Education* (1977) (unreported) it was held that the tribunals have no power to order a respondent to answer a questionnaire.

Enforcement

A person who believes that they have suffered discrimination contrary to the SDA 1975 may commence a claim in the employment tribunal. Unlike unfair dismissal there is no qualifying employment requirement. A complaint must be presented to the tribunal within three months of the act complained of: s76 SDA 1975.

Remedies

If an employment tribunal finds in favour of the complainant, s63 SDA 1975 provides that the tribunal may do one or more of the following:

1. make an order declaring the rights of the complainant and the respondent in relation to the act to which the complaint relates;

2. make an order requiring the respondent to pay compensation to the complainant;
3. make a recommendation that the respondent take appropriate action to obviate or reduce the adverse effect on the complainant of any act of discrimination to which the complaint relates.

The Sex Discrimination and Equal Pay (Remedies) Regulations 1993 provide that there is no limit placed on the amount of compensation that a tribunal may award. In determining the amount of the award, the tribunal must take into account all losses suffered and may include an amount representing interest. The tribunal can also make an award for injury to feelings, although it should be noted that this part of an award does not attract any interest. In the case of *Vento v Chief Constable of West Yorkshire Police (No 2)* [2003] IRLR 102, the Court of Appeal laid down guidelines with respect to the amount of compensation that should be awarded for injury to feelings. Mummery LJ considered that awards should be made in line with three broad bands of compensation. The range in the top band would be between £15,000 and £25,000 and would only be awarded in the most serious of cases of discrimination where, for example, there had been a prolonged campaign of harassment or discriminating treatment. Awards in the middle band range between £5,000 and £15,000 and should be awarded in cases which, although serious, do not merit an award from the highest band. The third band comprises of awards between £500 and £5,000 which would be made in less serious case where the alleged act of discrimination is a one-off event. Mummery LJ acknowledged that there is a great deal of flexibility within each band which will allow tribunals to make awards that are fair and reasonable, taking into account all the circumstances of each individual case.

It should be noted that there is a distinction between compensation for injury to feelings and an award for psychiatric injury. An award for the former will not exclude an award for the latter.

Time limits

An application must be made to the employment tribunal within three months of when the act complained of was done. However, s76(5) SDA 1975 provides that 'a court or tribunal may nevertheless consider any such complaint, claim or application which is out of time if, in all the circumstances of the case, it considers that it is just and equitable to do so'. This section confers upon the tribunals a wide discretion to hear a complaint out of time. When considering whether to exercise its discretion the tribunal should, when taking into account 'in all the circumstances of the case' as required by s76(5), limit itself to the circumstances relating to why it was not reasonably practicable to submit the application within the three months.

Difficulties can arise in determining the date upon which the three-month time limit begins to run. Where discrimination takes place over an extended period of time s76(6)(b) provides that 'any act extending over a period shall be treated as done at the end of that period'. However, it is not always easy to ascertain when such a period of discrimination ends. The matter was considered by the Court of Appeal in *Cast* v *Croydon College* [1998] IRLR 318. Mrs Cast was a full-time employee. In March 1992, whilst pregnant, she asked her employers if she could return to either a job share or part-time working after she returned from maternity leave but her request was rejected on 26 March 1992. Mrs Cast subsequently went on maternity leave and returned to work on 12 March 1993. On 16 March and on 10 May she requested yet again if she could work part time but the requests were refused. On 11 May she asked the College to record their refusal in writing and also said that according to the College's development plan job-sharing was to be introduced. On 14 May the College replied that it was essential for a person in her position to work full time.

On 7 June 1993 Mrs Cast resigned and on 13 August 1993 presented a complaint to the employment tribunal that she had been discriminated on grounds of sex.

The tribunal held that any act of sex discrimination happened on 26 March 1992 when her original application was refused and that further rejection was merely a repetition of that request and refusal. In the circumstances there was no continuing act of discrimination. The tribunal concluded that the presentation of the claim was made out of time. The applicant appealed to the EAT which also dismissed her claim, taking the view of the tribunal that the complaint ran from the original refusal. Mrs Cast appealed to the Court of Appeal.

In allowing the appeal the Court of Appeal held that both the employment tribunal and the EAT had erred in holding that the time to make the complaint ran from the original request. They stated that the employment tribunal should have found that the employer's refusal to a subsequent request to work part time was a continuing 'act extending over a period' within the meaning of s76(6)(b) SDA 1975 and therefore had to be treated as 'done at the end of that period'. The case involved a number of requests and refusals, each decision amounting to a fresh refusal of a fresh request. Therefore, the most recent refusal was relevant for the purpose of time-scale and the case was remitted to the employment tribunal.

6.2 Race discrimination

Introduction

During the 1960s concern was raised about the generally low status of black people, Asian and other non-white employees. This led to the introduction of the Race Relations Act 1965 which was later extended to include protection from racial discrimination in the field of employment. However, such protection was limited and did not provide the opportunitiy for an individual employee to seek redress in the employment tribunals.

The late sixties and early seventies saw an increase in racial tension and it became clear that more broadly based legislation which provided better means of

178   *Discrimination in Employment*

enforcement was required. To meet these requirements to protect all people from discrimination on the grounds of ethnic origin the Race Relations Act (RRA) 1976 was introduced. Part II of the Act specifically seeks to eliminate discrimination in the field of employment and to promote equal opportunities for all employees at all stages of employment. The RRA 1976 also established the Commission for Racial Equality (CRE) whose objective is to work towards the elimination of racial discrimination and to promote equal ooportunities.

The CRE is able to offer advice to individuals on racial matters and may also enforce some of the provisions of the RRA 1976 on behalf of individual employees.

The major provisions of the RRA 1976 and the Sex Discrimination Act 1975 are broadly similar, with many of the general principles such as the prohibition of indirect discrimination being applicable to both pieces of legislation.

The RRA 1976 has recently undergone some significant legislative changes which were brought into effect by the Race Relations Act 1976 (Amendment) Regulations 2003 (SI 2003/1626) which came into force in July 2003 as required by the EC Racial Treatment Directive of July 2000. The Regulations help to bring the RRA 1976 in line with the Sex Discrimination Act (SDA) 1975.

The RRA 1976 does not apply to discrimination on the grounds of religious belief and to overcome this omission the Employment Equality (Religion or Belief) Regulations 2003 (SI 2003/1660) were introduced and will be considered later in this chapter.

Direct discrimination

Section 1(1) RRA 1976 provides that:

> 'A person discriminates against another in any circumstances relevant for the purposes of any provision of this Act if –
> (a) on racial grounds he treats that other less favourably than he treats or would treat other persons; or
> (b he applies to that other a requirement or condition which he applies or would apply equally to persons not of the same racial group as that other but –
> (i) which is such that the proportion of persons of the same racial group as that other who can comply with it is considerably smaller than the proportion of persons not of that racial group who can comply with it; and
> (ii) which he cannot show to be justifiable irrespective of the colour, race, nationality or ethnic or national origins of the person to whom it is applied; and
> (iii) which is to the detriment of that other because he cannot comply with it.'

Thus, where an employer discriminates against a person purely on the grounds of his racial origin his conduct will be unlawful.

The Race Relations Act 1976 (Amendment) Regulations 2003 introduced a new definition of indirect discrimination into the RRA 1976. Section 1(1A) which provides:

> 'A person also discriminates against another if, in any circumstances relevant for the

purposes of any provision referred to in subsection (1B), he applies to that other a provision, criterion or practice which he applies or would apply equally not of the same race or ethnic or national origins as that other, but –
(a) which puts or would put persons of the same race or ethnic or national origins as that other at a particular disadvantage when compared with other persons,
(b) which puts that other at that disadvantage, and
(c) which he cannot show to be a proportionate means of achieving a legitimate aim.'

Section 1(1A) has broadened the scope of what constitutes indirect race discrimination. It will no longer be necessary for a claimant to show that a requirement or condition imposed by an employer is one that he could not comply with and therefore acted as a complete bar. A claimant will only have to establish that a provision, criterion or practice is one which has an adverse impact and disproportionate effect on the complainant's racial group.

Further, with respect to employment, s4(1) provides that:

'It is unlawful for a person, in relation to employment by him at an establishment in Great Britain, to discriminate against another –
(a) in the arrangements he makes for the purpose of determining who should be offered that employment; or
(b) in the terms on which he offers him that employment; or
(c) by refusing or deliberately omitting to offer him that employment.'

Difficulties may arise where a person's colour or ethnic origin are just some of the factors that have given rise to alleged discrimination. An employee who believes that he has been subjected to race discrimination must show that race is the effective and substantial reason for the discriminatory treatment. In *Seide* v *Gillette Industries Ltd* [1980] IRLR 427 a Jewish employee alleged that he had been discriminated against because, following anti-semitic remarks made by a colleague, he had been moved to an alternative shift with some loss of pay. Mr Seide was moved again when another colleague on the new shift asked to be moved because the applicant hummed incessantly and tried to make him take sides on the issue of race. The tribunal and the EAT found that the treatment of the applicant by the employers had not been motivated by racial or anti-semitic considerations and that the decision of the employers to move him had been to preserve good working relationships within the company.

If an employer puts forward other grounds which may also have been a factor in the treatment of an employee it is for the tribunal to consider whether the alleged discriminatory treatment is because of the factors alleged or because of discrimination.

In *Owen and Briggs* v *James* [1982] ICR 618 Miss James applied for a job as a typist with a firm of solicitors. She was interviewed but was not offered the position. A few weeks later she saw the same job advertised and was offered an interview. When she arrived the person conducting the interviews realised that she had been interviewed previously and refused to interview her again. Later the same day a white girl with less qualifications than Miss James was interviewed and offered the position. During the course of the interview the interviewer commented that he did not understand why he would take on a coloured person with so many English girls available for work. Miss James made an application to the employment tribunal claiming that the reason she had not been offered the job was because of her racial origin. The respondents argued in their defence that Miss James's colour was only one factor in their refusal to offer her the position.

It was held by the Court of Appeal that if race is a substantial reason for the alleged discrimination then the tribunals may find any such conduct unlawful, and that in the instant case the tribunal had been correct in finding that the main reason for the respondents' refusal to offer Miss James a job was her colour and that the conduct of the respondents had been unlawful.

Motive

The motive of an employer when subjecting a person to unfavourable treatment is irrelevant and an employer may be liable for direct discrimination even though he is not motivated by racial prejudice: *Din v Carrington Viyella Ltd (Jersey Kapwood Ltd)* [1982] IRLR 281.

A person can suffer direct discrimination even though he is not a member of a minority racial group. In *Showboat Entertainment Centre Ltd v Owens* [1984] IRLR 7 a manager of an amusement arcade refused to follow his employer's instructions not to allow young coloured black people into an amusement arcade. He was dismissed and claimed that he had been discriminated against contrary to s1(1) RRA 1976. The EAT held that the words 'on racial grounds' in s1(1) are capable of covering any action that is based on race whether it is because of the race of the person so affected or because of the race of others. The EAT was clearly influenced by the fact that, if it found for the defendant, employees could be placed in the position where they had to choose between disobeying the law and disobeying an order from an employer and risk losing their job.

Meaning of racial group

The definition of 'racial grounds' and 'racial group' can be found in s3 RRA 1976. Section 3(1) provides that:

> 'In this Act, unless the context otherwise requires –
> "racial grounds" means any of the following grounds, namely colour, race, nationality or ethnic or national origins;
> "racial group" means a group of persons defined by reference to colour, race, nationality or ethnic or national origins, and references to a person's racial group refer to any racial group into which he falls.'

Section 3(2) provides:

> 'The fact that a racial group comprises two or more distinct racial groups does not prevent it from constituting a particular racial group for the purposes of this Act.'

This means that a racial group may comprise people who are the same colour but different nationalities and two groups may comprise of people of the same nationality but different racial groups.

An issue which has been more difficult to determine is whether the RRA 1976 extended to 'ethnic origin'. This is potentially a broad term but one that can be used to define persons who share the same common belief and culture. The leading authority is the case of *Mandla v Dowell Lee* [1983] ICR 385 which was a case of indirect discrimination. The House of Lords held that a school rule forbidding the wearing of turbans could amount to indirect discrimination against Sikhs. In determining whether Sikhs were covered by the RRA 1976 Lord Templeman said:

> 'In my opinion, for the purposes of the Race Relations Act a group of persons defined by reference to ethnic origins must possess some of the characteristics of a race, namely group descent, a group of geographical origin and a group history. The evidence shows that the Sikhs satisfy these tests. They are more than a religious sect, they are almost a race and almost a nation.'

Lord Fraser further identified two essential characteristics that should be satisfied before an ethnic group would be covered by the RRA 1976 and five characteristics that should be taken into consideration.

Essential characteristics
1. A long shared history of which the group is conscious as distinguishing it from other groups, and the memory of which it keeps alive.
2. A cultural tradition of its own, including family and social customs and manners, often but not necessarily associated with religious observance.

Relevant characteristics
1. Either a common geographical origin, or descent from a small number of common ancestors.
2. A common language, not necessarily peculiar to the group.
3. A common literature peculiar to the group.
4. A common religion different from that of neighbouring groups or from the general community surrounding it.
5. Being a minority or being an oppressed or a dominant group within a large community, for example a conquered people (say, the inhabitants of England shortly after the Norman conquest) and their conquerors might both be ethnic groups.

In *Crown Suppliers v Dawkins* [1993] ICR 517 the Court of Appeal held that the refusal to offer employment to a Rastafarian because of his refusal to cut his hair did not amount to racial discrimination because Rastafarians do not constitute a racial group for the purposes of the RRA 1976. The Court of Appeal accepted that they had a shared history of more than 60 years but considered that this was insufficient to set them aside from other members of the Afro-Caribbean community.

The issue of whether the English and Scots are separate racial groups was considered in the case of *Northern Joint Police Board* v *Power* [1997] IRLR 610. Mr Power applied for the post of chief constable of a Scottish constabulary. He was not short-listed and believed that this was because he was English. He complained to an employment tribunal that he had been discriminated against on the grounds of race.

At a preliminary hearing the tribunal held that English and Scots were separate racial groups by reference to their national origins for the purposes of s1(1) RRA 1976 and that there had been discrimination. The police board appealed to the EAT stating that England and Scotland were both parts of the same nation and that Parliament had not intended the RRA 1976 to cover discriminatory claims relating to individual parts of the UK. The EAT upheld the preliminary ruling of the tribunal and remitted the matter to the tribunal to determine whether the applicant had English national origins and whether he had been discriminated against because of those origins.

Detriment

In a claim for race discrimination it is necessary to establish that the applicant has suffered a detriment. In *Ministry of Defence* v *Jeremiah* [1980] IRLR 436 it was said that a detriment means being at a disadvantage. There is no need to show that the employer was hostile: all that is necessary is for the applicant to prove that he or she was in some way disadvantaged by the employer. The test is generally objective: would the reasonable worker consider that he or she has been disadvantaged; *De Souza* v *Automobile Association* [1986] IRLR 103. In *Barclays Bank* v *Kapur* [1995] IRLR 87 it was said that an unjustified sense of grievance could not amount to a detriment. A person can be subjected to a detriment if their reputation is lowered in the eyes of others, even though the employee may be unaware of the fact: *Garry* v *London Borough of Ealing* [2001] IRLR 681.

Continuing treatment

An act of discrimination may be a single act or form part of continuing pattern of conduct. Where an employee is subjected to continuing discrimination this may be regarded as a continuing act for the purposes of limitation: *Owusu* v *London Fire & Civil Defence Authority* [1995] IRLR 574.

In *Derby Specialist Fabrication Ltd* v *Burton* [2001] IRLR 69, the EAT considered that an employee had been subjected to a 'climate of racial abuse'. The employer had been aware of the treatment but had failed to do anything about it. The failure of the employer to prevent racial abuse was held by the EAT to amount to continuing conduct. In *Hendricks* v *Commissioner of Police for the Metropolis* [2003] IRLR 96 Mummery LJ expressed concern that too literal a view was being adopted by the tribunals when looking at what amounts to a 'continuing act' and said that 'The concepts of policy, rule, practice, scheme or regime ... should not be treated as a complete and constricting statement of the indicia of "an act extending over a period".'

Harassment

The issue of racial harassment was not expresslly referred to in the RRA 1976 as originally enacted. However, the Race Relations Act 1976 (Amendment) Regulations 2003 (SI 2003/1626) amend the RRA 1976 and provide that it is unlawful to subject a person to racial harassment: s3A RRA 1976. Regulation 6 amends s4 RRA 1976 to provide protection to employees from racial harassment by an employer.

In *Burton and Rhule* v *De Vere Hotels* [1996] IRLR 596 the applicants, who were both black, worked as waitresses at the defendant's hotel. One evening the entertainment was provided by Bernard Manning who made offensive jokes and comments about coloured people. The applicants claimed that they had been subjected to racial harassment. The EAT held that because the employer was aware that Mr Manning was known for his racially offensive remarks they could have prevented the harassment and was therefore liable.

In order for an employer to be vicariously liable for any racial harassment of an employee by other employees it is necessary to establish that the harassment was carried out in the course of employment within the meaning of s32 RRA 1976.

This issue of vicarious liabilty was considered by the Court of Appeal in *Jones* v *Tower Boot Co Ltd* [1997] IRLR 168. The applicant, Mr Jones, was employed by the respondents as a machine operator from 16 April 1992. He resigned a month later. He complained to an employment tribunal that during the time of his employment he had been subjected to racial harassment from his fellow workers. He had been burnt on his arm with a hot screwdriver, his legs had been whipped with a piece of welt, he had metal bolts thrown at him and had a notice 'chipmonks are go' stuck on his back. Furthermore, he had repeatedly been called 'chimp', 'monkey' and 'baboon'.

The tribunal held that the acts complained of had been carried out 'in the course of employment', falling within the meaning of s32 RRA 1976. The employers were therefore vicariously liable for the harassment.

The employers appealed to the EAT which allowed their appeal. They held that they could not be liable for the harassment as it was not done in the course of employment. The EAT applied the common-law test for whether an act is done in the course of employment – whether the unauthorised wrongful act of the employee was so connected with that which he was employed to do as to be a mode of doing it. In applying this test it could not accept that the acts complained of were an improper mode of performing authorised tasks. The EAT remitted the case to an employment tribunal on the grounds that the management had subjected the complainant to a detriment in allowing the said abuse to continue. The employers appealed against the decision to remit and the employee appealed against the decision to set aside the decision of the employment tribunal.

The Court of Appeal held that the employment tribunal had erred in applying the common-law test and that for the purpose of s32 RRA 1976 the words 'in the course of employment' should be interpreted broadly. They considered that it would be wrong to allow an employer to escape liability for racial discrimination on the scale suffered by the employee by using the common-law test.

Thus, in *Jones* the Court of Appeal gave a purposive construction to s32 RRA 1976 which requires a broad interpretation of the the words 'in the course of employment' so that they are interpreted in the sense in which they are used in everyday speech. This will mean that in deciding whether an employer is vicariously liable it will be a question of fact to be determined by a tribunal on a case-by-case basis.

Victimisation

An employee who has previously raised a race issue with his employer should not be treated less favourably because of his previous complaint. Section 2 RRA 1976 provides that such victimisation is unlawful:

> '(1) A person ("the discriminator") discriminates against another person ("the person victimised") in any circumstances relevant for the purposes of any provision of this Act if he treats the person victimised less favourably than in those circumstances he treats or would treat other persons, and does so by reason that the person victimised has –
> (a) brought proceedings against the discriminator or any other person under this Act; or
> (b) given evidence or information in connection with proceedings brought by any person against the discriminator or any other person under this Act; or
> (c) otherwise done anything under or by reference to this Act in relation to the discriminator or any other person; or
> (d) alleged that the discriminator or any other person has committed an act which (whether or not the allegation so states) would amount to a contravention of this Act ...'

In order for there to be discrimination by means of victimisation two tests have to be satisfied. First, the discriminator must treat the person victimised less favourably than he would treat other persons and, second, the discriminator treats the person victimised less favourably because of the previous complaints made by the 'victim'.

In *Nagarajan* v *London Regional Transport* [1999] 3 WLR 425 the appellant, Mr Nagarajan, had been employed by London Underground Ltd (LUL) from June 1979 until December 1988. He was then employed by London Regional Transport (LRT), a holding company for LUL, for four months as a travel consultant and then from May 1989 until October 1989 as a duty train manager.

During his employment with LUL and LRT the appellant brought several complaints of race discrimination and victimisation.

In 1992 the appellant applied for the post of word-processor operator with LUL that had been advertised. He received no response to his application and contacted the company's solicitors. He was advised that his application had not been received but to reapply when other posts were advertised. The appellant believed that the reason he had not received a response to his application was because of the complaints that he had previously brought and he complained to the employment tribunal.

The tribunal upheld his claim, holding that his application had disappeared despite being sent to the correct address, although the tribunal did not draw any adverse inference in respect of the disappearance. However, the tribunal did draw an adverse inference from the fact that the appellant was not advised to submit a fresh application for the post for which he had applied. The employers appealed and their appeal was allowed at the EAT and the Court of Appeal. Mr Nagarajan further appealed to the House of Lords.

The appeal was allowed (Lord Browne-Wilkinson dissenting). The House of Lords held that a person can discriminate on racial grounds under s1(1)(a) RRA 1976 even though the discriminator was not consciously motivated and therefore ss1(1)(a) and 2(1) should be read in the same way albeit that the terms used are different. A complainant can therefore be victimised under s2(1) even though the discriminator was not consciously motivated by the complainant's previous claims. In this case it was held that the finding of the employment tribunal that the discriminator had been 'consciously or subconsciously' motivated when interviewing the complainant and in rejecting his application was sufficient to find discrimination under s2(1).

Scope of the Race Relations Act 1976

In the context of employment, the Race Relations Act 1976 applies not only to employees but also expressly applies to contract workers: s7 RRA 1976. Section 7 therefore has the effect of making the end user of a worker's services potentially liable in the event of discrimination. An example of the application of s7 can be found in the case of *Harrods Ltd* v *Remick* [1997] IRLR 583. In this case Harrods granted licences to various companies to sell goods in their store. The concessionaires employed their own staff, but those staff had to be approved by Harrods and were required to conform to Harrods' dress code and rules of conduct. A failure to conform to these standards could lead to Harrods withdrawing 'approval' which would mean that the individual concerned would no longer be allowed to work in the store. The case arose out of three unrelated concessionaire arrangements involving women who had either lost their approval or had failed to be approved in the first place. The applicants claimed race discrimination. The issue for consideration was whether Harrods had discriminated against the women in the capacity of principal contrary to s7(1) RRA 1976 and whether the women were carrying out work for Harrods within the meaning of s7(1). The Court of Appeal held that Harrods were liable for race discrimination. It did not matter that the employees were employed by a concessionaire; the fact was that each concessionaire had a contract with Harrods and the work was performed for the principal. The goods sold by the concessionaire belonged to the store at the moment of sale and the monies received were credited to Harrods. Taking these factors into account, along with the dress code requirement and rules relating to conduct, the reality was that the ladies were working for Harrods.

Whilst it is clear that contract workers are covered within the scope of the RRA 1976 the Act does not cover those persons who are self-employed. In *Mingeley* v *Pennock and Another (t/a Amber Cars)* [2004] ICR 727 the Court of Appeal held that the employment tribunal was correct in holding that it did not have jurisdiction to hear a claim under the RRA 1976 because Mr Mingeley was not in employment within the definition of s78(1) of the 1976 Act, where employment means:

> 'employment under a contract of service or of apprenticeship or a contract personally to execute any work or labour ...'

In this case Mr Mingeley was a taxi driver who owned his own vehicle. He had an arrangement with the respondents whereby for £75 per week he was provided with a radio and access to a computer system which allocated customers to drivers. Although he was required to wear a uniform and charge fares set by the respondents, all other factors indicated that he was self-employed. Accordingly, he was not therefore in the employment of the respondents and his claim was dismissed.

Illegality

In accordance with general contractual principles a claimant will find it difficult to rely upon an illegal contract to found a claim of race discrimination. This issue was considered recently by the EAT in the case of *Vakante* v *Governing Body of Addey and Stanhope School (No 2)* [2004] ICR 279. The claimant was an asylum-seeker who was given limited permission to remain in the country. One of the restrictions imposed upon him was that he was not allowed to work without permission from the Home Office. The claimant, in breach of the condition, commenced work with the respondent. He was subsequently dismissed and claimed that he had been discriminated against contrary to s4(2) RRA 1976. At tribunal the claimant was successful, despite the argument advanced by the employer that the claimant was not entitled to rely upon an illegal contract. However, on appeal the EAT remitted the case back to the employment tribunal to determine whether the claim of discrimination was closely linked with the issue of illegality, in which case he would not be able to rely upon the contract. At the remitted hearing the tribunal held that the claim which related to access to training, benefits and his dismissal was inextricable linked with the conduct of the claimant and therefore his claim failed. Mr Vakante appealed to the EAT where it was held that the illegality of the contract was attributable to the conduct of Mr Vakante, it was he who had breached the conditions under which he was allowed to be in the country and therefore he would not be allowed to succeed in his claim of race discrimination.

Vicarious liability

At common law an employer will normally only be vicariously liable for the wrongful acts of employees if they are committed in the course of employment. The common law test is whether the unauthorised wrongful act of the employee was so connected with that which he was employed to do, as to be a mode of carrying out his duties. The problem that arises is that the more serious the misconduct of the employee the easier it is for the employer to argue that it is not connected with his employment. Section 32 RRA 1976 provides that an employer will be vicariously liable for discriminatory acts committed by his employees unless he can show that he took such steps as were reasonably practical to prevent the employees carrying out the discriminatory act.

However. in the case of *Jones* v *Tower Boot Co Ltd* [1997] IRLR 168 the Court of Appeal said that the common law test was not appropriate in discrimination cases. In this case Mr Jones, who was only employed by the respondents for one month, claimed that he had been subjected to the most horrendous racial harassment by his fellow workers. He had been burnt on his arm with a hot screwdriver, his legs had been whipped with a piece of welt, he had metal bolts thrown at him and a notice saying 'chipmonks are go' pinned on his back. Furthermore, he had repeatedly been called 'chimp', 'monkey' and 'baboon' by his fellow workers. At the employment tribunal it was held that the conduct of the fellow workers had taken place within the 'course of employment' and, accordingly, the respondents would be vicariously liable for the discrimination. However, on appeal the EAT applied the common law test for whether an act is done in the course of employment and held that the misconduct of the fellow workers could not be considered as an improper mode of carrying out their authorised duties. There was a futher appeal to the Court of Appeal where it was held that the EAT had erred in applying the common law test and that for the purposes of s32 RRA 1976 and the corresponding s41 Sex Discrimination Act 1975 the words 'in the course of employment' should be interpreted broadly.

Genuine occupational qualification

Section 5 RRA 1976 provides that with respect to certain jobs an employer may raise a defence to a race claim by establishing that being a member of a particular racial group is a genuine occupational qualification. It would therefore be lawful for the owner of a Thai restaurant to employer Thai waiting staff. Section 5(2) specifies the circumstances and jobs in which the defence will apply and these include actors, models, waiting staff where a waitress or waiter of a particular racial group is required for reasons of authenticity and jobs which involve providing personal services which promote the welfare of persons of their own racial group.

The Race Relations Act 1976 (Amendment) Regulations 2003 provide a new defence for an employer where race is a 'genuine and determining requirement' for the job. This defence can be found in s4A RRA 1976. However, it must be noted that an employer will have to show that being of a particular race is proportionate in the circumstances.

Questionnaire

An employe who believes that he has been racially discriminated against can present a questionnaire to his employer to ask questions relating to his treatment under the Race Relations (Questions and Replies) Order 1977 (SI 1977/842).

This questionnaire can be used in evidence at a subsequent tribunal hearing. The questionnaire is in a set form. If the claimant wants to advance the questionnaire and its answers at the tribunal hearing, the questionnaire must generally have been served within three months of the discriminatory act. The respondent must respond to the questionnaire within eight weeks unless he can show that more time was required to reply to properly respond.

Time limits

The time limit for submitting a claim to the employment tribunal is three months from the date of the discriminatory act. However, tribunals do have the power to exercise discretion and extend the time limit for presenting a claim. This was recently considered by the Court of Appeal in *London Borough of Southwark* v *Afolabi* [2003] IRLR 220.

Mr Afolabi was employed by the council from 1973 in several different accounting positions. Following a re-grading in 1998 Mr Afolabi presented a race discrimination complaint on the grounds that he had been treated less favourably than white colleagues. In April 1999 Mr Afolabi inspected his personal file for the first time and discovered what he believed to be a further act of discrimination which dated from 1990. He presented a further a claim of race discrimination within three months of reviewing his file. The employment tribunal considered that it was just and equitable to hear the complaint even though it was presented almost nine years after the expiry of the statutory time limit. This decision was upheld by the EAT. At a further appeal hearing the Court of Appeal held that the employment tribunal had not erred in exercising its discretion to hear the complaint despite the length of time between the act of discrimination and the presentation of the complaint.

Time limits do also apply to the serving of questionnaire's as detailed above.

Burden of proof

To bring the burden of proof for race discrimination in line with the Sex Discrimination Act 1975, the Race Relations Act 1976 (Amendment) Regulations 2003 reversed the burden of proof so that if a claimant is able to establish a prima facie case of indirect discrimination, the burden shifts to the respondent to prove that the act complained of was not racial discrimination.

Compensation

Since the removal of the statutory limit for successful race discrimination claims in 1994 the employment tribunal can award unlimited compensation. In cases where the discrimination has been extremely serious the tribunals can make very substantial awards. In *D'Souza* v *London Borough of Lambeth* [1997] IRLR 677 the EAT made an award of £358,288. This consisted of £3,000 for injury to feelings, £2,000 exemplary damages, £18,269 for loss of pension rights and over £300,000 was for loss of future earnings. In *Yeboah* v *Crofton* [2002] IRLR 634 the tribunal made an award of £380,000.

Compensation can be awarded for injury to feelings in race discrimination cases. Guidance as to how such compensation should be awarded was set out by the Court of Appeal in *Chief Constable of West Yorks* v *Vento (No 2)* [2003] IRLR 102. The guidelines apply to claims of sex, race and disability discrimination and provide that award in excess of £25,000 should only be made in exceptional cases. The lowest award should be no less than £500

An employer will be liable for all losses which flow from the discriminatory act of the employer and it is not necessary to show that such losses are foreseeable. In *Laing Limited* v *Yessin Essa* [2004] IRLR 313 Mr Essa was employed as a labourer at the Millennium Stadium site in Cardiff in June 1999. He was subjected to petty acts of humiliation and, on 28 July 1999, a foreman made a particularly offensive remark about him in front of a gang of other men. Mr Essa was very distressed and complained to his employer. The company apologised to Mr Essa. However, the nature of the remark and continued harassment by other workers caused Mr Essa severe trauma with the result that he left his employment on the 5 August 1999. The company disciplined the foreman, who was given a final written warning on 6 August 1999, but by this time Mr Essa had already left the site. Mr Essa was not satisfied with the company's response and brought a claim of race discrimination.

The employment tribunal heard from two psychiatrists that Mr Essa had undergone a personality change as a result of his experience. Mr Essa gave up representing Wales as an amateur boxer because the incident had such an effect on him. The tribunal upheld his claim against Laing, and awarded compensation of £5,000 for injury to feelings and just over £500 for financial loss. The tribunal restricted the amount of financial loss on the basis that the employers 'are only liable for such reasonably foreseeable loss as was directly caused by the discriminating act'. Mr Essa appealed against the amount of the award, arguing that he should only have to prove a causal link between the act of discrimination and the loss, and was not required to prove reasonable foreseeability. The EAT agreed with Mr Essa and Laing appealed to the Court of Appeal. A majority of the Court of Appeal held that the employment tribunal had erred in concluding that the applicant was not entitled to full compensation under the Race Relations Act 1976 because the loss was not reasonably foreseeable. A claimant who has suffered direct discrimination in the form of racial abuse is entitled to be compensated for all losses which arises naturally and directly from the wrong, and it is not necessary for the claimant to show the loss was reasonably foreseeable.

In *Laing* the Court of Appeal was split on the issue and this case cannot be regarded as a decisive change in the law with respect to recovery for psychiatric injury that is not foreseeable. Furthermore, the Court of Appeal has restricted its finding to claims of racial abuse and Pill LJ commented that 'It is possible that, where the discrimination takes other forms, different considerations will apply.'

If an employer fails to deal properly with an employee who commits a racial act, such a failure may amount to an aggravating feature with the result that the claimant may be awarded additional aggravated damages. In *British Telecommunications plc v Reid* [2004] IRLR 327 Mr Reid, an Afro Caribbean, was subjected to racial abuse whereby one of his colleagues threatened him by saying that he knew people with baseball bats and that he 'will get someone to put him back in his cage'. Mr Reid was too distressed to continue working and left his duties. He raised a grievance with his employers which took 14 months to complete and during that time the colleague who had made the threat was promoted. Meanwhile BT disciplined Mr Reid for abandoning his duties on the day of the incident. Mr Reid brought a claim of race discrimination against BT. At tribunal it was held that the comment 'I will get someone to put you back in your cage' amounted to an act of race discrimination for which BT was vicariously liable. The tribunal awarded Mr Reid £6,000 for injury to feelings and £2,000 for aggravating damages. In determining the amount of compensation to be awarded, the tribunal took into account the fact that following the incident Mr Reid was subjected to the indignity of a totally unjustified disciplinary investigation. Furthermore, as a result of the incident Mr Reid suffered from stress which resulted in him taking a considerable amount of time off work sick. The tribunal also took into account the fact that Mr Reid had to wait 14 months for his grievance to be dealt with by his employer. BT unsuccessfully appealed to the EAT against the amount of compensation awarded and further appealed to the Court of Appeal. The Court of Appeal held that the award for aggravated damages would stand. The Court of Appeal considered that the failure of BT to punish the employee who had made the threat amounted to an aggravating feature. Furthermore, the Court of Appeal held that the award of £6,000 for injury to feelings was not inconsistent with the approach taken by the Court of Appeal in *Chief Constable of West Yorkshire Police v Vento (No 2)* [2003] IRLR 102.

Tribunals can order interest to be paid on awards made under the RRA 1976: the Employment Tribunals (Interest on Awards in Discrimination Cases) Regulations 1996 (SI 1996/2803).

Employment Equality (Religion or Belief) Regulations 2003

The Employment Equality (Religion or Belief) Regulations 2003 (SI 2003/1660) came into force in December 2003 and make it unlawful to discriminate against an employee or potential employee on grounds of religion or belief. The Regulations, which implement the EC Equal Treatment Framework Directive (2000/78/EC) into UK law, apply to all businesses, irrespective of size.

In the UK, unlike many other European countries, there was no legislation protecting employees against religious discrimination until the implementation of the Human Rights Act 1998. Previously, attempts had been made to use the Race Relations Act 1976 to cover religious discrimination, but because of the requirement of belonging to an ethnic group Jews and Sikhs were protected but Hindus, Buddhists, Christians and Muslims were not. The Regulations apply widely to 'any religion, religious belief or similar philosophical belief'.

The Regulations apply to vocational training and all aspects of employment – including recruitment, terms and conditions, promotions, transfers, dismissals and training – and include employees, apprentices, self-employed and contract workers.

The Regulations provide that it is unlawful to directly or indirectly discriminate against any person because of their religion or belief. It is therefore unlawful to treat them less favourably than others or to apply a criterion provision or practice which disadvantages people of a particular religion or belief unless it can be objectively justified: reg 3.

Regulation 4 makes it unlawful to victimise a person because they have made, or intend to make, a complaint or allegation in relation to a complaint of discrimination on the grounds of religion or belief. This provision also includes persons who have given, or intend to give, evidence in relation to a complaint of discrimination on the grounds of religion or belief.

The Regulations also provide protection for employees from harassment: reg 5. Harassment is unwanted conduct that violates a person's dignity or creates an intimidating, hostile, degrading, humiliating or offensive environment for them, having regard to all the circumstances including the perception of the employee.

Regulation 7 provides a defence for employers with respect to job applicants (in other words failing to offer them the job for which they have applied) if the employer can prove that possessing a particular religion or belief is a genuine occupational requirement. The criteria of what constitutes a genuine occupational defence are likely to be strictly interpreted. Therefore it is likely that the requirement of being a Christian for the position of chaplin in a Christian church would be regarded as being a genuine occupational requirement, whereas such a requirement for a gardener or maintenance worker for the same church would not attract the defence.

The Regulations also extend to post-termination discrimination. Regulation 21 provides that it is unlawful to discriminate against a person after the working relationship has ended where the discrimination or harassment arises out of, and is closely connected to, that relationship.

The first case to be heard under the new Regulations is *Mohmed* v *Virgin Trains* (2004) (not reported) in which Mr Mohmed claimed that he was treated unfavourably because he was sacked by the respondents for failing to trim his eight-inch long beard. The respondents successfully established that the reason for his dismissal was not relate to his beard but because of a 'general lack of enthusiasm'.

6.3 Disability discrimination

Introduction

The Disability Discrimination Act (DDA) 1995 provides that it may be unlawful to discriminate against a person because of a disabilty. The DDA 1995 covers discrimination in the fields of employment, occupational pensions, contract workers, insurance providers, trade organisations, education, property, public transport facilities and services. The employment provisions of the Act which are found in Pt II came into effect in December 1996.

The DDA 1995 has been has been amended by the Disability Discrimination Act 1995 (Amendment) Regulations 2003 (SI 2003/1673) and the Disability Discrimination Act 1995 (Pensions) Regulations 2003 (SI 2003/2770), which both came into effect on 1 October 2004. These changes implement the provisions within the EC Equal Treatment Framework Directive (2000/78/EC) with respect to equal treatment for workers in employment.

Section 1 Disability Discrimination Act 1995

Section 1(1) provides that for the purposes of the Act a person has a disability if he has a physical or mental impairment:

> '... which has a substantial and long-term adverse effect on a person's ability to carry out normal day-to-day activities.'

Section 1(2) defines 'disabled person' as meaning 'a person who has a disability'.

'Impairment'
Although impairment is not defined it will include physical impairments affecting the senses, such as sight and hearing, and mental impairments including mental illness and learning disabilities. The Disability Discrimination (Meaning of Disability) Regulations 1996, which came into force in 1996, provide that addiction to alcohol, nicotine or other drugs are excluded from the scope of DDA 1995. Hayfever and disfigurement resulting from tattoos or body piercing are also excluded. The 1996 Regulations also exclude some personality disorders such as a

tendency to arson, theft, physical or sexual abuse. However, in *Murray* v *Newham Citizens Advice Bureau* [2003] IRLR 340 the EAT held that where a person suffers from one of the excluded impairments because of a disability within the meaning of s1 DDA 1995, this will amount to a disability. In this case Mr Murray, who suffered from scizophrennia, a disability within the meaning of s1 DDA 1995, applied for a position as a volunteer with Newham Citizens Advice Bureau. His application was rejected on the grounds that his illness had caused him to be violent in the past. His claim of disability discrimination was rejected by the tribunal on the grounds that because he had a tendency to violence this was excluded from the DDA 1995 and therefore he was not disabled within the meaning of s1 DDA 1995. The EAT allowed the appeal by Mr Murray and remitted the matter to another tribunal to determine whether the discrimination was justified.

The Act covers progressive conditions such as cancer, HIV infections, MS and muscular dystrophy where impairments are likely to become more severe with time.

Section 2 DDA 1995 provides that if a person has suffered from a disability within the meaning of s1, but has since recovered, they will also be covered by the DDA 1995. This section is particularly important for persons who believe that they are being discriminated against because of past illnesses, particularly those who have suffered from a mental impairment. A mental impairment is defined in Sch 1 DDA 1995 as including 'an impairment resulting from or consisting of a mental illness only if the illness is a clinically well-recognised illness'. Stress on its own is not a disability, but where it manifests itself in the form of a recognised mental illness it will be amount to a disability.

It may be difficult for a tribunal to determine whether a person who is suffering from stress is suffering from a disability for the purposes of s1 DDA 1995. In *Morgan* v *Staffordshire University* [2002] IRLR 190 the applicant, who was engaged by the respondents as a catering worker, was assaulted by a supervisor. She was offered alternative positions but the respondents could not guarantee that she would not come into contact with the supervisor who had assaulted her. The applicant resigned claiming that she had been constructively dismissed and mentioning that she had suffered stress and anxiety. Her claim was later amended to include a specific claim of disability discrimination. The question for determination was whether the stress and anxiety of the applicant amounted to a mental impairment, and therefore a disability, for the purposes of s1 DDA 1995. At a preliminary hearing the applicant produced some medical notes but offered no other medical evidence to support her claim. The tribunal held that the applicant was not suffering from a mental disability within the meaning of the DDA 1995. The applicant appealed to the EAT. The EAT set out guidelines for determining when an applicant is suffering from a mental impairment. The EAT said that a mental illness could be established in the following ways.

1. Proof of a mental illness specified in the World Health Organisation's International Classification of Diseases (WHOICD).

2. Proof of a mental illness specified as such in established medical publications.
3. Proof by other means of a medical illness recognised by a respected body of medical opinion.

The applicant in this case had therefore failed to establish that she was suffering from a mental impairment within the meaning of the DDA 1995.

In determining whether a person has a disability within the meaning of s1 DDA 1995 the tribunal are entitled to take into account their own experience if they suffer from a similar disability: *Kirkton* v *Tetrosyl* [2002] IRLR 840.

It will sometimes be difficult for a tribunal to determine what is a disability without medical assistance. This was acknowledged by the EAT in *Foster* v *Hampshire Fire and Rescue Service* (1998) 43 BMLR 186 where the applicant suffered from asthma and classical migraines. She was dismissed because of her poor attendance record at work. She brought a claim for unfair dismissal. The tribunal found that she did not have a disability within the meaning of s1 DDA 1995 in that the degree of impairment did not have a substantial effect on her day-to-day activities. The applicant appealed to the EAT where the EAT considered that tribunals would sometimes be facing the dilemma of deciding medical questions without the assistance of expert medical opinion. However, in the instant case the EAT considered that the tribunal had been correct in holding that asthma and migraines was not a disability within the 1995 Act.

To assist the tribunals the Disability Discrimination (Guidance and Code of Practice) (Appointed Day) Order 1996 (SI 1996/1996) introduced Formal Guidance which sets out guidelines to enable tribunals to determine whether an illness or inability to carry out day-to-day activities amounts to a disability.

'Substantial'
The effect of disability has to be substantial and although this is not defined it must be more than minor and it must be a limitation that is considerably more than would be found amongst a random group of people. An inability to see traffic clearly enough to cross a road, or an inability to turn on taps, would be likely to be considered substantial.

In *Goodwin* v *Patent Office* (1998) The Times 11 November the applicant suffered from schizophrenia and was dismissed by the respondents following complaints by other employees about his behaviour. The applicant had not been on his normal medication at the relevant time. At the employment tribunal it was held that although the applicant's concentration was adversely affected by his illness, the effect on his normal day-to-day activities was not sufficiently 'substantial' to bring him within the meaning of disability and s1(1) DDA 1995 and therefore the tribunal had no jurisdiction to hear his complaint. The applicant appealed to the EAT which held that the tribunal had erred in holding that because the appellant was able to cope with day-to-day activities his illness was not a disability within s1(1) and the matter was remitted to the employment tribunal.

In *Cruickshank* v *Vaw Motorcast Ltd* [2002] IRLR 24 the EAT held that the correct approach in determining whether an employee's illness has a substantial effect on his normal day-to-day activities is to consider the medical condition of the applicant at the time of the alleged discriminatory act, and not his condition at the time of the tribunal hearing.

In *Abadeh* v *British Telecom plc* [2001] ICR 156 the EAT held that the issue of whether an impairment is substantial is a decision for the tribunal based on medical evidence, not a matter to be decided by a medical practitioner.

The Guidance (see above) considers that 'normal day-to-day activities' are those activities which are normal for most people and is 'not intended to include activities which are normal only for a particular person or group of people'. In *Commissioner of Police of the Metropolis* v *Ekpe* [2001] IRLR 605 Ms Ekpe brought claims of race and disability discrimination against her employer. The disability claim was based on the fact that she was required to use a keyboard and mouse at work which Ms Ekpe found difficult because she was suffering from a wasting of the muscles in her right hand. The tribunal had to consider whether the effect of this impairment was sufficiently substantial so as to bring her within the meaning of disability. In considering Ms Ekpe's claim the tribunal looked at the things she could and could not do. The tribunal accepted that she was not able to put rollers in her hair or apply her make-up but said these were not normal day-to-day activities and therefore concluded tha the claimant was not suffering from a disability. The tribunal went on to consider that even if they were wrong as to whether putting in rollers was a normal activity amongst women, nevertheless it was normal only for a particular group of people – women. This reasoning was based on the Guidance which states that the term 'normal day-to-day activities' is not intended to include activities which can only be regarded as normal for a particular person or group of people. Ms Ekpe appealed against the decision of the tribunal. The EAT considered that the approach adopted by the tribunal had been incorrect because the tribunal had considered what Ms Ekpe could do and not what she could not do. Furthermore, the tribunal had erred in holding that applying make-up and putting in rollers were not normal day-to-day activities.

'Long-term'

Long-term effects are those that have lasted, or are likely to last, 12 months or more or are likely to last for the rest of the life of the person affected. It will also include recurring disabilities. In determining whether a disability is long-term the tribunal must take into account any deterioration after the discriminatory act: *Greenwood* v *British Airways plc* [1999] ICR 696.

Discrimination

The DDA 1995 has, as already stated, been amended by the Disability Discrimination Act 1995 (Amendment) Regulations 2003. One of the areas that has seen significant changes is the part of the Act which deals with the meaning of disability. Prior to the changes s5, which has been repealed, set out the meaning of discrimination on the grounds of disability. However reg 4(2) Disability Discrimination Act 1995 (Amendment) Regulations 2003 inserts s3A into the DDA 1995, which provides that a person discriminates against a disabled person if, for a reason which relates to his or her disability, he treats him or her less favourably than he treats or would treat others and he cannot show that the treatment is justified. This is substantially the same as the old s5 definition. However, s3A(5) provides a new definition of direct discrimination:

> 'A person directly discriminates against a disabled person if, on the grounds of the disabled person's disability, he treats the disabled person less favourably than he treats or would treat a person not having that particular disability whose relevant circumstances, including his abilities, are the same as, or not materially different from, those of the disabled person.'

This new section provides that the appropriate comparator in a direct discrimination case is a non-disabled person whose abilities are the same as, or not materially different from, the abilities of the disabled person. The comparator is not a non-disabled person with a different level of ability. Furthermore, s3A(4) provides that the defence of justification will not apply to cases of direct discrimination.

It has already been stated that the new s3A(1)(a) and (b) defining discrimination are the same as the old s5(1)(a) and (b) wording, which was described by the Court of Appeal in *Clark* v *Novacold Ltd* [1998] IRLR 420 as linguistically ambiguous. The ambiguity of the wording suggests that there is a requirement for a comparator, an issue which was considered by the Court of Appeal in *Clark* v *Novacold Ltd*.

In this case the applicant injured his back at work in August 1996. In December 1996 the respondents obtained a medical report from the employee's doctor which said that because of the physical nature of the job it was difficult to anticipate when the applicant would be able to return to work. A further report was obtained from a consultant who said that whilst the injury would improve over a 12-month period it was not possible to state when the applicant would be fit for work. The applicant was dismissed from his job in January 1997 and presented an application to an employment tribunal claiming that he had been discriminated against on the grounds of his disability. The tribunal considered that the back injury was a long-term disability within the meaning of the DDA 1995 but rejected the applicant's claim that he had been discriminated against. The applicant appealed to the EAT and then to the Court of Appeal.

The Court of Appeal held that the tribunal and the EAT had erred in the approach that they had taken in determining a comparator for the purposes of s5(1) DDA 1995. The Court said that it was a mistake to take the same approach in determining the question of discrimination as under the Sex Discrimination Act 1975 and the Race Relations Act 1976, and that to take the same approach would be positively misleading. The Court therefore adopted a purposive approach to the issue and said that it was probable that Parliament meant the words 'a reason' to refer only to the facts which gave rise to the reason and the treatment and did not include the requirement of a causal link with the disability.

In essence what the Court of Appeal was saying is that the test of less favourable treatment is based on the reason for the treatment and not the fact of the person's disability.

Justification

Section 3A(1)(b) provides that in cases other than those concerning direct discrimination an employer may be able to defend a claim by establishing that the alleged discriminatory treatment was justified. Section 3A(3) provides that treatment is justified if the reason for the treatment is both material to the circumstances of the particular case and substantial.

The Disability Rights Commission Code of Practice published in October 2004 provides guidance as to treatment which may be regarded as being justified. The example given is that of a man unable to bend because of severe back pain who is rejected for a job a carpet fitter. Self evidently the job requires the fitter to be able to bend to fit carpets, a requirement which is both material and substantial to the circumstances of the case.

In *Morse* v *Wiltshire County Council* [1998] IRLR 352 (a case considered under the old s5) the EAT considered the issue of justification. Mr Morse had been employed as a road worker from 1963 until his dismissal by reason of redundancy in 1997. Following a road-traffic accident in 1986 Mr Morse was left with a 20 per cent disability which, inter alia, left him prone to blackouts. As a result Mr Morse refused to continue to drive a vehicle because of the risk of passing out. In 1996, following financial difficulties, the council conducted a review of its workforce to reduce numbers and improve flexibility, and Mr Morse and other non-drivers were selected for redundancy. Mr Morse argued that the reason he had been selected for redundancy was for a reason related to his disability. At the industrial tribunal it was accepted that his dismissal had been related to his disability but that it was justified in that the requirement of the council that employees should be fit and able to drive a vehicle was 'material to the circumstances of the particular case and substantial'. Mr Morse appealed against the decision of the tribunal.

The EAT held that tribunal had erred in holding that the dismissal was not contrary to the DDA 1995.

In determining what is material and substantial to the case the tribunal must consider whether the decision of the employer falls within the 'band of reasonable responses'. In *Post Office* v *Foley* [2000] IRLR 827 the Court of Appeal held that in applying the law of unfair dismissal in s98 ERA 1996, tribunals should continue to adopt the 'band or range of reasonable responses' approach to the issue of the reasonableness or unreasonableness of a dismissal as expounded in *Iceland Frozen Food Ltd* v *Jones* [1982] IRLR 439. In *Jones* v *The Post Office* [2001] ICR 805 the

Court of Appeal said that the same approach could be taken with respect to the issue of what is material and substantial. It is therefore for the employer to decide what is material and what is substantial, and the tribunal's job is merely to consider whether the employer's decision fell within the range of reasonable responses to the known facts. An employment tribunal may not substitute its own view for that of the employer by making its own appraisal of the medical evidence or making its own risk assessment

Reasonable adjustment

Section 3A(2) DDA 1995 provides that a person also discriminates against a disabled person if he fails to comply with a duty to make reasonable adjustments imposed upon him in relation to the disabled person. The duty to make reasonable adjustments prior to the implementation of the new Regulations was under s6 DDA 1995 which has also been repealed. Nevertheless many of the principles established by the courts will apply to the new s3(A)(2), although it must be noted that a failure to make a reasonable adjustment can no longer be justified.

An employer must make reasonable changes to their premises or employment arrangements if these disadvantage a disabled employee or prospective employee, compared to a non-disabled person. The changes include adjustments to premises, allocating some of a disabled person's duties to another employee, altering working hours, assigning a disabled person to another place of work and allowing a person to be absent from work for the purpose of rehabilitation. The Disability Rights Commission has set out in its Code of Practice (issued in October 2004) a comprehensive list of adjustments which an employer may be required to make to accommodate a person with a disability.

The requirement to make reasonable adjustments applies to job applicants, and the terms and conditions of employees

When an employer interviews a potential employee he will not always be aware of any disability. The EAT in *Ridout* v *TC Group* [1998] IRLR 628 held that there had to be some limitation placed on the duty of an employer to assess a candidate's disability before an interview. In *Ridout* the applicant has stated in her CV that she suffered from a rare type of photosensitive epilepsy. She was invited for an interview and arrived wearing sun glasses around her neck. The interview room had bright fluorescent lights and the applicant commented that this may put her at a disadvantage but the respondents thought that the applicant was making the comment for the purpose of explaining why she had her sunglasses with her. During the course of the interview the applicant did not wear her sunglasses, nor did she complain about being unwell. She subsequently complained that the respondents had failed to make reasonable adjustment with respect to the arrangements for the interview contrary to s6 and that she had been discriminated against. Her claim was dismissed by the tribunal and she appealed to the EAT.

The EAT considered that whilst it was not appropriate for disabled persons to be obliged to give detailed explanations to prospective employers about their disability simply to encourage an employer to make adjustments which ought to have made in the first instance, it was not reasonable to expect an employer to anticipate problems with respect to rare or little known disabilities simply from studying a CV or medical form and therefore her appeal was dismissed.

In *Archibald* v *Fife Council* [2004] IRLR 651, a case concerning a lady road sweeper who became disabled and unable to carry out her contractual duties, the House of Lords considered the obligation upon the council to move her to an alternative position. Lord Hope of Craighead considered the scope of the duty to make any adjustment and said:

> 'The making of adjustments is not an end in itself. The end is reached when the disabled person is no longer at a substantial disadvantage, in comparison with persons who are not disabled, by reason of any arrangements made by or on behalf of the employer or any physical features of premises which the employer occupies.'

In this case the House of Lords also held that in certain circumstances an employer may positively discriminate in favour of a disabled employee. Ms Fife claimed that a policy of the council which required her to go into open competition with other job applicants for sedentary duties which she could carry out put her at a disadvantage and amounted to a failure to make reasonable adjustments. The concept of positive discrimination is at odds with the Sex Discrimination Act 1975 and the Race Relations Act 1976 because under these two statutes positive discrimination is unlawful. However, in *Dixon* v *The Automobile Association Ltd* [2004] All ER (D) 127 the EAT placed a limit on this positive duty and said that it does not mean that an employer has to dismiss another employee to make way for a disabled person.

In *Nottinghamshire County Council* v *Meikle* [2004] IRLR 703 the employer council failed to make reasonable adjustments which would have allowed a partially sighted teacher to carry out her duties. The teacher found it increasingly difficult to work and took sick leave. In accordance with her contract, after the expiry of 100 days her sick pay was reduced to half her normal pay. The Court of Appeal held that the failure to pay Ms Meikle her full pay also amounted to a failure to make reasonable adjustments.

A lack of necessary training may also amount to a failure to make reasonable adjustments. In *Williams* v *J Walter Thompson Group* [2005] EWCA Civ 133 the Court of Appeal held that a failure to provide adequate equipment and training so as to allow a blind lady to carry out her duties as an IT consultant was a failure to make reasonable adjustments.

Section 4A(3) DDA 1995 provides that the duty to make 'reasonable adjustments' does not apply 'if the employer does not know, and could not reasonably be expected to know' that the disabled person has a disability. However, where an employer ought to be aware of an employee's disability but is not he may be liable for any subsequent discrimination: *Kent County Council* v *Mingo* [2000] IRLR 90 (EAT).

Difficulties can arise when an employer believes, on the basis of medical reports, that an employee will not be able to return to work. In *Fu* v *London Borough of Camden* [2001] IRLR 186 Ms Fu was employed as a housing officer. She suffered two accidents at work with the result that she was off work for a year. Upon her return to work in 1994 she was able to walk with the assistance of a walking stick, but after a further accident in 1997 apart from a brief return to work she remained off work. A medical report stated that it would not be possible to say when Ms Fu would be able to return to work. Camden Council obtained a further medical report which suggested that Ms Fu would not be able to return to work. On the basis of this report they decided to offer her a choice of taking ill-health retirement or being dismissed. Although Ms Fu did not want to retire, nevertheless given the choice as presented to her, she chose retirement. Her claim to the employment tribunal failed. However, the EAT found that the employer had failed to consider the possibility of making reasonable adjustments, which would have included a voice-activated computer, a hands-free telephone and a specially adapted chair, and had therefore failed in its duty. The employer had unsuccessfully argued that the medical opinion was that Ms Fu would be unable to return to work. The correct approach should be to look at whether reasonable adjustments would allow a person to return to work, and having viewed all the possibilities only then to come to a decision as to whether ill-health retirement is necessary.

Sometimes it may be necessary to make physical alterations to a building to accommodate a disabled person. In determining what is reasonable the tribunal must take into account the cost of such alterations and the ease with which they can be made. If planning permission or statutory consent is required to alter a building and such consent or permission is not granted an employer will not be obliged to make any necessary adjustments: s59 DDA 1995.

Some employers have argued that they have been prevented from making physical alterations to premises by their landlords. However, the Disability Discrimination (Employment Field) (Leasehold Premises) Regulations 2004 (SI 2004/153) prevent landlords from withholding consent for alterations to be made where the purpose of the alteration is to enable an employer to comply with obligations under the DDA 1995.

Section 6(3) provides examples of steps which an employer may have to take in relation to a disabled person and these include making adjustments to a premises, allocating some of a disabled person's duties to another, altering his working hours, assigning him to a different place of work and allowing him to be absent from work during working hours for rehabilitation.

If an employer fails to make reasonable adjustments this may also constitute discrimination. Section 5(2) provides:

'For the purposes of this Part, an employer discriminates against a disabled person if –

(a) he fails to comply with a section 6 duty imposed upon him in relation to the disabled person; and
(b) he cannot show that his failure to comply with that duty is justified.'

In *Clark* v *Novacold Ltd* (above) the Court went on to say that a failure to make adjustments may also constitute an act of discrimination against a person and liability for that is not contingent upon the finding of unfavourable treatment under s5(1). They are different causes of action even though they may overlap.

In order to show that the treatment of a disabled person was justified, an employer would have to show that it was both material to the circumstances of the particular case and substantial: s5(3). If an employer thinks that there may be a relevant and substantial reason for less favourable treatment towards a disabled person a prudent employer ought to consider whether that reason can be overcome or whether a reasonable adjustment, for example modification to premises, could make the reason less substantial.

The duty of the employer to make reasonable adjustments may be extremely onerous and this has been acknowledged by the EAT. In *Kenny* v *Hampshire Constabulary* (1998) The Times 22 October the applicant suffered from cerebral palsy. He applied for a job as a computer analyst with the respondents and was offered the post subject to the respondents being able to arrange assistance for the applicant with respect to using the toilet. There were no volunteers within the constabulary and so the respondents applied for a grant from the Access to Work scheme. They were advised that such an application took some time to process and as the respondents needed to fill the vacancy urgently they withdrew the job offer. The applicant presented a claim to the tribunal where it was held that the respondents had been justified in withdrawing the offer. He appealed to the EAT which accepted the argument put forward by the respondents that the old s6(1)(a) was limited to arrangements made in relation to the job undertaken by the disabled employee and did not impose a duty upon a prospective employer to provide full-time care for a disabled person.

The extent of the duty owed under s6 to provide alternative employment was also considered in the case of *British Gas Services Ltd* v *McCaull* [2001] IRLR 60. The applicant, a service engineer, was employed to service central heating systems in customers homes. Whilst driving, the applicant had an epileptic fit which caused him to black out and have an accident. The applicant was off work for some time after the accident and, after a medical examination, the employers' occupational health service advised that he could no longer drive. The respondents advised him that he could not return to his previous position: however, he could be employed as a customer service adviser. The applicant rejected the offer of the alternative job because it meant a reduction in salary of up to 30 per cent and claimed that he had been discriminated against contrary to the DDA 1995. The EAT held that the employers had complied with their s6 duty even though the employer was unaware of that duty. The question is: what steps did the employer actually take? The EAT also held that the tribunal had erred in finding that the offer of an alternative position at a much lower salary was unfair; given the circumstances the employer had done all that it could reasonably be expected to do.

In determining whether an employee has been discriminated against because of his disability the tribunals may take into account the treatment of the employer over a period of time.

In *British Sugar plc* v *Kirker* [1998] IRLR 624 the applicant was a visually impaired shift chemist and had been employed by the respondents for 17 years. He hadn't been promoted and during his time with the respondent managers had frequently made an issue of his eyesight. The respondents sought to reduce its workforce and set up a selection procedure. The applicant scored poorly on the performance and potential criteria even though he had not previously been criticised in respect of performance. He also scored badly with respect to absences; however, these were all connected to his disability. He was made redundant and complained to the employment tribunal.

The tribunal held that there had been discrimination under s5(1) on the grounds that the criteria applied were subjective and that they favoured employees who were not disabled. The employer appealed to the EAT which held that the tribunal had been correct in its decision and rejected the respondents' argument that the tribunal had taken into account factors which had occurred before the DDA 1995 had come into force. The EAT said that the tribunal was entitled to consider the applicant's history of employment in order to determine whether the same approach had continued with respect to the selection criteria for redundancy.

Scope of the Disability Discrimination Act 1995

Section 4 of the DDA 1995 provides that it is unlawful to discriminate against a disabled person from recruitment through to the end of the employment relationship, including:

1. interview arrangements;
2. recruitment;
3. terms on which employment is offered;
4. promotion, transfer and training;
5. dismissal;
6. post-termination obligations.

Prior to the implementation of the Disability Discrimination Act 1995 (Amendment) Regulations 2003 (SI 2003/1673) in October 2004, the DDA 1995 only applied to employer who employed more than 15 employees. The Regulations have now removed that exemption with the effect that the Act covers all employers. The Regulations have also extended the DDA to cover occupations which previously had been exempt from the DDA 1995.

Fire fighters, prison officers, police officers, members of the ministry of defence police, the British Transport Police and the Royal Parks Constabulary, all of whom were previously exempted from the original DDA, are now fully protected by the Act. Barristers were also previously excluded because like police officers they were not regarded as being in employment or employees within the meaning of the DDA 1995. However, since October 2004 barristers are protected from disability discrimination committed during the course of carrying out their duties. The new Regulations also provide that partners in a partnership and applicants for a partnership will have the same protection under the DDA 1995 as employees: s6A DDA 1995. Members of Her Majesty's armed forces are however, still excluded from the protection afforded by the DDA 1995.

Harassment

Section 4(3) provides that it is unlawful to subject a disabled person to harassment and this is defined in a new s3B, as inserted by the new Regulations, as follows:

'... a person subjects a disabled person to harassment where, for a reason which relates to the disabled persons disability, he engages in unwanted conduct which has the purpose or effect of –
(a) violating the disabled person's dignity, or
(b) creating an intimidating, hostile, degrading, humiliating or offensive environment for him.'

Constructive dismissal

Section 4(2)(d) DDA 1995 provides that it is unlawful to dismiss an employee if the reason is attributable to his disability. The question that has arisen is whether a dismissal can also include constructive dismissal. In *Commissioner of Police of the Metropolis* v *Harley* [2001] IRLR 263 the EAT held that s4(2)(d), which provides that an employer will discriminate against a disabled person 'by dismissing him, or subjecting him to any other detriment', does not apply to constructive dismissal. However, in the more recent case of *Catherall* v *Michelin Tyres plc* [2003] IRLR 61 the EAT considered that a purposive approach should be adopted to the DDA 1995 and that 'dismissal' in s4(2)(d) could include constructive dismissal.

The issue was finally settled by the Court of Appeal in *Nottinghamshire County Council* v *Meikle* [2004] IRLR 703, where it was held that s4 DDA 1995 does include constructive dismissal. The time limit for presenting a claim of constructive dismissal is three months from the date of the employee's resignation, not the act of the employer which caused the employee to leave.

Post-termination obligations

The scope of the DDA 1995 extends to post-termination obligations. This means that in accordance with the principle established by the House of Lords in *Relaxion*

Group plc v *Rhys Harper* [2003] IRLR 484 and s16A DDA 1995 as inserted by the 2003 Regulations, any discriminatory act committed by an employer after the termination of employment will be regarded as being within the scope of the DDA 1995 if there is a substantive connection between the employment relationship and the discriminatory conduct.

Time limits

A person who believes that they have suffered disability discrimination has three months from the act of discrimination to present a claim to the employment tribunal: Sch 3, Pt 1(3) DDA 1995. A tribunal may consider an application which is submitted after the three-month time limit if, in all the circumstances, it is just and equitable to do so.

Burden of proof

When a disability discrimination claim is heard by am employment tribunal the complainant will have to establish facts from which it may be presumed that discrimination has taken place. The burden of proof will then be upon the employer to prove that there has been no discrimination: s17A(1C) DDA 1995.

Remedies

If a complaint to an employment tribunal is successful, s17A provides that the tribunal can take the following steps:

1. make a declaration as to the rights of the complainant and the respondent in relation to matters to which the complaint relates;
2. order the respondent to pay compensation;
3. recommend that the respondent takes reasonable action within a specified period of time to eliminate or reduce the adverse effect on the complainant of any matter to which the complaint relates.

Any compensation awarded by the tribunals is calculated by applying the principles used in calculating damages in tort and may include a sum representing injury to feelings. The largest payout for a disability discrimination claim was recently made in the case of *HM Prison Service* v *Beart* [2005] IRLR 171, a case which illustrates how a failure to make reasonable adjustments can prove to be an expensive mistake. In this case an altercation between Mrs Beart and her line manager caused her severe depression, with the result that she had to take sick leave. A medical report stated that Mrs Beart could possibly return to work if she were redeployed. Mrs Beart had a business interest in a local shop and the Prison Service received reports that she was seen working in the shop whilst claiming sick pay. The Prison Service engaged private investigators to see whether in fact she was working.

The investigators submitted a report to the appellants with the result that Mrs Beart was dismissed. At tribunal it was held that Mrs Beart had been unfairly dismissed and had suffered disability discrimination and was awarded £400,000 compensation. The Prison Service unsuccessfully appealed against the findings of the tribunal and the award.

Following the decision of the EAT a spokesperson for the Disability Rights Commission said that this case 'should sound alarm bells in every workplace in Britain which is ignoring the Disability Discrimination Act.'

Victimisation

Section 58 DDA 1995 provides that it is unlawful to victimise disabled people who make use of, or try to make use of, their rights under the Act. An employer will be held to have discriminated against an employee if he treats him less favourably than he treats or would treat another person in the same circumstances if the reason includes any of the following:

1. the employee has brought proceedings against his employer under the Act;
2. the employee has given evidence, or supplied information, in proceedings connected with the Act;
3. the employee has assisted a disabled employee who is covered by the Act.

Section 55 therefore provides protection to employees who are not themselves disabled.

Liability of employers and principals

Section 58 DDA 1995 provides that an employer may be vicariously liable for anything done by a person during the course of his employment whether or not it was done with the approval of the employer. An employer will be liable for the actions of agents such as recruitment agents unless the agents worked outside their authority. In any proceedings brought under the Act an employer will be able to defend a claim if he can show that he took such steps as were reasonably practicable to prevent the employee from doing that act.

7

Equal Pay

7.1 Introduction

7.2 Equal Pay Act 1970

7.1 Introduction

European Union law has played a significant role in trying to eliminate discrimination between men and women in the workplace and one of the areas in which women have suffered great inequality is in the area of pay. In an attempt to address this issue art 119 of the EC Treaty and the Equal Pay Directive (75/117/EEC) provided the principle that men and women should receive equal pay for equal work and that all discrimination on the grounds of sex with respect to all aspects of remuneration should be eliminated. In the UK the Equal Pay Act 1970, which came into force in 1975, was enacted to ensure that women who carried out the same or similar work to men received equal pay. If, however, there is any conflict between domestic law and EU law it is European Union law which will prevail.

In May 1999 the Treaty of Amsterdam came into force which, inter alia, provided a more broad article to replace art 119. The new article, art 141 EC, strengthens the sex equality provisions and brings the EC Treaty in line with the Equal Pay Directive by defining the principle of equal pay as 'equal pay for equal work or work of equal value'. For simplicity reference will be made to the new art 141, as opposed to article 119, throughout this chapter.

Article 141 EC is directly enforceable by any person because it is of direct effect. The Equal Pay Directive is directly enforceable by employees of public authorities and indirectly enforceable by other employees because the Equal Pay Act 1970 is to be interpreted so as to give effect to the Equal Pay Directive.

7.2 Equal Pay Act 1970

The Equal Pay Act (EPA) 1970 provides that there should be equal treatment in terms of pay for men and women in the same employment. If there is no such equality, then an equality clause will be implied into the contract. There is no age limit or minimum qualifying period for the enforcement of rights under the Act. However, it should be noted that the Act only applies to terms of employment and does not apply to any discrimination prior to employment. Where there has been discrimination and the EPA 1970 does not apply it will be necessary to consider the provisions of the Sex Discrimination Act (SDA) 1975.

Remuneration takes many forms and the 1970 Act applies to all terms of the contract and is not just limited to pay. It will include working hours, holidays, sick pay and other benefits. In *Barber* v *Guardian Royal Exchange Assurance Group* [1990] IRLR 240 it was held by the ECJ that a pension paid under an occupational pension scheme constitutes pay for the purposes of art 141 EC and is therefore subject to the principle of equal pay for equal work. It was therefore contrary to art 141 for a man who was made redundant to only be entitled to a deferred pension when a woman in the same position would be entitled to an immediate pension. Further, in *Mediguard Services Ltd* v *Thame* [1994] IRLR 504 the EAT held that compensation for unfair dismissal is 'pay' for the purposes of art 141.

Whilst the Act was originally enacted to bring the pay and conditions of women in line with those of male colleagues who had traditionally been paid more for the same work, the Act applies to both men and women. In this chapter, for simplicity, claimants will, however, be women. The EPA 1970 operates on the basis of a female (or male) worker comparing herself with a male (or female) worker who is called the comparator and claiming the same terms and conditions as a contractual right.

The Act applies to employees and to those who work under a contract for services (s1(6) EPA 1970) and is designed to deal with equality of pay rather than the issue of whether pay is fair: *Glasgow City Council* v *Marshall* [2000] ICR 196.

Equality

Section s1(1) EPA 1970 provides that if the terms of a contract under which a woman is employed do not include an equality clause then such a clause will be implied into the contract.

There are three ways in which a women can bring a claim under the 1970 Act. A claim can be brought if she considers that she is doing work of a similar nature to a male comparator; alternatively, she may bring a claim if her work has been evaluated as equivalent to that of a male under a job-evaluation scheme; and, finally, she can claim that her work is of equal value to a male comparator.

'Like work'

Section 1(2) provides that:

'(2) An equality clause is a provision which relates to terms (whether concerned with pay or not) of a contract under which a woman is employed ... and has the effect that –
(a) where the woman is employed on like work with a man in the same employment –
(i) if ... any term of the woman's contract is or becomes less favourable to the woman

than a term of a similar kind in the contract under which that man is employed, that term of the woman's contract shall be treated as so modified as not to be less favourable, and
(ii) if ... at any time the woman's contract does not include a term corresponding to a term benefiting that man included in the contract under which he is employed, the woman's contract shall be treated as including such a term.'

When a situation arises where a woman claims that she is employed on less favourable terms than a man, one of the first issues for consideration is whether the man and woman are carrying out 'like work'.

Section 1(4) provides that a woman is to be regarded as employed on like work if her work and the work of a man is of the same or a 'broadly similar nature', and any differences are not of 'practical importance'. The approach adopted by the tribunals to s1(4) is fairly broad and they will not examine in minute detail whether or not there are minor differences in the work, nor will they consider that work is not of a 'like kind' simply because there are insubstantial differences.

In *Capper Pass Ltd* v *Lawton* [1976] IRLR 366 the EAT, when considering whether a female cook carried out 'like work' to two male assistant chefs, gave guidance as to the approach to be adopted. It was held that a woman is employed on like work with a man within the meaning of s1(4) if their work is of the same nature, or a broadly similar nature, and that trivial differences should be disregarded. This approach was more recently affirmed by the EAT in *Morgan* v *Middlesborough Council* [2004] EAT/0375/04. In *Coomes (Holdings) Ltd* v *Shields* [1978] IRLR 263 the Court of Appeal considered whether the differences in the duties of male and female employees were of practical significance.

In this case the applicant, who worked in a bookmakers, claimed that she was doing 'like work' to a male employee and therefore was entitled to equal pay. The employer argued that because the shop was located in an area where there might be trouble the male employee was also employed as a security guard and therefore there was a difference between their duties. The Court of Appeal held that the reality of the situation was that the applicant and the comparator worked alongside each other carrying out the same duties and that each of them dealt with awkward customers. The Court stated that the security role of the comparator did not amount to such a difference that it was of practical importance and therefore did not justify a difference in pay.

Where, however, there are differences which are more than trivial the work will not be considered to be 'like work'. In *Eaton* v *Nuttall* [1977] IRLR 71 a claim by a female scheduler that she carried out like work to a male colleague was rejected. The EAT took into consideration the fact that the job carried out by male employee carried with it a greater degree of responsibility in that any error on his part carried with it more serious results.

Any difference in the time when a job is done will not of itself justify a differential in pay and should be disregarded. The EAT in *Dugdale & Others* v *Kraft Foods Ltd* [1976] IRLR 368 held that where men work a night shift or unsociable hours they can be compensated by an additional 'shift payment'.

However, any 'like work' that is carried out during the daytime should be paid at the same rate that is paid to female employees to ensure genuine equal pay. In *Kerr v Lister Co Ltd* [1977] IRLR 259 women day-shift workers claimed that they were entitled to the same rates of pay as men and women who carried out the same work during the course of a night shift. Their claim was rejected on the basis that the justification for the differential was that a higher rate of pay was necessary to attract workers to carry out the night shift.

In *National Coal Board* v *Sherwin* [1978] IRLR 122 a female canteen worker was paid a lower basic rate of pay than a male canteen worker on the night shift. Her claim for equal pay was upheld by the EAT who affirmed *Dugdale & Others* v *Kraft Foods Ltd* (above) and held that employees who suffered the disadvantages of working at night should not be over compensated, although the EAT did acknowledge that working at night could bring with it extra responsibilities and that these should be factors to take into consideration.

In order to determine whether work is broadly similar the courts will consider whether there is any difference in contractual obligations. However, where the contract of a man provides that additional or alternative duties may be carried out the court will look beyond the terms of the contract and look at what happens in practice. In *Electrolux Ltd* v *Hutchinson & Others* [1976] IRLR 410 the employer argued that the female applicants who carried out broadly similar duties to their male colleagues were not entitled to equal pay because the contracts of the male comparators provided that they may be required to transfer between jobs and to work overtime, night shifts and Sundays. The EAT held that it was necessary to consider the extent to which the additional contractual obligations were actually performed and that in this case because the additional obligations were rarely carried out the women were entitled to equal pay.

Work rated as equivalent

In order to prevent claims by employees that they are not being paid equal pay for equal work, and thus avoid potential liability, an employer can evaluate particular functions – such as the scope, content, level of responsibility, knowledge etc – by means of a job-evaluation scheme, although it must be noted that an employer is under no obligation to do so.

A job-evaluation scheme is able to assess different jobs against predetermined criteria. Factors that can be taken into account include skill requirements, level of responsibility, scope of decision-making and knowledge. Each job is given a score based on a detailed job description to determine a level and consequent pay scale for the job. Any job-evaluation scheme must be analytical, with appropriate scores given for different skills and must be done on an objective basis. An approach which takes into account the 'whole job' or what feels right would not generally be acceptable: *Bromley & Others* v *H & J Quick Ltd* [1988] IRLR 456.

If the jobs of men and women have been rated as equivalent under a job-evaluation scheme then both groups are entitled to the same rates of pay and conditions and s1(2)(b) EPA 1970 provides that the term of the contract which is less favourable 'shall be treated as so modified as not to be less favourable'.

If the jobs have been evaluated as being equal there can be no claim for equality under the EPA 1970 unless the basis upon which the job was evaluated was sexually biased. The question which may arise is whether certain criteria may be considered to be biased in favour of one sex. In *Rummler* v *Dato-Druck GmbH* [1987] ICR 774 the ECJ was asked to consider whether a job-classification scheme which took into consideration characteristics more commonly found in men – in this case physical strength – was discriminatory. It was held that such a scheme which had physical effort as one of its criteria would not be discriminatory, provided that the employer took into account criteria which favoured the other sex.

It has already been stated that an employer is not under an obligation to carry out a job-evaluation scheme. However, the question that has arisen is whether once a job-evaluation scheme has been carried out an employer is under an obligation to implement the findings.

In *O'Brien & Others* v *Sim-Chem Ltd* [1980] ICR 573 the employer set up a job-evaluation committee comprising management and trade union representatives. Once the evaluation was completed the applicants were informed of their new grades and salary which were to take effect in April. However, before the new grades were implemented the government imposed a 'pay freeze' and the applicants were paid their original contractual rates. The applicants sought to have the new grades under the job-evaluation scheme implemented.

The House of Lords held that once the job-evaluation study had been undertaken, which resulted in the jobs of men and women being given an equal rating, the women became entitled to have their contracts modified so that their terms and conditions were no less favourable than the terms and conditions of the men. It was held that, once discrimination has been established, s1(2)(b) should come into effect regardless of whether the employer has implemented the job-evaluation scheme.

In *Arnold* v *Beecham Group Ltd* [1982] ICR 744 the EAT held that where an employer undertakes a job-evaluation scheme the evaluation study is not complete until it is adopted by the employers. In this case there was an agreement between the employers and the union to publish the results of a job-evaluation study. However, later objections resulted in a failure to implement the scheme, leaving the applicant on a lower rate of pay than she would have been if the scheme had been implemented. On the facts it was held by the EAT that the union and the employers had accepted the validity of the scheme and it was irrelevant that they had subsequently decided not to use it as the basis for a new pay structure.

Work of equal value

The third way in which a woman can bring a claim under the EPA 1970 is to claim that the work that she carries out is of equal value to that carried out by a man. This entitlement was introduced into the EPA 1970 by means of the Equal Pay (Amendment) Regulations 1983, which was implemented to bring the 1970 Act in line with art 141 EC. In *EC Commission* v *United Kingdom* Case 61/81 [1982] ICR 578 it had been held by the ECJ that the EPA 1970 did not conform with art 141 because it did not provide that employees could require a judicial body to order or carry out a job-evaluation scheme. This was remedied by the Equal Pay (Amendment) Regulations 1983, although the procedure that was put in place to resolve a claim of work of equal value is complex and time-consuming.

Section 1(2)(c) EPA 1970 provides that where a woman is employed to carry out work which is, in terms of the demands made on her such as skills, effort and responsibility, of equal value to that of a man in the same employment any terms and conditions which are less favourable to her than terms and conditions in the man's contract will be modified so that they are not less favourable.

Claims under the EPA 1970 for work of equal value can be extremely complex and time-consuming, and although the number of such claims is low they can have far reaching consequences for employers. A recent example of this can be seen in the case of *Wilson* v *North Cumbria Acute NHS Trust*, which was settled in early 2005, eight years after the claim was presented to the employment tribunal. The case is not of legal importance because clearly as it was settled there is no binding precedent. Nevertheless, it is extremely interesting because of its potential impact. The case concerned 1,500 women who were employed in a range of different duties from clerical officers and catering assistants to nurses and porters. The women claimed that the work that they carried out was of equal value to that of craftsmen, joiners, building labourers, works officers, craftsmen supervisors and maintenance assistants. Pay rates, hours of work, pensions, weekend working rates and sick pay were all included in the comparisons, which showed that the women were being paid less than their comparators. The case was settled and each of the women stand to gain between £35,000 and £200,000. The cost to the NHS is likely to be about £3 million. The women were supported in their claim by their union Unison, which estimates that there could be a further 100,000 further claims against the NHS.

In October 2004 changes were introduced to tribunal procedures in equal value claims to overcome some of the inherent difficulties. The Employment Tribunals (Constitution and Rules of Procedure) (Amendment) Regulations 2004 (SI 2004/2351) introduced the changes which include the use of new powers for the Employment Tribunal Presidents to appoint tribunal panels with specialist knowledge of equal value cases and new equal value rules of procedure that are more user-friendly. The Regulations also provide for the early exchange of factual information, with a requirement that the parties set out in advance of the hearing factual areas of agreement and areas of disagreement. The procedures relating to the use of experts in equal value claims are also amended to ensure that they receive relevant information at an early stage and provide early disclosure of their written expert evidence and so that less time is spent on cross-examination at tribunal.

A woman who wishes to make a claim under s1(2)(c) must first of all present her claim to the employment tribunal. The tribunal will consider as a preliminary matter whether there are reasonable grounds for determining whether the work is of equal value – this is known as a 'stage 1 equal value hearing'. In a case where a job evaluation scheme has rated the work of the claimant and the comparator with different values, the tribunal must determine that the work is not of equal value unless it has reasonable grounds for suspecting that the scheme discriminated on the grounds of sex, or was otherwise unsuitable. If the claimant has not been given an opportunity to make oral representations, she may do so before the tribunal decides whether or not it will dismiss the claim. If the tribunal is satisfied that there are reasonable grounds for bringing the claim, it may then proceed to determine the matter or require a member of a panel of independent experts to prepare a report with respect to the question of whether the work is of equal value. It is a matter of good practice for the tribunal to invite the parties to apply for an adjournment to give them the opportunity to settle the matter. However, an adjournment will not be granted to allow the employer to carry out a job-evaluation scheme.

The tribunal will also discontinue hearing an application if a job-evaluation scheme has taken place which has resulted in different values being given to the work of the applicant and the comparator. This may be the case at any time up to the time of the final hearing: *Dibro Ltd* v *Hore* [1990] IRLR 129.

If the parties are unable to reach a settlement and the tribunal requests an independent expert report, the expert is chosen from a panel which is nominated by ACAS. The role of the expert is inquisitorial, although his powers are limited particularly as there is no right of access to the employer's premises. If the tribunal has requested an independent expert to prepare a report, the parties must send to appointed expert all the information which they are required by the tribunal to disclose or facts which have been agreed between each other. At this stage the tribunal will also fix a date for the 'stage 2 equal value hearing'. Under the new Regulations the tribunal will have much more control over the time limits and procedures relating to the submission of the expert's report. Prior to the Regulations it was not uncommon for a report to take two years to complete. However, it is now expected that the time limit from the stage 1 hearing to the submission of the expert's report should be no longer than 18 weeks, although clearly this may be waived in more complex cases. The expert must take into account all representations that are made to him and send a summary of these representation to all parties inviting further representations to be made. Once the report is submitted the tribunal is under a duty to consider whether all procedural requirements have been satisfied in the preparation of the report and whether the conclusion that has been reached is a reasonable one and not in any way perverse. If the tribunal has grounds for the believing the report to be in any way defective, or the conclusion perverse, it may not accept the report and may require another report to be undertaken by another expert. The report can also be challenged by either party to the proceedings.

If the report is accepted it will be presented at the tribunal hearing. However, the Northern Ireland Court of Appeal held in *Tennants Textile Colours Ltd* v *Todd* [1989] IRLR 3 that although the report of an independent expert will inevitably carry significant weight a tribunal is not bound by the report.

One of the first cases to be decided after the implementation of the Equal Pay (Amendment) Regulations 1983 was *Hayward* v *Cammell Laird Shipbuilders Ltd (No 2)* [1988] AC 894. Here the applicant worked as a canteen assistant and claimed that her work was of equal value to others employed at the ship yard and chose as her comparators a painter, a joiner and an insulation engineer, all of whom were paid £30 per week more than the applicant. The applicant's claim was upheld by an independent expert. However, although the tribunal held that an equality clause operated, the parties could not agree the new terms of the contract. At a further hearing the employers argued that although the applicant received a lower basic rate of pay, additional benefits such as sick pay and meal allowances made her overall compensation package more favourable than that of her comparators. The argument put forward by the employers was accepted by the tribunal, the EAT and the Court of Appeal.

The House of Lords held that where a woman is performing work which has been rated as work of equal value to a comparator she is entitled to the same basic pay as the man, and that the word 'term' in s1(2)(c)(i) should be given its natural meaning so that it is a distinct part of the contract which can be compared with a similar provision in the contract of the comparator. The relevant terms should then be compared individually rather than treating the term relating to basic pay as part of a larger term embracing all of her contractual entitlements.

One of the effects of this decision is that the male comparators were then entitled to bring a claim on the basis that the applicant in this case was now on a better overall compensation package. However, this can be justified on the basis that one of the objective of the EPA 1970 is to bring about harmonisation of all terms and conditions for those employees carrying out work of equal value.

Choosing the comparator

In order to imply an equality clause into a woman's contract of employment the woman must be able to compare herself with a male worker who is employed in like work, work rated as equivalent or work of equal value.

The claimant chooses the man with whom she wishes to be compared. However, choosing the right comparator can sometimes be difficult. In *Ainsworth* v *Glass Tubes & Components Ltd* (1976) The Times 19 November the EAT held that a tribunal had erred when it substituted the male comparator nominated by the applicant with a comparator of their choice. An applicant will not be prevented from pursuing a claim of 'equal value' even if there are men other than the comparator carrying out 'like work' and being paid the same rate as the claimant.

In *Pickstone & Others* v *Freeman plc* [1988] 3 WLR 265 five women were employed as 'warehouse operatives' on a lower rate of pay than others employed as 'checker warehouse operatives'. They claimed that they were entitled to the same rate of pay as the male checker warehouse operatives who earned £4.22 more than them per week. Freemans argued that they were prevented from pursuing their claim because there were male warehouse operatives doing the same job as them at the same rate of pay.

It was held by the House of Lords that the women were not prevented from claiming that they were carrying out work of equal value to men because they were being paid the same rate as men who were warehouse operatives. Although it could be argued that s1(2)(c) appeared to exclude the right to bring a claim of 'equal value' where a women is employed on the same terms and conditions as a man who carries out the same work, the provision should be given a purposive interpretation – the purpose of the provision being to comply with art 141 EC.

Section 1(6) EPA 1970 provides that a woman may use as a comparator a man who is employed at the same establishment of her employer or an associated employer or a man at another establishment in Great Britain at which common terms and conditions of employment are observed. The rationale behind the implementation of s1(6) was put very succinctly by Lord Slyn in *British Coal Corporation* v *Smith* [1996] 3 All ER 97 where he said:

> 'The reason for this is obvious, since otherwise an employer could so arrange things as to ensure that only women worked at a particular establishment or that no man who could reasonably be considered as a possible comparator should work there ...'

A similar approach was taken by the Scottish Court of Session in *Morton* v *South Ayrshire Council* (2002) The Times 1 March. In this case female head teachers of primary schools claimed equal pay with secondary school head teachers. The applicants claimed that 75 per cent of primary school head teachers were female, whilst 75 per cent of secondary school head teachers were male. The salary scale for primary school heads was lower than that for secondary school heads. The applicants claimed that there was discrimination contrary to the EPA 1970 because they were engaged in the same 'service' within the meaning of art 141 EC. The respondents argued that the applicants could not use as their comparator head teachers who were employed by a different education authority. The Court of Session, having regard to the case of *Defrenne* v *Sabena (No 2)* Case 43/75 [1976] ECR 455, held that in determining whether there was inequality of pay the scope of enquiry was not always confined to the applicant's own workplace or indeed to his own employer. In this case pay scales were negotiated by the Scottish Joint Negotiating Committee and any settlement was to be regarded as a national settlement to be implemented by each education authority. The Court therefore concluded that a comparator employed by another education authority was permissible. The case was remitted to a tribunal for a full hearing on the facts.

The scope of art 141(1) EC has also been considered by the ECJ in *Lawrence* v *Regent Office Care Ltd* [2002] IRLR 822 where the rates of pay of female catering and cleaning staff working for North Yorkshire County Council were increased following a job evaluation scheme which had rated the work of the female employees of equal value to the work of men engaged in activities such as gardening and refuse collection. The work of the catering and cleaning staff was contracted out to a private contractor and their pay was cut. The female employees claimed equal pay, using as their comparators the male employees who were still employed by the council. The employment tribunal held as a preliminary issue that the applicants could not compare themselves with the men because the men were working for a different employer. The matter was subsequently referred to the European Court of Justice by the Court of Appeal, where it was held that whilst there was nothing in the wording of art 141(1) EC to limit the scope of that provision to situations in which men and women worked for the same employer, where the work of both the applicant and the comparator could not be attributed to a single source art 141 would not apply. There was no single entity that could remedy the alleged inequality in pay and therefore the application failed.

In determining what are 'common terms' for the purpose of s1(6) a broad approach has been adopted by the House of Lords. In *Leverton* v *Clwyd County Council* [1989] 2 WLR 47 a qualified nursery nurse employed by Clwyd County Council claimed that her work was of equal value to men employed at various council sites. The claimant and the comparators were employed under the conditions of service of the NJC for Local Authorities' Administrative, Professional, Technical and Clerical Services (the 'Purple Book'), which details the appropriate salary scales by which their pay was calculated. The council argued that because the claimant worked less hours than the comparators and had significantly more holiday entitlement she could not be considered to be in the same employment and on common terms.

It was held by the House of Lords that because the claimant and comparators were employed under the terms of the 'Purple Book', they were employed on common terms and conditions. The difference in hours and holidays did not prevent the claimant and the comparators from being regarded as employed in the same employment for the purposes of s1(6).

This broad approach taken by the House of Lords can also be seen in the more recent case of *British Coal Corporation* v *Smith* (above) where it was held by their Lordships that for a comparator to be regarded as being in the 'same employment' for the purposes of s1(6) it is not necessary for the applicant to show that the terms and conditions of employment of the comparator are identical to her own; it is sufficient to show that the terms are broadly similar.

The requirement to show 'common terms' only applies to a comparator who is employed at another establishment to the claimant. Where both are employed at the same establishment there is no such requirement.

When choosing a comparator a women can use a man who was employed in the same position prior to her appointment. The Court of Appeal in *Macarthys* v *Smith* [1980] ICR 672 held that art 141 EC provides that the principle of equal pay applies where a woman who carries out equal work to her predecessor and is paid less by her employer.

Where a female employee seeks to make a maternity-related equal pay claim the requirement of a male comparator can prove to be an impossible task! In *Alabaster* v *Barclays Bank and the Secretary of State for Social Security* [2005] EWCA Civ 508 Mrs Alabaster claimed sex discrimination when her employer failed to reflect a pay increase in the calculation of her statutory maternity pay (SMP). Mrs Alabaster became pregnant in May 1995, and the reference period upon which the level of earnings-related maternity pay is based was eight weeks prior to 31 October 1995. In December, prior to her maternity leave, Mrs Alabaster was given a pay rise and she argued that the salary increase should have been taken into account in calculating her SMP. The case, which went from the tribunal to the EAT and Court of Appeal and then to the ECJ and back to the Court of Appeal took nine years. The ECJ held that the increase in salary should have been reflected in Mrs Alabaster's maternity pay. To deny a woman on maternity leave the benefit of a pay rise which is awarded prior to taking maternity leave is discriminatory and contrary to art 141. The ECJ reasoned that if the appellant had not been pregnant she would have had the benefit of the pay rise. The Court of Appeal held that in order to give effect to the decision of the ECJ and the entitlement to increased maternity pay it was necessary to disapply s1 EPA 1970, the requirement for a male comparator, because pregnancy is a uniquely female condition. Brooke LJ said:

> 'In our judgment the appropriate way to proceed is to follow the example shown by the House of Lords in *Webb* and disapply those parts of s1 of the EPA which impose the requirement for a male comparator. In this way Mrs Alabaster can succeed in her claim for sex discrimination without the need for such a comparator, just as she would have done automatically if her claim had not related to the payment of an amount of money that was regulated by her contract of employment and had fallen within the SDA regime instead.'

Clearly this decision brings the EPA 1970 in line with the position under the Sex Discrimination Act 1975, as established by the House of Lords *Webb* v *Emo Air Cargo (UK) Ltd* [1994] QB 718.

The genuine material factor defence

An employer may have a successful defence to an equal pay claim if he can prove that the disparity between the pay of the applicant and the comparator is attributable to a material factor other than the difference in sex.

This defence is provided by s1(3) EPA 1970 which states:

> '(3) An equality clause shall not operate in relation to a variation between the woman's contract and the man's contract if the employer proves that the variation is genuinely due to a material factor which is not the difference of sex and that factor –
> (a) in the case of an equality clause falling within subsection (2)(a) or (b) above, must be a material difference between the woman's case and the man's; and

(b) in the case of an equality clause falling within subsection (2)(c) above, may be such a material difference.'

In order to successfully raise this defence the burden is upon the employer to prove that there is some objectively justifiable reason for the disparity claimed by the applicant: *Byrne & Others* v *Financial Times Ltd* [1991] IRLR 417.

It can be seen from s1(3) that with respect to 'like work' and 'work rated as equivalent' the employer needs to show that the material factor which causes the disparity is a material difference. However, with respect to 'equal value' the employer only has to show that it may be a material difference. It can be argued that following the decision of the House of Lords in *Rainey* v *Greater Glasgow Health Board Eastern District* [1987] AC 224 that this distinction no longer serves any practical purpose and that an employer can rely upon any factor (other than the difference of sex) to justify a pay differential if such a factor creates a genuine need for a pay differential.

In *Rainey* the health board decided to establish a prosthetic fitting service within the NHS. To attract prosthesists who had previously worked for private contractors to the NHS it was decided to offer them employment at the rate that they were receiving within the private sector, even though it was acknowledged that the normal rate for the job within the NHS was much lower. The applicant, who was recruited directly from training and was employed on the normal NHS rate which was of course significantly lower than the rate for those recruited from the private sector, claimed parity with her male colleagues from the private sector.

The House of Lords held that to determine whether a material factor constituted a material difference for the purposes of s1(3) it was necessary to go beyond the 'personal equation' of the applicant and her comparator and take into account all the circumstances of the case, including objectively justified economic factors. In this case in order for the Health Board to attract appropriately qualified prosthetists to set up this new service it was necessary to offer them higher salaries than the normal NHS rate and that this constituted a genuine material factor for the purposes of s1(3) EPA 1970.

The applicant in this case relied heavily upon a decision of the Court of Appeal in *Clay Cross (Quarry Services)* v *Fletcher* [1979] ICR 1 where it was held that when considering a defence of 'material difference' under s1(3) any consideration should be confined to the 'personal equation' between the applicant and the comparator. By this the Court of Appeal meant that only factors such as length of service, superior skill or qualifications, productivity or other personal circumstances such as preserving the wages of an employee's previous job (which is known as 'red-circling') should be taken into account. Lord Denning considered that to consider other external factors would render the Equal Pay Act virtually inpotent and said 'An employer cannot avoid his obligations under the Act by saying "I paid him more because he asked for more" or "I paid her less because she asked for less".'

However, the House of Lords held in *Rainey* that the guidance given by Lord

Denning, who said that the tribunal 'is not to have regard to any extrinsic forces which have led to the man being paid more', was too restrictive.

Although an employer may be able to rely upon the genuine material factor defence if for the purposes of recruitment a higher or indeed lower salary is to be paid, there may be some limit placed upon the amount of time such a defence will be operative.

In *Benveniste* v *University of Southampton* [1989] ICR 617 the Court of Appeal held that although the university may have been able to originally justify paying a female mathematics lecturer less because at the time she was recruited they were subject to serious financial restraints, the defence of 'genuine material factor' could not be relied upon if at a later stage the financial pressures that existed at the time of recruitment had been eased.

Collective bargaining

In some cases there may disparity between the pay of men and women that can result from separate collective bargaining. According to the decision of the European Court of Justice in *Enderby* v *Frenchay Health Authority* [1993] IRLR 591 this will not amount to a genuine material factor for the purposes of s1(3).

In *Enderby* senior speech therapists claimed that they were employed on work of equal value to clinical psychologists and pharmacists. The health authority rejected the argument that the work was of equal value, but argued that even if it was they would have a s1(3) defence because the rates of pay for the applicant and her comparators had been negotiated by different bodies and amounted to a genuine material factor.

The ECJ held that the fact that the rates of pay of the applicant and the comparators were decided by different collective bargaining processes was not sufficient objective justification for the difference in pay between the two jobs.

The reasoning behind the decision of the ECJ was that if an employer could show that there was no discrimination within the different bargaining processes then to allow the fact that the pay of a woman and her comparator had been negotiated separately to amount to a genuine material factor defence would allow employers to circumvent the legislation by using separate bargaining processes.

The ECJ in this case also held that where a prima facie case of sex discrimination is established upon the presentation of statistics which show an appreciable difference in pay for work of equal value between men and women, the burden of proof moves from the applicant to the employer. The Court appreciated that market forces will on occasions lead to inequality of pay but said that such inequality can only be justified in so far as they are objective and not the result of discrimination.

The approach adopted by the ECJ in *Enderby* had also been adopted by the Scottish EAT in *Barber & Others* v *NCR (Manufacturing) Ltd* [1993] IRLR 95 where it was held that where collective bargaining untainted by sex discrimination caused a pay differential, such a differential could not be justified purely on the grounds of collective bargaining.

Experience and qualifications

Long service, better qualifications and experience may amount to a material difference for the purposes of s1(3) EPA 1970.

In *Baker & Others* v *Rochdale Health Authority* (1994) (unreported) a group of nurses claimed that they were being paid less for like work than a male colleague. The health authority argued that the difference in pay was because the male nurse was experienced in fitting male catheters – an experience he had gained purely because of the policy of the health authority that only male nurses should carry out male catheterisation. Furthermore, the male nurse was able to train others in male catheterisation.

The Court of Appeal held that the experience of the male nurse and his ability to train others was a material factor and that, whilst there was a sexual basis for the policy that enabled him to gain the experience, the training should be treated as an independent factor for which he should be paid accordingly.

Grading structures

A grading structure, whether or not part of a collective agreement may operate as a genuine material factor defence. It was held by the Court of Appeal in *National Vulcan Engineering Insurance Group* v *Wade* [1978] ICR 800 that a grading scheme will not breach the EPA 1970 provided that the scheme is applied fairly regardless of sex.

Part-time workers

The Part-time Workers (Prevention of Less Favourable Treatment) Regulations 2000 introduced new rights for part-time workers to ensure that employees engaged on part-time contracts are not treated any less favourably than their full-time colleagues simply because of their part-time status. The Regulations provide that part-time employees are entitled to the same rates of pay (including sick pay), the same access to company pension schemes, the same entitlements to annual leave and should be treated no less favourably in the opportunities for training than their full-time counterparts. The Regulations also provide that part-time workers should have the same entitlement to annual leave, maternity leave, paternity leave, adoptive leave and parental leave but on a pro-rata basis. The Regulations provide that any unfavourable treatment between full-time and part-time workers must be objectively justified by the employer.

The Regulations were amended in October 2002 by the Part-time Workers (Prevention of Less Favourable Treatment) (Amendment) Regulations 2002 (SI

2002/2035). The amendments made two significant changes to the Regulations. The first important change is with respect to comparators. Under the original regulations a claimant had to compare herself with a full-time worker on the same type of contract, so that a part-time worker on a fixed-term contract had to use a comparator who was also on a fixed-term contract. The implementation of the Fixed-Term Employees (Prevention of Less Favourable Treatment) Regulations 2002, which make it unlawful to treat an employee less favourably because that employee is on a fixed-term contract, would appear to make it irrelevant as to whether a part-time worker uses as her comparator a fixed-term employee or a permanent employee. To avoid over-complication the Regulations have been amended so that a worker can compare herself with a full-time colleague irrespective of whether either the claimant or comparator's contract is permanent or fixed-term.

The second important change was to comply with the judgment of the House of Lords in *Preston v Wolverhampton Healthcare NHS Trust (No 2)* [2001] ICR 217 following the decision of the ECJ in *Preston & Others v Wolverhampton Healthcare NHS Trust & Others; Fletcher & Others v Midland Bank plc* Case C–78/98 [2000] IRLR 506 which considered the question of what rights a part-time worker has in relation to claiming retrospective benefits under a pension scheme.

In these joined cases, the claimants who worked part-time had been employed for a number of years. At various times in the past, because the claimants were on part-time contracts they had not been entitled to become members of their employer's occupational pension scheme. However, they were later entitled to membership of the various schemes. The claimants commenced proceedings on the grounds that they had been unlawfully discriminated against contrary to art 119 (now 141 EC) of the Treaty of Rome because they could not bring proceedings more than six months after terminating their employment, as a result of s2(4) EPA 1970; they could only claim entitlement to a pension scheme for the two-year period prior to commencing proceedings in the tribunal irrespective of the length of their employment, as a result of s2(5) EPA 1970; and, where they worked periodically for the same employer but under successive contracts, they could only instigate proceedings within six months of the end of each contract under s2(4).

The claims were rejected by the employment tribunal, the EAT and the Court of Appeal. However, the House of Lords referred the matter to the ECJ. The ECJ held that the six-month time limit for commencing a claim after the termination of employment was not incompatible with EU law; however, the ECJ held that it was incorrect to restrict a claimant's entitlement to join a pension scheme to the two-year period prior to commencing proceedings. The ECJ held that the claimants were entitled to claim their rights to become members of a pension scheme back to 1976, when art 119 had been enacted. Furthermore, the ECJ held that where workers are employed on a series of successive new contracts (umbrella contracts) the six-month time limit for commencing a claim should run from the date of the last contract and they were not required to bring a claim within six months from the end of each separate contract.

The House of Lords held that two-year time limit on backdating a part-time worker's entitlement to join a pension scheme was contrary to EU law and the Part-time Workers Regulations were subsequently amended to remove the two-year time limit.

Following *Preston* a further issue has developed which concerns the time limit for commencing a claim for entitlement to membership of a company pension scheme in the event of a transfer of the undertaking. We have already seen that pension rights do not transfer under TUPE. However, if there was a pension scheme from which a claimant was precluded because of her part-time status, the question is whether the six-month time limit for commencing a claim under the EPA 1970 runs from when her employment with the original employer (the transferor) ceased, which would be the date of the transfer, or whether time should run from the date when her employment with the new employer (the transferee) comes to an end.

In *PowerHouse Retail Ltd & Others* v *Burroughs, Bartlett & Others* [2004] EWCA Civ 1281 the Court of Appeal held that time starts to run from the date when the contract with the original employer ceases, in other words the time limit is six months from the date of the transfer of the undertaking.

Time limits

A claimant must present an equal pay claim to the employment tribunal either during her employment, or within six months after the termination of employment: s2(4) EPA 1970. 'During her employment' means any time up until the effective date of termination of her employment with the relevant employer, regardless of when she ceased doing the particular job to which her claim relates. In *National Power plc* v *Young* [2001] ICR 328, the applicant worked for National Power from 1969 until 1996 when she was made redundant. After leaving her employment she brought an equal pay claim relating to a job she had ceased to carry out in May 1995. The Court of Appeal held that the six-month time limit started from the end of her employment rather than from when she ceased doing the particular work which was the subject of her claim.

Section 2ZA EPA 1970 sets out the qualifying date in relation to bringing equal pay proceedings in cases of concealment, stable employment and where a claimant is disabled. Where there is stable employment, including persons who work on a series of short-term contracts or where an employee has worked at regular intervals for the employer, the time limit is six months from the date upon which the employment relationship ended. If the employer deliberately concealed any fact relevant to the claim, or if claimant is suffering from a disability, a claim must be presented within either six months of the termination of the relationship or six years after the discovery of the inequality or the disability ceasing. Disability for the purposes of the EPA 1970 means that the claimant was under age or mentally incapable and not the definition laid down in the Disability Discrimination Act 1995.

Claims for arrears

A claimant who is successful in an equal pay claim will be entitled to equal pay with immediate effect. However, the claimant will also wish to claim for the difference between her old rate and new rate of pay for a period of time prior to the hearing of her claim. The EPA 1970, as originally enacted, provided that claims for arrears were limited to a period of two years. This meant that in many cases were women had worked for more than two years at a different pay scale to their comparator they were not fully compensated for their losses. However, in *Levez* v *T H Jennings (Harlow Pools) Ltd* [2000] ICR 58, a case concerning a betting-shop manager who was paid £600 per year less than her male comparator, the EAT held that the two-year limit was contrary to art 141 EC and said that the period for which arrears could be claimed would be six years. As a result, the EPA 1970 was amended by the Equal Pay (Amendment) Regulations 2003, increasing the limit on backdated pay to six years in most cases.

Red-circling

Where an employee is moved to a lower paid job his employer may offer him some protection and continue to pay him the same rate as the previous job – this is called red-circling. The question has arisen as to whether the fact that a woman is paid less than her male comparator because his wages have been red circled is contrary to the EPA 1970 and whether the defence of genuine material difference will apply. In *Snoxell and Davies* v *Vauxhall Motors Ltd* [1977] ICR 700 the EAT gave guidance as to the approach that should be adopted by the courts when considering a s1(3) defence of material difference because the pay of male comparators has been red circled. The EAT held that the fact that the wages of a comparator have been red circled will not automatically give rise to the defence, and that a tribunal should look at all the circumstances including the factors which gave rise to the red circle and whether there is any evidence of sex discrimination.

Questionnaires

Section 42 of the Employment Act 2002 provides for the use of questionnaires by employees who are considering bringing an equal pay claim. Questionnaires are already used in race and sex discrimination claims and it is expected that equal pay questionnaires will allow for a potential applicant to be given information on pay schemes operated by the employer to enable him to decide whether or not to commence proceedings.

The use of questionnaires is intended to assist employees who believe that they have not received equal pay to request key information from their employers. It is hoped that the use of the questionnaires will assist in the resolution of disputes in the workplace without the need for a tribunal hearing. In the event that the matter is not resolved and the case proceeds to a tribunal hearing, the information should enable the complaint to be made more effectively, because the disputed issues will have been identified in advance.

The questionnaire seeks to establish whether an individual is receiving less pay and whether the employer agrees that the comparator is doing equal work. The questionnaire includes:

1. a statement of why the applicant believes that they are not receiving equal pay, followed by a statement of who they believe is the appropriate comparator;
2. questions to ascertain whether they are receiving less pay than their comparator and, if so, the reasons why;
3. questions on whether the employer agrees that the people being compared are doing equal work or work of equal value; and
4. space for the applicant's own questions.

An employer has eight weeks to respond to a questionnaire and a failure to do so can lead to the tribunal drawing an adverse inference. Employers are required to answer the questions posed as fully as possible: however, sometimes they may be required to provide information that is confidential, such as the salary of another employee.

If the information is confidential, and the comparator employee does not want his salary to be disclosed, the employer will need to consider how much information can be given without breaching confidentiality. If the case proceeds to tribunal, disclosure of relevant information may be ordered if the tribunal is of the opinion that it is in the interests of justice to do so.

8

Employment Law and the Family

8.1 Introduction

8.2 Ante-natal care

8.3 Maternity rights

8.4 Parental leave

8.5 Time off for dependants

8.1 Introduction

In the White Paper *Fairness at Work* published in 1998, the government put forward proposals to balance the competing interests of work and family life. It stated that in future 'it will become increasingly important to enable employees to balance satisfactorily family responsibilities and work'. In March 2000 the 'Work-Life Balance' campaign was launched to persuade employers of the economic benefits of work-life balance and to convince employers of the need for change.

Many of the 'family friendly' policies of the government have now been given statutory effect with a new simplified framework of maternity leave and pay, and an entitlement to parental and adoption leave. New provisions have recently been implemented providing for paternity leave and the right to ask for flexible working arrangements. Employees also have the right to take time off work to deal with domestic emergencies.

8.2 Ante-natal care

An employee who is pregnant has a statutory right to take time off for ante-natal care. Section 55 ERA 1996 provides:

'(1) An employee who –
(a) is pregnant, and
(b) has, on the advice of a registered medical practitioner, registered midwife or registered health visitor, made an appointment to attend at any place for the purpose of receiving ante-natal care,

is entitled to be permitted by her employer to take time off during the employee's working hours in order to enable her to keep the appointment.'

Section 55(2) ERA 1996 provides that an employee is not entitled to take time off for ante-natal care if her employer requests her to produce a certificate from a registered medical practitioner, registered midwife or registered health visitor stating that the she is pregnant, and an appointment card or some other document showing that the appointment has been made, and she fails to produce the documents requested.

An employee's working hours for the purpose of time off for ante-natal care is any time when, according to her contract of employment, she is required to be at work.

Any pregnant women who takes time off for ante-natal care is entitled to be paid by her employer for the period of absence at her normal hourly rate. Section 56(2) ERA 1996 provides details as to how an hourly rate is to be calculated in various different circumstances.

If an employer refuses a pregnant employee time off for ante-natal care, or has not paid her the sums that are due to her by virtue of s56 ERA 1996, the employee may present a complaint to the employment tribunal. Any application must be made within three months beginning with the date of the appointment concerned, or within such further period as the tribunal considers reasonable in a case where it is satisfied that it was not reasonably practicable for the complaint to be presented earlier.

8.3 Maternity rights

The Employment Relations Act (ERA) 1999 introduced new rules governing maternity rights which were intended to simplify the rules under the old scheme. Additional Regulations have been introduced to further enhance the maternity rights of female employees. The Maternity and Parental Leave (Amendment) Regulations 2001 and 2002 amend the Maternity and Parental Leave etc Regulations 1999, which implemented many of the provisions in the ERA 1999. Furthermore, the Employment Act 2002, which received Royal Assent on the 8 July 2002, provides for further Regulations to amend the law relating to maternity leave.

Ordinary maternity leave

Section 7 ERA 1999 inserts a new s71 into the ERA 1996 and provides that all female employees will have the right to maternity leave regardless of the length of time that the woman has been employed by the employer. A woman who exercises her rights under s71 is entitled to have the benefit of the terms and conditions of employment which would have applied had she not been absent and is entitled to return to the job in which she was employed before her maternity leave. The

Maternity and Parental Leave (Amendment) Regulations 2002, which came into force in November 2002, provide that the period of ordinary maternity leave is extended from 18 weeks to 26 weeks.

To assist in the calculation of maternity leave and notice periods, the dates are generally calculated from the expected week of confinement (EWC), in other words the week upon which the baby is due to be born, beginning with the Sunday. Confinement is defined in s171(1) Social Security Contributions and Benefits Act 1992 as 'labour resulting in the issue of a living child or labour after 24 weeks of pregnancy resulting in the issue of a living child whether alive or dead'.

The 2002 Regulations also amend the 1999 Regulations with respect to the notice that an employee must give to her employer. An employee must advise her employer before the end of the fifteenth week before the expected week of confinement of the date upon which she intends her maternity leave to begin – this is a significant increase in notice; prior to the new Regulations the notice period was just 21 days before the intended start date. Clearly the longer notice period will enable an employer to make suitable alternative arrangements to provide cover for the absent employee. If an employer requests a medical certificate stating the EWC the employee must provide one: however, an employer must make his request for a certificate clear.

The Maternity and Parental Leave (Amendment) Regulations 2002 further amend the 1999 Regulations to provide that an employer who has been notified of the commencement of an employee's ordinary maternity leave must notify the employee of the date upon which it will end: reg 8(c). Furthermore, if an employer fails to notify the employee of the date upon which her maternity leave ends, he cannot prevent the employee from returning before the end of her maternity leave and the employee is protected against any detriment or dismissal if she fails to return on the due date.

A woman may choose when to commence her maternity leave at any time from the eleventh week prior to the EWC. However, any pregnancy-related absence from work will cause an employee's ordinary maternity leave period to begin automatically if the absence is after the beginning of the fourth week before the expected week of confinement. If a woman has not taken maternity leave, and gives birth to her baby, the leave will begin automatically when the baby is born.

The entitlement to maternity leave only applies to those women who work under a contract of service and does not apply to those who are self-employed.

Entitlement to paid annual leave and other benefits should continue to accrue during maternity leave. Any rights under an occupational pension scheme should also continue.

Additional maternity leave

Section 73 of the ERA 1999 and the Maternity and Parental Leave etc Regulations 1999 replace ss79–84 ERA 1996, and have themselves been amended by the Maternity and Parental Leave (Amendment) Regulations 2002.

Section 73 (as amended) provides that any woman with 26 weeks continuous service with her employer at 15 weeks prior to the EWC will be entitled to 26 weeks additional unpaid maternity leave which will commence immediately after the period of ordinary maternity leave.

The 2002 Regulations have increased the period of additional maternity leave so that the period will end 26 weeks after the end of ordinary maternity leave, rather than 29 weeks after the week of childbirth. This means that an employee who has been in continuous employment for more than one year may take 52 weeks maternity leave.

An employee who is returning from additional maternity leave is entitled to return to a position on terms and conditions not less favourable than those which would have applied if she had not been absent.

An employer is under a duty to notify the employee of the date upon which her maternity leave ends and a failure to do so will result in the same sanctions as in the case of ordinary maternity leave.

Redundancy during maternity leave

Section 74 ERA 1996 as inserted by the Employment Relations Act 1999 and Maternity and Parental Leave etc Regulations 1999, provides that where an employee is absent on maternity leave and a redundancy situation arises so that it is not practicable for her employer to continue to employ her under her existing contract of employment, and where there is a suitable available vacancy, the employee is entitled to be offered the alternative employment: reg 10. Further, an employee who is dismissed by reason of redundancy and can show that reg 10 has not been complied with is to be regarded as being unfairly dismissed: reg 20.

Health and safety

Under the Management of Health and Safety at Work Regulations 1999, which were implemented to comply with the Pregnant Workers Directive, all employers must carry out a risk assessment and safety checks to ensure the health and safety at work of new or expectant mothers.

In the event of any risk an employer must take preventative action to prevent a pregnant worker from suffering any harm by:

1. altering working conditions;
2. offering suitable alternative work.

In the event that there is no suitable alternative work an employer must suspend the employee on normal pay.

In *Day* v *T Pickles Farms Ltd* [1999] IRLR 217 the EAT held that there is no requirement that an employee is pregnant to trigger off the assessment; it is sufficient if there is, in the workforce, a woman of child-bearing age. This was a common sense approach by the EAT because where there is a risk to a pregnant worker the recognition of such a risk may be too late once a woman is pregnant.

Interestingly, the EAT held that a failure to carry out a risk assessment can amount to a detriment within the meaning of the Sex Discrimination Act 1975. This is a more broad and effective individual remedy than relying upon a breach of the 1999 Regulations to establish a right to paid suspension or compensation for injury.

Compulsory maternity leave

The Pregnant Workers Directive required that a woman who had given birth must not work for at least two weeks after the birth. This requirement was originally implemented by the Maternity (Compulsory) Leave Regulations 1994 but can now be found in s72 ERA 1996. The employer is obliged to ensure that a woman does not return to work during the period of compulsory maternity leave and a failure to do so will be a criminal offence punished by a fine.

Maternity pay

A woman who takes maternity leave is entitled to one of two types of statutory maternity benefit:

1. statutory maternity pay (SMP) – this is paid by employers and is dependent upon eligibility;
2. maternity allowance (MA) – this is paid by the Benefits Agency.

To receive SMP a woman must be over the age of 16, work under a contract for service and pay Class One National Insurance contributions and satisfy the other conditions as detailed below. A self-employed woman will not be entitled to SMP but may be entitled to maternity allowance. In order to qualify for SMP an employee must satisfy the following criteria.

1. She must have 26 weeks continuous service up to and including the fifteenth week before the EWC.
2. She must earn an average sum which is sufficient to make it relevant for National Insurance purposes (currently £79 per week).
3. The employee must have given her employer at least four weeks notice of her intention to stop work.
4. She must have reached the eleventh week before the EWC.

Women who are entitled to SMP and whose EWC began after 6 April 2003 will receive the allowance for a period of 26 weeks. Women will be paid 90 per cent of their earnings for the first six weeks, which will be followed by £106 a week or 90 per cent of the woman's average earnings if this is less than £106 a week for the remaining 20 weeks. A woman will only receive SMP if she is not at work: however, if she has more than one job she may receive SMP from each employer.

A woman will be entitled to SMP regardless of whether or not she intends to return to work following the birth of her baby.

Maternity allowance is payable to women who are self-employed and have paid the requisite National Insurance contributions or women who do not satisfy the requisite conditions for SMP. However, in order to receive maternity allowance a woman must earn an average of at least £30 per week. The benefit is paid by the Benefits Agency and may be paid for up to 26 weeks. Maternity allowance is currently £106 per week or 90 per cent of earnings if this is less than £106 per week.

Paternity leave

Section 1 of the Employment Act 2002 inserts new provisions into Pt VIII of the ERA 1996 to make provision for fathers to take time off work following the birth of a child and inserts s80A into the ERA 1996. The details of the entitlement are set out in the Paternity and Adoption Leave Regulations 2002 (SI 2002/2788) which came into force in December 2002.

The Regulations provide that working fathers are entitled to two weeks' paid paternity leave following either the birth of a child after 6 April 2003 or the placement of a child for adoption. The entitlement to leave is subject to certain conditions.

1. The employee must have been employed by the employer from whom he is requesting leave for at least 26 weeks ending with the week immediately preceding the fourteenth week before the expected week of the child's birth.
2. The employee must be the father of the child or must be married to or be a partner of the child's mother and is expecting to have responsibility for the upbringing of the child.

An employee may choose to take either one week's leave or two consecutive weeks' leave which must be taken within 56 days of the birth of the baby. Notice must be given to the employer of the intention to take paternity leave and must specify the following:

1. the expected week of the child's birth;
2. the length of the period of leave that the employee has chosen to take;
3. the date upon which the leave is to commence.

Notice should be given to the employer on or before the fifteenth week prior to the expected week of the child's birth or, in cases where it is not reasonably practicable to do so, as soon as it is reasonably practicable. If an employee wishes to vary the time of his leave he may give notice of the variation to his employer provided that such notice is given either 28 days before the expected week of the birth of the child, if leave is to commence on the day of the birth, or 28 days before the date of commencement of leave. The entitlement to paternity leave is in addition to parental leave, which is detailed below.

Any person entitled to paternity leave will be paid the same rate as statutory maternity pay, which is currently £106 per week, or 90 per cent of average weekly earnings where these are less than £106.

Adoption leave

Adoptive parents who are newly matched with a child by an approved adoption agency and who have at least 26 weeks' continuous service at the time of the placement will be entitled to 26 weeks' paid leave and a further 26 weeks' unpaid leave. The leave may commence from the date of the placement or up to 14 days before the expected date of placement. Only one of the adoptive parents will be entitled to adoption leave: the other will be entitled to paternity leave. Statutory adoption pay will be paid at the same rate as SMP and those wishing to take such leave must inform their employer within seven days of being notified that they have been matched with a child, unless such notice is not reasonably practicable.

Flexible working

To further its 'family friendly' policies the government has now introduced the Flexible Working (Procedural Requirements) Regulations 2002, which came into effect on 6 April 2003. These provide that parents of children under the age of six, or disabled children aged under 18, have the right to apply to work flexibly and their employers will have a duty to consider these requests seriously. Employers will now have a statutory duty to consider any application by a qualifying parent seriously. The employer is under no duty to accede to any such request, but must consider the application, hold a meeting with the employee if he intends to refuse the request, and put the reasons for refusal in writing.

8.4 Parental leave

The Employment Relations Act 1999 inserts a new s76 into the ERA 1996 which implements the Parental Leave Directive (96/34/EC). The new s76 and the Maternity and Parental Leave etc Regulations 1999 came into force on 15 December 1999 and provide that an employee who has been continuously employed for a period of not less than a year and has, or expects to have, responsibility for a child, may take leave to care for that child: reg 13.

Regulation 13(2) provides that:

'(2) An employee has responsibility for a child, for the purposes of paragraph (1), if –
(a) he has parental responsibility or, in Scotland, parental responsibilities for the child; or

(b) he has been registered as the child's father under any provisions of s10(1) or 10A(1) of the Births and Deaths Registration Act 1953 or of s18(1) or (2) of the Registration of Births, Deaths and Marriages (Scotland) Act 1965.'

An employee is only entitled to parental leave in respect of a child born on or after 15 December 1999 unless the child is adopted, in which case the entitlement applies if the child is placed with the employee after that date: reg 13(3).

An employee is entitled to 13 weeks' unpaid leave up to the child's fifth birthday or, in the case of a child who is entitled to disability-living allowance, up to the child's eighteenth birthday. In the case of an adopted child the period of leave may be taken up to the fifth anniversary of the placement of the child with the adoptive parent or the date of the child's eighteenth birthday whichever is the earlier.

During the period of parental leave an employee is entitled to the benefit of terms and conditions of the contract which relate to notice, redundancy and disciplinary and grievance procedures.

An employee who wishes to take parental leave must generally give his employer at least 21 days' notice and must specify the date upon which the leave is to begin and end. If a male employee wishes to take leave immediately following the birth of the child he must give notice to his employer stating the expected week of childbirth and such notice should be served 21 days before the expected week of the birth. An employer may postpone a period of parental leave if he considers that the operation of the business would be unduly interrupted. However, the employer must advise the employee within seven days of receiving notice from the employee that he intends to postpone the period of leave and state the reasons for the postponement.

The minimum period of leave that may be taken is one week and the maximum that can be taken in respect of any one child is one year.

Right to return to work

An employee who takes parental leave for a period of four weeks or less is entitled to return from leave to the job in which she was employed before her absence: reg 18(1). However, this entitlement will not apply to an employee who takes parental leave of four weeks or less following additional maternity leave.

Where an employee takes parental leave of more than four weeks she is entitled to return either to the job in which she was employed before the absence or, if it is not reasonably practicable for the employer to permit her to return to that job, to another job which is both suitable for her and appropriate for her to do in the circumstances: reg 18(2).

A person who returns to work following a period of parental leave should do so on terms and conditions no less favourable than those which would have been applicable had the employee remained at work.

Protection from detriment

Regulation 19 provides that an employee is entitled under s47C ERA 1996 not to be subjected to any detriment as a result of taking parental leave.

Flexible working

Eligibility

The Flexible Working (Eligibility, Complaints and Remedies) Regulations 2002 (SI 2002/3236) make provision for parents of young or disabled children to make a request to their employer to vary their working hours or arrangements.

In order to make a request under the Regulations an employee must be an employee (as opposed to working under a contract for services or an agency worker) and have a child aged under six, or under 18 in the case of a child who is disabled. The employee who is requesting a change in their working pattern must be either the child's mother, father, adopter, guardian or foster parent, or married to or the partner of the child's mother, father, adopter, guardian or foster parent. The employee must also have worked with their employer continuously for at least 26 weeks at the date of the request.

The employee who is making the request must have, or expect to have, responsibility for the child's upbringing and should be making the application to enable them to care for the child.

Entitlement

Eligible employees will be able to request that the employer changes the number of hours that they are required to work, or request a change to the times when they are required to work, or request to work from home.

Application

It is up to the employee to make a considered application in writing. Employees are only able to make one application a year under the Regulations, and accepted applications will result in a permanent change to the employee's own terms and conditions of employment unless otherwise agreed between both parties. It is important, therefore, that, before making an application, the employee gives careful consideration to which working pattern will help them best care for their child; any financial implications it might have on them in cases where the desired working pattern will involve a drop in salary; and any effect it will have on their employer's business, and how these matters might be accommodated.

The Regulations also provide for the following.

1. When an employer agrees to a request for flexible working he must provide a written note of the contract variation that has been agreed by the parties, along with the date on which it is due to take effect.

2. The employer must hold a meeting with the employee within 28 days of receiving the request.
3. When a meeting is held, the result and, if appropriate, any reasons for refusal must be given to the employee in writing within 14 days of the meeting.
4. An employee has a right of appeal from an employer's refusal of a request for more flexible working.
5. An employee has the right to be accompanied at any meeting.

Employers' responsibilities and best practice
An employer must take a request for flexible working seriously and should follow the guidance given by the Department for Trade and Industry in its publication, *The Right to Request and the Duty to Consider*.

1. To consider requests properly in accordance with the set procedure.
2. To ensure they adhere to the time limits contained within the procedure.
3. To provide the employee with appropriate support and information during the course of the application.
4. To only decline a request where there is a recognised business ground and to explain to the employee in writing why it applies.
5. To ensure that any variation with the procedure is agreed in advance with the employee and recorded in writing.

Business grounds for refusing a request
The right to request flexible working is just as it says; it does not provide an automatic right to flexible working. However, an employer can only refuse a request if it falls into one of the following reasons for refusal:

1. Burden of additional costs.
2. Detrimental effect on ability to meet customer demand.
3. Inability to reorganise work among existing staff.
4. Inability to recruit additional staff.
5. Detrimental impact on quality.
6. Detrimental impact on performance.
7. Insufficiency of work during the periods the employee proposes to work.
8. Planned structural changes.

What kind of changes can be applied for?
There is scope to apply for a wide variety of different types of working pattern.
   Eligible employees can request to:

1. change the hours they work;
2. change the times when they are required to work; or
3. work from home (whether for all or part of the week).

Remedies and compensation

An employment tribunal or ACAS binding arbitration, which finds in favour of the employee, will be able to order the employer to:

1. reconsider an application by following the procedure correctly; and/or
2. pay an award to the employee.

The level of compensation will be an amount that ACAS or the employment tribunal feels to be just and equitable in all the circumstances, limited to a maximum amount. The maximum level is eight weeks' pay which is currently limited to £270 per week.

In addition, where an employer is found to have prevented the employee from being accompanied either at the meeting to discuss the application or appeal meeting they may make a separate award of up to two weeks' pay. Again, the week's pay is capped, as set out above.

8.5 Time off for dependants

Section 8 ERA 1999 inserts a new s57A into the ERA 1996 which provides that an employee is to be allowed to take a reasonable amount of time off work to deal with domestic emergencies concerning dependants. Section 57A provides as follows:

'(1) An employee is entitled to be permitted by his employer to take a reasonable amount of time off during the employee's working hours in order to take action which is necessary –
(a) to provide assistance on an occasion when a dependant falls ill, gives birth or is injured or assaulted,
(b) to make arrangements for the provision of care for a dependant who is ill or injured,
(c) in consequence of the death of a dependant,
(d) because of the unexpected disruption or termination of arrangements for the care of a dependant, or
(e) to deal with an incident which involves a child of the employee and which occurs unexpectedly in a period during which an educational establishment which the child attends is responsible for him.'

The above entitlement will only apply if the employee notifies his employer of the reason for his absence as soon as reasonably practicable and advises his employer of how long he intends to remain off work.

A dependant in relation to the employee is defined in s57A(3) as a spouse, child, parent or a person living in the same household other than an employee, tenant, lodger or boarder.

Section 57A(1)(a) and (b) will also apply to any person who reasonably relies upon the employee for assistance on an occasion when the person falls ill or is injured or assaulted, or reasonably relies upon the employee to make arrangements for the provision of care in the event of illness or injury: s57A(4).

Section 57A(1)(d) will also apply to any person who reasonably relies upon an employee to make arrangements for the provision of care.

Whilst s57A does not state that time off will be without remuneration, when read with other provisions of the ERA 1996 it is clear that this is the case. An employee who believes that his employer has refused to allow a reasonable amount of time off work in accordance with s57A may present his claim to an employment tribunal and should do so within three months of the refusal by the employer.

9

Remuneration

9.1 Introduction

9.2 Statement of pay

9.3 Payment of wages/deductions from wages

9.4 National minimum wage

9.5 Guarantee payments

9.1 Introduction

Generally most people who enter into a contract of employment have as one of their primary objectives the receipt of remuneration for the work undertaken. This chapter will consider obligations imposed upon an employer to provide employees with a pay statement, the protective measures that prevent an employer taking unlawful deductions from wages, the national minimum wage and guarantee payments.

9.2 Statement of pay

Most employees have a right conferred by s8 ERA 1996 to receive from their employer an itemised pay statement on or before the day of payment.

Section 8(2) provides that the statement shall contain particulars of:

'(a) the gross amount of the wages or salary,
(b) the amounts of any variable, and ... any fixed, deductions from that gross amount and the purposes for which they are made,
(c) the net amount of wages or salary payable, and
(d) where different parts of the net amount are paid in different ways, the amount and method of payment of each part-payment.'

Sections 8 and 9 provide that with respect to fixed deductions an employer may give either of the following statements:

1. a statement which specifies the amount and purpose of every fixed deduction; or
2. a statement which specifies the aggregate amount of all fixed deductions.

If an employer chooses the second option he must provide the employee with a standing statement of fixed deductions. This statement must be in writing and must state the amount and interval at which a deduction is to be made for each fixed deduction. This statement must be given to employees before or at the time of issuing any pay statment and must be re-issued incorporating any amendments at least every 12 months.

Certain classes of employees are not covered by s8 and these include independent contractors, members of the police force, merchant seamen and employees who ordinarily work outside the Great Britain.

Section 11 ERA 1996 provides that if an employer fails to provide an itemised pay statement an employee may make an application to an employment tribunal. If the employee has ceased his employment with the employer any application must be made within three months of the effective date of termination.

9.3 Payment of wages/deductions from wages

The payment of wages were originally governed by the Truck Acts 1831–1940 which were once described by Kahn Freund as 'the oldest piece of social legislation ... in force'. One of the aims of the Truck Acts was to ensure that workers were paid in the coin of the realm and made payment in the form of goods or tokens unlawful. Another objective was to regulate situations when employers deducted money from the wages of employees for bad workmanship. The Truck Acts did not protect all categories of workers and impeded those employers who wanted to pay wages directly into an employee's bank. Further legislation was required to meet modern needs and in 1986 the Truck Acts were repealed by the Wages Act 1986. Today the law relating to the payment of wages and deductions from wages is to be found in Pt II of the ERA 1996.

Scope of Pt II

Part II ERA 1996 is broad in its scope and s230(2) provides that it applies to employees and those working under a contract for services.

In *Blackstone Franks Investments Management Ltd* v *Robertson* (1998) The Times 4 May the Court of Appeal held that commission payments in respect of future wages were recoverable even though the employment relationship had been terminated.

There is no qualifying period of service and therefore Pt II applies to all employees regardless of the length of time they have been employed with the employer. However, persons who ordinarily work outside the UK are excluded from Pt II ERA 1996 by s196(2) ERA 1996.

Deductions

Section 13(1) of the ERA 1996 provides that:

'(1) An employer shall not make a deduction from wages of a worker employed by him unless –
(a) the deduction is required or authorised to be made by virtue of a statutory provision or a relevant provision of the worker's contract, or
(b) the worker has previously signified in writing his agreement or consent to the making of the deduction.'

An employer may lawfully deduct wages if authorised by statute, for example the deduction of tax and National Insurance. A court may also authorise an attachment of earnings order in respect of maintenance, fines, debts etc for which a person has been found to be liable in court. The order is sent to the employer who will be authorised to deduct the sum required in the order from the employee's wages. A similar order may be made under the Child Support Act 1991, and again the employer will be required to make the deduction before the employee receives his wages.

An employer may also deduct wages if there is a contractual term which allows him to do so. The term may be express or implied and may be oral or in writing. Surprisingly such provision in employees contracts have been interpreted broadly and in *Higgins* v *Cables Montague Contracts Ltd* [1993] EAT/564/93 it was held by the EAT to include a collective agreement which had been incorporated into the employee's contract of employment. However, an employer is under an obligation to notify an employee of the existence of a contractual term which allows for deductions to be made from his wages. In *Kerr* v *The Sweater Shop (Scotland) Ltd* [1996] IRLR 424 the EAT held that the display of a notice on a notice board was not sufficent and an employer should notify each worker individually in writing before any deduction is made.

If a worker expressly agrees in writing that money may be deducted from his wages an employer who deducts the sum agreed will do so lawfully. The agreement does not have to be part of the contract and would cover a situation where an employee is granted a loan for the purchase of a car. Here, the employer can deduct an agreed amount in respect of the loan, provided the agreement is clearly stated in writing.

The requirement of a clear written agreement was considered by the EAT in the case of *Potter* v *Hunt Contracts Ltd* [1992] IRLR 108 where an employee had signed a letter stating that if he left the company he would repay some of the costs of his HGV training. The EAT held that the letter was not sufficiently clear and that the employee had not expressly stated that the money was to be repaid from his wages.

An employer cannot lawfully deduct wages in respect of conduct or losses that occurred prior to the written agreement. In *Discount Tobacco and Confectionary Ltd* v *Williamson* [1993] IRLR 327 Mr Williamson was employed as a retail manager. Between December 1988 and February 1989 stock shortages were discovered. In

March 1989 he signed an agreement authorising his employer to deduct the sum of £3,500 from his wages at a rate of £20 per week.

Section 14 ERA 1996 provides that s13 will not apply to a deduction that is made in respect of an overpayment of wages or expenses that have been paid to an employee.

Payments

Section 15 ERA 1996 provdes similar provisions to s13 but this time with respect to payments to an employer. An employer shall not receive a payment from an employee unless the payment is required or authorised by a statutory provision or a relevant provision of the worker's contract, or the worker has previously signified in writing his agreement or consent to the making of the payment. Section 16 ERA 1996 further provides that s15 does not apply to a payment received from a worker by his employer where the payment is the reimbursement of an overpayment of wages or expenses.

Wages

For the purposes of Pt II, s27 ERA 1996 defines wages as:

'(1) ... any sums payable to the worker by his employer in connection with his employment, including –
(a) any fee, bonus, commission, holiday pay or other emolument referable to his employment, whether payable under his contract or otherwise,
(b) statutory sick pay under Part XI of the Social Security Contributions and Benefits Act 1992,
(c) statutory maternity pay under Part XII of that Act,
(ca) statutory paternity pay under Part 12ZA of that Act,
(cb) statutory adoption pay under Part 12ZB of that Act,
(d) a guarantee payment (under s28 of this Act),
(e) any payment for time off under Part VI of this Act or s169 of the Trade Union and Labour Relations (Consolidation) Act 1992 (payment for time off for carrying out trade union duties etc),
(f) remuneration on suspension on medical grounds under s64 of this Act and remuneration on suspension on maternity grounds under s68 of this Act,
(g) any sum payable in pursuance of an order for reinstatement or re-engagement under s113 of this Act,
(h) any sum payable in pursuance of an order for the continuation of a contract of employment under s130 of this Act or s164 of the Trade Union and Labour Relations (Consolidation) Act 1992, and
(j) remuneration under a protective award under s189 of that Act,
but excluding any payments within subs(2).
(2) Those payments are –
(a) any payment by way of an advance under an agreement for a loan or by way of an advance of wages (but without prejudice to the application of s13 to any deduction made from the worker's wages in respect of any such advance),

(b) any payment in respect of expenses incurred by the worker in carrying out his employment,
(c) any payment by way of a pension, allowance or gratuity in connection with the worker's retirement or as compensation for loss of office,
(d) any payment referable to the worker's redundancy, and
(e) any payment to the worker otherwise than in his capacity as a worker.'

Furthermore, s27(3) provides that where an employee is entitled to a non-contractual bonus that will be considered to be wages for the purpose of Pt II ERA 1996.

Meaning of deduction

There has been considerable debate over the scope of Pt II ERA 1996 and the precise definition of 'deductions' for the purpose of this Part. One of the key questions has been whether a deduction is a part payment, or does it include a total withholding of monies due to an employee?

In *Delaney* v *Staples* [1992] 1 All ER 944 the employee was dismissed from her employment and at the time of her dismissal she was owed £18 commission and £37.50 holiday pay. Ms Delaney received a cheque for £82 as payment in lieu of notice but this cheque was stopped when the employer had reason to believe that she had taken away confidential information. Ms Delaney made an application to the tribunal for payment of all the monies owing to her.

The Court of Appeal held that the non-payment of the sums of £18 and £37.50 amounted to a deduction of wages for the purposes of Pt II ERA 1996 and ordered that the sums be paid to her. The Court also considered the issue of the payment in lieu of notice and said that sums which fall due to an employee during the period of the contract are wages. However, in this case Ms Delaney had been summarily dismissed and therefore the contract was terminated during the period of notice which meant that any claim had to be one of damages for wrongful dismissal. In the Court of Appeal Nicholls LJ was firmly of the opinion that danages for wrongful dismissal did not fall within the defintition of wages The case proceeded to the House of Lords on the issue of payment in lieu of notice, where the decision of the Court of Appeal was confirmed.

Retail workers

Employees who are employed in the retail trade may be required to make payments to their employer in respect of stock shortages or cash shortages. From the employer's perspective this is one way to ensure that employees take care of stock and cash thus protecting the employer from petty theft by employees.

An employer who considers that it may be necessary at some point in the future to make deduction must ensure that there is a provision in the contract of employment which makes it clear to the employee that such deductions may be made. Furthermore, there are limits placed on the amount of money that can lawfully be deducted from wages. Section 18 ERA 1996 provides that where an employer makes a deduction in respect of a cash shortage or stock deficiency the amount of the deduction cannot exceed one-tenth of the gross amount of the wages payable to the worker on that day.

Time limits

In the event of an unlawful deduction from wages an employee can present an application to the employment tribunal. Section 23(2) ERA 1996 provides that an application must be presented:

> '... before the end of the period of three months beginning with –
> (a) in the case of a complaint relating to a deduction by the employer, the date of payment of the wages from which the deduction was made, or
> (b) in the case of a complaint relating to a payment received by the employer, the date when the payment was received.'

Where a complaint is brought in respect of a series of deductions or payments time will begin to run from the date of the last deduction. Where an application is presented outside the three-month time limit the tribunal can exercise its discretion to hear the application if it is satisfied that it was not reasonably practicable for the complaint to be presented before the end of the three-month time limit.

An employee who is still working for his employer may not wish to present a complaint to the employment tribunal for fear of losing his job. However, s104 ERA 1996 provides that an employee who is dismissed for exercising a statutory right will be regarded as automatically unfairly dismissed.

Jurisdiction

One of the problems raised by the case of *Delaney* v *Staples* was that the tribunals did not have jurisdiction to consider a claim for a breach of contract. This was remedied by the Employment Tribunals Extension of Jurisdiction (England and Wales) Order 1994 (SI 1994/1623) which provides that a tribunal will have jurisdiction to hear a claim for breach of contract provided that the following requirements are met.

1. The employment has been terminated.
2. The claim arises or is outstanding at the time of the temination of employment.
3. The claim relates to a breach of contract and a sum due under that contract.

One of the risks that an ex-employee faces when bringing a claim for breach of contract in the tribunals is that the employer may present a counterclaim – in other words an employer who believes that the employee owes him money can seek to recover such sums. A counterclaim can only be presented if there is a claim from an employee.

9.4 National minimum wage

The Labour government which was elected in 1997 decided that there should be a national minimum wage, the effect of which would make it unlawful to employ a person at a rate below the set rate. It was considered that this should not be based on a rigid formula but should be determined with the assistance of a low pay commission. The Low Pay Commission was established on a statutory basis under the provisions of the National Minimum Wage Act 1998.

Members of the Low Pay Commission are drawn from representatives of employers' groups, employees' organisations, trade unions and independent bodies.

The national minimum wage came into effect on 1 April 1999. The rate for adults from 1 October 2005 is £5.05 and for 18–21 year olds it is £4.25.

A new minimum wage of £3.00 per hour was introduced in October 2004 for those aged 16 and 17.

Calculating pay

If an employee is employed on a simple hourly rate then it will be easy to determine if the employer has complied with the national minimum wage. However, for many employees the situation is more complex and therefore there has to be a mechanism for calculating which components of an employee's pay should be included for the purposes of the national minimum wage. If an employee is paid a low basic rate but is able to top this up with performance-related pay, bonuses and tips paid through an employer then these will be included in determining the hourly rate of pay. Regional allowances and overtime will not be included. The reason that overtime payments are not included is because an employee should not have to work additional hours to earn the minimum wage.

In addition to calculating an hourly rate it is necessary to work out the number of hours that a worker must be paid. This will vary according to the type of work undertaken.

Time work

The employee will be paid for the hours he has worked. Hours do not need to be regular. To calculate whether the rate paid complies with the minimum wage the number of hours worked in the payment reference period, which cannot be longer than one month, are divided by the total sum received.

Salaried hours work

The number of hours worked each year will be divided by the pay reference period which will be 12 or 52. The resulting figure will then be used to divide the pay received.

Output work
Workers are paid acording to their productivity. The employer must make a fair estimate of the number of hours worked and pay the minimum wage for that work.

Unmeasured work
This includes workers for whom there are no set hours or measurement of their output. An agreement can be made between the employer and employee as to the average number of hours worked each day. If there is no agreement the minimum wage must be paid for the actual number of hours worked.

Exemptions

The national minimum wage does not apply to the following classes of workers:

1. independent contractors;
2. persons under 18;
3. volunteers;
4. apprentices over 18 but under 26 in the first 12 months of their apprenticeship;
5. members of the armed forces;
6. people who work and live as part of a family.

Enforcement

The national minimum wage is enforced by the Inland Revenue, who may issue an enforcement notice requiring the employer to pay the employee the appropriate rate. The issue of the scope of an enforcement notice was recently considered by the EAT in the case of *Inland Revenue Wales and Midlands* v *Bebb Travel plc* [2002] IRLR 783, where an enforcement notice was served upon an employer in respect of employees who had already left the company. Section 19(1) of the National Minimum Wage Act 1998 provides: if an officer acting for the purposes of this Act is of the opinion that a worker who qualifies for the national minimum wage has not been remunerated for any pay reference period by his employer at a rate at least equal to the national minimum wage, the officer may serve a notice (an 'enforcement notice') on the employer requiring the employer to remunerate the worker for pay reference periods ending on or after the date of the notice at a rate equal to the national minimum wage.

An enforcement notice may also require the employer to pay to the worker within such time as may be specified in the notice the sum due to the worker in respect of the employer's previous failure to remunerate the worker at a rate at least equal to the national minimum wage.

The employers in this case successfully argued that the enforcement notice was not valid because it did not apply to a pay reference period ending on or after the date of the notice, because the affected employees were not employed at the time the notice was served. The EAT considered that an enforcement notice can only be issued with respect to current workers and not those who have already left the employment of the employer.

If an employee is not paid the national minimum wage this will be considered to be a breach of a contractual right, and the employee may make an application to the Inland Revenue or bring a claim for an unlawful deduction of wages in the employment tribunal or county court.

In *Inland Revenue Commissioners* v *St Hermans Estate Co Ltd* [2002] IRLR 788 the respondents appealed against an enforcement notice on the grounds that the amount specified in the notice was incorrect. The EAT held that if an enforcement notice specifies an amount which is not correct it is for the tribunal to rectify the error. In this case the tribunal had declined to do so because the records detailing the entitlement of the employees were unsatisfactory. The EAT said that, in such a situation, the correct approach is for a tribunal to make a best estimate on the evidence that is has before it.

An employer is under a duty to keep accurate records of payments to employees, and the decision of EAT in the above case is logical because an employer should not be able to escape liability because he only has incomplete or inaccurate documentation pertaining to payment made to employees.

A worker who is dismissed or victimised for asserting a right under the National Minimum Wage Act 1998 may also present a claim to the employment tribunal for unfair dismissal or victimisation.

9.5 Guarantee payments

If an employer is unable to provide work for an employee during a day when he would ordinarily work, s28 ERA 1996 provides that the employer may be entitled to a guarantee payment if there is a reduction in the requirements of the employer's business for work of the kind which the employee is employed to do or there is any other occurence which affects the normal working of the business in relation to the particular type of work.

A guarantee payment can only be made in respect of a complete working day that is lost: s28(3). The employee is under an obligation to comply with any reasonable request by the employer to ensure that he is available for work.

Section 29 ERA 1996 provides that certain workers are excluded from the right to guarantee payment, and these include the following.

1. An employee who has not been continuously employed for a period of one month.
2. An employee who is employed under a contract for a fixed term of three months or less.
3. An employee who is employed under a contract made in contemplation of the

performance of a specific task which is not expected to last for more than three months.

Additionally, a right to a guarantee payment is denied if the failure to provide the employee with work for that day occurs in consequence of a strike, lock-out or other industrial action involving any employee of his employer or of an associated employer.

An employee will also loose his right to a guarantee payment if he refuses a reasonable offer of suitable alternative work – this does not necessarily have to be work that he is contractually bound to undertake; the emphasis is on the fact that it must be reasonable.

Limit on entitlement

The entitlement to a guarantee payment is limited to five days in any three-month period. However, if an employee is normally required to work less that five days in a week the entitlement during the course of a three-month period will not exceed the number of days the employee is required to work in a week.

Calculation of payment

The guarantee payment for any day is calculated by multiplying the number of normal working hours for the day that the employee was laid off by the employee's hourly rate: s30 ERA 1996. This amount is subject to an upper limit which is £18.90 per day from February 2006.

10

Health and Safety

10.1 Introduction

10.2 Common law duty

10.3 Statutory regulation

10.4 Working Time Regulations

10.1 Introduction

The issue of health and safety in the workplace has been one of considerable change and, because of the impact of European legislation and other proposals to modify the law, it will continue to evolve. The number of accidents at work and work related injuries demonstrates the continuing need for further development. In 2004/2005 there were 220 deaths, a rate of 0.75 per hundred thousand workers. In 2003/2004, 159,809 work-related injuries were reported, which is a rate of 629.1 per hundred thousand workers. In 2003/2004 approximately 39 million working days were lost; 30 million due to work-rleated ill health and nine million resulting from injuries sustained whilst at work. In addition, about half a million accidents at work resulted in employees taking three or more days off work. The prevention of accidents at work and stress-related illnesses caused by work-related issues is something which employers and trade unions are continuing to take very seriously. The cost of such a large number of employees being unable to work is something that individual employees and employers would like to see reduced.

The health and safety of employees in the work environment is governed by common law and statute and both will be considered in this Chapter.

10.2 Common law duty

There are two implied terms in the contract of employment which are particularly relevant to the matter of health and safety. The first is an implied term that the employer will take all reasonable care to ensure the health and safety of his employees and the second is that an employee owes his employer a duty to use reasonable care when carrying out his duties. An employer also has a duty in tort to take reasonable care for the safety of his employees. However, where there is a contractual duty the courts are reluctant to impose tortious liability.

Duty of employer

The implied contractual duty to provide a safe working environment was categorised by Lord Wright in *Wilsons and Clyde Coal Co Ltd* v *English* [1938] AC 57 as a three-fold duty:

1. to employ reasonably competent staff;
2. to provide reasonably safe equipment and materials;
3. to provide a reasonably safe system of work.

In *General Cleaning Contractors Ltd* v *Christmas* [1952] 2 All ER 1110 the House of Lords held that an employer was negligent in failing to provide both a safe system of work and adequate training. In this case an employee, who was cleaning windows by standing on the window ledge outside, was injured when the window fell onto his hand causing him to loose his balance and fall.

The implied term has developed to take into account the changing working environment. In *Waltons & Morse* v *Dorrington* [1997] IRLR 488 the EAT held that there is an implied term that an employer will provide and monitor for his employees, so far as is reasonably practicable, a working environment which is reasonably suitable for the performance by them of their contractual duties and an employer, as in this case, who required an employee to work in a smoke-filled environment, would in breach of the implied term. Conversely, in *Dryden* v *Greater Glasgow Health Board* [1992] IRLR 469 the EAT said there was no term that could be implied into a contract of employment based on custom and practice which entitled an employee to smoke at work.

There is an implied term in an employment contract that an employer will act reasonably in dealing with matters of safety. In *British Aircraft Corporation Ltd* v *Austin* [1978] IRLR 332 the failure of an employer to respond to an employee's concerns about wearing safety goggles over her glasses was held to be a breach of the implied term which gave rise to a successful claim of constructive dismissal.

Where an employee is particularly vulnerable to the risk of injury and the employer is, or should reasonably be, aware of that vulnerability the standard of care required from the employer will be greater. In *Paris* v *Stepney Borough Council* [1951] 1 All ER 42 the plaintiff, who worked in a garage, had only one eye. He was not supplied with goggles at work and was blinded when he was struck in his only eye by a splinter from a bolt. The House of Lords held that although the original disability did not increase the risk of further injury, there was an increase in the risk of a very serious consequence and therefore the employers were in breach of their duty as a result of their failure to supply the plaintiff with goggles. If an employer is unaware of the risk of injury he will not be liable: *Roe* v *Minister of Health* [1954] 2 All ER 131.

The extent of the duty of care owed by an employer was considered in the case of *Pickford* v *Imperial Chemical Industries plc* [1998] IRLR 435. Miss Pickford was employed as a full-time secretary by the defendants in 1984. Her duties included typing on a word processor and other secretarial duties. She had estimated that her time was split fairly evenly between her typing and other duties. In 1988 she began to experience pain in her hands and in 1989 she sought medical treatment but without success. By 1990 her condition had worsened; she tried working as a filing clerk but this proved too painful and in September 1990 the defendants, who were unable to offer her alternative employment, dismissed her. She claimed damages in respect of her injury from the defendants. The Court of Appeal, reversing the judgment of the High Court, held that the employers had breached their duty of care by failing to give Miss Pickford the same advice and instructions with respect to taking breaks etc that they had given typists in another department. They also held that the judge had been incorrect in holding that the burden of proof was upon the plaintiff to show that the cause of her condition was organic rather than psychogenic. The defendants appealed.

It was held by the House of Lords that the Court of Appeal had erred in reversing the decision of the High Court. The burden of proof was upon the plaintiff to show that the cause of her injury was organic and this she had failed to do. The House of Lords also held that the employers had not breached their duty of care towards the plaintiff. The plaintiff, by her own calculation, spent only 50 per cent of her day typing and she was therefore able to organise her day so that she did not spend long periods of time typing. She was, according to Lord Hope, an employee who 'did not need to be told what to do'.

A controversial attempt by the Court of Appeal to extend the scope of the duty of care to cover liability for psychiatric injury for police officers who suffered post-traumatic stress disorder was rejected by the House of Lords in *White & Others* v *Chief Constable of South Yorkshire* [1998] 3 WLR 1509. This case arose out of the Hillsborough Disaster in April 1989 when 96 Liverpool football supporters were crushed to death. The plaintiffs were police officers who claimed damages from their employer in respect of psychiatric injury sustained after witnessing horrific scenes at the football stadium.

Most of the plaintiffs were on crowd duty on the day of the incident and others were drafted into the stadium from elsewhere to tend to the dying and injured and to assist relatives in identifying victims in a temporary mortuary. At first instance the plaintiffs' claim was rejected on the ground that the duty of care owed by the chief constable in respect of psychiatric injury did not arise when a police officer was a secondary victim, nor could police officers fall into the category of rescuers simply because of their professional status. The plaintiffs successfully appealed to the Court of Appeal which held, inter alia, that the distinction between primary and secondary victims did not apply where there was an employer/employee relationship. The defendants were granted leave to appeal to the House of Lords.

The House of Lords held that the employees were to be treated as secondary victims and therefore the duty of care owed by the defendants did not extend to cover situations where police officers suffered post-traumatic stress disorder as a result of witnessing traumatic scenes in the course of duty.

A further limit on the duty owed to employees who suffer from a psychiatric disorder can be seen in the case of *Sutherland* v *Hatton* [2002] IRLR 263 where the Court of Appeal held that an employer would only be liable for a stress-related illness if such an illness was reasonably foreseeable. In this case Mrs Hatton taught French at a comprehensive school in Liverpool. In October 1995 she was signed off from work because of depression and debility and never returned. She retired on ill-health grounds in August 1996. She brought a claim on the grounds that the school authorities had failed to take reasonable steps to protect her from suffering her stress-related psychiatric illness. At trial she was awarded the sum of £90,765.83 in damages and the defendants appealed. The appeal was successful. The Court of Appeal held that the stress caused to Mrs Hatton was not reasonably foreseeable. Mrs Hatton had not brought difficulties that she was facing in school to the attention of the authorities and her workload was no greater than that of any other teacher in a similar school. Furthermore, her stress was also attributable to factors outside the workplace. Lady Justice Hale considered that 'Her workload and her pattern of absence taken together could not amount to a sufficiently clear indication that she was likely to suffer from psychiatric injury as a result of stress at work such as to trigger a duty to do more than was in fact done'. Lady Justice Hale went on to say:

> 'This is a classic case where no-one can be blamed for the sad events which brought Mrs Hatton's teaching career to an end. It was sought to meet some of the obvious difficulties in her case by the argument that teaching is such a stressful profession and that by 1995 all employers should have had in place systems which would overcome the reluctance of people like Mrs Hatton to reveal their difficulties and seek help. We have already explained why we take the view that, although an employer who does have such a system is unlikely to be found in breach of duty, it is not for this Court to impose such a duty upon all employers, or even upon all employers in a particular profession.'

The Court of Appeal laid down important guidelines as to what may or may not amount to workplace stress, which will provide much needed assistance in this difficult area of employment law.

Difficulties may arise where an employee has worked for several employers and later discovers that, because of unsafe working practices adopted by his employers, he has contracted a disease. The principal reason for such difficulties is the problem of establishing a causal link between the negligence of the defendant and the harm suffered. In *Fairchild* v *Glenhaven Funeral Services Ltd* [2002] 3 WLR 89 the claimant suffered mesothelioma, a form of cancer, as a result of negligently being exposed to asbestos by the defendants. The difficulty facing the claimant was that, because he had worked for more than one employer, and each had exposed him to the risk of contracting mesothelioma, it was difficult to prove which of the employers had exposed him to the asbestos fibres which did, in fact, cause his disease. The Court of Appeal, in applying the 'but for' test, rejected the claim because the evidence did not prove which of the defendants had caused the harm. The claimant appealed. It was held by the House of Lords that, because each of the defendant employers had negligently exposed the claimant to the risk of a disease which he contracted, each employer had materially increased the risk of the claimant suffering from that disease.

An employer may face a situation where an employee is working in a position or in an environment which is putting his health at risk: nevertheless, the employer may not have any other suitable alternative post for the employee. The question that arises is: to what extent is the employer under a duty to dismiss the employee, and would any such dismissal be considered as a fair dismissal? This question was partly answered by the Court of Appeal in *Coxall* v *Goodyear Great Britain Ltd* (2002) The Times 5 August. In this case the claimant, who worked as a paint and line operator at the defendant's factory, suffered from occupational asthma. In 1996 the defendant changed the product which was used to spray the inside of tyres, and following concerns by those engaged in the spraying, including the claimant, the defendant issued the workers with appropriate protective equipment. The claimant had a mild predisposition to asthma which was aggravated by the fumes from the new product. In April 1996 the claimant saw the company doctor who, in a memo, advised the team leader that the claimant should not work with the new paint. The memo did not reach the team leader and the claimant continued to work with the paint. In May 1996 the claimant was considered unfit to work and was later dismissed. At trial the claimant was awarded damages for the occupational asthma and the defendant appealed. The Court of Appeal dismissed the appeal and held that where an employee is at risk the employer is under a duty to ensure the health and safety of that employee and dismiss the employee if a suitable alternative position cannot be found. Simon Brown LJ said that the principle laid down in the case of *Withers* v *Perry Chain Co* [1961] 1 WLR 1314 that there is no legal duty on an employer to dismiss an employee who wishes to continue to work (even though there may be a risk to the health of the employee) is still relevant today. However, Simon Brown LJ also recognised that there will still be situations where an employer will be under a duty to dismiss an employee because he is in physical danger. The Court of Appeal considered that these two competing principles could only be resolved on a case-by-case basis.

Duty owed by an employee

An employee must take reasonable care in carrying out his duties. The extent of this implied terms can be seen from the decision of the House of Lords in *Lister* v *Romford Ice and Cold Storage Co* [1957] AC 555 where it was held that there is an implied contractual term that an employee will perform his duties with proper care and that an employer is entitled to recover damages from the employee for breach of this contractual term. Mr Lister had negligently run over a fellow employee who was also his father. The employer was vicariously liable for compensation to be paid to the father and sought to recoup the damages paid from tortfeasor. The House of Lords also held that the damages could be recovered because there is no implied term that the employee is entitled to be indemnified by the employer.

10.3 Statutory regulation

The implied common law duty of an employer to provide a safe working environment is reinforced by statute and regulations. Statutory regulation of health and safety within the workplace is governed by the Health and Safety at Work etc Act (HSWA) 1974. The Act provides the general principles for the protection of the health and safety of employees and established the Health and Safety Commission and the Health and Safety Executive. These bodies are responsible for the regulation of risks to health and safety of workers within the United Kingdom.

The HSWA 1974 imposes duties not only on employers to ensure the safety of their employees but also on employees and independent contractors. It should be noted that the HSWA 1974 applies to persons and not to workplaces. The Act itself is written in general terms and provides for more specific requirements to be set out in regulations.

The Health and Safety Commission

The Health and Safety Commission (HSC) is responsible for the health and safety of workers and must take appropriate steps to protect the health and safety of employees and others with respect to work-related activities. The HSA is sponsored by the Department of Works and Pensions and is accountable to Parliament. The Commission comprises a chairperson and nine other members who represent employers' organisations, trade unions and other organisations such as local authorities and professional bodies. The Commission must review health and safety legislation and promote training and research.

Duty of employer for employees

Section 2(1) HSWA 1974 provides that:

> 'It shall be the duty of every employer shall ensure, so far as is reasonably practicable, the health, safety and welfare of his employees.'

In particular, employers must (s2(2)):

1. provide and maintain plant and systems of work so that they are, so far as is reasonably practicable, safe and without risks to health;
2. make arrangements for ensuring, so far as is reasonably practicable, that articles

and substances are used, handled, stored and transported safely and without risks to health;
3. provide the necessary information, instruction, training and supervision to ensure, so far as is reasonably practicable, the health and safety at work of employees;
4. maintain any place of work under the employer's control, so far as is reasonably practicable, in a safe condition and without risks to health, including safe access and egress; and
5. provide and maintain a working environment which is, so far as is reasonably practicable, safe and without risks to health and provided with adequate facilities and welfare arrangements.

It can be seen that this duty is very similar to the common law duty owed by an employer to his employees. When determining what is reasonably practicable the courts will take into account the cost and practicality of implementing certain safety measures and the benefit that would be derived out of the particular safety measure.

The issue of whether a company can be held liable under s2(1) for the acts of an employee was considered by the Court of Appeal in *R v Gateway Foodmarkets Ltd* [1997] IRLR 189. In this case a Mr Finn was employed by the appellants as a section manager in a grocery store. At the store there was a lift which was regularly maintained by a reputable firm of lift contractors. Despite regular maintenance their had been a problem with the lift for some time which resulted in the lift getting stuck. The problem was caused by a faulty electrical contact which could be cured manually. When the lift became stuck, rather than call out the contractors the manager or one of the section managers would go up to the lift control room and free the contact.

In April 1993 the contractors had carried out their regular maintenance and the following day the lift became stuck. Mr Finn went up to the control room to free the lift but unfortunately the contractors had left open the trap door in the control room and Mr Finn fell through the trap door to the floor of the lift shaft. The company was charged under s2(1) HSWA 1974.

The judge in the Crown Court ruled that the offence was one of strict liability, subject to the defence of reasonable practicability, and concluded that the defendants were guilty under s2(1). The employers appealed to the Court of Appeal on the ground that s2(1) only applies to those who represent 'the directing mind' of the company and unless the failure to ensure the safety of others can be directly attributed to them there can be no breach of s2(1).

The appeal by the employers was dismissed. Evans LJ decided that the approach adopted by Lord Hoffmann in *R v Associated Octel Co Ltd* [1997] IRLR 123 to s3(1) HSWA 1974 should be adopted in respect of s2(1). He said that the duty imposed upon the employer by both ss2(1) and 3(1) is one of strict liability and is a duty to ensure the health and safety at work of all his employees, and if that duty is broken the employer is guilty of an offence.

The submission by the company that Parliament cannot have intended that a company would be liable for the acts or omissions of even its most junior employees was rejected. The fact that at senior management level all reasonable precautions had been taken to ensure the safety of employees was not sufficient to avoid liability because there was a failure at store management level to do likewise.

In *Walker* v *Northumberland County Council* [1995] IRLR 35 the defendant local authority was held to be liable for psychiatric damage caused to one of its employees who was a social worker because of its failure to take reasonable steps to prevent the employee suffering a second nervous breakdown as a result of pressure of work. The employee had advised the employer after his first breakdown that he would only be able to continue in his post if his workload was reduced. The Court considered that it was reasonably foreseeable that if the council failed to reduce his workload he would suffer a further breakdown.

The High Court said that there was no reason why the risk of psychological damage should not be taken into consideration when reviewing an employer's duty to provide employees with a reasonably safe system of work. However, the Court did acknowledge that claims involving psychiatric damage may cause difficulty, particularly with respect to causation.

Written safety policy

All employers with five or more employees must prepare a written health and safety policy and revise this policy as often as is appropriate: s2(3) HSWA 1974. The policy should set out in detail any hazards which are present in the workplace. The policy should also clearly state the names of persons within the organisation who are responsible for health and safety and set out arrangements for monitoring the effectiveness of the policy.

Consultation with safety representatives

Where an employer recognises a trade union for the purposes of collective bargaining, s2(4) of the Act makes provision for regulations to be made giving recognised trade unions the right to appoint safety representatives.

Section 2(6) provides that an employer must consult with appointed safety representatives:

> '... with a view to the making and maintenance of arrangements which will enable him and his employees to co-operate effectively in promoting and developing measures to ensure the health and safety of the employees, and in checking the effectiveness of such measures.'

The Safety Representatives and Safety Committees Regulations 1977, as amended, contain the details of the appointment of the representative and the duties of the employer to enter into consultation over safety matters. If two or more safety representatives request that an employer set up a safety committee then the employer should do so.

Duty of employer to independent contractors and others

Section 3(1) HSWA 1974 provides that it is the duty of an employer:

> '... to conduct his undertaking in such a way as to ensure so far as is reasonably practicable, that persons not in his employ who may be affected thereby are not exposed to risks to their health or safety.'

This section aims to safeguard any persons other than employees, including members of the public, from hazards within the workplace. The extent of the duty has been the subject of much discussion following the case of *R v Swan Hunter Shipbuilders Ltd* [1981] IRLR 403, where the Court of Appeal held that the duty under s3(1) extends to the provision of information, instruction and training to those who are not employees or in a contractual relationship with the employer if it is necessary to ensure the health and safety of all persons.

The matter has more recently been considered by the House of Lords in the case of *R v Associated Octel Co Ltd* (above). Associated Octel operated a chemical plant and during the summer 'shut down' maintenance and repair work was undertaken. During the 1990 shut down Associated Octel had arranged for an independent contractor who regularly carried out repair work at the plant to repair the lining of one of the tanks. The task was assigned to one of the contractor's employees and involved the use of acetone. Whilst the employee was inside the tank the bulb of a light that he was using broke and the electric spark ignited the acetone causing a flash fire. The employee of the contractor was seriously injured and Associated Octel was prosecuted under s3(1) HSWA 1974.

The company argued that control was essential before liability could be imposed under s3(1), and because it did not exercise any control over the way that independent contractors worked it should not be liable. This argument was rejected by the court at first instance and by the Court of Appeal. Associated Octel appealed to the House of Lords.

The House of Lords held that the company had been properly convicted under s3(1). The work carried out by the employee of the independent contractor fell within the scope of the employer's duty 'to conduct his undertaking in such a way as to ensure so far as is reasonably practicable, that persons not in his employ who may be affected thereby are not exposed to risks to their health or safety'.

Lord Hoffmann considered that whether the activity which has caused the risk amounts to part of the conduct by the employer of his undertaking must in each case be a question of fact. In this case the tank that was being repaired was part of Octel's chemical undertaking, the work formed part of a maintenance programme planned by Octel and the men who did the work, although employed by a contractor, were integrated into Octel's operation and, crucially, Octel provided their safety equipment and lighting.

The decision of the House of Lords appears at first to impose an enormous burden on employers with respect to the conduct of others. However, Lord Hoffmann did not envisage that all repairs, cleaning or maintenance that were necessary for the employer's business would attract the duty imposed by s3(1). When considering whether the employer has sufficient control, one of the crucial factors would be the place where the activity takes place.

The duty of employees

The HSWA 1974 also puts an obligation on employees to take care of their own health and safety and the health and safety of other people at work: s7. Employees are also under a duty to co-operate with an employer if the employer is required to carry out health and safety obligations. An employee who interferes with safety equipment will generally be in breach of contract and may find himself liable on criminal conviction to pay a fine.

Protection from detrimental treatment

An employee has a right conferred by s44 of the ERA 1996, as amended, not to be subjected to any detriment by any act or deliberate omission by his employer on the grounds that:

1. having been designated by the employer to carry out activities in connection with preventing or reducing risks to the health and safety of employees at work, he carried out, or proposed to carry out, such activities; or
2. being a health and safety representative or member of a safety committee, he performed or proposed to perform any functions in that capacity; or
3. he took part (or proposed to take part) in consultations with the employer, or in an election of representatives of employee safety; or
4. in the event there is no representative or safety committee, or it is not reasonably practicable to raise the matter through those means, he reasonably brought to his employer's attention circumstances which he reasonably believed were harmful or potentially harmful to health and safety; or
5. in circumstances of serious or imminent danger which he could not reasonably be expected to avert, he left, or proposed to leave, his place of work or any dangerous part of his place of work; or
6. in circumstances of serious or imminent danger, he took, or proposed to take, appropriate steps to protect himself or other employees from the danger.

In *Shillito* v *Van Leer (UK) Ltd* [1997] IRLR 495 Mr Shillito, a union official, was disciplined for a failure to follow correct procedure following complaints by workers of an odour given off by a solvent. Mr Shillito claimed that he has suffered a detriment because of his performance of his duties as a safety representative. The employment tribunal dismissed his complaint because they considered that he had acted unreasonably in trying to embarrass the employer. The EAT held that the protection afforded to a safety representative against action short of dismissal under s44 ERA 1996 does not require that the safety representative must act reasonably. However, the EAT upheld the decision of the tribunal on the grounds that Mr Shilito was not the safety representative for the area affected and was not pursuing a genuine health and safety matter but was motivated by a desire to embarass the employer.

Section 48 ERA 1996 provides that where an employee believes that he has suffered a detriment under s44 he can present a complaint to an employment tribunal. Any application must be made within three months of the act, or the failure to act of which he complains or where that act or failure is part of a series of similar acts or failures three months from the last act or ommission. If the tribunal finds in favour of the applicant it can order compensation to be paid to the employee.

Enforcement of health and safety legislation

Health and Safety legislation is enforced by the Health and Safety Executive (HSE) and local authority environmental health officers. HSE inspectors and environmental health officers have the power to enter premises to investigate health and safety issues. If they believe it necessary improvement notices can be served upon an employer directing him to make certain improvements within a specified period of time. If there is the possibility of imminent danger a prohibition notice can be served which will direct that the employer ceases to carry out the activity or process which is giving rise to the danger. If an employer breaches health and safety provisions he may incur criminal liability and civil liability.

European legislation and health and safety regulations

European Union legislation has had a significant impact on health and safety law within the UK. Most legislation has been in the form of directives made under art 138 EC. When a directive is passed the HSC has the responsibility of setting out proposals for the government to implement the directive.

To encourage improvements for the health and safety of workers throughout the European Union the Framework Directive (89/391/EEC) on health and safety was adopted in 1989. The Framework Directive has spawned several other directives and the following regulations have been passed to give effect to the directives.

The Management of Health and Safety at Work Regulations 1992 and 1999

The 1992 Regulations were passed to give effect to the Framework Directive and were broadly similar to the requirements of the HSWA 1974. The Regulations did, however, require that employers should carry out risk assessments to determine what protective measures should be in place to protect employees in the workplace. Any required measures and arrangements for implementing those measures must be recorded. As a result of amendments in 1999 to comply with the Pregnant Workers Directive the Management of Health and Safety at Work Regulations 1999 (SI 1999/3242) were introduced. The 1999 Regulations have modified the earlier Regulations including the requirement that employers must carry out health and safety checks with particular reference to new or expectant mothers.

The Regulations provide that where a pregnant female employee is at risk the employer should:

1. take preventative action to ensure the safety of the mother and child;
2. offer alternative working conditions;
3. offer suitable alternative work;
4. if there is no suitable alternative the employer must suspend the woman on normal pay.

In *Day* v *T Pickles Farms Ltd* [1999] IRLR 217 the EAT held that there is no requirement that an employee is pregnant to trigger off the assessment. It is sufficient if there is, in the workforce, a woman of child-bearing age. This is common sense because it may be too late once a woman is pregnant.

Workplace (Health, Safety and Welfare) Regulations 1992 (SI 1992/3004)
These came into full force at the beginning of 1996. The Regulations, which apply to all permanent workplaces, require an employer to maintain, organise and repair the workplace to a standard that will ensure the health and safety of employees. The premises should be adequately lit, ventilated and heated. An employer must also ensure that there are adequate toilet facilities and washrooms. Workstations should be arranged in such a way that they are suitable for the purpose for which they are used and proper seating must be provided.

Provision and Use of Work Equipment Regulations 1998 (SI 1998/2306)
These regulations aim to ensure that all machinery and tools used in the workplace are suitable and of a good standard, and that they are maintained to that standard to provide employees with the safe use of work equipment.

Personal Protective Equipment at Work Regulations 1992 (SI 1992/2966)
Where a risk cannot be avoided these Regulations state the type and standard of personal protective equipment (PPE) to be used by employees. In *Fytche* v *Wincanton Logistics plc* [2004] IRLR 817 the House of Lords held that the protection afforded by the Regulations does not extend to include a situation where a worker suffers an injury of a kind which the protective equipment was not designed to afford protection. In this case Mr Fytche, who drove a milk tanker, was provided with steel-capped boots which were designed to protect his feet in the event that a

milk churn or anything heavy fell on his toes. Whilst driving in snowy conditions one day Mr Fytche and his tanker became stranded. The appellant spent several hours in the snow digging out his lorry. Unfortunately his boots leaked, with the result that he suffered frost bite in his small toe. His claim against his employer failed because the Regulations provide that employers must ensure that workers have appropriate protective equipment to protect them from injury from foreseeable risks, but do not include unforeseeable risks. In this case it was not foreseeable that Mr Fytche would require waterproof boots because the nature of his job did not ordinarily bring him into contact with water for prolonged periods of time.

Health and Safety (Display Screen Equipment) Regulations 1992 (SI 1992/2792)
These provide minimum health and safety standards for the design and use of VDU workstations. Employers must assess and review the health and safety risks of the use of VDUs and reduce any such risks as much as reasonably practicable.

These Regulations were slightly amended in 2002 by the Health and Safety (Miscellaneous Amendments) Regulations 2002 (SI 2002/2174).

10.4 Working Time Regulations

The Working Time Regulations 1998 (SI 1998/1833) came into force on 1 October 1998 and limit the number of hours that a worker can work in an average week. In essence the Regulations provide that a worker's average working time, including overtime, must not exceed 48 hours per week, unless the employee decides to waive his right to protection from the Regulations.

The Regulations implement the EC Working Time Directive (93/104/EC) which should have been implemented by Member States by the 23 November 1996. The UK government was in breach of its EU obligations to implement the Directive within the prescribed time limit.

In August 2004 the EC Working Time Directive and the Horizontal Amending Directive (2000/34/EC) were revoked and consolidated into EC Working Time Directive (2003/88/EC). The consolidation of the two Directives did not involve any substantive changes.

The general philosophy behind the Working Time Directive was to protect the health and safety or workers throughout the European Union. Prior to the implementation of the Directive employers in the UK were under an implied duty to prevent workers from working long hours if to do so was likely to affect their health and safety: *Johnstone v Bloomsbury Health Authority* [1991] 2 WLR 1362. However, there was no statutory duty to do so.

The implementation of the Working Time Regulations was therefore a significant move forward in protecting workers and a robust approach has been taken by the courts in giving a purposive interpretation to the Regulations.

In *Barber & Others* v *RJB Mining (UK) Ltd* [1999] IRLR 308 the High Court ruled that the Working Time Regulations are to be implied into an employee's contract of employment, and therefore if an employer compels an employee to work in excess of 48 hours he will be in breach of contract.

In *Barber* the plaintiffs were employed as pit deputies at coal mines operated by the defendants. The plaintiffs' contracts of employment provided, inter alia, that they would have a 42-hour working week. However, they frequently worked longer hours to keep mines operative. Following the implementation of the Working Time Regulations the plaintiffs worked in excess of 48 hours for the first 17 weeks. The defendants asked them to sign a reg 5(1) 'opt out' (see below) agreement but they refused to do so until a wage claim had been settled. It was held that the Working Time Regulations impose a contractual obligation upon an employer to limit the average working week of an employee to no more than 48 hours. Regulation 4(1) is free-standing and does not have to be read in conjunction with reg 4(2) and therefore it is clear that reg 4(1) imposes legal rights and obligations into the employment contract.

The court granted a declaration that the plaintiffs had exceeded the number of hours permitted under the Working Time Regulations, but in the circumstances refused to grant an injunction restraining the employers from requiring the plaintiffs to work until the average number of hours fell below 48 hours per week.

Reference period

The Regulations provide that an employee's average number of working hours per week will be calculated over a period of 17 weeks – this is known as the 'reference period'. This has the effect of allowing some flexibility for the employer, whilst protecting an employee from working excessive hours over a long period of time.

The reference period may be extended to 26 weeks in certain circumstances.

Exemptions

When the Regulations were originally implemented there were a large number of groups of workers who were excluded. However, since 1999 a number of new regulations have been implemented to include most workers within the protection of the EU Directive.

Calculation of working time

The average working time is calculated by dividing the total number of hours worked in the reference period by 17 (or 26 where appropriate). However, difficulties can arise if the employee is absent during part of the reference period. Regulation 4 provides that in certain circumstances absences during the reference period will not count and extra working time must be added to the total number of hours worked as compensation. This will include the following:

1. holidays;
2. sick leave;
3. maternity leave;
4. any days where the employee has agreed to have the Regulations disapplied.

Waiver

If an employee currently wishes to work an average of more than 48 hours a week he can 'opt-out' of his right to protection from the Regulations by notifying his employer in writing. The agreement to waive an employee's rights must allow for the employee to bring the agreement to an end if he so wishes and may contain a notice period of up to three months to bring it to an end. If no notice period is specified in the agreement the employee is obliged under reg 5 to give seven days' notice. Any notice to bring the agreement to an end must be given in writing to the employer.

If there is an agreement between an employer and an employee to disapply the Regulations the employer must keep records of this and make them available for inspection by the Health and Safety Executive or an environmental health officer who are empowered to enforce the Regulations.

The Working Time Directive allows EU members to permit workers to 'opt out' of the protection afforded by the Directive. The United Kingdom is the only EU member to have introduced this provision.

The effect of the 'opt-out' is undoubtedly to dilute the effect of the Regulations. Some employers require employees to sign an 'opt out' when signing their contract of employment and it is argued that this is contrary to the purpose of the Directive.

Negotiations are currently taking place in the European Parliament to remove the 'opt out'. The British government is strongly opposed to this change but it is likely that the 'opt out' will eventually disappear so that all workers covered by the Regulations will be limited to working 48 hours a week.

Night workers

A person who works at night is limited to working an average of eight hours in each 24-hour period over the reference period of 17 weeks. An employee is deemed to be a night worker if his daily working time includes at least three hours of 'night time'. 'Night time' is defined as a period of at least seven hours which includes the period from midnight to 5 am.

In *R* v *Attorney-General for Northern Ireland, ex parte Burns* [1999] IRLR 315 Miss Burns worked as a production operative on a shift pattern which required one week of each three-week shift cycle to be worked from 9 pm to 7 am. The applicant had difficulty working at night and claimed that it was having a detrimental impact upon her health. She requested that she be put on a permanent day-shift pattern but her employers rejected her application. In 1997 she resigned from her position on medical advice but did offer to withdraw her resignation if her employer put her onto day shifts. However, the employers were unable to accept this offer. Miss Burns made an application for judicial review claiming, inter alia, that the UK government was in breach of its obligations under European law in that it failed to implement the Directive within the prescribed time limit and that she was a 'night worker' within the definition within the terms of the Directive.

It was held the UK government was in breach of Community law by failing to implement the Directive within the prescribed time limit. The court further held that the applicant was a 'night worker' for the purposes of the Directive. Article 2(4) defines a 'night worker' as 'any worker, who during the night time, works at least three hours of his daily working time as a normal course'. It was argued that because the applicant only worked during the night time on one shift out of three she was not a 'night worker' but this was rejected by the court. Kerr J said:

> 'The Directive contemplates that a night worker may be someone who works as little as three hours during the night time. It is inconceivable, therefore that the definition of night worker should be confined to someone who works night shifts exclusively or even predominantly.'

Regulation 6A provides that employers should ensure that no young workers (ie between the ages of 15 and 18) shall work at night, although there are exceptions for those working in hospitals or engaged in sporting, artistic, cultural or advertising activities. A night worker cannot opt out of the night-work limit set by the Regulations.

Daily rest breaks

Regulation 10 provides that an adult worker is entitled to a rest break of 11 hours in each 24-hour period. An adolescent worker is entitled to a 12-hour rest break in each 24-hour period.

Rest periods

An employee who works over a specific period of time is entitled to a rest period away from his place of work. Regulation 12 provides that an adult worker is entitled to a 20-minute rest period where the working day is longer than six hours. A young worker is entitled to a 30-minute rest period if they work for more than four-and-a-half hours. Employers are under a duty to make sure that workers can take their rest break but they are not required to ensure that workers do in fact take their break. The rest break must be taken during the six-hour period (four-and-a-half hour period in the case of young workers) and not at the beginning or end of the working period. Mobile workers, who are defined as 'any worker employed as a member of travelling or flying personnel by an undertaking which operates transport services for passengers or goods by road or air' are excluded from the normal rest break entitlement. However, Regulation 24A provides that they must have 'adequate rest'. This is rest which is sufficiently long and continuous to ensure that tiredness does not cause workers to injure themselves or others or have short or long-term effects on their health. A worker is also entitled to a rest period of not less than ll consecutive hours between each working day: reg 10. There are some exceptions to reg 10, including where an employer and workers agree that the 11-hour limit may be varied provided that the worker is allowed to take 'compensatory rest' which is a period of rest equivalent to the period of rest that was missed.

Weekly rest periods

Regulation 11 provides that an adult worker is entitled to an uninterrupted rest period of 24 hours a week, although this may be averaged over a two-week period.

Holiday entitlement

Since 23 November 1999 most employees are entitled to four weeks' paid holiday per annum provided that they have worked for the employer for a period of 13 weeks or more.

In *Gibson* v *East Riding of Yorkshire Council* [1999] IRLR 358 the appellant was employed as a swimming instructor by the respondents from April 1996. During the school holidays the appellant was not required to work and therefore did not receive any pay for that period. The appellant brought a claim on the basis that under the terms of the Working Time Directive she was entitled to four weeks' paid leave. The defendants argued that her hourly rate had been negotiated partly on the basis that she was not entitled to paid leave. Her application was dismissed by the employment tribunal and she appealed to the EAT.

The EAT held that art 7 of the Directive, which provides that an employee is entitled to four weeks' paid annual leave, is sufficiently precise and unconditional so as to have direct effect. The appellant, who worked for an 'emanation of the state', was therefore entitled to rely upon the Directive. The contractual rights of the appellant were varied by the Directive from the date that the Directive should have been implemented in the UK, ie 23 November 1996, and the appellant was therefore entitled to four weeks' paid annual leave from 23 November.

An employee is entitled to be paid holiday pay at his normal contractual rate. However, difficulties may arise in determining exactly what an employee should be paid. In *Bamsey* v *Albon Engineering Ltd* [2004] IRLR 457 Mr Bamsey was contracted to work 39 hours per week. His contract provided that he could also be required to work up to nine hours' over-time; however, there was no obligation on his employer to provide over-time work. Mr Bamsey worked on average 58 hours a week, earning £329.99. When Mr Bamsey took his paid annual holiday entitlement his holiday pay was calculated at the rate of 39 hours per week, with the result that he was paid £198.51, which his employer said were his 'normal working hours'. Mr Bamsey presented a claim to the employment tribunal for unpaid holiday under the Working Time Regulations. He argued that since the aim of the Working Time Directive was to ensure the health and safety of workers, this objective would be diminished if workers received an amount of holiday pay that was significantly below the rate they would receive when at work, as this would clearly act as a disincentive for an employee to take his or her full annual leave entitlement. The employer argued that the aim of the Working Time Directive was only to provide minimum requirements and not to guarantee equivalence between holiday pay and amounts received when actually at work. Mr Bamsey's claim failed at both the employment tribunal and the EAT and he further appealed to the Court of Appeal.

The Court of Appeal held that his claim must fail. In coming to its decision that the calculation of holiday pay does not require an employer to take account of compulsory but non-guaranteed overtime, the Court of Appeal considered that this was not contrary to the purpose of the EU Working Time Directive which has been implemented in the UK by the Regulations. The Court of Appeal considered that if non-contractual overtime was to be included in holiday pay the effect of this would be that workers would receive more pay during their annual leave than that which they are contractually entitled to earn while at work. The Court of Appeal accepted the argument that the express inclusion of ss221–224 ERA 1996 in reg 16 automatically incorporates s234. Section 234 defines 'normal working hours' by reference to contractual hours and to contractually agreed overtime; it does not allow voluntary overtime to be taken into account.

This decision has been subject to criticism because it is argued that the purpose of the Working Time Directive was to encourage workers to take holidays, and if they receive less money than if they were at work workers may be less inclined to do so. However, it should be noted that the Court of Appeal said that there was no evidence to show that workers who only receive basic pay as holiday pay were not taking their full annual leave entitlement.

'Rolled-up' holiday pay

Recently, difficulties have arisen because employers, particularly in high-turnover industries, provide a 'rolled-up' hourly rate which includes basic pay and an element for holiday pay. When the employee takes his holiday, the employer does not pay his holiday pay because in theory the employee has already received it.

In *College of North East London* v *Leather* (2001) judgment of 30 November (not reported), Ms Leather was employed as a part-time lecturer at the College of North East London. Her contract contained the following term: 'There is no entitlement to paid holiday under this contract'. Ms Leather claimed that reg 13 of the Working Time Regulations entitled her to holiday pay. The employers claimed that her hourly rate of pay included a sum which represented an element in respect of holiday pay which amounted, pro rata, to an equivalent sum received by full-time lecturers. In upholding the complaint the tribunal concluded that the contract between the parties was for an hourly payment which was solely in respect of hours worked. The respondent could not unilaterally vary the contract to apportion part of the hourly rate to holiday pay, as the EAT considered that that would defeat the provisions of the Regulations. The contract specifically stated that there was no entitlement to holiday pay and therefore it followed that no payments were made under the contract for holiday pay.

The issue of 'rolled-up' holiday pay was further considered by the Court of Appeal in *Blackburn* v *Gridquest Ltd (t/a Select Employment)* [2002] IRLR 604. In this case the employees were employed by different employment agencies who supplied workers for Ford Motor Company. They claimed that they had not been paid holiday pay in accordance with the Working Time Regulations. The tribunal found that holiday pay had been paid, but as part of the rolled-up rate of pay: however, this fact had not been communicated to the workers. The EAT remitted the case to a new tribunal, but the employees appealed to the Court of Appeal. It was held that the appeal would be allowed and the decision of the EAT in *Leather* affirmed. Lord Justice Pill said:

> 'A week's pay is the amount payable by the employer under the contract of employment for the normal working hours in a week. Only if it is agreed between employer and employee that the weekly payment includes an amount for something else, such as holiday pay, can it be held to do so. An employer cannot unilaterally decide that the week's pay is a payment not only for the hours worked during the week but includes an element of holiday pay. The claim that holiday pay was "in fact" paid amounts to an assertion that the employer can decide unilaterally what is included in the weekly payment.'

It is clear that the Court of Appeal was concerned with transparency – if an employee is paid a rolled-up rate it must be made clear to him that his rate of pay includes a sum which represents holiday pay. The Scottish Court of Session has also considered the position of an employee who was advised that his weekly rate of pay included an 8 per cent allowance for holiday pay. He claimed that the allowance was unlawful. In *MPB Structure Ltd* v *Munro* [2003] IRLR 350 the Scottish Court of Session held that a 'rolled-up' rate of £10 per hour, which represented £9.25 salary and £0.75 holiday pay, was unlawful. The Court of Session ruled that this was contrary to the Regulations, and that the company was still obliged to make a payment of holiday pay during the four weeks' paid holiday under the Working Time Regulations. Furthermore, the court held that the employer could not offset the payment of £0.75 per hour which had represented holiday pay against the sum owed.

However, in *Marshalls Clay Products Limited* v *Caulfield* [2004] IRLR 564 the Court of Appeal considered that paying holiday pay on a 'rolled up' or 'up front' basis does not breach the Working Time Regulations and may be legitimate. The Court of Appeal referred the matter to the European Court of Justice (ECJ) because of the inconsistency between the decision of the Scottish Courts of Session in *MPB Structures Limited* v *Munro* and the present case. Essentially the Court of Appeal referred three questions to the ECJ:

1. Does rolled up holiday pay violate a worker's rights under the Working Time Directive? Is it necessary, to comply with the Directive, to pay for holidays in the pay period during which they are taken?
2. Is there any difference if the worker was paid the same before and after the rolled-up arrangement came into force (ie the effect of the arrangement was only to attribute part of the wages already payable to the worker to holiday pay)?
3. If rolled-up holiday pay is not permissible, can employers receive credit for payments already made in this way?

Although the decision of the Court will not be published until 2006 the Advocate-General has issued an opinion on the matter and considers that rolled up holiday pay can be lawful and consistent with the Directive's objectives, but only if there are clear systems in place to ensure that the workers affected actually take holidays. It would be for the national courts to examine in each case whether workers have an effective possibility of taking annual leave. With respect to the second question referred by the Court of Appeal the opinion re-confirms the position set out in *Marshalls Clay* v *Caufield* that for rolled-up holiday pay to be effective there must be a genuine increase in the rate of pay to take account of the holiday element and that increase must be transparent to enable the worker to see what proportion is holiday pay. On the final question, the Advocate-General considered that where an arrangement to pay holiday pay does not comply with the Directive an employer will not be prevented from receiving credit for sums already paid to workers under that arrangement. Although the ECJ is not bound by the opinion of the Advocate-General, nevertheless weight is attached to the opinion that is given.

Extension

The Working Time Regulations 1998 were amended in August 2003 to extend working time provisions to some of the groups who were previously excluded, including all non-mobile workers in road, sea, inland waterways and lake transport, workers in the railway and offshore sectors, and to all workers in aviation who are not covered by the Civil Aviation (Working Time) Regulations 2004. The Regulations also included doctors from 1 August 2004.

Flight and cabin crews

The Civil Aviation (Working Time) Regulations 2004 implement EU Directive 2000/79/EC and apply to flight and cabin crew

The Regulations provide that workers are entitled to four weeks' paid annual leave or pro rata if a worker has worked for less than one year. A week's leave should be equivalent to the time that a worker would normally work in a week. If the worker has irregular hours, which is generally the case with flight and cabin crew, workers wil be entitled to leave which would allow them to be away from their place of work for a week. Annual leave must not be replaced by a payment in lieu, except in circumstances where the employment is terminated.

The Regulations provide that the workers must be given a medical assessment when they begin work for an employer and at regular intervals thereafter. They also provide for annual maximum working and flying hours which will include time spent on standby. Employers must allow workers to have at least seven rest days each month and at least 96 rest days throughout the year. The Civil Aviation Authority has the responsibility for the enforcement of the Regulations.

Doctors
The Working Time Directive (Amendment) Regulations 2003 provide that doctors in training, who were previously excluded from the Working Time Regulations 1998 are subject to weekly working time limits.

These new limits are currently being phased in as follows:

1. 58 hours from 1 August 2004 to 31 July 2007;
2. 56 hours from 1 August 2007 to 31 July 2009;
3. 48 hours from 1 August 2009.

Junior doctors can 'opt out' of the Regulations but because of restrictions within their contracts can not exceed more than 56 hours of actual work each week. The reference period to calculate the average weekly hours for this category of workers in 26 weeks; however, sick days and annual leave must be excluded from the calculation. Working time is time when a worker is required to be at their place of work.

Road transport workers
The Road Transport (Working Time) Regulations 2005 (SI 2005/639) end the exclusion from the Working Time Directive for road transport workers. The Regulations affect drivers and other 'mobile workers' who are those who are subject to the Community Drivers' Hours Regulation (3820/85/EEC).

Enforcement

The Working Time Regulations are enforced in a number of different ways, with the possibility of both criminal sanctions as well as civil liability. The limits of the Regulations are enforced by the Health and Safety Executive (HSE). The HSE is also charged with the responsibility of ensuring that night-time workers receive appropriate health assessments. The Civil Aviation Authority has responsibility for the enforcement of the Civil Aviation (Working Time) Regulations 2004 and the Vehicle and Operator Services Agency will enforce the Regulations in respect of workers engaged in the road transport industry.

11

Trade Unions

11.1 Definition and legal status

11.2 Trade unions and their members

11.3 Trade union membership and employers

11.4 Employment Relations Act 2004

11.5 Trade union duties

11.6 The government of trade unions

11.7 Collective bargaining

11.8 Union recognition

11.1 Definition and legal status

Definition

A trade union is an unincorporated association at common law, which means that it has no legal identity of its own and only operates through its members. A trade union is defined by s1 Trade Union and Labour Relations (Consolidation) Act (TULR(C)A) 1992 as:

'... an organisation (whether temporary or permanent) –
(a) which consists wholly or mainly of workers of one or more descriptions and whose principal purposes include the regulation of relations between workers of that description or those descriptions and employers or employers' associations ...'

In order for an organisation to be a trade union the principal purpose of the organisation must fall within the definition in s1 TULR(C)A 1992. In *Midland Cold Storage* v *Turner* [1972] ICR 230 it was held that a shop stewards' committee from several unions was an 'organisation of workers'. However, because the organisation was not involved with negotiations with employers, nor had it sought recognition by them as a bargaining agent, it was not a trade union, since its principal purposes did not include regulating relations between employers and employees.

Certification officer

A list of all trade unions who satisfy the definition in s1 TULR(C)A 1992 is maintained by the certification officer (CO), a post that was created by the Employment Protection Act (EPA) 1975. The CO is appointed by the Secretary of State and is charged, inter alia, with the duty of issuing certificates of independence to all listed trade unions. If the CO refuses to issue a certificate to a trade union, or if he proposes to remove a name from the list, an appeal can be made to the EAT. The CO also has powers to deal with complaints by trade union members with respect to breaches of trade union rules and regulations. Section 29 Employment Relations Act (ERA) 1999 has widened the powers of the CO considerably and an officer may now make orders in areas of trade union law, whereas prior to the ERA 1999 he could only make declarations.

Independence

In order to benefit from certain rights and privileges a trade union must be independent. Section 5 TULR(C)A 1992 provides that an:

> '... "independent trade union" means a trade union which –
> (a) is not under the domination or control of an employer or group of employers or of one or more employers' associations, and
> (b) is not liable to interference by an employer or any such group or association (arising out of the provision of financial or material support or by any other means whatsoever) tending towards such control; ...'

In *Squibb UK Staff Association* v *Certification Officer* [1979] ICR 235 it was held that a union is liable to interference tending towards employer control when it is exposed to the risk or reasonable possibility of such interference. In this case the Court of Appeal held that a staff association, comprising 'white collar' staff from the company which was recognised by management as the sole negotiating body for the staff, was not sufficiently independent because there was a risk of interference from the employer.

In order to determine whether a trade union is sufficiently independent the CO will take into account certain criteria as follows.

History

If a union was set up by the employer or set up with management help it is unlikely that the CO will consider it sufficiently independent. If, however, there is a significant period of time during which there has been no influence from the employer then a certificate of independence may be granted. In *Blue Circle Staff Association* v *Certification Officer* [1977] ICR 224 the EAT held that in deciding whether a union is independent the CO has a duty to look beyond the form of that union's constitution to discover whether an employer in fact exercises domination or control. In this case the employer had dominated the association for a significant period of time and the association was not free from paternal control.

Membership
If a union is formed from employees of one company it is more vulnerable to interference from the employer than a union who recruits from several companies.

Finance
If a union receives a subsidy from the employer it is less likely to be perceived as being independent.

Facilities
If an employer provides a trade union with facilities, such as offices, phones and computers prior to an application for a certificate of independence, the union is less likely to be granted such a certificate. Once a certificate has been granted an employer is encouraged to make available such facilities for trade union officials.

Collective bargaining
To gain a certificate of independence a trade union must demonstrate a robust approach to negotiations.

Organisation and structure
A union should be structured in such a way as to allow individual members to play an active role in union affairs and should preclude any involvement by the employer in the organisation of the union.

The main advantages of a certificate of independence are that members and officials have the right to be members of a trade union and to take part in union activities. An employer must also consult with union representatives prior to making employees redundant or when he is considering a transfer of the business under TUPE. Furthermore, an employer is under a duty under s181 TULR(C)A 1992 to disclose information to union representatives that is necessary for the union to carry out collective bargaining. This information would include pay, benefits, conditions of service, company performance and financial information.

Status of trade unions

As an unincorporated association a trade union cannot own property in its own name, although it can do so through trustees. However, it has been argued that a trade union does have a quasi-corporate status and can be sued in tort. This was considered in the case of *Taff Vale Railway Company* v *Amalgamated Society of Railway Servants* [1901] AC 426 where Lord Halsbury decided that although trade unions were unincorporated associations they could be held liable in tort in their own name. Lord Brandon was prepared to ascribe full corporate status to trade unions. However, his view was in the minority. In order to facilitate the day-to-day operations of trade unions ss10 and 12 TULR(C)A 1992 confer upon trade unions many of the characteristics of legal corporations.

1. A trade union is capable of making contracts.
2. A trade union is capable of suing and being sued in its own name, whether in proceedings relating to property or founded on contract or tort or any other cause of action.
3. Proceedings for an offence alleged to have been committed by a trade union or on its behalf may be brought against it in its own name.
4. All property belonging to a trade union shall be vested in trustees in trust for it.
5. A judgment, order or award made in proceedings of any description brought against a trade union is enforceable against any property held in trust for it to the same extent and in the same manner as if it were a body corporate.

Section 10(2) TULR(C)A 1992 quite clearly states, however, that a trade union shall not be treated as if it were a body corporate. In *EEPTU* v *Times Newspapers* [1980] QB 585 the question arose as to whether a trade union could pursue a claim in defamation. However, the High Court held that a union was prevented from having a corporate or quasi-corporate personality and so it was not possible to bring defamation proceedings.

Union accounts

The obligations imposed upon trade unions and employers' associations in respect of the conduct of their financial affairs are also similar to the obligations imposed upon limited companies. Section 28 TULR(C)A 1992 provides that a trade union must keep proper accounting records and establish and maintain a satisfactory system of control of its accounting records.

Members of a union are entitled to inspect their union accounts. This entitlement is provided by s29 which imposes a duty upon a trade union to keep records available for inspection. The accounts must be kept available for inspection for a period of six years from their creation. Where a trade union member requests access to the accounts the union must allow him to inspect the records within 28 days of the request being made: s30. The union member may be accompanied by an accountant; however, s30(5) protects the confidentiality of the accounts and provides that the union may not allow the member to be accompanied by an accountant if the accountant fails to enter into such agreement as the union may reasonably require for protecting the confidentiality of the records.

If a union refuses a member access to accounts within 28 days he may by virtue of s31 TULR(C)A 1992 apply to the court for an order to require the union to allow him to inspect the accounts.

The union's accounts are of interest not only to the union and its members but also to the CO. Section 32 TULR(C)A 1992 states that the trade union shall send to the CO annual returns signed by such persons as required by the CO.

The annual returns must include:

1. revenue accounts indicating the income and expenditure of the trade union;

2. a balance sheet;
3. other accounts as the CO may require;
4. an auditors report.

The union is also obliged to provide the CO with details of the salary paid and other benefits provided to each member of the union executive, the president and the general secretary.

Section 32 also provides that a union must provide a statement of the number of names on the union's register as at the end of the period to which the return relates and the number of those names which were not accompanied by an address. Furthermore, the union should also include a note of all the changes in the officers of the union and of any change in the address of the head office of the union.

Restraint of trade

Prior to 1875 it was a crime to belong to a trade union. This criminality was largely removed by the Conspiracy and Protection of Property Act 1875 where recognition was given to trade unions, but judicial hostility towards unions remained. Unions were perceived as interfering in the contractual relationship between an employer and his employees which, it was argued, amounted to a restraint of trade under contract law. The effect of the doctrine of restraint of trade was nullified initially by the Trade Union Act 1871 and is now to be found in s11 TULR(C)A 1992 which provides that 'No rule of a trade union is unlawful or unenforceable by reason only that it is in restraint of trade.'

Trade union rules

The trade union rule book lays down the constitution of the union and forms the basis for the contract between the member and the trade union. Whilst Parliament and the courts have traditionally been reluctant to interfere in the constitutions of unincorporated associations they have been more inclined to do so in the case of trade unions.

The principal reason for intervention is that the unions have more power than other unincorporated associations and prior to the abolition of the closed shop some employees needed to belong to a trade union in order to secure employment.

If a dispute arises between a union member and his union the courts will look to the rule book to determine the contract. Most rules which form the basis of the contract between the employer an employer are expressly stated. Difficulties arise where the rule book is silent on the issue for determination. In *Heatons Transport (St Helens) Ltd v Transport & General Workers' Union* [1972] 3 WLR 431 the House of Lords looked at custom and practice in order to decide whether the union was vicariously liable for a tort committed by one of its shop stewards. Such an approach was necessary because the rule book was silent on this point. However,

Lord Wilberforce pointed out that rule books are not drafted by experienced draftsmen and that courts should resist the temptation to interpret them as if they were.

Illegality

In accordance with general contractual principles a rule that is unlawful at common law will be void.

Closed shop

The concept of the closed shop was a prominent feature of industrial relations during the course of the 1960s and 1970s. A closed shop existed where there was an agreement between a trade union and an employer that employees carrying out specific duties within a company were required as a condition of employment to join a relevant trade union. The effect of the closed shop was that 100 per cent of certain groups of the workforce belonged to the same trade union.

The existence of the closed shop was controversial. Trade unions argued that it offered trade union members protection from employers, whilst others argued that it removed individual freedom and that members may be forced into industrial action through fear of losing their membership. The Donovan Report of 1968 agreed that the operation of a closed shop could operate against the interests of individuals and the workforce as a whole. However, they rejected the call for a law to ban closed-shop agreements.

Despite several attempts to outlaw closed shop agreements it was not until the Employment Act 1990 that the final remnants of legal support were removed, making it impossible to operate a closed shop. This can now be seen in s137 TULR(C)A 1992 which will be discussed in more detail below.

11.2 Trade unions and their members

Membership

A trade union is a voluntary association which will have its own conditions for membership which are generally laid out in the union's rules. A trade union is allowed to specify classes of persons who are not entitled to join a union. In *Faramus v Film Artistes' Association* [1964] 1 All ER 25 a union refused to accept the plaintiff as a member once it was known that he had a criminal conviction. The House of Lords held that although it is in restraint of trade for a union operating a closed shop to have a rule forbidding membership to anyone who has ever been convicted of a criminal offence, such a rule may be saved by statute.

A trade union cannot discriminate against a person who applies for membership purely on the grounds of race, sex or disability.

Contractual rights of members

It has already been stated that membership of a trade union gives rise to contractual rights and obligations. If a member of a trade union believes that his rights have been breached he may bring a claim in the courts for breach of contract.

In *Hopkins* v *National Union of Seamen* [1985] ICR 268 the plaintiff, a member of the National Union of Seamen, applied for an injunction restraining the defendants from imposing a levy on union members' wages. The levy had been imposed by the executive council of the union, whereas the union's rules expressly reserved the right to impose such a levy to general meetings. The High Court held that the executive council had acted ultra vires in imposing the levy.

The courts will treat the union rule book like any other contract and may also imply terms into the contract between the union and its members. An example of this can be seen in the case of *MacLelland* v *National Union of Journalists* [1975] ICR 116 where a member of a union was disciplined according to the union rule book for failing to attend all of a three-day mandatory meeting called by his union. The courts implied a term of reasonable notice which had to be given to all members when the union intended to call an important meeting. In the event the union had only given members a couple of hours' notice and therefore it was held that there never was a valid mandatory meeting.

If a union member has a grievance with his union, the rule book may provide that internal remedies should be exhausted before an application can be made to the courts. In *White & Others* v *Kuzych* [1951] AC 585, a Canadian case, the Privy Council held that a trade union could enforce an express contractual term which provided that members will not seek redress in the courts until all internal remedies have been exhausted. It should however be noted that in this case the rule was not unduly prejudicial to the plaintiff. A much more robust approach is taken where there is an attempt by the rule book to prevent a member seeking redress in the courts.

In *Lee* v *Showmen's Guild of Great Britain* [1952] 2 QB 829 the Court of Appeal held that union rules which purport to preclude the courts from intervening in union matters are contrary to public policy and therefore void.

The decision in *Lee* v *Showmen's Guild of Great Britain* is supported by s63 TULR(C)A 1992 which provides that a trade union member is not to be denied a right of access to the courts. The section provides that if a member of a union, or an ex-member of a union, has made a valid application in accordance with union rules for determination of a matter, and that matter has not been determined within a period of six months beginning with the day on which the union received the application, then any rule which provides that internal remedies must be exhausted will be regarded as irrelevant.

Disciplinary proceedings

The union rule book may provide that if a member breaches union rules, for example refusing to take industrial action, he may face disciplinary action by the union. Disciplinary action can include fines, forfeiture, expulsion from the union or any other detriment. If the union rules provide a procedure for disciplinary hearings such procedure must be adhered to strictly.

A trade union member also has a right not to be unjustifiably disciplined by his unions: s64 TULR(C)A 1992. If a trade union member is disciplined for certain types of conduct which are laid down in s65(2), including a failure to participate in or support industrial action, then he will be deemed to have been unreasonably disciplined.

In *NALGO* v *Killorn and Simm* [1990] IRLR 464 union members were suspended from their union for breaking a strike during a pay dispute. A circular was issued to other union members stating that they should not communicate with those suspended. Simm and Killorn wrote to the branch chairman about the circular but they did not receive a satisfactory response. They decided to lodge a complaint with the employment tribunal alleging, inter alia, that one of the union's purposes in issuing the circulars was to cause them embarrassment. The tribunal upheld their complaint and the union appealed against the decision. The EAT held that publishing the names of strike-breakers and circulating these to all other members of a branch with the intention of causing embarrassment to those named could reasonably be regarded as subjecting those members to a detriment and that the complainants had been unjustifiably disciplined.

It can be seen that in disciplining members who have breached union rules a trade union is acting in a quasi-judicial capacity. In *Lawlor* v *Union of Post Office Workers* [1965] Ch 712 the High Court held that when a disciplinary committee of a union is deciding whether to discipline a member, it must act judicially and with regard to the rules of natural justice. Although the statutory requirement that a union should act in accordance with the rules of natural justice have been repealed, nevertheless a union should still abide by common law principles.

In *Roebuck* v *National Union of Mineworkers (Yorkshire Area)* (1976) The Times 28 July a newspaper printed a defamatory article about Arthur Scargill, an area president of the union. At trial Mr Roebuck, a union member, gave evidence on behalf of the newspaper. The matter was referred to the union's executive council and an investigation was ordered to determine whether Mr Roebuck's conduct had been detrimental to the union. The chairman of the panel was Arthur Scargill. Mr Roebuck was found guilty and was suspended from the union for two years. Mr Roebuck brought an action claiming that the executive committee of the union had acted contrary to the rules of natural justice. The High Court held that the rules of natural justice disqualified Arthur Scargill from chairing the disciplinary hearings because he had been the complainant who brought charges.

A union member who believes that he has been unreasonably disciplined may make an application to the employment tribunal. Section 66 TULR(C)A 1992 provides that an application must be made within three months of the date of the making of the determination claimed to infringe the right, or where the employment tribunal is satisfied that it was not reasonably practicable for the complaint to be presented before that time within such further period as the tribunal considers reasonable.

In *NALGO* v *Killorn and Simm* (above) the EAT considered that the three-month time limit could be extended where the delay was due to a reasonable attempt to appeal against the determination.

A person who makes an application to the tribunal must wait until all union procedures are fully concluded before making an application. Section 64 provides that 'an individual is "disciplined" by a trade union if a determination is made, or purportedly made, under the rules of the union'. In *TGWU* v *Webber* [1990] ICR 711 it was held by the EAT that a recommendation by the TGWU that a member be expelled was not a determination for the purposes of s64 because the decision had yet to be confirmed.

Where the employment tribunal finds that the complaint is well founded, it will make a declaration to that effect. Furthermore, s67 TULR(C)A 1992 provides that an individual whose complaint under s66 has been declared to be well founded may make an application for an award of compensation to be paid to him by the union. Section 67(8) provides that the amount of compensation shall not exceed:

'(a) an amount equal to 30 times the limit for the time being imposed by s227(1)(a) of the Employment Rights Act 1996 (maximum amount of a week's pay for basic award in unfair dismissal cases), and
(b) an amount equal to the limit for the time being imposed by s124(1) of that Act (maximum compensatory award in such cases) ...'

If a declaration is made by the employment tribunal and the trade union fails to take any or sufficient action to remedy the situation the member may make an application to the EAT. In order to give the union time to carry out any remedial action an application to the EAT cannot be made until after four weeks of the employment tribunal's determination. Any application must be made within six months of the tribunal's declaration.

Exclusion

Section 174(2) TULR(C)A 1992 provides that an individual shall not be excluded or expelled from a trade union unless:

'(a) he does not satisfy, or no longer satisfies, an enforceable membership requirement contained in the rules of the union,
(b) he does not qualify, or no longer qualifies, for membership of the union by reason of the union operating only in a particular part or particular parts of Great Britain,
(c) in the case of a union whose purpose is the regulation of relations between its members and one particular employer or a number of particular employers who are

associated, he is not, or is no longer, employed by that employer or one of those employers, or

(d) the exclusion or expulsion is entirely attributable to conduct of his (other than excluded conduct) and the conduct to which it is wholly or mainly attributable is not protected conduct.'

Any person who is expelled or excluded from a trade union has the right to bring the complaint before the employment tribunal. Section 175 provides that an application must be made to the tribunal within six months of the exclusion or expulsion or where the tribunal is satisfied that it was not reasonably practicable for the complaint to be presented before the end of that period, within such further period as the tribunal considers reasonable.

Where a person makes a successful application to the tribunal under s174 the tribunal shall make a declaration to that effect and s176 provides that the applicant may make an application for an award of compensation to be paid to him by the union. The amount of compensation awarded will be such sum as the employment tribunal considers just and equitable in all the circumstances. However, in any event an award by the employment tribunal shall not exceed (s176(6)):

'(a) an amount equal to 30 times the limit for the time being imposed by s227(1)(a) of the Employment Rights Act 1996 (maximum amount of a week's pay for basic award in unfair dismissal cases [which is currently £280]), and

(b) an amount equal to the limit for the time being imposed by s124(1) of that Act (maximum compensatory award in such cases [which is currently £56,800]) ...'

If, following a declaration by the employment tribunal a person is not admitted or readmitted to the trade union an application may be made to the EAT. An application must be made within six months and any compensation awarded shall not be less than £6,300.

In *Bonsor* v *Musicians' Union* [1956] AC 104 a professional musician was expelled by the branch secretary for being in arrears with his subscriptions. Only the branch committee had the power to expel members and therefore the expulsion was wrongful. It was held by the House of Lords that unions have sufficient legal status to be sued for breach of contract and therefore the plaintiff was entitled to damages for wrongful expulsion.

One issue that has recently been addressed by the EAT is whether membership of a political party is conduct within the meaning of s174(2)(d). In *ASLEF* v *Lee* [2004] EAT/0625/03 a union member was expelled from his union for writing articles for a BNP magazine and standing as a BNP candidate in local elections. His claim to the employment tribunal was unsuccessful and he appealed to the EAT. The EAT held that there is a crucial distinction between expulsion from a trade union because of the individual's membership of a trade union and expulsion because of his conduct and activities which are associated with his membership of a particular political party. The expulsion for mere membership is unlawful, whereas expulsion for conduct relating to membership may be lawful. The EAT referred the case back to the employment tribunal to determine whether the expulsion had been for membership or conduct.

Right to terminate membership of union

Parliament has also intervened to give union members rights with respect to terminating their membership of a trade union. Section 69 TULR(C)A 1992 provides that:

> 'In every contract of membership of a trade union, whether made before or after the passing of this Act, a term conferring a right on the member, on giving reasonable notice and complying with any reasonable conditions, to terminate his membership of the union shall be implied.'

In *Ashford* v *Association of Scientific, Technical and Management Staffs* [1973] ICR 296 two union employees purported to resign from their union. One member gave seven days' notice and the other resigned summarily. However, the union rules provided that members could only resign by filling in the appropriate proforma which would be put before the executive who would then decide whether the resignation was to be approved. It was held that union members may resign from the trade union whether or not the union approves, but reasonable notice must be given.

In *Badger* v *Transport & General Workers Union* [1974] ITR 80 the NIRC upheld a tribunal's view that 13 weeks was a reasonable period of notice on the basis that, under TGWU rules, a member more than 13 weeks in arrears was deemed no longer to be a member.

11.3 Trade union membership and employers

Legislation has imposed certain obligations upon employers to protect trade unions and their members and to ensure that an employee does not suffer discrimination because he is a member of a trade union.

One of the principal forms of protection is provided by s137 TULR(C)A 1992 which states that it is unlawful to refuse a person employment because he is or is not a member of a trade union. A requirement by an employer that a person take steps to become or cease to be, or to remain or not to become, a member of a trade union, or to make payments or suffer deductions in the event of his not being a member of a trade union will also be unlawful.

If an employer breaches s137 and unlawfully refuses employment the employee or potential employee has a right of complaint to an employment tribunal.

Section 137(5) states that a person shall be taken to be refused employment if he seeks employment of any description with a person and that person:

1. refuses or deliberately omits to entertain and process his application or enquiry;

2. causes him to refuses or deliberately omits to offer him employment of that description;
3. makes him an offer of such employment but withdraws it or causes him not to accept it.

Refusal of employment includes advertising a job in terms which indicate that the job is only open to members of a union or non-members of a union, refusing or deliberately omitting to process an application or causing an applicant to withdraw or cease to pursue his application or enquiry. If an employer makes an offer of a position to a prospective employee on such employment terms which are such as no reasonable employer who wished to fill the post would offer then this, too, will be deemed to be a refusal of employment.

Difficulties have arisen when a person who has been involved in trade-union activities changes employer and the potential employer refuses to employ him because of his trade-union activities.

In *Birmingham District Council* v *Beyer* [1977] IRLR 211 the applicant was a noted trade-union activist. He had applied on two different occasions to the district council in order to obtain employment. On the first occasion he had used a false name and a bogus reference. When this was discovered he was summarily dismissed for gross misconduct. On the second occasion he did not disguise his identity but he was able to obtain employment on a site where he was unknown. When, within a couple of hours, the officials of the corporation discovered the true facts, he was again dismissed on the grounds that he had grossly deceived the corporation when he made his previous application. The EAT held that the protection afforded by statute only applied to activities in the employment of the employer from which the applicant has been dismissed and therefore a dismissal because of previous activities would not be unfair.

However, in *Fitzpatrick* v *British Railways Board* [1991] IRLR 376 the Court of Appeal held that a complainant must show that union activities had taken place at an 'appropriate' time and this could include previous union activities.

The protection afforded by s137 only applies to employment under a contract of service and therefore will not apply to self-employed persons. Another exception is the employment of trade union officials by trade unions – it is not unlawful for a trade union to require an employee to be a member of the union.

Employees are also afforded protection by virtue of s146 TULR(C)A 1992 which originally provided that if a person is subjected to action which is short of dismissal on grounds related to union membership or activities this will also be unlawful. Thus, if an employee is refused the opportunity for promotion, training or some other employment benefit because of his membership or non-membership of a trade union, in the event that the matter cannot be resolved through internal procedures he will be able to make an application to an employment tribunal.

Section 146 as originally enacted caused difficulties in cases where an employer treated a trade union member less favourably but it did not amount to action short of a dismissal. This loophole was highlighted by two lengthy cases involving Mr Wilson, a member of the NUJ, and his employer, Associated Newspapers Ltd, and Mr Palmer, a member of the RMT, and his employer, Associated British Ports. In both cases the men had been offered a financial incentive in the form of a pay rise if they gave up their rights to have terms and conditions set by collective bargaining. Both men, supported by their union, were successful in the Court of Appeal. The Conservative government responded by implementing s148, the 'Ullswater amendment' to TULR(C)A 1992, which overturned the decision of the Court of Appeal The effect of the amendment was to exclude from liability an employer whose objective was to further a change in the relationship with all or any class of his employees. The cases reached the House of Lords, where it was held that s146 TULR(C)A 1992 protecting trade union members against action short of dismissal only applied to 'acts' and not to the 'omission' of not offering a pay rise to union members who wanted their terms and conditions to be negotiated as part of collective bargaining. This loophole was partially closed by an amendment to s146 by substituting the words 'action short of a dismissal against him' for a more broad approach which was that an employee had the right not to 'be subjected to any detriment as a individual by an act, or any deliberate failure to act, by his employer'.

The case progressed to the ECHR and in *Wilson & Another* v *United Kingdom* [2002] IRLR 568 it was held that their right to freedom of association as provided by art 11 of the European Convention on Human Rights (ECHR) had been breached. The ECHR said that trade unionists must be free to organise industrial action to persuade an employer to enter into collective bargaining and free to instruct their representatives to make representations to their employer. However, the Court did not go so far as to say that the Convention imposes an obligation employer to engage in collective bargaining.

To comply with the judgment of the ECHR s146 was amended by the Employment Relations Act 2004. Section 29 inserts new ss145A–145F into TULR(C)A 1992 to protect workers from being persuaded by an employer not to join a trade union, take part in the activities of the trade union or to take advantage of its services by some inducement or bribe. To further ensure that inducements or bribes being made to trade union members to forego union rights the 'Ullswater amendment' (s148(3)–(5) TULR(C)A 1992) is repealed. This brings the UK into compliance with the judgment of the European Court of Human Rights in *Wilson & Another* v *United Kingdom*.

In *Robb* v *Leon Motor Services Ltd* [1978] IRLR 26 the EAT held that the transfer of an active shop steward coach driver to other duties in an attempt to keep him away from fellow employees constituted action short of dismissal. The EAT also held in *Carlson* v *Post Office* [1981] ICR 343 that the refusal of car-parking facilities to members of a union which was not recognised by the Post Office unions was capable of being action short of dismissal.

In *Associated Newspapers Ltd* v *Wilson* [1995] 2 AC 454 the House of Lords held that the right of an employee not to have action short of dismissal taken against him did not extend to an omission to act on the part of the employer. The effect of this decision meant that an employer could confer a benefit upon an employee who was not a member of a union but omit to confer the same benefit on employees who were members of a union without breaching s146. However, this decision has been overturned by the Employment Relations Act 1999 which has amended s146 by substituting the words 'be subjected to any detriment as an individual by any act, or any deliberate failure to act, by his employer if the act or failure takes place' for 'action short of dismissal against him'.

Section 146(1) provides that every employee has the right not to be subjected to any detriment as an individual by any act, or any deliberate failure to act, by his employer, if the act or failure takes place for the purpose of:

1. preventing or deterring him from being a member of an independent trade union, or penalising him for being so; or
2. preventing or deterring him from taking part in the activities of an independent trade union at an appropriate time, or penalising him for doing so; or
3. compelling him to become a member of a trade union.

Detriment, for the purpose of this section, is detriment short of dismissal.

Members of trade unions are therefore protected from any form of detriment be it an act or omission which prevents him from taking part in the activities of his union. Difficulties have also arisen with respect to the interpretation of the phrase 'activities of an independent trade union'.

The type of activities which will attract protection will depend upon the status of the employee. If the person is a union member s146 will only protect him in respect of activities which are closely associated with union membership. However, if the employee is a union official he will be able to carry out a wider range of activities.

Section 146 only operates if the activities carried out by an employee are carried out at an appropriate time; generally this will be either within his working hours, with the express or implied consent of his employer, or outside working hours.

In *Marley Tile Company Ltd* v *Shaw* [1980] ICR 72 the Court of Appeal held that an employer's consent to employees taking part in union activities can be implied from the previous conduct of the parties and that express permission is not necessary. However, in this case because the management had not accepted the accreditation of the shop steward, consent could not be implied and therefore the dismissal was not contrary to s146.

An employer's agreement that activities be carried out at an appropriate time can be implied by taking into account what has been normal custom and practice. However, an employer's agreement cannot be inferred from silence on the part of the employer.

Furthermore, in *Brennan & Ging* v *Ellward (Lancs) Ltd* [1976] IRLR 378 it was held by the EAT that protection will not be afforded to an employee who suddenly downs tools and leaves the premises to consult a union official elsewhere when the employer has expressly forbidden him to do so.

If an employee is required to take his meal or tea breaks on the premises of his employer he is entitled to engage in union activities without the consent of the employer: *Zucker* v *Astrid Jewels Ltd* [1978)] ICR 1088. If an employer allows his employees to engage in general conversation whilst working he cannot prevent them from discussing union-related matters. If, however, the discussion interferes with the completion of work, or causes disruption to others, the employer can prohibit such conversations.

In *British Airways Engine Overhaul Ltd* v *Francis* [1981] ICR 278 a union official was reprimanded by her employer for issuing a press statement criticising her union without prior consultation with the employer. It was held by the EAT that the statement was issued on the instructions of a clearly defined group of union members and was a union activity, even though the subject matter was criticism of the union and therefore the applicant had been unlawfully disciplined.

In 1998 ACAS issued a new Code of Practice on Time Off for Union Duties replacing the Code of 1991.

11.4 Employment Relations Act 2004

Following a government review of the Employment Relations Act 1999, which provided, inter alia, for the statutory recognition of trade unions, the general consensus was that the Act was working reasonably well but required further refinement. These refinements can be seen in the Employment Relations Act (ERA) 2004 which received Royal Assent on 16 September 2004. The Act will be introduced in stages. However, the first sections have already been implemented by the Employment Relations Act 2004 (Commencement No 1 and Transitional Provisions) Order 2004 which came into effect on 1 October 2004.

The ERA 2004 is divided into seven parts:

1. Union Recognition: ss1–21.
2. Law relating to industrial action: ss22–28.
3. Rights of trade union members, workers and employees: ss29–43.
4. Enforcement of minimum wage legislation: ss44–47.
5. The Certification Officer: ss48–51.
6. Miscellaneous (relating to internal affairs of trade unions: ss52–55.
7. Supplementary provisions: ss56–59.

Union recognition

Part 1 of the ERA 2004 provides for clarification of issues surrounding the determination of the appropriate bargaining unit and communications between a union and relevant workers.

Section 3 provides that if a trade union has made a recent application to the

Central Arbitration Committee (CAC) the employer must, within five days, provide to the union the following information:

1. a list of the categories of workers in the proposed bargaining unit;
2. a list of the workplaces in which the workers in the proposed bargaining unit actually work; and
3. the number of workers the employer reasonably believes to be in each category at each workplace.

Furthermore, additional power is given to the CAC to require that employers and trade unions provide relevant information to assist in identifying the relevant bargaining unit. However, this power does not extend to the disclosure of confidential information.

The CAC must require the holding of a ballot of those within the proposed bargaining unit if it has credible evidence that a significant number of union members within the unit do not want the union (or unions) to conduct collective bargaining on their behalf.

Section 51 ERA 2004 reconfirms the position in the ERA 1999 that if an application for recognition is refused the union will be prevented for applying for recognition for a three-year period. The section also confirms that there is no right to appeal against a decision of the CAC other than through an application for judicial review.

Industrial action

The notice and ballot procedures have, not surprisingly, given rise to more litigation than any other collective issue. To overcome some of the burdensome provisions of the original Trade Union and Labour Relations (Consolidation) Act (TULR(C)A) 1992 relating to the identification of workers to be included in a ballot, the 1999 and 2004 Acts have amended TULR(C)A 1992 to relax the requirement that the union specify particular employees who would be entitled to take part in the ballot, for a notice which should contain 'such information in the union's possession as would help the employer to make plans and bring information to the attention of those employees who will be entitled to vote': s226A(2)(c) TULR(C)A 1992. These notices must state the total number of workers to be involved in the proposed ballot, the number of workers in each category, and the number of workers at each workplace, but will not have to reveal the names of individual union members.

Similarly with respect to the requirement to give written notice of industrial action, a union is required to give information to the employer of the numbers category and workplace of those union members who intend to take part in industrial action: ss234A(3)(a) and (5A).

Section 24 confirms the current position as laid down by the House of Lords in *P v National Association of School Masters* [2003] ICR 386 that small and accidental failures in the balloting procedure will not automatically lead to a loss of statutory immunity for potential tortuous liability.

The protection afforded to workers who participate in industrial action that any dismissal within an eight-week period of the commencement of a strike will be unfair remains the same, although s26 ERA 2004 provides that any lock-out days are to disregarded in calculating the eight-week period.

Rights of trade union members, workers and employees

Section 41 ERA 2004 extends the list of unlawful reasons for dismissing an employee who is taking part in unofficial industrial action to include a reason related to exercising the right to request flexible working under s104C Employment Rights Act 1996. There is no qualification period for making a claim on this ground.

Jurisdiction of Employment Appeal Tribunal

Section 38 ERA 2004 extends the jurisdiction of the Employment Appeal Tribunal to cover claims under the National Minimum Wage Act 1998 and the Employment Relations Act 1999.

Enforcement of minimum wage legislation

Sections 44–47 ERA 2004 amend the provision for the enforcement of the national minimum wage. When the provisions come into effect enforcement officials will have the right to disclose information obtained from an employer to a worker and vice versa.

11.5 Trade union duties

An employer is statutorily bound to allow an official from a recognised trade union to have time off for trade union duties.

Section 168 TULR(C)A 1992 provides that:

'(1) An employer shall permit an employee of his who is an official of an independent trade union recognised by the employer to take time off during his working hours for the purpose of carrying out any duties of his, as such an official, concerned with –
(a) negotiations with the employer related to or connected with matters falling within s178(2) (collective bargaining) in relation to which the trade union is recognised by the employer, or
(b) the performance on behalf of employees of the employer of functions related to or connected with matters falling within that provision which the employer has agreed may be so performed by the trade union, or
(c) receipt of information from the employer and consultation by the employer under s188

(redundancies) or under the Transfer of Undertakings (Protection of Employment) Regulations 1981.'

A union official who takes time off to carry out union duties is entitled to be paid. Where a person is on piecework, or his pay is dependent upon the amount of work done, his pay will be calculated by reference to the average hourly earnings of that employee.

An employer is obliged to allow an official time off work for union duties as long as these duties are related to collective bargaining as laid down in s178 TULR(C)A 1992. Matters which fall within s178 include: terms and conditions of employment, the physical conditions in which any workers are required to work, engagement or non-engagement of staff and allocation of work or the duties of employment between workers or groups of workers.

The time that an official can take off will include preparatory meetings prior to negotiations with an employer. In *London Ambulance Service* v *Charlton & Others* [1992] ICR 773 the EAT held that union officials were entitled to paid time off for the purposes of attending a union meeting to prepare for negotiations with the employer. The EAT considered that there was a sufficient nexus between the preparatory meeting and the issue of collective bargaining and that it did not matter that only union members were at the meeting.

An employer should allow a union official to take time off for union duties if it is reasonable in the circumstances. If an employer refuses a union official time off, the employee can make an application to the employment tribunal for a declaration and compensation. The ACAS Code of Practice on Time Off for Union Duties provides that consideration should be given to the operational requirements of the business, including the size of the workforce.

When considering whether time off is reasonable in the circumstances an employer can take into account previous time away from the workplace. In *Wignall* v *British Gas Corporation* [1984] ICR 716 a part-time NALGO official, who sat on no less than 22 committees, was permitted to take 12 weeks a year off to carry out his union duties. He was invited to produce a new magazine for the union and applied for additional days off but his request was refused by his employer on the ground that 'enough is enough'. The EAT held that an employer need not treat each application on its own merit but may look at all the circumstances, including time off that had already been granted to the employee.

The obligation upon an employer to allow time off for union duties does not include time off to lobby Parliament over proposed legislation. In *Luce* v *London Borough of Bexley* [1990] ICR 591 the EAT held that lobbying Parliament did not constitute a 'trade union activity' for the purposes of allowing time off work.

Section 168(2) provides that an employer is obliged to allow a trade union official time off during his working hours to undergo training in aspects of industrial relations. The training must however be relevant to his duties concerning industrial relations between the official and his employer. In *Menzies* v *Smith & McLaurin Ltd*

[1980] IRLR 180 a union official requested time off to attend a course on job security. The leave was granted by his employer but they refused to pay him during the time off because the course syllabus was too wide and general to be of any direct assistance to him in his capacity as a union official. The EAT held that although the term 'industrial relations' is not to be construed too narrowly, the course was not directly related to the union officials duties and therefore it would not be reasonable to expect the employer to pay the official for the time that he was off work.

An employer must also allow an employee who is a member of an independent trade union recognised by the employer to take time off during his working hours to take part in activities of the union. This entitlement which is conferred by virtue of s170(1) TULR(C)A 1992 does not extend to activities which themselves consist of industrial action. The amount of time off which an employee can take will be what is deemed reasonable in all the circumstances having regard to the provisions of the Code of Practice issued by ACAS.

11.6 The government of trade unions

We have already seen that a trade union had a quasi-corporate status. It is therefore necessary to have persons acting in an official capacity to 'manage' the union and its affairs. During the course of the 1960s and 1970s the growing power of the unions persuaded Parliament that it ought to act in respect of the governance of trade unions and set down statutory requirements. Elections must be held for various union posts, including members of the national executive.

Section 46 TULR(C)A 1992 imposes a statutory obligation upon trade unions to hold elections for members of the executive and certain positions, and that a person who holds such a position must be elected every five years. Section 46 does not apply to the president and general secretary of a trade union if the holder of such office is neither a voting member of the executive nor an employee of the union.

Any member of a trade union who wishes to hold an official union post should be able to stand as a candidate. However, if a person belongs to a class of persons who are excluded from standing for election by the rules of the union then he may be excluded: s46. No pressure should be put upon a member of a union who wishes to be a candidate to join a particular political party.

Election addresses

A trade union must provide every candidate in an election for a union post with the opportunity of preparing an election address in his own words: s48 TULR(C)A 1992. This address should be given to the union to be distributed to all members who are entitled to vote in the election. The union must try as far as is reasonably practical to ensure that a copy of every election address which is submitted in time is distributed with voting papers for the election. The cost of the production and distribution of election addresses should be borne by the union and not the candidate. The union should also ensure, so far as reasonably practicable, that the same facilities with respect to the preparation of an election address are provided equally to each candidate.

Appointment of independent scrutineer

In order to ensure that elections are carried out in accordance with correct procedures, s49 TULR(C)A 1992 provides that before an election for a post on the executive committee is held, the union must appoint a qualified independent person as a scrutineer. A person is a qualified independent person if he satisfied the requirements of the Trade Union Ballots and Elections (Independent Scrutineers' Qualifications) Order 1988.

Entitlement to vote

The general principle is that all members of a trade union should be entitled to vote, although the union rules may exclude such entitlement to members who are not in employment, who are in arrears in respect of any subscription or contribution due to the union or who are apprentices, trainees or students or new members of the union.

The rules of the union may also restrict entitlement to vote to members who fall within a class determined by reference to a trade or occupation, geographical area, or a class which is by virtue of the rules of the union treated as a separate section within the union.

Voting

Each union member who is entitled to vote should receive a voting paper at his home address and should register his vote by appropriate marking of the voting paper. Each voting paper must state the name of the independent scrutineer and clearly specify the address and the date by which the paper is to be returned. Each voter must be allowed to vote without interference from the union or any of its members and should, so far as is reasonably practicable, be able to do so without incurring any direct cost to himself.

After voting has taken place s52 TULR(C)A 1992 provides that the independent scrutineer must provide a report stating the following:

1. the number of voting papers distributed for the purposes of the election;
2. the number of voting papers returned to the scrutineer;
3. the number of valid votes cast in the election for each candidate;
4. the number of spoiled or otherwise invalid voting papers returned;
5. the name of the person or persons appointed under s51 TULR(C)A 1992 to count the votes.

The scrutineer's report shall also state whether he is satisfied that all correct statutory procedures were followed and that the arrangements made with respect to the production, storage, distribution, return and security of the voting papers were correct.

The trade union cannot publish the result of the election until it has received the scrutineer's report.

11.7 Collective bargaining

One of the primary functions of a trade union is to protect the rights of individual workers in the workplace. One of the ways in which these rights are protected is through negotiations between the employer and the union – this is known as collective bargaining. There are also advantages from an employer's perspective; it can be much easier to negotiate the terms and conditions for a large number of workers with trade-union representatives than with each worker individually.

The definition of collective agreements and collective bargaining can be found in s178 TULR(C)A 1992 where it is stated:

> '(1) In this Act "collective agreement" means any agreement or arrangement made by or on behalf of one or more trade unions and one or more employers or employers' associations and relating to one or more of the matters specified below; and "collective bargaining" means negotiations relating to or connected with one or more of those matters.
> (2) The matters referred to above are –
> (a) terms and conditions of employment, or the physical conditions in which any workers are required to work;
> (b) engagement or non-engagement, or termination or suspension of employment or the duties of employment, of one or more workers;
> (c) allocation of work or the duties of employment between workers or groups of workers;
> (d) matters of discipline;
> (e) a worker's membership or non-membership of a trade union;
> (f) facilities for officials of trade unions; and
> (g) machinery for negotiation or consultation, and other procedures, relating to any of the above matters, including the recognition by employers or employers' associations of the right of a trade union to represent workers in such negotiation or consultation or in the carrying out of such procedures.'

There are two distinct forms of collective bargaining. First, there is the normative function which regulates the contractual terms and conditions of individual workers; and, second, the procedural function which regulates the relationship between the employer and the trade union.

There are also different levels of collective bargaining. These can take place at national level where an agreement may be struck between one or more unions and a single employer or employers' association which will be binding on all represented workers throughout the country. National bargaining tends to deal only with minimum terms and conditions that are to apply to workers and therefore it may be necessary to negotiate at a local level to consider more specific terms and conditions based on local custom and practice.

11.8 Union recognition

We have seen from s178(2)(g) TULR(C)A 1992 that collective bargaining includes negotiations relating to the recognition of trade unions by employers for the purpose of representing union members.

One of the difficulties that has dogged industrial relations has been the recognition of trade unions by employers. Recognition in relation to a trade union is defined by s178(3) TULR(C)A, as 'the recognition of the union by an employer, or two or more associated employers, to any extent, for the purpose of collective bargaining'.

Many employers have refused to recognise the right of a trade union to represent the workforce and have preferred to negotiate terms and conditions individually with their employees. The Industrial Relations Act 1971 introduced some compulsion on the part of the employer to recognise a union but only where a majority of the workforce were in favour of union recognition for the purposes of collective bargaining. This requirement was further complicated by the Employment Protection Act 1975 which required ACAS to make the decision on recognition where there was no voluntary agreement between the union and employer. The procedures under the Employment Protection Act were abolished by the Employment Act 1980.

During the time of the Conservative government there was a significant weakening in the power of the trade unions and therefore it was not considered necessary to put into place any statutory requirement that an employer recognise a trade union for the purposes of collective bargaining. However, the Labour government in the White Paper *Fairness at Work* (1998) acknowledged that 'the collective representation of individuals at work can be the best method of ensuring that employees are treated fairly, and it is often the preferred option of both employers and employees'.

In order to address the belief by the government that 'every employee should be free to decide to join a trade union. But equally every employee should be free not to join', the government invited representations from the CBI and the TUC following which proposals for reform with respect to a new system of trade union recognition were formulated.

Recognition and the Employment Relations Act 1999
Basic outline
Section 1 and Sch 1 of the Employment Relations Act (ERA) 1999 insert a new

Chapter (Chapter VA) and a new Schedule (Sch A1) into the Trade Union and Labour Relations (Consolidation) Act (TULR(C)A) 1992.

Schedule A1, Pt I TULR(C)A 1992 provides that a trade union seeking recognition is entitled to make a request to the employer to conduct collective bargaining on behalf of a group of workers. In order to make such a request three requirements need to be satisfied.

1. The union must have a certificate of independence.
2. The employer must employ at least 21 employees on the day the request is made
3. The request must be received by the employer.

To deter employers who suspect that a request for union recognition is to be made from defeating such a request by reducing their workforce to below 21 on the relevant day, para 7(1)(b) of Sch A1 provides that as an alternative to the requirement of 21 there must be an average of 21 workers in the 13 weeks ending with the day upon which the request is made.

Agreement
If the employer and the union agree the appropriate bargaining unit 'and that the union is to be recognised as entitled to conduct collective bargaining on behalf of the unit' (para 10(1) of Sch A1), then provided such agreement is made before the end of the first period which is ten days following receipt of the request by the employer no further steps are to be taken.

Agreement to negotiate
If, before the end of the first period the employer informs the union that the employer does not accept the request for recognition as it stands but is willing to negotiate, the parties may conduct negotiations with a view to agreeing a bargaining. The union will then be recognised as entitled to conduct collective bargaining on behalf of the agreed bargaining unit. It may be that a union present a request to an employer for recognition in respect of shop-floor workers and administrative staff. The employer may be prepared to grant recognition in respect of the shop-floor workers and if this accepted by the union then provided such agreement is reached before the end of the second period which is 20 working days after the end of the first period, no further steps need be taken.

Either party may request ACAS to assist in conducting negotiations: para 10(5) of Sch A1.

Rejection by the employer
If the employer rejects the request by the union or fails to respond within ten days of the request being made, the union may apply to the Central Arbitration Committee (CAC), see below, to determine whether the bargaining unit proposed by the union is appropriate and whether the union has the support of the workers within that bargaining unit: para 11 of Sch A1.

If the employer rejects the request by the union but informs the union that he is prepared to negotiate such agreement must be reached within the 20-day second period. A failure to agree will entitle the union to apply to the CAC to determine whether the bargaining unit proposed by the union is appropriate and whether the union has the support of the workers within that bargaining unit: para 12 of Sch A1.

Where an employer agrees to negotiate the request of the union, and before the end of the second period a bargaining unit has been agreed but no agreement has been reached on the right of the union to conduct collective representation, the union may apply to the CAC to decide whether or not the union has the support of the majority of the agreed bargaining unit.

The Central Arbitration Committee

The Central Arbitration Committee (CAC) has been given a significant role in respect of assisting the parties to agree an appropriate bargaining unit. If there is no agreement between the parties the CAC can issue a declaration stating that the bargaining unit proposed by one of the parties is appropriate or it may propose an alternative bargaining unit. If the CAC is not satisfied that the majority of the workers in the bargaining unit are members of the union seeking recognition, or if union members have represented that they do not want the union to conduct collective bargaining, it may not issue a declaration if it considers that a ballot should be held 'in the interests of good industrial relations'. If an application is made under paras 11 or 12, in order to determine the level of support, the CAC must apply the 10 per cent test. Paragraph 14(5) of Sch A1 provides that the 10 per cent test is satisfied if members of the union constitute at least 10 per cent of the workers constituting the relevant bargaining unit.

If the CAC is satisfied that the bargaining unit proposed by the agreement of the parties or a bargaining unit decided upon by the CAC has the support of the majority of union members it must issue a declaration that the union is recognised for the purposes of collective bargaining. In the event of a declaration being issued the parties have 30 days in which to agree the method by which they intend to conduct collective bargaining.

Method of collective bargaining

Once a bargaining unit and the right to recognition has been established the next consideration is the method by which by which the employer and the union will conduct collective bargaining.

If the CAC issues a declaration that the union is to be recognised the parties have 30 days, starting with the day after the parties are notified of the declaration, to negotiate a method by which they will conduct collective bargaining. If no agreement is reached either the employer or the union may apply to the CAC for assistance.

Schedule A1 TULR(C)A 1992 provides that the CAC has two roles to play with respect to the method of collective bargaining. First, para 31(2) provides that:

'The CAC must try to help the parties to reach in the agreement period an agreement on a method by which they will conduct collective bargaining.'

Second, para 31(3) provides:

'If at the end of the agreement period the parties have not made such an agreement the CAC must specify to the parties the method by which they are to conduct collective bargaining.'

If the parties have made a voluntary agreement for recognition a similar process to the above is applied to determine a method of collective bargaining.

From the day after the parties have reached agreement there is a negotiation period of 30 days during which time the parties will consider the method of collective bargaining: para 58. The 30-day negotiation period may be extended with the agreement of both parties. If the parties cannot reach agreement either of the parties may apply to the CAC for assistance.

An employer or union may also apply to the CAC for assistance if the parties have agreed a method by which they will conduct collective bargaining and one of the parties fails to carry out the agreement as to method: para 59.

Multiple applications

It is possible that more than one union may submit a request for recognition and that the relevant bargaining units proposed by each of the unions comprises of some of the same employees. If the employer refuses to negotiate the union must then submit its application to the CAC. Upon receipt of more than one application where the bargaining units overlap, para 14 of Sch A1 provides that the CAC must apply the 10 per cent test. If more than one application satisfies the 10 per cent test the CAC must reject all applications. The most appropriate course of action for the unions to pursue in such a situation would be to resubmit a joint application. If none of the applications satisfy the test, the CAC will again have to reject the applications. If the CAC decides that the 10 per cent test is satisfied by only one application the CAC must proceed with the application and reject the other applications.

Termination

Once the parties have voluntarily agreed to recognition, or if a declaration has been made by the CAC, the recognition of the union for the purposes of collective bargaining may not be terminated by the employer for a period of three years starting with the day after the date of the agreement. After three years an employer may terminate the agreement either with or without the consent of the unions. The union may, however, terminate the agreement at any time with or without the consent of the employer.

Derecognition

If the CAC has issued a declaration that the union is to be recognised or has specified a method of collective bargaining, the derecognituion procedure in Pt IV of Sch A1 applies. An employer can only apply for derecognition after a period of three years since the CAC declaration has elapsed.

An employer may wish to apply for derecognition if he employees less than 21 employees. In such a case the employer would have to comply with the procedure laid down in para 99 which provides, inter alia, that the employer must give notice to the union or unions and the CAC. The CAC will consider such an application.

Alternatively, an employer may just wish to bring the agreement to an end because he considers that there is no benefit to be derived from such an agreement. In such a case the employer must give notice in writing to the union. If the union is in agreement that the collective bargaining be terminated then no further steps need be taken under Pt IV. If, however, the union still wishes to conduct collective bargaining, the union or the employer can seek assistance from ACAS or the employer can apply to the CAC to conduct a secret ballot to establish whether there is support from the workforce for collective bargaining. The CAC will then determine whether on the evidence provided collective bargaining should continue.

It is also possible that a worker who falls within the relevant bargaining unit may apply to have the bargaining arrangements terminated. Again such an application can only be considered after a three-year period has elapsed. Notice of the request must be given to the employer and union.

Detriment and unfair dismissal

Paragraph 156 of Sch A1 provides that a worker has a right not to be subjected to any detriment if, inter alia, the worker has acted with a view to obtaining or preventing recognition of the union or for giving support to, or not supporting, recognition. A worker is also protected if he voted in a ballot or influenced others to vote or abstain from voting.

Similarly, a worker will also be protected from unfair dismissal if he has asserted rights under the Act.

12

Industrial Action

12.1 Introduction

12.2 Inducing a breach of contract

12.3 Statutory immunity

12.4 Trade dispute

12.5 Secondary action

12.6 Picketing

12.1 Introduction

From the earliest days of the industrial society the relationship between the employer and the workforce has generally been one that has been prone to contention and difficulty, although there have been exceptions such as the paternalistic approach towards workers which was employed by the Cadbury family. Relationships were often exploitative, resulting, not surprisingly, in a reaction by the workforce which led progressively to the development and growth of militant trade unionists. Over time this inevitably extended the power and influence of the trade unions up until the 1980s.

A simplistic assessment of how this environment affected industrial relations and collective bargaining was to cause a swing from the powerful Victorian owner/employer to all powerful multi-million member trade unions. Collective bargaining was essentially a trial of strength and not the intended constructive negotiation. Within key large industries collective bargaining enmeshed in both politics and the 'class war', further distorting the constructive debate on employment matters. It is therefore not difficult to understand that negotiations and collective bargaining at times prove to be extremely difficult. Trade unions try to exercise their collective strength by threatening an employer with industrial action unless their terms are met.

We have already seen that the law regards the employment relationship as a contract of employment and this in theory reduces the scope for trade unions to take industrial action because any action that they do take could be regarded as interfering with the contract between the employer and his employee.

The contractual nature of the employment relationship was largely created by the judiciary in the nineteenth century at a time when there was much judicial hostility towards the idea of trade unions. Prior to 1875 most industrial action amounted to a criminal conspiracy by those participating, leading to the possibility of criminal sanctions, including imprisonment and deportation. However, by 1875 the trade unions had become a significant feature of British industry and the Conspiracy and Protection of Property Act 1875 removed many of the sanctions regarding trade union membership and trade union activity.

The response of the judiciary to the Conspiracy and Protection of Property Act 1875 was still hostile and they responded by developing tortious liability to control the actions of trade unions. Criminal sanctions had merely created martyrs out of those engaging in industrial action such as the Tolpuddle martyrs. However, civil sanctions threatened the finances of trade unions through damages, sequestration of assets etc and these could prove to be much more damaging to trade unions.

12.2 Inducing a breach of contract

It is a tort for a third party to induce a party to a contract to breach that contract. This well established principle was applied in *Lumley* v *Gye* (1853) 2 E & B 216 where an opera singer was induced to breach her contract with one theatre by the owner of a rival theatre. The High Court held that it was a tort to induce someone to breach a contract. Although this tort had not been developed to specifically control the action of unions it proved to be a particularly powerful tool for the judiciary to use to control trade-union activity. The principle of *Lumley* v *Gye* that each of the parties to a contract has a right to the performance was extended by Lord Macnaghten in *Quinn* v *Leathem* so that each of the parties has a right to have his 'contractual relations' with the other duly observed.

In *Quinn* v *Leathem* [1901] AC 445 the House of Lords held that trade-union pressure exerted upon a customer of Mr Leatham, a butcher, not to purchase meat from him because he was using non-union workers amounted to an actionable conspiracy. Lord Brampton said that a civil conspiracy consists of an unlawful combination of two or more persons acting contrary to law; the means used are unimportant since it is the wilful doing of the mischief, coupled with the resulting damage, which constitutes the cause of action.

Although the judiciary had developed new torts the unions were not unduly concerned. It was widely considered at the end of the nineteenth century that because unions were unincorporated associations the torts which were being developed could only be pursued against individual members of a union and not against the union as a body. This was to change in *Taff Vale Railway Company* v *Amalgamated Society of Railway Servants* [1901] AC 426 where Lord Halsbury decided that although unions were unincorporated associations they could be held liable in tort. Indeed, Lord Brampton went one step further and ascribed to the unions full corporate status. The trade unions lobbied successfully for a change in the law and in 1906 the Trade Disputes Act gave trade unions immunity from the torts of conspiracy and inducing a breach of contract of employment.

The immunity of trade unions granted by the Trade Disputes Act 1906 was subject to an important condition. In order to be granted immunity the union had to be acting 'in contemplation or furtherance of a trade dispute' – this became known as known as the 'golden formula'.

It became quite clear that if a union persuaded workers to go on strike as a result of a trade dispute they would be immune from liability in tort. However, trade disputes take several forms including putting pressure on the suppliers, customers or distributors of the employer with whom the union is in dispute and such pressure can lead to a situation where it is impossible for one party to a contract to fulfil his contractual obligations.

In *Thomson* v *Deakin* [1952] Ch 646 the unions were in a trade dispute with Thomson. Thomson had a contract with Bowaters to supply them with certain goods. Some of the drivers used by Bowaters belonged to the same union that were in dispute. The union instructed these drivers not to make deliveries from Bowaters to Thomson. Furthermore, the union wrote to Bowaters advising them of the dispute and the instruction that had been given to the drivers. Thomson sought an injunction preventing the blacking.

The Court of Appeal held that the union had not induced a breach of contract between Bowater and Thomson. The Court held that a union would only be liable if it had induced the breach of contract either directly or indirectly. The Court considered that there had been no direct inducement to Bowater to breach the contract; the letter written to the company had merely been passing on information. Furthermore, the Court considered that there had not been any indirect inducement because the union had not used unlawful means to further their dispute.

An essential element of the tort of indirect inducement is that unlawful means are used to induce a party to the contract to breach that contract. The importance of the distinction between lawful and unlawful means was stated by Lord Denning in *Torquay Hotel Co Ltd* v *Cousins* [1969] 2 Ch 106 where it was held that notifying a party to a contract that performance will be hindered or prevented is actionable in tort as a direct interference with the contract. In this case because there was no trade dispute between the plaintiff and the union the defendants were not protected by the Trades Dispute Act and therefore the matter was determined according to common law principles.

Lord Denning said:

'I have always understood that if one person deliberately interferes with the trade or business of another, and does so by unlawful means, that is, by an act which he is not at liberty to commit, then he is acting unlawfully, even though he does not procure or induce any actual breach of contract.'

Provided that the means used to interfere with a contract are unlawful that will be sufficient to impose liability even though there is no breach of contract. In *Rookes v Barnard* [1964] AC 1129 the defendants threatened a strike if the plaintiff, who was not a union member, was not dismissed. It was held that the union had interfered with the employment of Rookes by unlawful means by the intimidation of his employers. They were held to be acting unlawfully, even though the employers committed no breach of contract as they gave Rookes proper notice.

Similarly, in the case of *Stratford* v *Lindley* [1965] AC 307 the defendant union instructed its members to refuse to handle the plaintiffs' barges. The union was angered by an agreement made between a subsidiary company of the plaintiffs and a rival union. Customers who had hired barges from the plaintiffs were unable to return them with a consequent breach of contract between the plaintiffs and their customers. The House of Lords held that the defendants were acting unlawfully at common law even with regard to new business which was not subject to contract. Lord Reid said:

> 'The respondents' action made it practically impossible for the appellants to do any new business with the barge hirers. It was not disputed that such interference is tortious if any unlawful means are employed.'

The fact that damage is caused to another as result of industrial action will not automatically mean that there is the tort of conspiracy. In *Crofter Hand-Woven Harris Tweed Co* v *Veitch* [1942] AC 435 the TGWU instructed dockers to refuse to handle imported yarn which was to be used by the plaintiffs to make tweed. The House of Lords held that if the predominant purpose of a combination of workers is the lawful protection or promotion of any lawful interest of the combiners, and no illegal means are used, the combination is not a tortious conspiracy even though it causes damage to another.

Despite the protection afforded to trade unions by the Trade Disputes Act 1906 the development of tortious liability made it difficult for trade unions to carry out their legitimate functions. In 1974, when the Labour government was restored to power it repealed the Industrial Relations Act 1971 and introduced the Trade Union and Labour Relations Act (TULRA) 1974 which has itself been repealed and replaced by the Trade Union and Labour Relations (Consolidation) Act (TULR(C)A) 1992.

12.3 Statutory immunity

Statutory immunity is now given against certain economic torts by s219 TULR(C)A 1992. Section 219 provides that:

> '(1) An act done by a person in contemplation or furtherance of a trade dispute is not actionable in tort on the ground only –
> (a) that it induces another person to break a contract or interferes or induces another person to interfere with its performance, or

(b) that it consists in his threatening that a contract (whether one to which he is a party or not) will be broken or its performance interfered with, or that he will induce another person to break a contract or interfere with its performance.'

This section provides immunity from liability in tort for any person who calls a strike or threatens industrial action, provided that such action is in furtherance of a trade dispute – this has been described as the 'golden formula' by Wedderburn. The immunity from liability granted in s219(1)(a) and (b) covers any contract, not just employment contracts. However, s219 does not give immunity against liability for other torts which may be committed during industrial action such as nuisance, trespass and defamation, nor does it grant immunity for any criminal acts that may be committed.

In *News Group Newspapers Ltd* v *SOGAT 82* [1986] IRLR 337 the plaintiffs intended to move production of the *London Post* from central London to Wapping. Negotiations with the union broke down and the members of the union engaged in the picketing of the plaintiffs' premises in Wapping. The picketing also included demonstrations, obstruction of the highway and intimidation of workers. It was held by the High Court that the picketing and demonstrations were at times an unreasonable use of the highway and actionable in tort as a private nuisance. Furthermore, the picketing also amounted to a public nuisance.

Section 219 refers only to inducing a breach of contract. Immunity will not be granted if there is an inducement to breach a statutory duty. In order to determine whether there is any liability it is necessary to determine whether on the true construction of the appropriate statute whether the tort has been committed. In *Lonrho* v *Shell Petroleum Ltd* [1982] AC 173 the House of Lords held that contravention of the Southern Rhodesia (Petroleum) Order which made it a criminal offence to supply crude oil to Southern Rhodesia was a criminal offence. However, the breach did not give rise to an action in tort because the prohibition was not imposed for the benefit or protection of a particular class, nor did it create a public right to be enjoyed by all.

In *Meade* v *Haringey London Borough Council* [1979] 1 WLR 637 parents pursued a claim against the council for the wrongful closure of schools which was in breach of the statutory duty on the local authority to ensure that sufficient schools should be available. It was held that where a body had acted ultra vires the a person who had suffered special damage was entitled to a remedy.

In *Barretts & Baird (Wholesale) Ltd* v *Institution of Professional Civil Servants & Duckworth* [1987] IRLR 3 it was held by the High Court that where a body has a statutory duty, and that duty is breached, those persons who are owed a duty of care and suffer as a result of a breach can pursue a claim in respect of that breach. An inducement or procurement of such a breach can amount to unlawful means for the purpose of establishing the tort of interference with a person's trade, business or employment contracts or with his commercial contracts. However, on the facts of this case, there was no arguable breach of statutory duty as a result of the breach, nor was there evidence to show that the predominant purpose of the strikes was to injure the plaintiffs.

Section 219(2) TULR(C)A 1992 provides that:

'An agreement or combination by two or more persons to do or procure the doing of an act in contemplation or furtherance of a trade dispute is not actionable in tort if the act is one which if done without any such agreement or combination would not be actionable in tort.'

This provision means that if an act which is carried out by one person is unlawful it will remain unlawful if carried out by more than one person. The section only provides immunity for those who use lawful means. The immunity granted by s219 has recently been subject to certain statutory restrictions and will only be available to unions and union members if appropriate balloting procedures are followed prior to industrial action. However, before these procedures are considered it is necessary to determine what amounts to a trade dispute for the purposes of Wetherburn's golden formula.

12.4 Trade dispute

A trade dispute is defined in s244 TULR(C)A 1992 as:

'(1) ... a dispute between workers and their employer which relates wholly or mainly to one or more of the following –
(a) terms and conditions of employment, or the physical conditions in which any workers are required to work;
(b) engagement or non-engagement, or termination or suspension of employment or the duties of employment, of one or more workers;
(c) allocation of work or the duties of employment between workers or groups of workers;
(d) matters of discipline;
(e) a worker's membership or non-membership of a trade union;
(f) facilities for officials of trade unions; and
(g) machinery for negotiation or consultation, and other procedures, relating to any of the above matters, including the recognition by employers or employers' associations of the right of a trade union to represent workers in such negotiation or consultation or in the carrying out of such procedures.'

There are several points to consider with respect to s244. First of all, only disputes concerning any of the matters listed above will attract the immunity granted by s219 TULR(C)A 1992. Second, in order for s219 immunity to come into effect the matter must relate 'whole or mainly' to one of the matters listed. This requirement was implemented by s18 Employment Act 1982 which narrowed down the previous requirement that a matter had to be 'connected' with a trade dispute. The effect of the change was considered by the Court of Appeal in *Mercury Communications Ltd* v *Scott-Garner* [1984] Ch 37 where it was held that to satisfy the definition of trade dispute in s219 a dispute must relate wholly or mainly to one of the matters listed in s219(1) and the definition was thus narrower than it had been before the change. In this case the Court of Appeal considered that the dispute was part of a political campaign against the decision of the government to break the monopoly of the Post Office with respect to telecommunications and did not relate 'wholly or mainly' to the possibility of redundancies.

The question of whether a boycott of national curriculum tests by teachers was in furtherance of a trade dispute was considered by the Court of Appeal in *Wandsworth London Borough Council* v *National Association of Schoolmasters and Union of Women Teachers* [1993] IRLR 344. The plaintiffs claimed that the boycott by the unions was primarily concerned with the educational merits of the national curriculum and therefore not a trade dispute. The trade unions claimed that this was a dispute about increased workloads and therefore related wholly or mainly to the terms and conditions of the contracts of employment of their members. The Court of Appeal held that although members of the unions had objected to the implementation of the tests on educational grounds, it was clear that the union had for some time been expressing concern with regard to the working hours of its members and the implementation of the national curriculum tests brought the matter to a head. The Court therefore considered that the boycott was in furtherance of trade dispute within the meaning of s244 and therefore attracted immunity.

Statutory restrictions on immunity

During the course of the 1980s the golden formula became subject to a number of statutory restrictions which had the effect of limiting further the immunity of trade unions. In order to attract the immunity conferred by s219, unions had to adhere to strict procedural requirements concerning notifying employers of possible industrial action and balloting members. These requirements were laid down in ss226–235 of TULR(C)A 1992 and were considered by the Labour government in its White Paper *Fairness at Work* (1998) to be 'unnecessarily complex and rigid'. A study showed that nearly 75 per cent of legal actions against trade unions concerned the ballot and notice provisions laid down in ss226–235. The complexity of the requirements of the relevant provisions has been relaxed a little by amendments made by the Employment Relations Act 1999.

Notice of industrial action

If a union decides to take industrial action in contemplation or furtherance of a trade dispute, in order to attract immunity the union must give advance notice to the employer in writing of the proposed ballot and industrial action.

The requirements of notice are laid down in ss226A and 234A TULR(C)A 1992. Section 226A requires that a trade union has to take such steps as are reasonably necessary to ensure that employers must receive seven days' written notice stating that the union intends to hold a ballot, specifying the date which the union believes will be the opening date of the ballot and giving details of persons who would be entitled to vote in any ballot.

In *Blackpool and The Fylde College* v *National Association of Teachers in Further and Higher Education* [1994] ICR 648 the House of Lords held that a union's written notice of ballot or strike action must enable the employer readily to ascertain the individual employees who will be involved in the action and that a notice which merely stated that all those members employed by the employers would be taking part would not be valid.

The Employment Relations Act 1999 has relaxed the requirement that the union describe the employees of the employer that would be entitled to take part in the ballot for a notice which should contain 'such information in the union's possession as would help the employer to make plans and bring information to the attention of those employees who will be entitled to vote': s226A(2)(c) TULR(C)A 1992.

Similarly, with respect to the requirement to give written notice of industrial action, a union is required to give information to the employer of the numbers, category and workplace of those union members who intend to take part in industrial action: s234A(3)(a) and (5A) TULR(C)A 1992.

Sample voting papers

Section 226A places further requirement on trade unions that no later than the third day before the opening of the ballot, a sample of the form of voting paper which is to be used be sent to relevant employers. Originally s226A(3)(b) required that where a union was balloting union members of different employers and different voting papers were to be used the union had to send samples of all the voting papers used to all affected employers. The Employment Relations Act 1999 has inserted a new s226A(3B) into TULR(C)A 1992 so that a union will only have to send a sample of the voting paper that is to be sent to the employees of an employer.

Scrutineers

If a union is to conduct a ballot they must appoint an independent scrutineer. The rules relating to scrutineers can be found in s226B and include the scrutineer taking such steps as appear to him to be appropriate for the purpose of enabling him to make a report to the trade union and making the report within four weeks of the ballot. Section 226C provides that where the number of members entitled to vote in the ballot do not exceed 50 there is no requirement for a scrutineer.

Entitlement to vote

Where a union intends to hold a ballot s227(1) TULR(C)A 1992 provides that entitlement to vote must be:

> '... accorded equally to all the members of the trade union who it is reasonable at the time of the ballot for the union to believe will be induced to take part or, as the case may be, to continue to take part in the industrial action in question, and to no others.'

If a trade union denies any person who is entitled to vote in a ballot the opportunity to exercise his right but then later induces him to take part in the industrial action the effect will be that the union will lose its immunity: s227(2).

In *London Underground Ltd* v *National Union of Rail, Maritime and Transport Staff* [1995] IRLR 636 the Court of Appeal held that a trade union will not be deprived of its statutory immunity if it has induced members who did not take part in a ballot to take part in industrial action, provided that they were not members of that particular union at the time the ballot was held.

However, a problem has arisen with respect to persons who were existing members of a particular union at the time a ballot was held but who were not part of the relevant workforce at the time of the ballot and who then subsequently change jobs. The original wording of s227(2) meant that a trade union could not induce these people to take part in industrial action without risking losing immunity. To mitigate against the hardships that s227(2) might inflict upon a union the Employment Relations Act 1999 has repealed s227(2) and inserted a new s232A into TULR(C)A 1992 which provides that a trade union will retain its immunity if it was not reasonably foreseeable at the time of the ballot that the trade union member in question might be induced to take part in industrial action.

Workplace ballots

One of the objectives of the conservative government in the 1980s and 1990s was to ensure greater democracy within the trade-union movement, particularly with respect to strike ballots. Prior to the implementation of ss226–234A TULR(C)A 1992 it was common practice for a decision to strike to be taken at a mass meeting of workers by a show of hands of those present. There were allegations of intimidation of those who voted against strike action and, it was argued, only those persons who were active trade unionists attended meetings and therefore any vote was unrepresentative of the workforce as a whole.

To overcome these difficulties s226 TULR(C)A 1992 provides that any inducement of a person on the part of a trade union to take part in industrial action will not attract s219 immunity unless the industrial action has the support of a ballot. In *Falconer* v *ASLEF and NUR* [1986] IRLR 331, a case decided under s10 of the Trade Union Act 1984, it was held that where a ticket-holder suffered financial loss and inconvenience as a result of a one-day rail strike called without a valid ballot he could recover damages from the defendant unions who organised the strike.

Separate workplace ballots

A trade union who intends to organise industrial action at more than one workplace must hold separate ballots at each workplace: s228(3) TULR(C)A 1992. Section 228(3) does not apply if the union reasonably believes that all members have the same workplace. However, s228A, as inserted by the Employment Relations Act

1999, provides that a union may hold a single ballot if one of the following is satisfied.

1. If the workplace of each member entitled to vote in the ballot is the workplace of at least one member of the union who is affected by the dispute.
2. If the entitlement to vote is limited to all members of the union who have an occupation of a kind and are employed by a particular employer or number of employers with whom the union is in dispute.
3. If entitlement to vote is accorded to, and limited to, all the members of the union who are employed by a particular employer, or by any number of employers with whom the union is in dispute.

A trade union can choose whether to ballot members who are oversees. However, union members who are in Northern Ireland will not be treated as working overseas if separate workplace ballots are held and the members' place of work is normally in Great Britain, or if there is a general aggregate ballot which involves members both in Great Britain and Northern Ireland.

Voting requirements
Another of the procedural requirement to which a union must adhere in order to attract s219 immunity in the event of industrial action is to conform with the voting requirements laid down in ss229–231B TULR(C)A 1992.

A person who is entitled to take part in a ballot must vote by the marking of a voting paper: s229(1A). Each voting paper must:

1. state the name of the independent scrutineer;
2. clearly specify the address to which, and the date by which, it is to be returned;
3. be given and marked with one of a series of consecutive numbers.

Section 229(2) requires that the voting paper must contain at least one of the following questions.

1. A question (however framed) which requires the person answering it to say, by answering 'Yes' or 'No', whether he is prepared to take part or, as the case may be, to continue to take part in a strike.
2. A question (however framed) which requires the person answering it to say, by answering 'Yes' or 'No', whether he is prepared to take part or, as the case may be, to continue to take part in industrial action short of a strike.
3. The voting paper must specify who, in the event of a vote in favour of industrial action, is authorised for the purposes of s233 to call upon members to take part or continue to take part in the industrial action.

Difficulties have arisen as to whether an overtime ban and a call-out ban constitute a strike or action short of a strike. The position has now been made clear by s229(2A) TULR(C)A 1992 as inserted by the Employment Relations Act 1999, which provides that for the purposes of s229(2) an overtime ban and a call-out ban constitute industrial action short of a strike. The distinction is important because if for example the union balloted its members on whether they would be prepared to strike, but the industrial action they pursue is an overtime ban, the union would not have carried out an appropriate ballot and the strike would be illegal.

The ballot paper must also contain the following statement:

'If you take part in a strike or other industrial action, you may be in breach of your contract of employment. However, if you are dismissed for taking part in a strike or other industrial action which is called officially and is otherwise lawful, the dismissal will be unfair if it takes place fewer than eight weeks after you started to take part in industrial action, and depending on the circumstances may be unfair if it takes place later.'

To ensure greater democracy every union member who is entitled to vote must be allowed to vote without interference from union officials, union members or fellow employees. A trade union will, however, be allowed to campaign for a vote in favour of industrial action (*Newham London Borough Council* v *NALGO* [1993] ICR 189) and such a campaign will not be treated as an unlawful call for industrial action before the ballot is carried out.

A trade union must ensure that as far as is reasonably practicable any person who wishes to vote should be able to do so without incurring any direct cost to himself.

With the exception of merchant seamen every person who is entitled to vote in a ballot must as far as it is reasonably practicable have a voting paper sent to him by post to his home address and be given a convenient opportunity to vote by post.

Post ballot requirements

As soon as is reasonably practicable after the holding of a ballot s231 TULR(C)A 1992 provides that the trade union shall ensure that all those who were:

'... entitled to vote in the ballot are informed of the number of –
(a) votes cast in the ballot,
(b) individuals answering "Yes" to the question, or as the case may be, to each question,
(c) individuals answering "No" to the question, or, as the case may be, to each question, and
(d) spoiled voting papers.'

The trade union is also obliged to take steps to ensure that as soon as is reasonably practicable every relevant employer is informed of the matters mentioned in s231 above.

The independent scrutineer must prepare a report which states that he is satisfied that the ballot was conducted in accordance with the required statutory procedures. Furthermore, under s231B he must state that he is satisfied with the arrangements made with respect to the production, storage, distribution, and return of the voting papers used in the ballot, and the arrangements for the counting of the votes, including all such security arrangements as were reasonably practicable for the purpose of minimising the risk that any unfairness or malpractice might occur, and that he has been able to carry out his statutory obligations under s226B(1) without any interference from the trade union or any of its members, officials or employees.

If, following a ballot a trade union calls for industrial action it will only be lawful if it is called by the person specified on the ballot paper and the ballot will only be effective for a four-week period beginning with the date of the ballot. To try to encourage negotiations between the employer and trade union this four-week period may be extended to eight weeks if all parties agree. Where more than one employer is effected the extension of the time limit to eight weeks must be negotiated with each individual employer.

During the course of the four-week period there may be a legal challenge by any relevant employer or employers with respect to the validity of the ballot and a court may prohibit industrial action by virtue of a court. If any such order subsequently lapses or is discharged the trade union may apply to the court for an order that the period during which the prohibition had effect shall not count towards the four-week or eight-week period.

Notice to employers of industrial action

Once a trade union has completed a ballot and has decided to call for industrial action the trade union will not be protected by s219 immunity unless the union takes such steps as are reasonably necessary to ensure that the employer receives a relevant notice within the appropriate period: s234A TULR(C)A 1992. The appropriate period is the period which begins with the day when the union notifies the employer of the result of the ballot and ends with the seventh day before the day specified in the relevant notice for the commencement of industrial action.

The notice must be in writing and must describe the employees of the employer who the union intends to induce or has induced to take part, or continue to take part, in the industrial action. There is no requirement for the union to name those employees who it intends to induce to take part in industrial action.

The notice must also state whether the industrial action is intended to be continuous or discontinuous, for example one-day stoppages. Where it is to be continuous, the union must inform the employer of the intended date for any of the affected employees to begin to take part in the action and, where it is to be discontinuous, the intended dates for any of the affected employees to take part in the action.

Once industrial action has begun generally negotiations will still take place between the employers and the trade unions concerned to secure some sort of agreement. To further encourage such negotiations between the parties, s234A(7A) and (7B), as inserted by the Employments Relations Act 1999, provide that industrial action can be suspended for the purpose of negotiations without the need for unions to issue a new notice to employers in the event that the negotiations fails and the industrial action resumes.

We have already seen that the issues under dispute must be identified on the ballot paper and that industrial action can only take place in respect of those issues.

If, however, there has ceased to be a dispute over the issues identified on the ballot paper, then continuing industrial action will not have the support of that ballot. In *Newham London Borough Council* v *NALGO* (above) the Court of Appeal held that if one side honestly and genuinely believes that the issues for dispute have not been resolved the ballot will still be effective. In *Newham London Borough Council* the Court considered that there was evidence to show that were sufficient differences between the parties to indicate that they genuinely felt that the balloted issues had not been resolved and therefore the industrial action was lawful.

12.5 Secondary action

When a trade union was in dispute with one employer it became a common feature of industrial conflict for that trade union to persuade other union members who worked for another employer, and who were not in dispute with that employer, to take industrial action in support of their fellow trade unionists. The aim of such action, which is called secondary action, was to put pressure on the employer with whom they were in dispute either directly or indirectly.

The effect of secondary action could have extremely damaging results – for example, where a customer or supplier of the employer in dispute with the trade union is prevented from receiving or supplying goods or services. To mitigate against the hardship of secondary action the statutory immunities granted by s219 have been removed by s224 TULR(C)A 1992 in respect of all secondary action other than in the course of lawful picketing.

Section 224(2) provides that there is secondary action in relation to a trade dispute when a person:

> '(a) induces another to break a contract of employment or interferes or induces another to interfere with its performance; or
> (b) threatens that a contract of employment under which he or another is employed will be broken or its performance interfered with, or that he will induce another to break a contract of employment or to interfere with its performance.'

The issue of secondary action was considered by the House of Lords in *Duport Steels Ltd* v *Sirs* [1980] 1 WLR 142 where a breakdown in wage negotiations between trade unions and the British Steel Corporation led to a strike by workers at the state-owned British Steel Corporation. In order to put pressure on the government the union threatened to call on strike their members in private-sector steel companies. The private companies affected applied for an injunction to restrain the trade unions from inducing their employees to breach their contracts. The question for consideration was whether the action bringing pressure on the government was in furtherance of a trade dispute. The House of Lords held that following the decision in *Express Newspapers* v *McShane* [1980] AC 672 the test of whether an act was in contemplation or furtherance of a trade dispute is a subjective one, and that if the unions believed that by creating a shortage of steel sufficient pressure would be brought to bear on the government so that they would provide sufficient money to the British Steel Corporation in order meet the unions' wage claim this would be considered to be in furtherance of the trade dispute with British Steel.

Secondary action will be only be lawful where it is done in the course of lawful picketing by a worker employed by the employer with whom there is a dispute picketing his own place of work, or by a trade union official: s224 TULR(C)A 1992. This allows for a worker to engage in peaceful picketing at his place of work and provides immunity if that worker tries to peacefully persuade others who are not employed by the employer in the dispute to breach their contract of employment. A good example of this would be where peaceful pickets persuade lorry drivers who are delivering goods supplied by another company to the employer to turn away without making their deliveries. This exception only applies to picketing at a trade union member's place of work and does not extend to picketing elsewhere.

12.6 Picketing

During an industrial dispute trade-union members who are taking industrial action may try to put pressure on the employer and other workers who are not engaged in industrial action by demonstrating at the site of an industrial dispute – this is called picketing. Secondary picketing occurs when others who are not parties to the dispute join in such a demonstration. Picketing can give rise to potential civil and criminal liability.

Potential liability

The criminal law generally plays a minor role in industrial conflicts – such matters are between employers and their workers and are generally not matters for the state. However, where numbers of workers are engaged in picketing there is significant potential for a wide range of public-order offences to be committed. During the miners' strike in the 1980s there was a great deal of picketing outside coal mines which lead to violence and the intimidation of those mineworkers who did not go on strike. Where such picketing leads to violence and intimidation it is quite clear that normal police powers to deal with such activities will apply. The potential for criminal offences can arise from the mere presence of a person on a picket line or any activities carried out by that person whilst picketing.

Obstruction of the highway
Where there are large numbers of pickets demonstrating on the highway outside their place of work it is likely that they will be obstructing the highway contrary to s137 of the Highways Act 1980.

In *Broome* v *DPP* [1974] AC 587 during a national building strike a picket tried to persuade a lorry driver to turn around and not enter a building site. The lorry driver was not dissuaded and so Mr Broome stood in front of the lorry and shouted at the driver in order compel him to listen. The driver asked Mr Broome to move but he refused to do so and was arrested and charged with obstruction of the highway. Although Mr Broome was acquitted by magistrates at first instance his later conviction was upheld by the House of Lords where it was said that picketing is only made lawful if attendance is for the purpose of peaceful persuasion. If, however, attendance is for any other purpose, such as preventing free passage on the highway or compelling other people to stop, then the picketing is unlawful.

The High Court in *Thomas and Others* v *National Union of Mineworkers* [1986] Ch 20 also held that pickets who were harassing working miners as they tried to use the highway to gain access to work were commiting an actionable nuisance. The court granted the plaintiffs an injunction restraining the union from picketing the workplace (other than a peaceful picket with six or less union members) and picketing the homes of working miners.

Obstructing a police officer and breach of the peace

If a picket fails to comply with a lawful order from a police officer he may be committing an offence under s51 Police Act 1964. The police also have a common-law power to take whatever action is deemed reasonable to prevent a breach of the police. These powers have been widely used by the police to control number and conduct on the picket lines. In *Piddington* v *Bates* [1960] 3 All ER 660 the High Court said that a police officer may take such steps as he thinks appropriate to control pickets and if he thinks it necessary to restrict their numbers in particular circumstances he may do so, although no arbitrary figure was laid down.

In *Kavanagh* v *Hiscock* [1974] QB 600 during the course of a dispute at St Thomas's Hospital by electricians, police officers who anticipated a breach of the peace prevented pickets from approaching a coach carrying working electricians. One of the pickets tried to push his way past the police and eventually punched a police officer. The picket was convicted of wilfully obstructing and assaulting constables in the course of their duty. The appellant appealed against his conviction, but it was held by the High Court that the police officers had reasonable grounds to believe that the pickets would force the coach to stop which could give rise to a breach of the peace and were therefore acting within the course of their duty in preventing the pickets from approaching the vehicle.

Public nuisance

Mass picketing on the public highway may also amount to a public nuisance.

Watching and besetting

These offences, which were originally contained in the Conspiracy and Protection of Property Act 1875, are now to be found in s241(1) TULR(C)A 1992 which provides

308 Industrial Action

that a summary offence will be committed where a person, with a view to compel someone to act or abstain from acting:

'(a) uses violence to or intimidates that person or his wife or children, or injures his property;
(b) persistently follows that person about from place to place;
(c) hides any tools, clothes or other property owned or used by that person, or deprives him of or hinders him in the use thereof;
(d) watches or besets the house or other place where that person resides, works, carries on business or happens to be, or the approach to any such house or place; or
(e) follows that person with two or more other persons in a disorderly manner in or through any street or road.'

A person who is found guilty of an offence under s241 is liable on conviction to imprisonment for a term not exceeding six months or a fine not exceeding level 5 on the standard scale, or both: s241(2) A police officer may arrest without warrant anyone he reasonably suspects is committing an offence under s241: s241(3).

In the Scottish case of *Galt* v *Philip* [1984] IRLR 156 where doctors were prevented from going into a laboratory because of the occupation of the laboratory by trade union members in furtherance of a trade dispute, the High Court of Justiciary held that the actions came within the meaning of s7(4) Conspiracy and Protection of Property Act 1875 and as they were done in order to prevent the doctors from doing what they had a legal right to do the respondents were guilty.

In order to be liable under s241 there must there must be compulsion as opposed to mere persuasion. The element of compulsion was considered by the High Court in *DPP* v *Fidler* [1992] 1 WLR 91 in a case concerning anti-abortionists trying to dissuade women from having abortions. The court considered that in order to be guilty of watching and besetting the conduct of the defendants must amount to compulsion.

Public Order Act 1986
A number of offences may be committed under the Public Order Act 1986 as a result of activities carried out by trade-union members who are picketing. Pickets who engage in threatening, abusive or disorderly behaviour within the sight of another person who is likely to be harrassed, harmed, or distressed may be found guilty of the offence of disorderly conduct contrary to s5 Public Order Act 1986. More serious offences that could be committed include riot (where more than 12 people use or threaten to use violence contrary to s1), violent disorder (s2) and affray: s3.

The Act also provides the police with wide powers to impose conditions for marches and demonstrations. The authorities can impose conditions on the location, duration and numbers participating in any march or demonstration, although the imposition of conditions will only apply to an assembly of more than 20 pickets.

Peaceful picketing

It is clear that there is potential criminal and civil liability for those trade-union members who either engage in picketing activity or take part in a picket line. There is therefore a need to provide a balance between the competing interests of trade unions who wish to exert pressure upon their employer in furtherance of a trade dispute and employers who wish to maintain business efficacy.

Section 220 TULR(C)A 1992 provides that:

> '(1) It is lawful for a person in contemplation or furtherance of a trade dispute to attend –
> (a) at or near his own place of work, or
> (b) if he is an official of a trade union, at or near the place of work of a member of the union whom he is accompanying and whom he represents,
> for the purpose only of peacefully obtaining or communicating information, or peacefully persuading any person to work or abstain from working.'

Section 220 only provides immunity from criminal or civil liability if a person attends his place of work; it does not provide protection in respect of any picketing activities. Furthermore, the right to immunity only applies to those who picket within the 'golden formula', ie in contemplation or furtherance of a trade dispute.

An employee's place of work is not defined in the 1992 Act but the ACAS Codes of Practice on picketing suggest that this will ordinarily be the site at which the picket works. Section 220(2) provides that if a person normally works at more than one place his place of work will be any premises of his employer from which he works or from which his work is administered.

In order for picketing to be lawful it has take place 'at or near' the place of work. This phrase was considered by the Court of Appeal in *Rayware Ltd* v *TGWU* [1989] 1 WLR 675 where union members had picketed at the entrance to a trading estate some 1,230 yards from the employer's premises. The Court of Appeal held that whether the picketing had taken place at or near the place of work was a question of fact and degree which had to be considered in the geographical sense, having regard to the circumstances of the case. In this case, because the pickets could not get any closer to the employer's premises without trespassing on a private road their action was conducted near their place of work.

13

Employment Tribunal Procedure

13.1 Introduction

13.2 Procedure

13.3 The hearing

13.4 ACAS unfair dismissal arbitration

13.1 Introduction

Employment tribunals, were first established by the Industrial Training Act 1964. Since 1964 the jurisdiction of employment tribunals has grown and now embraces a range of issues which could not have been imagined back in 1964. Employment tribunals can be found in most major towns and cities throughout the country. In 2003 it was announced that the employment tribunals and Employment Appeal Tribunal will form part of a unified Tribunal Service which will be created in the next few years.

Jurisdiction

The jurisdiction of the tribunals has also changed from that of a predominately appellate function in respect of administrative decisions concerning training levies, selective employment tax and enforcement notices under health and safety legislation, to that of an adjudicative tribunal dealing at first instance with disputes concerning employment rights between employees and employers.

The employment tribunals now deal with a variety of disputes, mainly arising from the contract of employment, including discrimination, terms and conditions, certain breach of contract claims, redundancy entitlements and unfair dismissal.

The employment tribunal is more proactive that the courts and more inquisitorial. A tribunal can of its own motion require attendance of any witness, including a party to the proceedings. This rule was affirmed by the EAT in *Clapson v British Airways* [2001] IRLR 184.

The increase in the jurisdiction of the tribunals, and the increased complexity of many of the new matters upon which the tribunals adjudicate, has resulted in the system becoming much more formal and legalistic than was originally intended.

Composition

Each tribunal panel normally consists of a chairman who is a lawyer of at least seven years' standing and two other panel members, one of whom will be from a panel representing employers' interests and the other from a panel representing the interests of employees, who will usually be associated with one of the trade unions.

Reform of tribunals

The employment tribunals have been subject to significant reviews and reform over recent years which reflects the increased workload and importance of the employment tribunal.

Following a review of the employment tribunals in 1994 the government produced a Green Paper which began a consultative process on the reform of the tribunals. The result of this consultation resulted in the Employment Rights (Dispute Resolution) Act (ER(DR)A) 1998. Part I of the Act was designed to improve procedures in order to make better use of tribunals' time and resources and Pts II and III were intended to provide an alternative means of resolving certain disputes.

Following the ER(DR)A 1998 further reviews of the tribunals were carried out. The Employment Act 2002 introduced further changes, many of which have been implemented by the Employment Tribunals (Constitution and Rules of Procedure) Regulations 2004 (SI 2004/1861) which came into force in October 2004.

Determinations without a full hearing

In order to cut down on costs and save time s2 ER(DR)A 1998 provides that the Secretary of State may make regulations to authorise the determination of proceedings without any hearing, which allows the tribunal to hear cases on written submissions alone. An application may be determined by written submissions in the following circumstances.

1. The parties give their consent in writing.
2. The respondent takes no steps to contest the case.
3. The applicant is seeking a form of relief to which he or she is not entitled.
4. The facts of the case are undisputed and the tribunal is bound by the decision of a superior court in another case.
5. The proceedings relate only to a preliminary issue.

Hearing by chairman alone

Similarly, financial constraints have gradually slimmed down the number of cases which must be heard by a full tribunal and in an increasing number of cases the employment tribunal consists of the chairman without the other two lay members.

The chairman can deal with all interlocutory stages. The Employment Tribunals (ETA) Act 1996, s4, provides that certain proceedings should be heard by the chairman alone.

1. Applications for interim relief in trade-union membership, health and safety and other cases under ss128, 131 and 132 ERA 1996 and ss161, 165 and 166 TULR(C)A 1992.
2. Applications under insolvency provisions: ss182 and 188 ERA 1996.
3. Complaints relating to unlawful deductions from wages: s23 ERA 1996.
4. Claims for compensation for breach of contract: s3 ERA 1996.
5. Proceedings where the complainant has given written notice withdrawing the claim.
6. Proceedings where the parties have given written consent to the case being heard by the chairman alone (even if they later withdraw their consent). This is provided by s4(2) ERA 1996, subject to s4(5) ERA 1996. However, where the chairman, having regard to whether there is a likelihood of a dispute arising on the facts, considers that it is a case which it is desirable should be heard before a full tribunal then the application should be heard by a full tribunal.

The EAT considered the discretion of the chairman in *Sogbetun v Hackney London Borough Council* [1998] ICR 1264 where the chairman of a tribunal who was sitting alone with the written consent of the parties found that the applicant had not been unfairly dismissed. The applicant appealed to the EAT, arguing that her case ought to have been heard by a full tribunal. It was held that because the originating application and the notice of appearance made it clear that there was a dispute on the facts a reasonable chairman ought to have exercised his discretion and constituted a full tribunal.

The chairman should also take into account any views expressed by the parties with respect to a hearing by a chairman alone. However, there is no obligation upon the chairman to consult with the parties.

Section 3 ER(DR)A 1998 widens the jurisdiction of a chairman sitting alone to determine matters arising from unauthorised deductions from wages for any reason, and also includes rights to redundancy payments, guarantee payments and relevant compensation. The 1994 Green Paper proposed that a chairman would have to determine certain issues sitting alone; in other words it would be mandatory. However, the 1998 Act has allowed the chairman to retain his discretion in the matter and it is thought that hearings by a chairman alone will continue to be the exception and will be confined to cases where there is little dispute between the parties on the issues of reasonableness and fairness.

13.2 Procedure

The originating application

If an employee wishes to makes an application to an employment tribunal the normal way is by means of a form called an ET1. Any application must be submitted on a standard ET1, which is available from job centres and on-line from the Employment Tribunals website.

Originating applications must generally be presented to the tribunal within three months of the date of dismissal or act complained of. However, the tribunals do have discretion to hear a case out of time if the tribunal considers that it was not reasonably practicable to present the complaint before the end of three months.

In *DPP v Marshall* [1998] ICR 518 the applicant, a transsexual, was offered a job with the CPS. He was interviewed as a male and offered the job. When the applicant accepted the job it was made clear that she would be taking the job in her new female identity. The offer of the position was withdrawn. Subsequently, the ECJ in *P v S and Cornwall County Council* [1996] IRLR 347 held that the Equal Treatment Directive applied to people who were discriminated against on the grounds of gender reassignment. The applicant presented a claim to the tribunal within three months of the decision in *P v S* but it was more than three months since the withdrawal of the job offer. The employment tribunal considered that they would grant an extension of the time limit because it was just and equitable to do so. The respondents not surprisingly appealed claiming that the tribunal had undermined the principle of legal certainty.

It was held that the tribunal had not erred in granting the extension. The discretion enjoyed by the tribunal was in the widest and most general of terms and required consideration of all relevant matters. These included the applicant's awareness of her right to bring a viable claim and the date upon which she became aware of that right.

The Employment Act 2002 (Dispute Resolution) Regulations 2004 (SI 2004/752) also provide that in certain circumstances where a complaint is presented to the tribunal and either the statutory disciplinary or grievance procedures are continuing, the normal time for presenting the claim may be extended for three months.

Notice of appearance

The defendant in the proceedings, who is normally referred to as the respondent and is generally the employer, will have an opportunity to put forward his case and this will generally be done by means of a notice of appearance or ET3. From April 2006 all responses must be submitted on the prescribed ET3.

The ET3, like the originating application, is not considered a formal pleading. There are several reasons for this but the most compelling one is that many respondents do not have the resources to employ a lawyer to assist them, and even if the undertaking has the resources the notice of appearance is frequently filled in by someone from human resources and not their legal representative.

If an employer considers that the originating application does not contain sufficient information to allow him to answer the case he can request from the applicant further and better particulars. This request should be copied to the tribunal, along with a request for additional time to enter the notice of appearance. If the applicant fails to respond adequately to the request, an application can be made to the tribunal to make an order requiring the applicant to respond.

Amendment

If one of the parties to the proceedings wishes to make a change to either the ET1 or ET3 generally a tribunal will allow such an amendment to be made, provided the other side is not prejudiced, although the chairman will consider whether any prejudice may be remedied by adjourning the proceedings or by an order for costs if the request for the amendment is made late in the day.

The guidelines for amendment were set out in *Cocking v Sandhurst (Stationers) Ltd* [1974] ICR 650.

1. Did the original application comply with the rules for presentation including the time limit – if not there is no power to amend.
2. If the proper procedures for submitting an application were followed the tribunal may allow amendment if they are satisfied that the mistake was genuine and not an attempt to mislead.
3. The tribunal should, when exercising its discretion, have regard to all the circumstances of the case.

Questionnaires

A person considering bringing a complaint under the Sex Discrimination Act 1975, the Race Relations Act 1976 or the Disability Discrimination Act 1995 should use the questionnaire procedure.

The forms consist of a questionnaire which the applicant or potential applicant may use to direct questions at the respondent about the reasons for doing or failing to do an act about which the applicant has a grievance.

The time limit for presenting a questionnaire is three months beginning with the date of the act complained of or, if the applicant has presented an originating application, 21 days from the day of presentation.

Provided the questionnaire is served within the relevant time limit the questionnaire, and any answers given, can be used as evidence at a tribunal hearing. A questionnaire served outside the time limits must be served with the leave of the tribunal if it is to be admissible as evidence. If a respondent fails to answer, or replies in an evasive fashion, this might itself be used as evidence of discrimination.

In many discrimination cases, particularly those involving indirect discrimination, statistical information about the respondent's workforce may provide the best evidence available from which to draw an inference of discrimination.

The tribunals are encouraging the use of questionnaires and, indeed, some tribunals have indicated that they will not order that information be provided by written answers where a questionnaire would be the most appropriate means for requesting the details concerned.

Further and better particulars

We have already noted that a party to proceedings may require further information in order for him to be able to present his case. Further information can be requested by an application for further and better particulars. The general principles to be applied by tribunals were laid down by Wood J in *Byrne & Others* v *Financial Times Ltd* [1991] IRLR 417:

> 'General principles affecting the ordering of further and better particulars include that the parties should not be taken by surprise at the last minute, that particulars should only be ordered when necessary in order to do justice in the case or to prevent an adjournment; that the order should not be oppressive; that the particulars are for the purpose of identifying issues, not for the production of evidence; and that complicated pleadings battles should not be encouraged.'

As a general rule a party should not be required to supply further and better particulars in respect of an issue upon which the other party bears the burden of proof. However, if a party puts forward a positive allegation, such as in a dismissal case where the dismissal itself is admitted but the applicant alleges a particular reason for the dismissal, the applicant will be required to supply further and better particulars of any positive assertion, although the burden of proving that the dismissal was fair is upon the employer.

Any request for further and better particulars should be made directly to the other party. Indeed, a tribunal will not generally entertain a request for an order for further and better particulars unless a direct application has been made to the other party.

However, if the other party refuses to provide the information requested on a voluntary basis, an application can be made to the tribunal which will be a chairman sitting alone to order further and better particulars.

Equal pay cases

In an equal pay case, where the respondent seeks to rely on the genuine material factor defence provided by s1(3) Equal Pay Act 1970, an applicant can request precise details of the percentage pay differentials which are said to be explained by the material factor relied upon.

13.3 The hearing

In many tribunal proceedings one, or possibly both, of the parties may be unrepresented and therefore the tribunals are not as formal as the courts and are not bound by normal rules of evidence. They must make inquiries of advocates and witnesses so as to clarify the issues and handle the proceedings. A tribunal has the power to call witnesses itself should it consider this to be necessary.

Challenge

The composition of the tribunal can be challenged and the most appropriate time to make an objection is before the hearing commences.

In *Halford* v *Sharples* [1992] 1 WLR 736 a member of the panel had 'specialist' knowledge of personnel practices in police forces and was specially chosen to sit on a claim of sex discrimination. The EAT held that the panel should be selected at random and not by reference to any specialist experience.

Absence of a member

If a member of a tribunal has to stand down or becomes indisposed the consent of the parties is necessary for the hearing to continue without him. One of the longest cases ever before a tribunal *Port of London Authority* v *Payne* [1994] ICR 555 was heard by a chairman and one member following the death of the other member. The claim of unfair dismissal on the grounds of trade-union activity raised by a dockworker shop steward lasted for 197 days with the absent member dying after just seven days of the commencement of the hearing.

Hearing in public

The hearing of the application must be in public. It can, however, be in private if a minister directs on the grounds of national security. The tribunal does have discretion to hear certain evidence in private.

Allegations of sexual offences and sexual misconduct

Provisions introduced by s40 Trade Union Reform and Employment Rights Act 1993 (now s11 Employment Tribunals Act (ETA) 1996) allow tribunals to restrict reporting of cases involving sexual misconduct and in disability discrimination cases evidence of a personal nature.

The circumstances in which the EAT can make a restricted reporting order were explored in *Chessington World of Adventures Ltd* v *Reed (Restricted Reporting Order)* [1998] ICR 55; [1998] IRLR 56. It was held that the EAT does not have a statutory power to make a restricted reporting order in an appeal against a decision on the question of liability. The only proceedings in which the EAT has a statutory power to make such an order are appeals from the employment tribunal's grant, or refusal to grant, an order or appeals from interlocutory decisions of the tribunal where it has made such an order. However, Morison J suggests that the EAT may have an inherent power to make an order in exceptional cases where it would be required for the administration of justice.

There are however limits to reporting restriction orders. In *R v London (North) Industrial Tribunal, ex parte Associated Newspapers Ltd* [1998] ICR 1212 the tribunal imposed a reporting restriction in respect of a case involving sexual misconduct. The order covered the victim, witnesses, the local authority employer and the chief executive of the local authority. An application to have the order quashed was successful – a blanket reporting restriction was contrary to legitimate public interest. Section 11(1) ETA 1996 is only intended to operate where the disclosure of the identity of a witness who fell within the definition of a 'person affected' would affect the proper conduct of the case.

Representation

There is no restriction on the kind of person who may represent a party at a tribunal hearing. Many employees who are unable to afford legal representation may be represented by a trade union official, a citizen's advice bureau representative or a friend. Legal representation may be either by a solicitor or counsel. It should be noted that where both parties are legally represented the hearing does generally become more formal.

Written representations

Written representations can be made to the tribunal. They should be sent seven days before the hearing, with copies to the other party, but the tribunal has power to consider them even if they have been submitted within seven days of the hearing. In practice the tribunals welcome presentation of written arguments in skeleton form – they save time and release the tribunal from making detailed notes on oral submissions.

The decision – enforcement and rights of appeal

The decision of the tribunal is formal; the tribunal must include the reasons for its decision which will either be in summary or extended form. The decision can be given orally at the end of the hearing or reserved, or a decision can be given with reasons to follow. If a losing party wishes to appeal a decision the application for appeal can only be made with extended written reasons.

Costs

To encourage the legitimate use of the employment tribunals costs are not normally awarded and so an employee can bring a claim against an employer without the fear of incurring costs in the event that he loses his case. However, costs can be awarded if the tribunal decides that a party has acted frivolously, vexatiously, abusively, disruptively or otherwise unreasonably in either bringing or otherwise conducting the case. The Employment Tribunals (Constitution and Rules of Procedure) Regulations 2001 (SI 2001/1171) have broadened the scope for tribunals to make a costs order so that an order can now be made where 'the bringing or conducting of the proceedings by a party has been misconceived'. A tribunal may also award the cost of an adjournment or postponement when the adjournment or postponement is requested at the last minute by either party with no good reason, or where it is necessary because a party has not come sufficiently prepared to deal with issues which may be expected to arise at the hearing.

If a tribunal is of the opinion that a party is pursuing a non-meritorious claim it may warn that party that a costs order may be made. Such a warning should only be given if there is a real risk of costs being awarded against the party, because the effect of such a warning will be to deny the party who has been given the warning the opportunity of a fair hearing. This issue was considered by the EAT in *Lewis* v *Kingston Royal London Borough Council* (2001) Judgment of 3 May (not reported) and more recently by the Court of Appeal in *Gee* v *Shell UK Ltd* [2003] IRLR 82. In both cases applicants withdrew their claims because of a costs warning that was issued by the tribunal. In *Gee* the Court of Appeal held that the applicant was denied a fair hearing after withdrawing her case because she was advised by the tribunal chairman that she was at risk of a 'substantial' costs order. The ultimate question, according to Scott LJ, is whether an applicant has been denied a fair hearing: he said 'The danger is that where a tribunal make or presses a costs warning that is not justified or in a manner that is not justified an applicant will be deprived of a hearing at all'.

Clearly, given that the tribunals do have more scope under the new Regulations to make a costs order, the dictum of Scott LJ must be borne in mind before making such an order to avoid a situation where potential applicants decide not to pursue their claim because of a fear of costs. The cost limit has been increased from £500 to £10,000. This is a significant increase but it is part of a package of measures designed to cut down on weak cases going to tribunal.

13.4 ACAS unfair dismissal arbitration

The number of cases coming before the employment tribunals has increased significantly and therefore to reduce the burden upon tribunals an alternative dispute resolution scheme was necessary.

Provision for ACAS to propose an arbitration scheme was contained in s212A TULR(C)A 1992, having been inserted by s7 Employment Rights (Dispute Resolution) Act 1998. The scheme has now been approved by the Secretary of State and several pilot schemes are now in operation.

In drawing up its proposals ACAS 'tried to adhere to the central features of trade dispute arbitration, which are that it is voluntary, speedy, informal, confidential and free from legal argument'.

The aim is to provide a distinct alternative to employment tribunals which will of course still remain attractive to parties in a proportion of unfair dismissal claims.

Access to the scheme

Parties may enter the scheme either through a settlement reached with the assistance of an ACAS conciliation officer or through a compromise agreement. In either case the unfair dismissal claim will be settled by the agreement to go to arbitration under the scheme. The operation of the scheme will be triggered when ACAS receives a copy of the conciliated settlement or compromise agreement and the ET1 and ET3 if these have already been completed.

Terms of reference

Arbitration under the scheme will be on standard, non-variable terms of reference. ACAS's proposed formulation is as follows.

1. The arbiter shall decide whether the dismissal was fair or unfair, and in doing so shall have regard to the ACAS Code of Practice, Disciplinary Practices and Procedures in Employment, and the ACAS advisory handbook, *Discipline at Work*. Where the dismissal is found to have been unfair, the arbitrator may award reinstatement, re-engagement or compensation.
2. The parties will have to agree that there is no dispute between them on any jurisdictional issue – for example, whether or not the applicant was an 'employee'. If any such disputes exists, the parties will be advised that the case can be heard only by an employment tribunal.

Hearing arrangements

ACAS will have no obligation to provide a hearing before an arbitrator unless they are notified of the parties' agreement to go to arbitration within six weeks after it was made, unless it was not reasonably practicable to comply with that limit.

The hearing will be arranged to take place as soon as is reasonably practicable, and the parties will normally be expected to agree a hearing date within two months of ACAS being notified of their agreement.

The parties will be expected to co-operate fully with the arbitration process by, for example, exchanging copies of documents and details of any witnesses they intend to call. The arbitrator will not have the power to make any witness or discovery orders, but will have the right to draw an adverse inference from the withholding of information.

Conduct of hearings

The arbitrator will be responsible for the conduct of the hearings. There will be no oaths or affirmations. The parties will be allowed to have representatives and to bring witnesses. Each party will have the opportunity to give a detailed explanation of their case, to comment on the other's case and to make a summing up statement.

The arbitrator will adopt an inquisitorial approach and, although there will be no direct cross-examination, questions between the parties may be addressed through the arbitrator.

Settlement of cases

The parties will be free to reach a settlement of the claim at any time before the end of the hearing, and may ask the arbitrator to endorse their signed agreement as an award. However, the arbitrator will not have the power to endorse agreements which go beyond the issue being determined by arbitration.

The arbitrator's award

The arbitrator's decision will be in writing, and will refer to the general consideration and reasoning taken into account in reaching the decision. Any questions regarding the decision will be dealt with only if they are referred to ACAS within 28 days. The amount of any compensation will take into account statutory limits imposed upon tribunals.

The decision, including the award, will be issued by ACAS to the parties involved and will not be published. However, ACAS will maintain confidential records of both cases and decisions for monitoring and evaluation purposes and may publish general summary data.

Appeals

There will be no appeal on a point of law in respect of the arbitrator's award which will be final and binding on the parties.

Appeals in respect of conduct of the arbitrator, the hearing process or the award will only be allowed on the grounds of serious irregularity. Appeals will be to the High Court in England and the Court of Session in Scotland.

Enforcing awards

Any award will be enforceable in the county courts. However, where an award for reinstatement or re-engagement is made and not complied with, the matter will be referred to an employment tribunal for appropriate compensation to be awarded.

Index

ACAS unfair dismissal arbitration, *318–321*
   access to scheme, *319*
   appeals, *320*
   award, *320*
      enforcing, *321*
   conduct of hearings, *320*
   hearing arrangements, *319–320*
   settlement of cases, *320*
   terms of reference, *319*
Agency workers, *20–23*
Alternative employment, *120–122*
Ante-natal care, *224–225*
Apprentices, *19–20*

Casual workers, *23–24*
Children, *20*
Closed shop, *272*
Collective agreements, *46–48*
   definition, *287*
   transfer of undertaking, and, *147*
Collective bargaining, *287–288*
   equal pay, and, *218–219*
   method of, *290–291*
Company directors, *17–18*
Company handbook/rule book, *48*
Concept of employment, *9–29*
   continuity and delegation, *16–17*
   employee or independent contractor, *9–16*
   fixed-term contracts, *24–29*
   special categories of workers, *17–24*
   vicarious liability, *29*
Constructive dismissal, *75–81, 203*
Contract of employment, *30–62*
   collective agreements, *46–48*
   company handbook/rule book, *48*
   express terms, *36*
   illegality, *31–33*
   implied terms, *36–46 see* Implied terms
   offer and acceptance, *30–31*
   post-termination obligations, *51–60 see* Post-termination obligations
   sources of terms of, *33*
   variation of contractual terms, *48–51*
      flexible working, *51*
   whistle-blowing, *61–62*
   written particulars of terms, *33–35*

Disability discrimination, *192–205*
   burden of proof, *204*
   constructive dismissal, *203*
   harassment, *203*
   justification, *197–198*
   liability of employers/prinicpals, *205*
   meaning, *195–197*
   post-termination obligations, *203–204*
   reasonable adjustment, *198–202*
   remedies, *204–205*
   scope of 1995 Act, *202–203*
   section 1 DDA 1995, *192–195*
      'impairment', *192–194*
      'long-term' *195*
      'substantial' *194–195*
   time limits, *204*
   victimisation, *205*
Discrimination in employment, *148–205*
   disability, *192–205 see* Disability discrimination
   race, *177–192 see* Race discrimination
   sex, *148–177 see* Sex discrimination
Dismissal, *63–113 see also* Redundancy
   automatically fair reasons for, *81–82*
      national security, *81*
      strike or lock-out, *81–82*
   automatically unfair reasons for, *83–87*
      assertion of a statutory right, *84*
      failure to carry out disciplinary procedure, *85*
      family friendly policies, *86*
      fixed term contracts, *85*
      health and safety, *84–85*
      jury service, *86–87*
      national minimum wage, *86*
      pregnancy, *83*
      spent offences, *83*
      transfer of undertakings, *83–84*
      unfair selection, *87*
      union membership, *84*
      whistle-blowing, *86*
      working time cases/Sunday working, *86*
   constructive, *75–81, 203*
   definition, *69–70*

Index

Dismissal (*contd.*)
  excluded categories, *95–100*
    age, *96–97*
    by agreement, *99–100*
    illegality, *97–98*
    persons employed outside Great Britain, *98–99*
  human rights, and, *105–106*
  notice, *107*
    withdrawal, *107*
  potentially fair reasons for, *87–95*
    capability, *88–89*
      counselling, *88*
      incompetence, *89*
      qualifications, *89*
      training, *88–89*
      warnings, *88*
    conduct, *89–93*
      gross misconduct, *90–93*
      conduct outside work, *93*
    other substantial, *94–95*
      business needs, *94*
      pressure from third parties, *95*
    redundancy, *93*
    statutory prohibition, *93*
  procedure, *100–107*
    disciplinary and grievance, *103–105*
    warnings, *107*
  reasonableness, *100–107*
  remedies, *110–113*
    compensation, *111–113*
    re-engagement, *111*
    reinstatement, *110–111*
  termination, *64–69*
    by agreement, *64–66*
    death, *66*
    frustration, *66–68*
    language of, *70–72*
    resignation, *68–69*
  time limits, *108–110*
  wrongful, *72–75*

Employee or independent contractor, *9–24*
  determining factors, *13–17*
    continuity, *16–17*
    delegation, *17*
    labels, *13–15*
    mutuality of obligations, *15–16*
  importance of distinguishing between, *9–10*
  special categories, *17–24*
    agency workers, *20–23*
    apprentices, *19–20*

Employee or independent contractor, special categories (*contd.*)
    casual workers, *23–24*
    children, *20*
    company directors, *17–18*
    minors, *20*
    office holders, *19*
    partnerships, *18*
    police officers, *19*
    trainees, *19–20*
  tests for determining, *10–13*
    control, *10–11*
    integrational, *11*
    multiple, *11–13*
Employment tribunals *310–321*
  composition, *311*
  determination without full hearing, *311*
  hearing, *316–318*
    absence of a member, *316*
    allegations of sexual offences/misconduct *316–317*
    by chairman alone, *311–312*
    challenge, *316*
    costs, *318*
    decision, *317*
    enforcement, *317*
    in public, *316*
    representation, *317*
    rights of appeal, *317*
    written representations, *317*
  jurisdiction, *310*
  procedure, *313–315*
    amendment, *314*
    equal pay cases, *315*
    further and better particulars, *315*
    notice of appearance, *313–314*
    originating application, *313*
    questionnaires, *314–315*
  reform, *311*
  role of, *133*
Equal pay, *206–223*
  Act of 1970, *206–223 see* Equal Pay Act 1970
  EC law and, *206*
  employment tribunals, and, *315*
Equal Pay Act 1970, *206–223*
  claim for arrears, *222*
  collective bargaining, *218–219*
  equality, *207*
  experience, *219*
  genuine material factor defence, *216–218*
  grading structures, *219*
  'like work', *207–209*
    comparator, *213–216*

Index

Equal Pay Act 1970 (*contd.*)
  part-time workers, 219–221
  qualifications, 219
  questionnaires, 222–223
  red circling, 222
  time limits, 221
  work of equal value, 210–216
    comparator, 213–216
  work rated as equivalent, 209–210
    comparator, 213–216
European Union, 3–8
  Human Rights Act 1998, 7–8
  institutions, 4–5
    Commission, 4
    Council of Ministers, 4–5
    European Court of Justice, 5
    European Parliament, 5
  introduction, 3–4
  sources of European law, 5–7
    directives and recommendations, 6–7
    Treaty articles, 6

Family, employment law and, 224–235
  ante-natal care, 224–225
  maternity rights, 225–230 see Maternity rights
  parental leave, 230–234
    flexible working, 230, 232–234
    protection from detriment, 232
    right to return to work, 231
  time off for dependants, 234–235
Fixed-term contracts, 24–29
  dismissal, 28
  equal treatment, 29–27
  notice, 27
  particular task, 27–28
  redundancy, 28–29

Garden leave, 58–60
Guarantee payments, 244–245

Health and safety, 246–266
  common law duty, 246–251
    duty of employer, 247–250
    duty owed by employee, 250–251
  statutory regulation, 251–258
    consultation with safety representatives, 253–254
    duty of employees, 255
    duty of employer,
      to employees, 251–253
      to independent contractors and others, 254–255

Health and safety, statutory regulation (*contd.*)
    enforcement, 256
    EU legislation, and, 256–258
    Health and Safety Commission, 251
    protection from detrimental treatment, 255–256
    written safety policy, 253
  Working Time Regulations, 258–266 see Working Time Regulations
Historical background, 1–3

Implied terms, 36–46
  as a matter of law, 38
  common law, 38–46
    common practice, 44
    duty of good faith, 39–44
    duty of obedience, 38–49
    duty of skill and care, 39
    duty to care for safety of employees, 44–45
    duty to provide pay, 46
    duty to provide work, 45
    notice period, 46
    smoking, 45
Industrial action, 293–309
  background, 293–294
  inducing a breach of contract, 294–296
  notice to employers of, 304–305
  picketing, 306–309 see Picketing
  secondary action, 305–306
  statutory immunity, 296–298
  trade dispute, 298–305 see Trade dispute

Maternity rights, 225–230
  adoption leave, 230, 232–234
  flexible working, 230
  health and safety, 227–228
  maternity leave,
    additional, 226–227
    compulsory, 228
    ordinary, 225–226
    redundancy during, 227
  maternity pay, 228–229
  paternity leave, 229–230
  returning to work, 231
Minors, 20

National minimum wage, 242–244

Office holders, 19

Partnerships, 18
Pay *see* Remuneration

Picketing, *306–309*
  besetting, *307–308*
  breach of the peace, *307*
  obstructing a police officer, *307*
  obstruction of the highway, *306–307*
  peaceful, *309*
  potential liability, *306–309*
  public nuisance, *307*
  Public Order Act 1986, *308*
  watching, *307–308*
Police officers, *19*
Post-termination obligations, *51–60*
  alterations to covenants, *54–56*
  garden leave, *58–60*
  geographical area, *53–54*
  previous customers, *54*
  restraint of trade, *51–52*
  seniority, *53*
  time, *52–53*
  trade secrets, *56–58*

Race discrimination, *177–192*
  burden of proof, *188–189*
  compensation, *189–191*
  continuing treatment, *182–183*
  detriment, *182*
  direct, *178–182*
  genuine occupational qualification, *187–188*
  harassment, *183–184*
  illegality, *186*
  meaning of racial group, *180–182*
  motive, *180*
  questionnaire, *188*
  religion/belief, *191–192*
  scope of 1976 Act, *185–186*
  time limits, *188*
  vicarious liability, *187*
  victimisation, *184–185*
Red circling, *122*
Redundancy, *114–147 see also* Dismissal
  alternative employment, *120–122*
    trial period, *121–122*
  consultation, *126–131*
    appropriate representatives, *127–128*
    duties of employers, *126–127*
    'establishment', *127*
    failure to consult, *130–131*
    process, *128–130*
    'proposing', *127*
  dismissal, *115–118*
    constructive redundancy, *116*
    for reason of redundancy, *116–118*
    leaving early, *115–116*

Redundancy (*contd.*)
  employment tribunal, role of, *133*
  lay-off, *123–124*
  misconduct, *122–123*
  payments, *124–126 see* Redundancy payments
  rationalisation, *118–120*
  restructuring, *118–120*
  selection criteria, *132*
  short-time working, *123–124*
  transfer of undertakings, *133–147 see* Transfer of undertakings
  transferred, *119–120*
Redundancy payments, *124–126*
  computation, *125*
  entitlement to, *124*
  making a claim for, *124*
  non-eligibility, *125*
  pay, *125*
  written statement, *126*
Remuneration, *236–245*
  deductions from wages, *238–241*
  definition, *240*
  jurisdiction, *241*
  time limits, *241*
  guarantee payments, *244–245*
    calculating, *245*
    limit on entitlement, *245*
  national minimum wage, *242–244*
    calculating, *242–243*
    enforcement, *243–244*
    exemptions, *243*
  payment of wages, *237–241*
  scope of Pt II ERA 1996, *237*
  statement of pay, *236–237*
  wages, definition, *239–240*

Sex discrimination, *148–177*
  advertisements, *164*
  burden of proof, *169–171*
  defences, *171–174*
  direct, *150–156*
    comparator, *155–156*
    discrimination against married persons/civil partners, *154–155*
    'less favourably', *151–154*
    motive, *150–151*
    treatment, *151*
  effect of EC law, *148–150*
  employment, and, *164*
  enforcement, *175*
  gender reassignment, *165–166*
  indirect, *156–161*

Sex discrimination, indirect (*contd.*)
    'considerably smaller', *158–159*
    'detriment', *159*
    'justification', *159–161*
    requirement or condition, *157–158*
  interviews, *163*
  positive, *174–175*
  post-termination, *168–169*
  questionnaires, *175*
  reference to ECJ, *168*
  remedies, *175–176*
  scope of 1975 Act, *163–177*
  sexual harassment, *164–165*
  sexual orientation, *166–168*
  time limits, *176–177*
  victimisation, *161–163*
Short-time working, *123–124*

Trade dispute, *298–305*
  entitlement to vote, *300–301*
  notice of industrial action, *299–300*
  sample voting papers, *300*
  scrutineers, *300*
  statutory restrictions on immunity, *299*
  workplace ballots, *301–305*
    notice to employers of industrial action, *304–305*
    post ballot requirements, *303–304*
    separate, *301–302*
    voting requirements, *302–303*
Trade union recognition, *288–292*
  agreement, *289*
    to negotiate, *289*
  basic outline, *288–289*
  Central Arbitration Committee, *290*
  derecognition, *291–292*
  detriment, *292*
  Employment Relations Act 1999, and, *288–292*
  method of collective bargaining, *290–291*
  multiple applications, *291*
  rejection by employer, *289–290*
  termination, *291*
  unfair dismissal, *292*
Trade unions, *267–292*
  accounts, *270–271*
  certification officer, *268*
  closed shop, *272*
  collective bargaining, *287–288*
  definition, *267*
  duties, *283–285*
  Employment Relations Act 2004, *281–283*
    enforcement of minimum wage legislation, *283*

Trade unions, Employment Relations Act 2004 (*contd.*)
    industrial action, *282–283*
    jurisdiction of EAT, *283*
    rights, *283*
    union recognition, *281–282*
  government, *285–287*
    appointment of independent scrutineer, *286*
    election address, *285–286*
    entitlement to vote, *286*
    voting, *286–287*
  illegality, *272*
  independence, *268–269*
  membership, *272–277*
    contractual rights, *273*
    disciplinary proceedings, *274–275*
    employers, and, *277–281*
    exclusion, *275–277*
    right to terminate, *277*
  recognition, *288–292* *see* Trade union recognition
  restraint of trade, *271*
  rules, *271–272*
  status, *269–270*
Trainees, *19–20*
Transfer of undertakings, *133–147*
  automatic transfer, *140–142*
  collective agreements, *147*
  consultation, *146–147*
  contracting-out, *134–137*
  dismissals, *142–144*
  employee protection, *137–140*
  meaning of undertaking, *134*
  non-commercial undertakings, *137*
  transfer of liabilities, *145–146*
  variation of contractual terms, *144–145*

Unfair dismissal *see* Dismissal; ACAS unfair dismissal arbitration

Wages *see* Remuneration
Whistle-blowing, *61–62, 86*
Working Time Regulations, *258–266*
  calculation of working time, *259–260*
  daily rest breaks, *261*
  enforcement, *266*
  exemptions, *259*
  extension, *265–266*
  holiday entitlement, *262–263*
    'rolled-up' holiday pay, *263–265*
  night workers, *260–261*
  reference period, *259*

Working Time Regulations (*contd.*)
  rest periods, *261–262*
    weekly, *262*
    waiver, *260*

Written particulars of terms, *33–35*
Wrongful dismissal, *72–75*

Unannotated Cracknell's Statutes for Use in Examinations

New Editions of Cracknell's Statutes

Only £11.95   Due 2005

Cracknell's Statutes provide a comprehensive series of essential statutory provisions for each subject. Amendments are consolidated, avoiding the need to cross-refer to amending legislation. Unannotated, they are suitable for use in examinations, and provide the precise wording of vital Acts of Parliament for the diligent student.

Company Law
ISBN: 1 85836 563 5

Equity and Trusts
ISBN: 1 85836 589 9

Constitutional & Administrative Law
ISBN: 1 85836 584 8

European Union Legislation
ISBN: 1 85836 590 2

Contract, Tort and Remedies
ISBN: 1 85836 583 X

Family Law
ISBN: 1 85836 566 X

Criminal Law
ISBN: 1 85836 586 4

Land: The Law of Real Property
ISBN: 1 85836 585 6

Employment Law
ISBN: 1 85836 587 2

Law of International Trade
ISBN: 1 85836 582 1

English Legal System
ISBN: 1 85836 588 0

Medical Law
ISBN: 1 85836 567 8

Revenue Law
ISBN: 1 85836 569 4

For further information or to place an order, please contact:

Customer Services
Old Bailey Press at Holborn College
Woolwich Road, Charlton
London, SE7 8LN
Telephone: 020 8317 6039
Fax: 020 8317 6004
Website: www.oldbaileypress.co.uk
E-Mail: customerservices@oldbaileypress.co.uk

Old Bailey Press

The Old Bailey Press Integrated Student Law Library is tailor-made to help you at every stage of your studies, from the preliminaries of each subject through to the final examination. The series of Textbooks, Revision WorkBooks, 150 Leading Cases and Cracknell's Statutes are interrelated to provide you with a comprehensive set of study materials.

You can buy Old Bailey Press books from your University Bookshop, your local Bookshop, directly using this form, or you can order a free catalogue of our titles from the address shown overleaf.

The following subjects each have a Textbook, 150 Leading Cases, Revision WorkBook and Cracknell's Statutes unless otherwise stated.

Administrative Law
Commercial Law
Company Law
Conflict of Laws
Constitutional Law
Conveyancing (Textbook and 150 Leading Cases)
Criminal Law
Criminology (Textbook and Sourcebook)
Employment Law (Textbook and Cracknell's Statutes)
English and European Legal Systems
Equity and Trusts
Evidence
Family Law
Jurisprudence: The Philosophy of Law (Textbook, Sourcebook and Revision WorkBook)
Land: The Law of Real Property
Law of International Trade
Law of the European Union
Legal Skills and System (Textbook)
Obligations: Contract Law
Obligations: The Law of Tort
Public International Law
Revenue Law (Textbook, Revision WorkBook and Cracknell's Statutes)
Succession (Textbook, Revision WorkBook and Cracknell's Statutes)

Mail order prices:	
Textbook	£15.95
150 Leading Cases	£12.95
Revision WorkBook	£10.95
Cracknell's Statutes	£11.95
Suggested Solutions 1999–2000	£6.95
Suggested Solutions 2000–2001	£6.95
Suggested Solutions 2001–2002	£6.95
101 Questions and Answers	£7.95
Law Update 2004	£10.95
Law Update 2005	£10.95

Please note details and prices are subject to alteration.

To complete your order, please fill in the form below:

Module	Books required	Quantity	Price	Cost
		Postage		
		TOTAL		

For the UK and Europe, add £4.95 for the first book ordered, then add £1.00 for each subsequent book ordered for postage and packing.
For the rest of the world, add 50% for airmail.

ORDERING

By telephone to Customer Services at 020 8317 6039, with your credit card to hand.

By fax to 020 8317 6004 (giving your credit card details).

Website: www.oldbaileypress.co.uk
E-Mail: customerservices@oldbaileypress.co.uk

By post to: Customer Services, Old Bailey Press at Holborn College, Woolwich Road, Charlton, London, SE7 8LN.

When ordering by post, please enclose full payment by cheque or banker's draft, or complete the credit card details below. You may also order a free catalogue of our complete range of titles from this address.

We aim to despatch your books within 3 working days of receiving your order. All parts of the form must be completed.

Name
Address

E-Mail
Postcode   Telephone

Total value of order, including postage: £
I enclose a cheque/banker's draft for the above sum, or

charge my   ☐ Access/Mastercard   ☐ Visa   ☐ American Express

Cardholder: ....
Card number

☐☐☐☐ ☐☐☐☐ ☐☐☐☐ ☐☐☐☐

Expiry date   ☐☐☐☐

Signature: ....Date: ....